The World's Story

Scenes in Roman Life, Painted by a Roman Artist. *(Made up from paintings which decorated the walls of one of the buried houses of Pompeii. The painter has endeavored to make every-day subjects more interesting by depicting the workers as little cupids. At the top they are dyeing; in the middle, gathering orchard fruits; and at the bottom, forging, casting, and working in metal.*

THE WORLD'S STORY

A Simple History for Boys and Girls

BY

ELIZABETH O'NEILL, M.A.

Book Design by Mary Jo Loboda

Cover design by Mary Jo Loboda

New images compiled by Margot Davidson

Originally published by T. Nelson & Sons, Ltd./T.C. & E.C. Jack, Ltd.

London, Edinburgh, New York, Toronto, and Paris, 1914

Editor's Note on the New Edition

We have attempted to faithfully reproduce O'Neill's original text with additional images that were not available to publishers and printers in the early 20th century. Please keep in mind, however, that the history in this book ends before the First World War and represents a colonial worldview. So, while this book lays a good foundation—in a style that will be appealing to children—a study of modern and current history should follow the reading of it.

Hillside Education

475 Bidwell Hill Road

Lake Ariel, PA 18436

www.hillsideeducation.com

Dedicatory Letter

Dear Doris,—You were kind enough to read a small part of this *Story of the World*, and to say that you liked it. I hope you will like also the parts you did not read. I could not tell you all the things which have ever happened in the world, but I have tried to tell you shortly about all the most important things from the very beginning, even before people had come into the World at all, right down to our own wonderful times. I have chosen the greatest men and women to tell you about, and in reading their stories I hope you will understand better something of what the times were like in which they lived, and what the other people too were like who were not so great and the kind of lives they led.

The pictures in the book are not like those in most of the books you see and read, because most of them are not pictures made by people who are alive now, but they are copies of pictures, and statues, and buildings made by the very people you are reading about in the book. When you are reading about the Egyptians you get a picture of a pyramid made by the Egyptians themselves 6000 years ago. When you read about the Greeks you find pictures of statues of great Greek statesmen made by great Greek artists long ago, and so on. In the 'Middle Ages' you are given pictures from the beautiful stained glass windows and the wonderful manuscripts which the people of the Middle Ages knew so well how to make. Sometimes the drawing may seem a little curious to you, but it is much more interesting for you to have these pictures than imaginative pictures made by people who are living now.[1]

Just as all the pictures are true so all the stories are true too. Indeed, there were many tales I could have told you which are often told to children as history, but are not true at all. I hope you will like those I have told just as well, for after all history *should* be true. Very affectionately I dedicate the book to you.

ELIZABETH O'NEILL.

---

[1] All the illustrations were chosen and arranged by Mr. S. G. Stubbs.

TABLE OF CONTENTS

CHAPTER I—THE COMING OF MAN

Long before men came into the world the earth existed, though it was very different from the earth as it is today. Men of science who can read a story in the rocks which make up the surface of the earth tell us that at one time it was so hot that nothing of any kind could live on it. It was a great round lump of melted stuff whirling round and round. By degrees it got a little cooler. The outside cooled first, and a crust was formed which broke and, perhaps, at first fell into the melted part underneath. Later on it stopped falling through and turned into a hard, cool skin, much like the earth as it is now, except that at first there was no living thing on it, not even the smallest flower or insect. But the inside of the earth has not cooled altogether yet, and we find that if we go down into it, for instance down a coal-mine, it grows hotter the lower we go. Sixty feet below the surface a thermometer would tell us that it is a degree hotter, another sixty another degree, and so on.

Still the outside has cooled, and when it had become cool enough for water to be on it then it was possible for plants and animals to live. Now the first plants and animals began to live so long ago that even the cleverest men cannot say exactly when it was. It must have been, in any case, hundreds and hundreds of thousands of years ago. We do not know even when the first man lived, and we do not know where. In the Bible we are told that the first man was Adam, and that he lived in a certain place which had four rivers flowing through it. Many people have thought that this place, the Garden of Eden, must be in Arabia, in the valley of a river called the Euphrates, where the Assyrians and Babylonians lived afterwards. But some of the greatest men of science now say that probably the first man lived in an island in the far East, which in those far-off days would not be an island at all, but a part of Southern Asia. One of the reasons for thinking this is that not many years ago a skull was found there which is thought to be that of the very first man. He must have been a very strange man. His forehead sloped back sharply from his eyebrows instead of going straight up and then gently

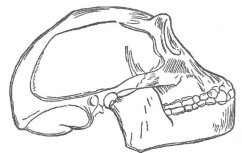

The Shape of the First Man's Head (From *the skull found in Java by Dr. Dubois*).

back as ours do. His head must have been smaller than that of any man now alive, but it was larger than the head of a certain kind of monkey called the 'Gibbon' monkey, though it was very much like it in shape. Learned men who think, as many of them do now, that men are descended from monkeys, say that this was probably the skull of the very first man, and would, therefore, naturally be very much like that of a monkey.

There are other reasons why men of science think that it was in Java that the first man was born, and one of them is that it could only be in a warm, moist climate such as we know existed there that man could first grow. If this is so, of course, it might almost as well be in the place where the Garden of Eden is supposed to have been, except that no traces of these far-off men have been found there. But we really do not know anything certainly about the first man, though we know a good deal about men who lived many thousands of years ago.

There are some signs of the existence of the first men even in Europe in far-off ages, when the land was covered with white glistening ice, and everything was dreadfully cold. We do not know how these men came to Europe. Nor do we know how many kinds of men there were at the time, but traces have been found of three kinds at least. We shall hear something of these presently.

Although we do not know where these first men came from, we know a good deal about them. They were cave-dwellers. They did not build houses as we do; but they moved about until they found some hole in the rocks which would keep out the cold winds and the hail and snow, and there they made their home—if they could. For sometimes they would find huge animals in the caves, and would have to fight for their lives. We think the elephant a very big animal, but the elephants of those days were much bigger. The elephants of today would look beside them as sheep beside horses. There were also other huge animals of different kinds with strange names and strange shapes. Besides these there were giant bears, lions, and wolves.

These ancient men had very poor weapons to fight with. They had not learned to make swords and spears of iron. Stone was all they could think of to make their axes, spears, knives, and swords. They would knock one piece of stone against another until they had made a sharp edge, and then after a long time it would look something like the head of an axe. A favorite place for caves chosen as homes by these wild men was the side of a steep cliff, or hill, probably because the great wild animals could not reach them there very easily. We know of several of these caves which, because of the things dug out of them, must have been the homes of wild, early men like these.

They stained themselves different colors with the juice of plants, just as the people did whom Julius Caesar found in Britain. They wore skins of wild animals for clothes, and they lived on the flesh of the animals they killed and on roots which they dug out of the earth. We find not only their rough stone weapons, but their bones lying side by side with those of the great rhinoceros, which they seem to have learned how to kill easily. They knew how to make fires, and they kept the wild beasts away at night by building up great fires made from the brushwood of the forests.

These men were not attractive to look at. Their foreheads went sharply back from their eyebrows, and these stood out like a shield over their eyes. Their chins also went back from their teeth instead of forward like ours. They were short men, and as we have seen did not know many things as yet. They must have been very cunning hunters, as that was the work they lived by, and some of their weapons were cleverly made. But at best they were not very different from monkeys.

These ancient men are called by some people 'Neander' men, because the first head of such a man was found in a cave in Germany called the Neander cave.

THE REINDEER MEN

Long after the Neander men lived we know that there was another sort of ancient men who are called 'Cromagnard' men, because their skulls were first found at Cromagnan in France. They are also sometimes called Reindeer men, because they lived at the time when reindeer roamed over the south of Europe. Now these Reindeer men, although, of course, they were savage men who lived thousands and thousands of years ago, must have been in some ways almost like the men of today. The climate had changed very much from that which the Neander men had had to put up with. It was now cold and dry. The ice had disappeared, and the climate was not very different from that in the north of Europe in winter now.

The Reindeer men were still cave-dwellers, and some of their traces have been found in caves in Devon and Derbyshire. But they had foreheads like those of men now, rising fairly gently from the eyebrows. The whole head and face of a Reindeer man must have been quite like those of men we meet every day. The size of his head was about the same. The only great difference was that the chin still went backwards from the teeth. They were tall men, too, with much better figures than the Neander men. But this is not all. Though they were hunters, and had only weapons of stone, their weapons were more finely made, and, strange to say, the Reindeer men were very fine artists. Curious, savage people though they were, covering their bodies with yellow and red paint, they could cut into ivory perfect little pictures of the things they saw around them. You can almost see the deer putting down its finely shaped legs when you look at some of these scenes in ivory. They could paint too. In a cave in the north of Spain there are painted on the walls in almost natural colors and in natural positions, buffaloes, wild boars, and horses. They were painted long ago by the Reindeer men. Sometimes they tried sculpture, and at this too they were very clever.

These paintings and sculptures and drawings are to be found not in one cave only, but in many in the south of France and in the north of Spain, so we cannot think they were the work of one artist among a number of savages, just like a genius among thousands of ordinary people today. They were a real race of artists, clever men in many ways though so savage in others. We know that they were clever in other ways too. They got their flints and stones to make weapons

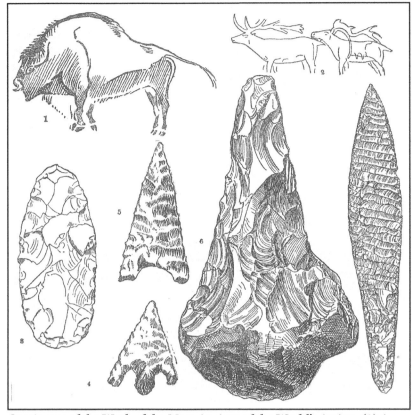

Specimens of the Work of the Most Ancient of the World's Artists. (1) A buffalo painted on a wall of a cave at Altamira, North Spain, perhaps 50,000 years ago; (2) Carvings on ivory by Reindeer men; (3) A tool carved out of flint found at a great camp of the New Stone Age in Sussex; (4) and (5) Beautifully carved flint arrow-heads of the same Age found in Ireland; (6) A flint pick found in the Thames; (7) A flint knife from Denmark.

from mines from which they dug them with axes sometimes made out of the horns of animals. We know, too, that they made lamps for themselves. Altogether, they must have been men whom we should have liked to know.

A strange thing about these Reindeer men is that we are almost certain that they were not descended from the rougher and ruder Neander men. It seems more probable that they came to the western parts of Europe when the terrible covering of ice had gone from it. But a still stranger thing is that the bodies of another kind of men still have been found, of the same sort as the negro of the present time. So here we see there are three kinds of men found living at the same time; the savage small Neander men, the artistic and clever and finely built Reindeer men, and the Negro men. But we know almost nothing about the Negro men. All these men lived in a time which the people who study these things call the 'Old Stone Age.' But the Reindeer men still lived in the New Stone Age—a time which is nearer to the days when real history begins.

The weather in the west of Europe was growing warmer still, so that new and different kinds of animals could live there. The reindeer had gone, but there was now the red deer which long afterwards the Red King loved to hunt in England.

THE LAKE-DWELLERS

The Reindeer men disappeared with the reindeer. Where they went to we do not know. Perhaps they just died out because the weather did not suit them as it did other men who now began to show themselves. So far as we know the new people did not come from the Reindeer men. The men of this new time began to build houses, sometimes of stone, sometimes of wood. A favorite place for houses was the middle of lakes. The men first drove heavy pieces of wood into the water, and then built their houses upon them. Lake-dwellers, as we call them, are known to have lived at Glastonbury in England. They began to collect herds of cattle and kept them for food. They also tilled the land and grew things. They built strange circles of stone, one of which may still be seen at Stonehenge in the South of England. We know, too, that they began to make pottery, but they could not draw and paint like the Reindeer men who had lived perhaps thousands of years before them. This seems a strange thing, as the new men were so much more civilized in other ways. The New Stone Age reaches the time of which real history begins to speak. It lasted until about four thousand years ago in some parts of Europe, but in Egypt even about seven thousand years ago the people had learned to make weapons of bronze, and a little later of iron. It is with these people that the most interesting part of the story of the world commences. Of the earlier peoples we can never know very much, and real history begins with the writing down of the doings of men who were very different from these savages—people who knew many things and wanted to know more, and so people whom we understand better and like to hear about.

When people learned to make weapons of bronze and iron instead of stone the wild animals were more frightened of them, and fled before them. When all the animals in one place had been killed or had run away the people moved on to another place to find more animals; so that in the very early days people were always moving from place to place. Families who were related to each other kept together and moved with each other. We call a number of families keeping together in this way a 'tribe.' Often two tribes would want to go to the same place, and then they would fight, and the tribe which won would have the land.

After many years men began to collect together sheep and cows, from which they got nearly everything they wanted. They killed some of them for meat to eat, and got milk from the cows to drink, and they made themselves clothes from the wool of the sheep. When there were so many animals the grass was soon eaten up, and so again the tribes had to move on to other places for fresh pasture land.

Sometimes when a tribe found land on which things grew very easily they stayed there, and instead of keeping so many sheep and cattle they kept only a few, and instead of letting grass grow all over the land they gave up some of the land to grow many other things. They built themselves houses to live and sleep in instead of the tents which they had used when they were always moving. So villages were made, and some of these grew into towns, and instead of all the men hunting or fishing or fighting or growing corn some began to do one thing and some another. Some men made boots, and others made weapons for the people who were looking after the land and had no time to do these things for themselves. But always for thousands of years there were tribes still moving, sometimes coming to fight the people who had settled down, and taking their lands from them. Most of the people in the hottest part of the earth had black skins and black hair. Those farther north were brown or yellow, and also had black or very dark hair. Then there were tribe upon tribe of white people, and more and more of these were ever pouring into Europe from Asia. We know most about the people of Europe, Asia, and the north of Africa, and more about some of these peoples than about others. With the story of the people who lived on the banks of two great rivers, the Nile and the Euphrates, real history begins.

How the World Began. *The world probably began as a great mass of glowing gas whirling round and round, which gradually, after millions of years, cooled down into solid matter. This photograph shows the mass of glowing gas in the Milky Way called the nebula of Andromeda, which is now in the state that our world was probably in at the beginning.*

Chapter II—The Jews and the Phœnicians

The rich lands on which things grew easily and where men first settled down to live without moving away were generally found on the banks of great rivers. People cannot live without water to drink, and the soil, too, must be watered before it will bear fruit. For thousands of years, while tribes were still swarming over Asia and passing into Europe, lasting settlements had existed near two great rivers, the river Nile in North Africa and the river Euphrates in Western Asia. The country round the banks of the Nile was called Egypt. The Egyptians were a brown people, with straight black hair and curious long dark eyes. The country on the right of the Euphrates was called Mesopotamia; the people there belonged to the lighter races.

In both these countries as the years went on the people had learnt to do many wonderful things which would have been impossible in earlier and wilder times. They learned to know something about the sun and stars; they could count and do sums in arithmetic, and they learned to build not only houses of brick, but great buildings of stone, and though they did not write as we do, and had not paper and ink, they had a picture-writing of their own which they scratched on stones and the walls of their buildings. Many of these pictures remain to this day, and clever men are able to read them and tell us what they mean. In Egypt the most wonderful buildings of all were great, pointed stone monuments, which the old Egyptians built over the graves of their dead kings to do them honor, lest they should be forgotten. These Pyramids were built nearly four thousand years before the Birth of Christ; and there they stand to this day, and people go from far-off countries to look at them as one of the wonders of the world. They are so big and wonderful that the people of today cannot imagine how they were built. The Egyptians, too, made beautiful stone statues, and they must have been very fond of beautiful things. But we must remember that not all the people could enjoy these things, for many of them were slaves and had to do all the work, and could be bought and sold like animals. It must have kept thousands and thousands of slaves busy cutting the great stones to build the Pyramids.

The Pyramid Tomb of King Khufu and the Great Sphinx at Gizeh, Egypt. *This is the greatest of the pyramids. It was built over 6500 years ago, and is 150 feet higher than St. Paul's Cathedral.*

More than a thousand years after the Pyramids were built, the Egyptians were conquered by a new people who came out of Arabia. These were a Semitic people, quite different from the Egyptians; it is to this race that the Jews and Arabs belong. All the Semitic peoples seem to have come from Arabia at first. After about two hundred years the Semites were driven out of Egypt. But long before these Semites went into Egypt others had crossed the country called Syria and conquered Mesopotamia. They found there a people much more civilized than themselves; but they soon became as civilized as the people round them, and set up great kingdoms.

The south-eastern part of Mesopotamia was called Babylon, and a great Semitic kingdom was founded there. One of its rulers, called Hammurabi, drew up some famous laws, which he had written down on a great block of stone, on which clever men today can read the laws of the Babylonians two thousand years before the Birth of Christ. These laws show that the Babylonians were very highly civilized indeed.

The part of Mesopotamia to the north-west of Babylonia was called Assyria, and was nearly always under the same ruler as Babylonia. The old writers used to call them both by the one name, 'Assyria,' but it was generally the Babylonians who were the more important people.

Clever men who are interested in the story of these old peoples have dug deep down in the ground at different places in these countries, which are now very lonely and wild. They have found there old forgotten temples and walls and tombs, and all sorts of vases and weapons, belonging to different times in the several thousands of years during which the greatness and civilization of the Assyrians and Babylonians lasted.

In the British Museum we can see the great bronze gates of a palace built nearly a thousand years before the Birth of Christ. They are covered with curious and beautiful sculpture. But many older things than these have been found, and some have been carried away to different countries of Europe.

It was in the time of Hammurabi that Abraham, of whom we read so much in the Bible, lived. Up to this time the people of Egypt and Mesopotamia, though they knew so many things, knew very little about each other and the rest of the world.

ABRAHAM

At last, one man travelled from beyond the Euphrates, right across the land of Canaan, which we now call Syria, and into Egypt. This was Abraham, the father of the Hebrew or Jewish people, who were to have such a wonderful history. Abraham was a very rich, wise man, the father of an immense family. He was a Semite who lived in the land of Mesopotamia, but he heard the Voice of God telling him to go out from his home, to leave his father and friends, and to go to the land that should be shown to him. In those days people worshipped many gods, but Abraham believed in the one God, and he handed on his belief to the people whose father he was. It was from the Jews that after hundreds of years nearly all the world learned to worship the one God.

Abraham travelled out of Mesopotamia into the land of Canaan. He was a rich man and the head of a tribe of about twelve hundred people, besides the family and followers of his nephew Lot who travelled with him. Abraham was head of all and led the rest. He went on before dressed in a bright scarlet robe. His wife and children probably rode on donkeys or camels. There were many of these, and on their backs the men-servants and maid-servants piled Abraham's great possessions—his clothing and that of his family, the tents in which they slept, food and the things with which to cook it, and what hangings and coverings were used. Other slaves drove the great herds of sheep and cattle belonging to Abraham and Lot. It was Abraham who said where they should travel and where they should stop. Generally they were moving up and down amidst the rich pasture lands and the beautiful groves of oak in the land of Canaan, which God had promised should belong to him and to his children's children for ever. Generally, too, Abraham and his people travelled under a cloudless sky of blue, and all must have been gay and happy. But there was a dark side to this free and happy life. Sometimes no rain would fall for many days, and the grass would dry up under the blazing sun, and there was no water for man or beast to drink. Corn would not grow, and there was little or nothing to eat. It was the dead time of famine.

At one time when famine fell thus upon the land Abraham led his people further and further south into the rich land of Egypt, where they could have water and bread. Here Abraham saw for the first time the wonderful land of the pyramids with its temples and its statues. It was even hotter in Egypt than in the land of Canaan. Half the year it had soft spring weather, and for the other half a scorching summer. But it was a rich land and generally had much corn. The great river Nile which runs through the land, and which the Egyptians worshipped as a god, overflowed its banks each year, and the water spread over the low lands, fertilizing the crops. Having done its work, the river shrank again to its ordinary size. Sometimes the Nile did not rise, and then the people were sad for nothing would grow; but there was so much corn in the years of plenty that it could be stored up to feed the people in the days of famine. It was at a time of famine in the land of Canaan that Abraham led his people into Egypt, where there was corn for all.

The Pharaoh or Egyptian king welcomed him and gave him corn and rich presents, and Abraham taught the Egyptians things about the stars which he had learnt in Mesopotamia and which the Egyptians did not know. When the famine was over Abraham went again out of Egypt into the beautiful land of Canaan. But he had now so many people that his servants and those of his nephew, Lot, quarrelled about the pasture lands, and Abraham thought it best that they should separate. He took his nephew to the top of a hill where they could look down upon all the land of Canaan, and told him to choose which part he would take for himself. Lot chose the rich country that lay round the banks of the river Jordan, and Abraham was content with another part of Canaan.

There were other tribes besides those of Abraham and Lot in the land of Canaan, and when one of these, called the Elamites, fought against Lot and carried him and his people off as prisoners, Abraham went to their rescue and brought them safely back. It was on his way back from this expedition that Abraham met Melchisedech, who was a priest and also ruler of one of the many cities which were spread about the land of Canaan. Melchisedech also worshipped the one God, and offered to Him a sacrifice of bread and wine, instead of animals or fruits which were the common sacrifices of the time. Melchisedech felt himself drawn to love Abraham, and offered him the tenth part of all he possessed, but Abraham would take nothing for himself or his own people, but only for the men who had joined their servants to his in the battle.

When Abraham had gone back to his home it was revealed to him that he should become the father of a great nation, to which the land of Canaan should belong in the end, though it must suffer much, and be carried into captivity after his death. Now Sarah, the wife of Abraham, had not any children. She was already ninety years old (for people lived to a great age in those days), and Abraham wondered how his children's children could become as many as the stars in heaven if he had not even one child. But Sarah had a son as had been promised, and they called him Isaac. Sarah lived to see her boy grow to be a man, and was buried at the age of one hundred and twenty-seven years in the cave of Hebron, which Abraham bought to be a burying-place for himself and his family. Through Isaac, Abraham was the father of the Jews, but he had other children with other mothers, and through these he became the father of other nations. His son Ishmael, whose mother was Sarah's handmaiden Hagar, was the first of

How an Ancient Egyptian Painted the Coming of the Israelites into Egypt *(From a painting on the walls of a tomb at Beni Hassan, Egypt, made nearly 4000 years ago. It may very easily represent Israelites as the Egyptians saw them when Abraham went with his people into Egypt in the time of famine).*

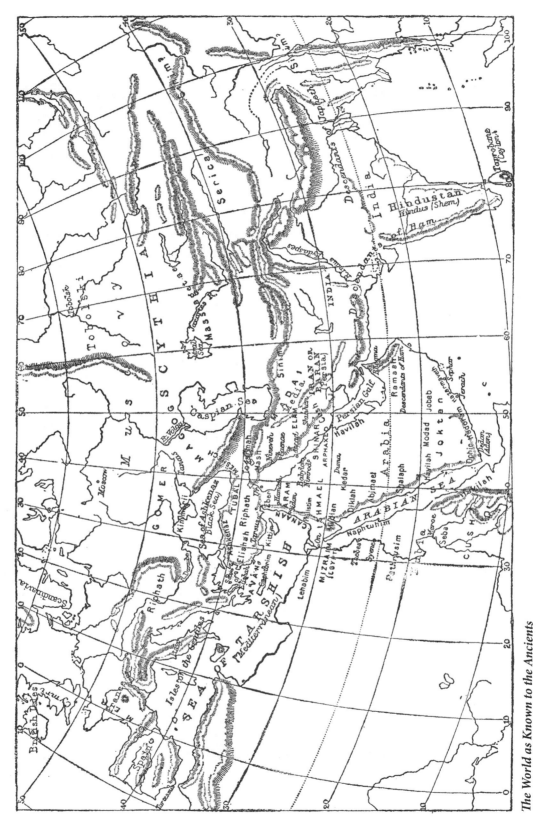

The World as Known to the Ancients

an Arab tribe, and six sons of Abraham by a second wife founded other tribes. These families went out from the land of Canaan, leaving it to Isaac, the son of Sarah.

When Isaac had grown to be a man, Abraham sent a servant to seek a wife for him in his old home in Mesopotamia. Men now travelled much oftener between Mesopotamia and Egypt across the land of Canaan. The servant prayed that he might have a sign to show him how to choose a wife for his master's son. He asked that the maid who was the one to choose should give him water to drink when he asked her, and offer to draw some from the well for his camels too.

One evening, when he had made his camels lie down near a well outside a town, he saw a beautiful girl coming to the well with a pitcher on her shoulder to draw water. He asked her to give him water to drink, and she immediately filled the pitcher and gave it to him and then drew more for the camels. The servant knew then that she was the wife whom he was seeking for Isaac. He went back with her to her brother's house and, bringing forth precious gifts of silver and gold, he asked that Rebecca might go back with him to be Isaac's wife. And so she did.

Esau and Jacob

Isaac and Rebecca loved each other at first sight. They had two sons, Esau and Jacob. Esau grew up to be a strong man. His skin was covered with hairs, and he loved hunting. He was his father's favorite, but Rebecca loved Jacob best. One day, when Esau came in tired and very hungry from hunting, he found Jacob cooking some food for himself and he begged him to give it to him. Jacob said he would if Esau would promise to give up to him his rights as eldest son. So Esau sold his birthright for a mess of pottage, and Jacob, though he was the younger son, became the head of the children of Abraham. Jacob, by covering himself with the skins of kids, pretended to his father Isaac that he was Esau, and Isaac gave him his solemn blessing.

Then Jacob went away to the land of Mesopotamia to find a wife. He loved Rachel, the younger daughter of his uncle Laban, and Laban promised her to him as his wife if he would work for him for seven years. Jacob did this, but Laban then said he would give him his elder daughter Lia and he must serve seven years more for Rachel. In those days men could have several wives. At the end of another seven years Jacob won Rachel, and he always loved her best. Lia had six sons and Rachel only two, Joseph and Benjamin, and these two Jacob loved best for their mother's sake. After the birth of Joseph, Jacob took his wives and children and all his possessions and went back again into the land of Canaan. Here his sons grew up, and Jacob always loved Joseph best. He loved to dress him in beautiful clothes, and he gave him a wonderful coat made of different colored stuffs.

Joseph had eleven brothers altogether. Some of them were jealous of Joseph and wanted to kill him. One day, when they were far away from home looking after their father's sheep,

Jacob sent Joseph with a message to them, but they took his beautiful coat from him and sold him to some merchants who were travelling into the land of Egypt. Then they dipped his coat in the blood of a kid which they had killed and sent it to their father. Jacob was brokenhearted, for he thought that a wild beast had killed and eaten Joseph, and that it was his blood which stained the coat.

But Joseph was sold in Egypt and became a servant to Potiphar, a captain in the palace of the Pharaoh. The Pharaoh at this time was probably one of the Semitic conquerors of Egypt, and so was friendly towards other Semites. Joseph had many strange adventures in Egypt. At one time he was shut up in prison through the wickedness of Potiphar's wife, who told her husband that Joseph had done wrong things which he had never done. While he was in prison he was able to tell some of the other prisoners the meaning of some strange dreams they had had. Then the Pharaoh had a dream which troubled him, and which none of the wise men in Egypt could explain to him. Pharaoh was told of this servant in prison who could tell the meaning of dreams. So Joseph was sent for to go before the Pharaoh and hear the dreams.

JOSEPH IN EGYPT

The Pharaoh had dreamed that he stood upon the bank of a river, and out of the river came seven beautiful fat cows and began to feed on the banks. Then again came seven thin ugly cows, and they ate the fat cows up but did not look any fatter themselves. Then the Pharaoh woke up, and fell asleep again and dreamed another dream. In this dream he saw a stalk of corn with seven full ears of grain on it. But besides these were seven small ears which spoiled the others. Then Joseph told the Pharaoh that the dreams meant that there would be seven years of plenty in Egypt, but that they would be followed by seven years of famine. He advised the Pharaoh to choose a wise man to rule over the land for him, and to store up corn in great barns during the years of plenty, so that there should be food for the people in the years of famine.

The Pharaoh was so pleased with Joseph that he said he should be the ruler. He took a ring from his own hand and put it on Joseph's finger, and dressed him in a beautiful robe of silk with a gold chain round his neck. And so Joseph was the greatest man in Egypt after the Pharaoh. During the seven years of plenty he stored up corn in barns; and then came the seven years of famine, and he gave the corn out to feed the hungry people.

But the famine spread over the land of Canaan too, and Jacob, hearing that there was corn in Egypt, sent his sons to see if they could buy some. They went to Joseph, who knew them at once, though they did not know him. He was so overcome at the sight of them and the memory of his father, that he turned away and cried. All the brothers had come except Benjamin, and Joseph gave them corn and put their money back again in the top of their sacks. But he said they must come again and bring their brother Benjamin (for he longed to see him, as he was his brother by the same mother). To make quite sure he kept one of the brothers, Simeon, saying he would not set him free until Benjamin should come.

So the brothers went sadly back to their father, for they knew it would be a great sorrow to him to let Benjamin leave him. Jacob was indeed sad when he heard that Simeon was left behind in Egypt, but he declared he could never let Benjamin go. But soon the corn they had brought was eaten, and the brothers reminded their father that they could only get more if they took Benjamin to the governor of Egypt, who was so strangely interested in him. Ruben, one of the brothers, who had tried to save Joseph when the others wanted to kill him, promised that, whatever happened, he would bring Benjamin safely back.

So they went again into Egypt, and Joseph received them with great kindness, though he had to leave them for a time to hide his tears, so overcome was he at the sight of his brother Benjamin. He again filled their sacks with corn, but told his servants to put a silver cup into Benjamin's sack. The sacks were placed upon the camels' backs, and the brothers started for home. But when they had gone part of the way Joseph sent servants after them to bring them back, saying they had stolen his silver cup. The brothers were indignant, and so sure of their own honesty that they said they would leave behind as slave to Joseph the one in whose sack the cup should be found.

The sacks were emptied and the cup found in Benjamin's sack. Then Joseph told the other brothers that they could go home but he would keep Benjamin. They fell on the ground and told him that they would rather all stay as slaves than face their father without the son he loved best. Then Joseph could no longer keep his secret, but sent every one else away, and then told his brothers that he was Joseph, whom they had sold into Egypt. At first they were afraid, but he told them not to fear and kissed them all, especially Benjamin. Then he sent them to bring his father to see him, and Jacob, full of joy, came with all his tribe and everything he had, and settled down in the land of Egypt: and here the Israelites, as his people were called, lived for many years, until long after Jacob and Joseph and all his brothers were dead, and many Pharaohs too had ruled and died.

THE STORY OF MOSES

The Israelites became so strong, and there were so many of them, that the new Pharaoh, who was probably an Egyptian and not a Semite, was afraid that they would become stronger than the Egyptians themselves. So he ordered that they should do all the hardest work— building cities for him and making bricks: but still the Israelites grew strong and there were more and more of them. Then the Pharaoh said that every baby boy born to the Hebrews, as the Egyptians called them, should be killed. He thought that through this there would be none among them to grow up to be men, and so the Hebrew people would be destroyed. But some of the mothers managed to hide their babies and keep them safe.

There was one woman who hid her baby until he was three months old, and then, when she found she could not do so any longer, she put him in a basket and laid him on the banks of the river Nile, among the bulrushes. She left him there, and his elder sister stood a little way off to see what would happen to him.

Just then an Egyptian princess, the daughter of the Pharaoh, came down to the river to bathe. She saw the basket, and sent one of her maids to bring it to her. When the princess saw the baby lying inside it crying, she felt very sorry for it, and said she would adopt it as her own. Then the baby's sister came and offered to find a nurse for the child. She brought her mother, and the princess gave her the baby to take care of until it was grown up. She called him Moses, and when he was grown up to be a young man he was taken to live at the palace. But he always remembered that he was a Hebrew, and he longed to save his people, who were still cruelly treated by the Egyptians.

At last Moses begged the Pharaoh to allow him to lead his people out of the land of Egypt into Canaan again. But the Pharaoh would not. Then all sorts of trouble fell on the Egyptians, and at last, fearing that God was angry with him because he would not let the Hebrews go, the Pharaoh said they might go, as they had asked, to sacrifice to God in the desert. But the Hebrews went forth at night out of the land of Egypt never to enter it again. They were led by Moses and his brother Aaron, who was a priest, and they started on the journey through the desert to the land of Canaan, which they called the Promised Land.

It was forty years after all before they reached it, and during all those years of wandering in the desert they had many strange adventures. Sometimes they would grumble against God and wish themselves back in Egypt. Sometimes they set up idols and worshipped them. This made Moses very angry and very sad. Once, while he was away on a mountain praying, the faithless people made an image of a calf out of brass and fell down and adored it. Moses was so angry when he came back that he smashed the calf to pieces and ground it to powder. Then he sprinkled it in water and made the people drink it as a punishment.

THE TEN COMMANDMENTS

It was while he was on the mountain praying that Moses was inspired to write down on tablets of stone the Ten Commandments, which have been handed down from generation to generation for good people to keep, even to our own day.

Moses never entered the Promised Land, but died within sight of it.

The Israelites settled down in it, and at first shared it with other strange tribes, but gradually won it for themselves. Many wonderful stories are told in the Bible of the battles with the other tribes, and the brave men, like Gideon and Samson, who helped to win the whole land of Canaan for the Jews.

Soon the Jews stopped wandering about with large flocks and herds, and instead became an agricultural people, and cultivated the land. They learned many things from the tribes round about, and became more and more civilized. In time they chose a king for themselves.

Their first king was Saul, a handsome man, taller than any of the people. He was a great fighter. While Saul was still alive there was a young boy called David, who killed a giant called Goliath and many other enemies of the people, so that the people sang, 'Saul has slain his thousands, but David his tens of thousands,' which made Saul very jealous. He tried to kill David, but Saul's son, Jonathan, loved David more than a brother, and helped to save him from the anger of the king. David became king after Saul, and Jonathan was content that it should be so. David did many wrong things, but he was always very sorry for them afterwards. He loved God very much, and many of the psalms, the beautiful hymns in the Bible, are said to have been written by David. The Bible calls him 'a man after God's own heart.'

Statue of David Defeating Goliath, Aix-en-Provence (France)

After David, his son Solomon became king. The Jews were by this time a great people. They had conquered their enemies, and Solomon was a man of peace. It was he who built the wonderful temple at Jerusalem. It was built of cedar wood, and overlaid with pure gold, and carved with wonderful statues and tracery. Solomon had had the cedar wood, and many of the other things which he used for the temple, brought from Phœnicia, a land which lay on the coast north of Canaan. Hiram, King of Tyre, one of the chief towns of Phœnicia, was a great friend both of David and Solomon.

The Phœnicians were Semites too, and a very rich people. They were the first people we know of who made boats for themselves and sailed away across the sea to strange lands. In the days of Hiram the Phœnicians had learned to build quite big ships. At first they had only known how to build little rough boats, and had sailed carefully along the coast of Canaan from place to place, carrying their precious woods to other people, and carrying back in exchange corn and oil and things which did not grow in their own land. Later, when new tribes like the Israelites poured into the land of Canaan, the Phœnicians were pushed nearer and nearer to the coast, and began to depend more and more on their trade with other lands.

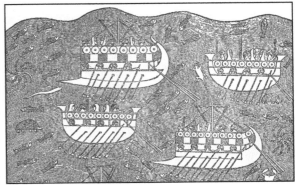

Ships of the King of Tyre in the Arabian Gulf (From an Assyrian stone carving made about 2500 years ago).

Gradually they ventured away from the coast across to the island of Cyprus, which they could see in the distance, and then gradually they sailed right through the Mediterranean Sea, touching at the coasts of North Africa and Spain, into what is now the English Channel, and from the South of Britain they carried back beautiful pearls to their own land. When Solomon saw how rich and great the Phœnicians had become through their trade he built himself a fleet of ships, and Hiram lent him men to build them. When they were made Hiram sent sailors to teach the Israelites how to manage them, and so Phœnicians and Israelites together sailed through the Red Sea to Arabia, and on to India, and from the wonderful East they brought back gold and silver and all kinds of precious things.

The reign of Solomon was the time during which the Israelites were richest and greatest. After his death the northern tribes broke away from the tribes of Judah and Benjamin, who lived in the south of Canaan. The North had one king and the South another, and in time they became separate peoples. The northern tribes mixed with other peoples in the land of Canaan, and together they became known as the Samaritans, whom we read of in the life of our Lord. The tribes of Judah and Benjamin, with their capital and glorious temple at Jerusalem, did not mingle with the other peoples, but remained a race apart, and to them the name of 'Jews' was left. They did not long remain an independent people. Before very long Assyria conquered nearly all the land of Asia round the rivers Tigris and Euphrates and westward to the sea.

The Jews fought hard against the Assyrian king, Sennacherib, and the Egyptians helped them. We read in the Bible how they were saved for a time, for a plague fell upon the Assyrians. But a hundred years later the Jews were carried captive into Babylonia, and kept there for seventy years, for the Assyrians and Babylonians often carried off whole nations whom they had conquered in this way. The ruler of Assyria at this time was Nebuchadnezzar. He was a great soldier, but he was also a great builder. He had made for him the hanging gardens of Babylon, which were one of the wonders of the world. Seventy-five arches were built, one on top of another, and at the top of all were gardens of trees and flowers. Nebuchadnezzar was a great builder of walls and temples too, and many of these have been dug out, and golden figures of gods and gold tables and ornaments have been found. The Jews were very unhappy in Babylon, as we read in the Bible, but at last they were allowed to go back to their own land.

During all this time the Jews often forgot the worship of the one God, and the observance of the law of Moses, and fell into idolatry, and all the wickedness of the people round about them. But they never quite forgot, and though they never again became a great people, it was from them that the great new religion of Christianity was in time to spread over the world. Meanwhile the Jews were subject to the new races, which one after another raised great conquering kingdoms in Europe or Asia or in both.

Hanging Gardens of Babylon by Martin Heemskerck.

CHAPTER III—THE GREEKS

Gradually the interest of early history moves from Western Asia and Northern Africa, where the two great early civilizations grew up, into Eastern Europe, and we begin to read about people who seem much more like ourselves. This is partly because they belong to the great race of which the English are one branch, viz. the Aryan race, which rolled in over Europe and almost swamped the earlier peoples already on the land. The Aryan race invaded the north of India too, and became the chief people there, as we know from the language still spoken in the north of India. It sounds very different from our own language, but it is quite plainly derived, like it, from the speech used by all the Aryan race before it was dispersed all over the world. Another great branch of the Aryan race was the Persian people, who swooped down upon the lands round the Tigris, the twin river to the Euphrates, and founded a great kingdom there, and then gradually conquered the whole of Western Asia and Egypt. The Persians, however, did not bring new ways into the lands they seized, but were content to learn from the people they conquered. So people went on building and teaching and doing most things in much the same way as they had done before the Persians came.

But in the east of Europe there rose up a great people belonging to the Aryan race who developed a very wonderful civilization of their own. These were the Greeks or Hellenes, as they were called at that time.

While the Jews had been wandering from Mesopotamia into the Promised Land these people had been pouring from the North into that land which we now call the Balkan Peninsula, and into the islands round about it.

The Greeks were a very wonderful people, clever and beautiful, full of curiosity about men and things. When we first hear about them they were already quite civilized. They lived in towns and built beautiful houses, and very early too they loved and made poetry. The first great poetry that the Greeks made was said to be written by a blind poet called Homer, but scholars now think that the Homeric poems were written by many men and handed down from one generation to another. They tell of the early days of Greece, and with some history is mixed much that is legend or mere story. The stories are interesting in themselves and because they show us what the early Greeks thought was great and good. But the stories of Ulysses, of Jason and the Golden Fleece, of the fair Helen and the great wooden horse in which the Greek soldiers hid themselves and so got within the walls of Troy, should be read merely as stories. Later the Greeks wrote plays and poems as great as any which have ever been written. Indeed, it is through Greece that the other countries of Europe have learned many of the best things they know. The climate of Greece was so soft and mild and the country so beautiful that the people were able to live very much out of doors. They were very healthy and happy, and they loved beautiful things. The Greeks tried to bring up all their children to be strong and beautiful, and most of them were so. Being used to seeing only beautiful people their artists and sculptors painted and modelled very fine figures, and some of the statues carved by these old Greek artists remain today among the world's greatest treasures.

The Greeks were very proud of their country and their people. To them the rest of the world were 'barbarians' or uncivilized. Their patriotism was fired by the religious festivals in which all the Greeks united to do honor to their gods. At first each Greek clan or tribe worshipped together. Each kindled and kept alight a sacred fire in honor of the gods. Never must the fire be allowed to go out under peril of great disaster through the anger of the gods. No barbarian stranger might bring fuel to the fire. The care of it was a sacred trust.

A Greek Solider in Homer's Days (From a very early painting on a Greek vase).

As time went on some shrines became more famous than others, and to the great temples there Greeks from all parts of Greece would go in great numbers. At Delos there was a great shrine, and a still more famous one at Olympia, a beautiful plain in South-Western Greece surrounded by mountains and forming a kind of natural theatre. Here every fourth year the Olympic games were held in honor of Zeus, the greatest of the gods honored by the Greeks. At the Olympic games the best runners from all parts of Greece ran races. Rich men brought their chariots and competed in racing too. Poets brought their offerings of hymns written and sung in honor of the gods. The victors in each contest, those whom the judges thought the best, were crowned before all the people with wreaths of wild olive, while the name of their fathers and the districts from which they came were cried aloud so that the people might do them honor.

Yet, though the Greeks could thus unite for worship and patriotism, they were not all joined together in one kingdom like the English or French today. Each town with the country round it had at first its own government. This was chiefly because the land was broken up by deep bays on the coast and by mountain ranges inland and it was difficult for the people in one part of the country to travel to another part. So there were many states such as Corinth, Delos, and Thebes, and more famous still than these, Sparta and Athens.

For a time after the Greek people had settled down each state had its king. The first king would probably be the bravest soldier who had led the people to victory in war, but when he died his son would become king, and then his grandson, and in time some of the kings were not brave men at all, and nearly everywhere in Greece the people said they would not have kings any longer, but chose several of the greatest men in the land to rule them instead. Government by a few great men was called by the Greeks an 'aristocracy.' Generally in time the states grew tired of the aristocracies too, if they became proud and selfish, and in most Greek states some one man seized power again. He was not a king, but was called a 'tyrant,' which did not mean a cruel and selfish person as it does now. Soon again in nearly every Greek state the tyrants were overthrown, and some states chose once more to be governed by an aristocracy. Sparta chose thus, and was so governed as long as she remained a state. But some of the states declared that all the people should have a share in the government, and these were called democracies.

The greatest of these was the state of Athens, whose people were perhaps the bravest and most beautiful, and certainly the cleverest in the whole of Greece. Athens was the most beautiful of all the Greek city-states. Every one of its people was educated, and every man had a vote and took a direct part in the government. The state was so small that all the men could meet together to choose their leader. It was a very vivid eager life which the Athenians led, all keenly interested in politics, in philosophy and in artistic things. In Athens, every Greek had time and opportunity to hear beautiful poetry, to see good plays acted in theatres open to the air. All took an interest in the building of temples and in the beautiful statues made to adorn them. Perhaps no nation in history has ever had so fine a people, so little poverty, and so much education. But it must be remembered that in Athens, as everywhere in Greece, there were many slaves, who did the hardest work, and so made possible the brighter lives of their masters. The Greek 'democracy' was not like the modern democracy which most people think is the best form of government. The Greeks did not consider the welfare of *all* the people, and in modern nations where all are free the problem of making all happy and comfortable is more difficult.

THE SPARTANS

Sparta, the other great city-state in the south of Greece, was not a democracy, but remained an aristocracy. Its people were sterner and not so bright perhaps as the Athenians. They believed that every man should be a soldier, and every boy was taken from his mother when he was seven years old and brought up with other boys and taught how to fight. A Spartan boy would never cry whatever happened. He never thought about being warm and comfortable, but wore the same clothes summer and winter and cared only to be strong and brave. This was the ideal of the Spartans, the thing they lived for. The women felt just the same as the men about it, and the mothers gave up their boys willingly for the sake of the state. The girls shared the games and races with the boys, and grew up strong and brave women. A mother would much rather that her son should die in battle than give in. 'Return *with* your shield or *upon* it,' she would say as her son went forth to battle.

Besides the Greeks in the Balkan Peninsula and in the islands round about it there were others who had gone forth across the sea and built cities on the coast west of the land now called Asia Minor.

Since the Phœnicians had led the way men knew much more about ships and how to sail the seas safely, and some of the more adventurous Greeks had sailed westwards and set up towns in Sicily and in the south of Italy. Some of these were very rich and beautiful. The towns on the coast of Asia Minor, too, flourished and grew rich, and were full of beautiful temples, for the Greeks during many hundreds of years worshipped many gods. It was a long time before their cleverest men realized that there could be only one God, and then the people were very angry with them for saying so. Meanwhile, they built their temples to Apollo the god of beauty, or to Diana the goddess, whom they pictured as a huntress, young, brave, and noble, armed with bow and arrow, and with fluttering graceful garments short to the knees. There was one famous temple of Diana at Ephesus, one of the chief Greek towns in Asia Minor. We read in the Bible how in later days St. Paul tried to teach the Ephesians about our Lord, and how they clung to the worship of their goddess. But long before this a great danger had threatened Ephesus and the other Greek settlements in Asia Minor, a danger which threatened Greece, too, and which was so great that in the end the Greeks joined together to resist it.

THE PERSIANS

For hundreds of years the Greek towns in Asia Minor, like those at home in Greece, and the colonies in Sicily and the south of Italy, were prosperous and free, but at length they fell under the power of the Lydians, a people who possessed the land near. The Lydian king, Croesus, had conquered most of Asia Minor, and had demanded tribute of the Greek cities there. Croesus was wonderfully powerful and rich, but he fell in his turn before the Persian power, which had now spread westward over Babylonia and on to the very coast. When, last of all, the Greek cities there were attacked by this great barbaric power, they sent distressful messages to their kinsmen in Greece proper, and Athens determined to send them help.

This decision of the Athenian people is one of the turning-points in the world's history. If Athens had not fought against Persia and won, the Persian power might have spread from Asia to Europe, and the whole history of the world would have been changed. The Persians belonged to the Aryan people, but they were quite unlike the Aryan people in Europe. They were brave men, but they had no idea of the freedom which was the ideal of the Greeks. With the Persians, as with most Eastern people before and since, the will of the king was the supreme law. On his word depended life and death. The greatest nobles bowed before him as though he had been a god. His court was full of beautiful things, and life seemed gay and brilliant, but there was a sense of uneasiness, for under a cruel or capricious king no man could feel that even his life was safe.

A story is told of the cruelty of one of these early kings. A nobleman had offended him, but the king pretended to forgive him and invited him to a feast. At the end of the meal the king asked him what he thought of the food, and when he had been assured that it was excellent, the king called for a basket and showed it to his guest. In it were the head, hands, and feet of the nobleman's own child, and the king maliciously told him that the food that he had eaten was his child's body.

The poor people were very poor and often unhappy. Women were hardly thought of as human beings, and children could be sold by their parents as slaves. The 'Great King' could lead great armies to battle, but the soldiers did not feel that they were fighting for their fatherlands. They won because of their great numbers, and because they were often fighting men very like themselves. But things turned out very differently when the Persians found themselves fighting with the Greeks, men who loved freedom and beauty and goodness, men who were full of pride in their people and respect for themselves.

When Croesus was conquered by the Persian king, Cyrus, the Greek cities had been forced to give in to him too. Instead of the mere tribute that they had paid to Croesus, they were placed under Persian governors and treated as a conquered people. One town, Miletus, was allowed some sort of independence, but even there the

The Royal Archers of King Darius of Persia (From some beautifully painted bricks on the walls of the ancient palace of Darius at Susa).

people never felt really safe. The tyrant of Miletus had been carried off into honorable captivity with the Persian king, but had left his son-in-law, Aristagoras, to govern Miletus. The rulers of the other cities had become mere servants of Persia, and so the people determined to get rid of them and set up democratic governments. This they did. Aristagoras took the lead in the movement, gave up his power into the hands of the people, and when, in the year 500 B.C., the Greek cities of Asia Minor announced that they would no longer live under Persian rule, it was Aristagoras who went over to Greece proper to ask help of the Greeks there for their kinsmen over the sea. He went first to Sparta, and told them first of the sad state of the Greeks in Asia Minor, and then of the riches of the Persians. It would be easy, he said, to conquer the Persians, barbarians who wore trousers and turbans, and then all the wealth of Persia would be theirs. But the Spartans refused to go.

Then Aristagoras went on to Athens, and again told his tale. The Athenians had but lately got rid of their tyrants. They were full of spirits and courage. Aristagoras reminded them that

Miletus, the chief town suffering under the Persians, had been founded by people from Athens. The Athenians determined to give them help, and sent twenty ships across the seas. The Lydian town of Sardis was accidentally burnt, and the Athenians, without giving further help, went back to their ships, and so home. It was afterwards said that the new Persian king, Darius, was so angry with the Athenians that he told one of his servants to remind him before every meal of the vengeance he was to take on them. But it was eleven years before Darius tried to revenge himself on the Athenians. Meanwhile he turned his anger against Miletus and the other rebel cities. Miletus was taken, and many of its men were killed. The others were sent with the women and children to a town far away on the river Tigris, and there had to live out their lives as exiles far from home and country. The other rebellious cities were badly treated too, and then, after eleven years, Darius turned to take vengeance on the Athenians who had dared to defy him. He sent messengers to Greece asking the states to send him earth and water, as a sign that they would consent to live under the yoke of the 'Great King,' as he called himself.

THE BATTLE OF MARATHON

Some of the states did so, but Athens and Sparta proudly refused; and it is said that Sparta threw the Persian messengers into a pit, and told them to find earth and water for themselves there. In the same year, 490 B.C., Darius prepared a great fleet of ships, filled them with soldiers, and sent them against the Athenians. Thousands and thousands of them clothed in mail poured from the ships into the plain of Marathon, which was twenty miles from Athens and belonged to it. The Athenians sent for help to Sparta, but were told that no help could be sent until after a religious festival, which was still some days off. The Spartans were never very ready to join with the Athenians, for the states were very jealous of each other. It is said that Pheippides, the runner chosen to carry the message to Sparta, ran all the way in two days. The distance was one hundred and fifty miles.

When he came back the Athenians stood on the mountains looking down upon the plain of Marathon, and the generals consulted together as to what should be done. Miltiades, one of the generals, advised an immediate attack, and the others gave up their power to him, and he arranged the battle according to his will. The Athenians by his orders plunged down from the mountains on to the Persian army in the plain. There were five times as many Persians as Greeks, but the shock was so great, and the Athenians fought so well, that the great awkward army of men, who had no knowledge of what freedom meant, were driven into the sea and back to their ships by the splendid Greek soldiers.

The Greeks clung on to the Persian ships, meaning to set fire to them, but the Persians slashed savagely at them. The brother of Æschylus, the great poet and writer of plays, who also fought at Marathon, had his hands cut off as he clung to a ship, and then he held on by his teeth. All but seven ships got away. The Persians sailed round to attack the harbor of Athens next morning, but the Greek soldiers, weary as they were from the battle, marched to meet them, and when the Persians saw the men who had just conquered them drawn up again to face them, they gave up the attack and sailed away in disgust.

So Athens saved Greece, and probably Europe; for Darius, if he had conquered Greece, might have spread his empire over the whole of Europe, and the ideas of freedom and art and beauty which the Greeks taught the world might have been lost. The Athenians built a great monument on the plain of Marathon to commemorate their victory, and they made the men of the little town of Platasa citizens of Athens. Platasa alone of the Greek states had helped the Athenians, and the thousand men whom they had sent were among the bravest and best fighters in the great battle.

A Soldier of Marathon (From a Greek tomb on the battlefield).

Miltiades, the victorious general, soon fell into disgrace. He asked the Athenians to fit out for him a fleet of ships, but begged them to allow him to keep as a secret the purpose for which he wanted them, promising to bring a great deal of money back. Then he sailed away to fight an enemy of his own who lived in Paros, an island near. He was not able to take the city, and sailed back again to Athens without having done anything and without the money he had promised. The Athenians were very angry, and Miltiades would have been put to death but for the memory of his courage and cleverness at Marathon. He was ordered to pay a fine of a large sum of money, but died before he had time to do so. Some people have blamed the Athenians for having been so severe against a man who had done so much for them, and they have said that people governed as democracies are always changeable. Still, Miltiades had no right to use his country's money to take revenge on his own enemies.

Yet the Athenians were perhaps a little changeable, for they showed it in their treatment of others. The two chief men in Athens after Marathon were Themistocles and Aristides. Themistocles was anxious that the Athenians should build a fleet, and so be able to fight on sea as well as on land, while Aristides would have preferred a policy of peace. In the end Themistocles got his way and Aristides was banished, for the Athenians had a custom of sending troublesome politicians into exile, so that they should not hamper the rulers at home. When the votes were being given as to whether Aristides should go or stay, one man at least was said to have voted against him because he was 'tired of hearing him called Aristides the Just.' Aristides was not long away, for Persia soon threatened again, and Athens was glad to call back all the exiles who had been sent away after Marathon.

THE PERSIAN INVASION OF GREECE

Darius went back to Persia determined to prepare a monster invasion of Greece and so take his revenge, but he died before he had time to carry it out, and the work was left for his son Xerxes, who became king after him.

Xerxes invaded Greece in the year 480 B.C. He had endless resources at his disposal in men and money. Fearing the stormy sea round the Cape of Mount Athos, which his fleet would have to pass on its way to the Greek peninsula, he ordered great gangs of men to cut a deep channel through it, so that two ships could easily sail through side by side. Then he ordered bridges of boats to be made across the Hellespont, and in the towns, all along the way by which his army would have to go, he stored great quantities of food. He meant to avoid all risk. The first bridge broke because the ropes were not strong enough, and Xerxes ordered that the men who had built it should be beheaded. In his mad anger he ordered, too, that the water of the Hellespont should be whipped with rods, receiving three hundred lashes for its defiance of the Great King.

Then the bridges were built again with stronger bonds, and in a fit of repentance or amiability Xerxes poured wine from a golden bowl into the Hellespont, and then flung the cup and a golden bowl and a sword into the water, at sunrise of the day when he was at length ready to lead his great unwieldy army into Greece. The baggage, with the camels and horses, crossed on one bridge and the soldiers on the other. The first to cross were ten thousand Persians, the flower of the army, brave strong men accustomed to conquer. Behind them went the sacred horses and a chariot, empty in honor of the gods, and Xerxes himself drove after. Behind him straggled an enormous host, to the number of at least a million men, drawn from the peoples conquered by the Persians, and with no heart for the fight. So great was the crowd that the two bridges were filled with men and animals crossing over during seven days and seven nights.

It is said that one old man who had sent four sons to the army begged that the fifth might stay at home, but Xerxes, instead of granting the favor, ordered that the boy should be killed, and the pieces of his body placed on both sides of the bridge as a warning to others who might wish to hang back. Any who were slow to cross were freely lashed with whips. Xerxes could not realize that fear will never lead an army to victory.

When the Greeks had seen the danger threatening from Persia, some of the states had been very anxious that the whole of Greece should join to resist it. A congress of the states was called to meet at the Isthmus of Corinth. The part of Greece south of the isthmus was called the Peloponnesus, and here Sparta was the chief state, and had great power over the others. So nearly all the Peloponnesians naturally joined with Sparta, though Argos, a Peloponnesian town, held aloof, declaring she would rather be ruled by the Persians than help Sparta, whom she hated. In the end very few of the states north of the Isthmus of Corinth joined in the defence. There was, of course, Athens and the people of Phocis, and the faithful little town of Platæa, and Thespiæ, another town near. But most of the northern Greeks held aloof, and some hastened to send earth and water to the Great King. Themistocles had his fleet ready, and was longing for a good sea fight, but as Sparta was the chief state in all Greece for the moment, the chief command was given to them both by land and sea.

The Story of Thermopylæ

As ranges of mountains stretch across the north of Greece, the Greeks knew that the Persian army must come through mountain passes. They decided to make a stand at the Pass of Thermopylæ, for if the Persians could get through that, there would be nothing to stop them until they reached the Isthmus of Corinth. A band of men were therefore set under the Spartan king, Leonidas, to guard the pass. More Spartans were to be sent later when a feast should be over. The Spartans would never let anything interfere with their sacred feasts. However, Leonidas knew that a few men could hold the pass easily against even the immense army of Xerxes, but unfortunately a treacherous Greek went to Xerxes and told him that to the west of the Pass of Thermopylæ was a path over a mountain which could not easily be defended. Leonidas had placed some Phocians there, but when they saw vast numbers of Persians advancing they turned and fled.

News came to Leonidas that the Persians were advancing, and he knew that there was no hope for those who should remain to guard the pass now that it would be attacked from both ends. So he told his army that those who wished might go away, but that he himself would stay and die fighting the enemy. Three hundred Spartan soldiers with their slaves, and seven hundred others chose to stay, only about a thousand men in all. The Spartans were never afraid, not even of death, and they spent their time making an elaborate toilet, combing out their thick hair, which they wore long, putting on dresses of bright scarlet, and polishing their weapons, so that they might face death with every sign of joy.

As the Persians poured into the plain south of the pass, Leonidas told his men to fight their way out of the northern end; and there he and his little band died fighting desperately, killing far more Persians than their own numbers. The Persians were astounded at such courage, and angry too that so many of their own men were killed by a mere handful of Greeks. Two brothers of the Great King himself were among the dead. Later the Greeks built monuments on the spot where the heroes of Thermopylæ had fought, and chief among them was a marble lion to honor the memory of Leonidas.

In spite of the heroism of Leonidas and his Spartans all Greece, as far as the Isthmus of Corinth, now lay open to the Persians, and as they marched south the states gave in their allegiance. Platæa and Thespiæ were beaten down to the ground, and the Athenians, seeing that there was no hope for them, took refuge on the fleet, and were carried off to Salamis and other places of safety. One of the oracles had advised them to trust to a wooden wall, and this they thought meant their wooden boats; but a few men remained behind in the Acropolis, the hill center of the town, which could not be entered when the gates were shut except at one side. Across this side the Athenians who remained placed great beams of wood to form a kind of wall, hoping thus to fulfil the words of the oracle, and take shelter behind a wooden wall. When the Persians advanced to attack them they threw great stones down on their heads. But it was of no use, for the Persians broke through the barrier, killed the Greeks, and practically destroyed Athens.

Thus the fate of the Greeks on land was sad enough, in spite of their great courage; but there was still the fleet, in which Themistocles had put so much trust. The Persian fleet, off the coast near Thermopylæ, had suffered much from storms, and in a fight they had with the Greeks, though the Greeks lost some ships, the Persians lost more. When the news came of the destruction of Athens the Greek fleet was at Salamis. Themistocles could not persuade the leaders to sail forth and attack the Persians. One of the generals said to Themistocles, 'O Themistocles, those who stand up in the game too soon are whipped' (referring to a rule in the Greek games); but Themistocles answered, 'Yes, but those who start late are not crowned.'

At length Themistocles had recourse to a trick. He sent word to the Persians that the Greek fleet was very frightened, and was going to sail away. The Persians then thought it would be best to attack the Greeks before they could escape, and one morning the Greek fleet found the whole Persian fleet drawn up to the east, ready to fight.

The Greeks then showed that they could fight on sea as well as on land, in spite of their hesitation. They dashed in and broke the front line of the Persian ships, and drove the two back lines in confusion upon each other. On sea, as on land, the Persian forces were too awkward and unwieldy. There was really not room for so many ships. The battle became fast and furious. When a Persian ship was sunk the men were drowned, for few of them could swim; while many Greeks even from ships which were destroyed saved themselves by swimming to the shore.

Xerxes had one ally who was a woman. Queen Artemisia of Halicarnassus in Caria. The Greeks had promised a prize to whomsoever should capture her; but when a Greek ship was chasing her she wilfully sank a Persian ship which came in her way. The Greek captain seeing this, and not knowing it was Artemisia's ship, gave up the chase, thinking that she had deserted from the Persians.

Xerxes sat on a great white marble throne on the shore and watched the battle. Even at the end the Persians had twice as many ships as the Greeks, but so many men and ships had been destroyed that they had no longer any heart for the fight. Orders were given that the fleet should sail away; and Xerxes himself, sick at heart with disappointment, collected what remained of his vast army, and crossed the Hellespont in haste, lest the Greek fleet should come to stop him. Three hundred thousand Persians remained in Greece under the general Mardonius to make one more attempt in the next year at the conquest of this small country, which had thus defied the giant armies of the Great King.

An Early Greek Warship (*From a painting on a Greek vase made in the sixth century* B.C.).

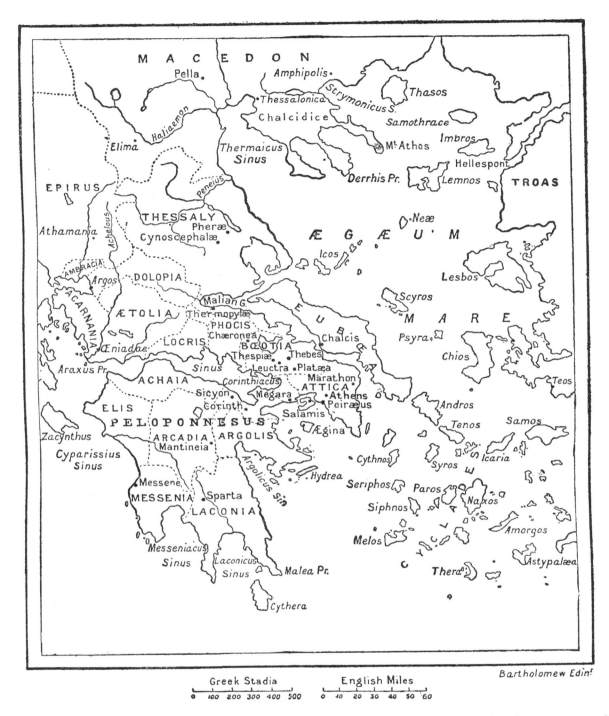

Bartholomew Edinᶠ

Greek Stadia   English Miles

Xerxes met with endless misfortunes on the journey home. The bridges across the Hellespont broke; the ice gave way on a frozen river as the army crossed it; provisions ran short and disease broke out. Men and animals died in thousands. Mardonius spent the winter in Thessaly, and in the spring started again towards Athens. Once more the Athenians withdrew to Salamis, and their city was again ravaged by the enemy. The Athenians sent indignant messages to the Spartans, who had again failed to help them, because their religious festivals held them back. Meanwhile they had built a strong wall across the Isthmus of Corinth. It is said that some one pointed out to them that the Athenians might in the end join the Persians against Sparta, and that their strong wall would be of little use if the Athenians with their magnificent fleet attacked them by sea.

At last the Spartans sent an army to join the Athenians, and Mardonius withdrew north into Bœotia, which was better country for his cavalry to fight in. Help from other Greek states now poured in, and Mardonius, anxious to break up the Greek army, sent Masistios, the commander second to himself, to attack Megara. The Athenians detached themselves from the general army and went to their aid. Masistios was a handsome man, and almost a giant in height. He wore a suit of golden mail, and over it a tunic of crimson. His white horse was shot under him, and though his mail resisted all arrows for a time, he was at last shot through the eye and killed. The Athenians won the victory, and the body of Masistios was carried in triumph along the lines of the Greek army that all might see it.

Mardonius waited several days before he ventured to attack the Greeks, and then one day, when the Spartans were making a change in their position, he led his army against them alone. The Athenians were surrounded by the Greeks, who were helping the Persians, and so the Spartans fought the famous battle of Platæa practically alone against the Persians. The splendid Persian cavalry tried to break the solid mass of the Spartan ranks, but failed. The heavily armed and mailed foot soldiers of Sparta broke down the hedge of shields, behind which the light-armed foot soldiers of the Persian army stood; and though it was a hard-fought battle, and the Persians were overwhelmingly greater in numbers than the Spartans, the splendid discipline of the Greeks won the day. Mardonius himself was killed, and the Persians fell back to their camp. Here another struggle took place; but the Athenians now came up to the help of the Spartans, and the Greek victory was complete.

All the precious vessels of gold and silver which Xerxes had been too hurried to take away, and so had left to his officers, now fell to the Greeks, and in some degree repaid them for the immense expenses of the war. It is said that only three thousand Persians were left alive out of the three hundred thousand of Mardonius's great army, while in all only one hundred and sixty Greeks died on the field.

On the afternoon of the day in which the battle of Platæa was fought in the morning, the Greeks won another great victory over the Persians at Mycale in Asia Minor. Here it was the Athenians who played the chief part, going to the help of the Greek cities in Asia Minor, who were still under the hated rule of the Great King. The Persian admiral drew up his boats on the shore, but the Athenians followed, landed, and fought against them on land, and won a great victory. So not only were the Persians driven out of Greece proper, and Europe saved from an invasion by an Eastern people, but the Greeks in Asia Minor were freed from their rule; and soon they were to be followed into their own strongholds, and the magnificence of the Great King was to be a thing of the past.

Chapter IV—The Athens of Pericles and Socrates

Athens had very nobly allowed the Spartans to take the lead in the great struggle with Persia, but once the danger was past the old jealousy between the two states broke out again. Pausanias, the Spartan leader, who had fought so bravely and won so glorious a victory at Platæa, soon proved himself unworthy of the position he held, and Athens took advantage of this to place an Athenian at the head of her fleet. Pausanias was found to be writing to the Persians, and even planning to give Greece up into the power of the Great King, if he himself should be allowed to marry the king's daughter, and if all sorts of riches were showered upon him.

When the Spartans sent messages to the Persians through Pausanias it was noticed that no answer ever came, and so a slave who was given a letter to take, opened it to see what it said. He found that it merely told the Persians to kill the messenger (himself). The slave took the letter to the judges at Sparta, and Pausanias, who had already been called back to Sparta, was condemned to death. He fled for shelter to the Temple of Athene; and as it was not considered right to kill a man in so holy a place, or even violently to drag him forth, the Spartans ordered that the doors of the temple should be blocked up, and the roof taken off, so that Pausanias soon died a miserable death through cold and hunger.

Meanwhile the Athenians had built very strong walls round their city and round their port at the Piræus. Now with such strong walls and their mighty fleet they had no need to fear anybody, and the Spartans were surprised and angry to find that the new leader they sent to Athens in place of Pausanias was sent back with the message that the Athenians had chosen a leader of their own.

After this there was a terrible enmity between Sparta and Athens. Athens was now quite equal in wealth and importance to Sparta, and she took steps to make herself still richer and more powerful. She kept up an immense navy, and many of the islands in the Ægean Sea, Thrace, and some of the Greek colonies in Asia Minor joined in a league with Athens. They were all to send

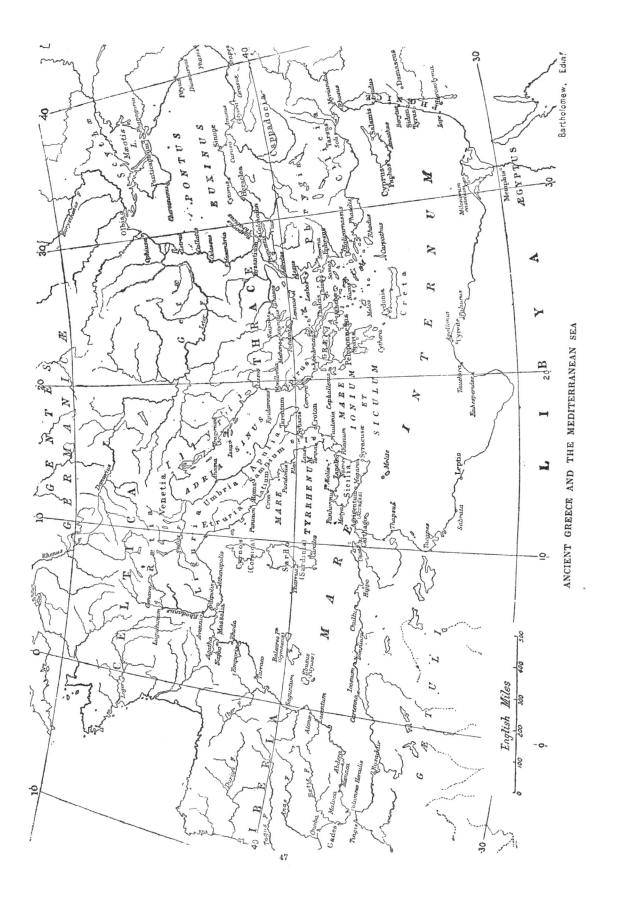

ANCIENT GREECE AND THE MEDITERRANEAN SEA

47

32

ships and sailors, and all to defend each other against any enemy. The League was called the Confederacy of Delos, and all the money belonging to it was kept at the Temple of Apollo at Delos, and each state sent men there to worship the god. But in time Athens often allowed the other states to send money instead of ships; and after a while she forgot that the other states had joined her of their own free will, and she began to think herself the chief state of a sort of empire, with the other states paying tribute to her. In the end this was very bad for Athens, for it made the other states angry and ready to help her enemies against her.

Bust of Pericles bearing the inscription "Pericles, son of Xanthippus, Athenian".

But this was not for a long time yet, and for many years Athens grew richer and richer. She kept up an immense navy; but there was more money than was needed for that, and some of this was spent on raising beautiful buildings in Athens and making life very easy for her people. Even the men who met in their parliament to rule the state were paid for their time and trouble. The Athenians became great traders, and sent their merchant-ships to all parts of Greece. Gold and silver were quite common.

But the Athenians were not like the Persians, who wasted their wealth on mere splendour and show. Nor had they any sympathy with the Spartans, who, however rich they might be, would never change from their plain, hard way of living. The Athenians loved beautiful things, and they spent their money in making their city perfect and in giving joy and pleasure to all the citizens.

PERICLES

The chief man in democratic Athens for many years after the Persian Wars was Pericles, one of the most famous men who have ever lived. He never trusted Sparta, and knew that a great struggle with that state must come some day. He was made 'general' of the Athenian people; but he was always careful to remember that he held power from the people,

The Greek Ideal. This beautiful sculpture, a portion of the frieze of the Parthenon now in the Louvre, represents, as only a Greek artist could, the bodily perfection towards which the Athenians strove.

The Parthenon and the Acropolis of Athens as They Probably Were in the Days of Pericles (*From a reconstruction in the British Museum*).

The Parthenon of Athens as It Is Today

who chose him to rule as their best and wisest citizen. Unlike so many of even the bravest Greeks, he was faithful and honest in small things as well as great. He was kind, too, and on his deathbed, when the men round him were talking of the great and noble things he had done, he reminded them that he was to be praised not for these things, but because he had never caused sorrow to a fellow-citizen. This was remarkable at a time when the Greeks were terribly cruel and revengeful to any one who offended them.

Yet Pericles had done wonderful things, for which his fellow-citizens might justly praise him. It was said that 'he found Athens of brick and left it of marble.' The whole city had practically to be built again after the Persian attack. A giant statue of the Goddess Athene made of bronze was made and placed on the highest point of the Acropolis. Then the Athenians planned and built the Parthenon, a beautiful temple of marble, the ruins of which remain today to show men how beautiful the buildings of Greece could be.

Right round the outside of the temple ran a frieze or band of sculpture, carved by Phidias, perhaps the greatest sculptor who has ever lived, and by his pupils. Bits of this frieze have since been carried off by other nations. Some may be seen in the British Museum in London, and others in the Museum of the Louvre in Paris. They are considered among our greatest treasures of art. Inside the temple was another immense figure of Athene, carved by Phidias himself from ivory and gold, as marble was not considered rich enough. The great public buildings were adorned with pictures telling of the legends of early Greece and of the wars of later times. A great theatre, too, was built. It was a fine building, and had no roof, so that the Athenians with their fine climate could see plays acted in perfect comfort.

Just as the age of Pericles was the time when the greatest artists of Athens lived, so, too, it was the age of the great Athenian play-writers. It seemed as though the joy of victory over the Persians had spread through the nation and inspired the cleverest men in the most wonderful way. This kind of thing has often been noticed in the history of nations. A nation

The Replica of Athene of the Parthenon (Nashville, TN), based on a Roman copy of the immense statue carved in ivory and gold by Phidias. The original has long been lost.

will grow strong and fight for its freedom, and it will be found that the age of great soldiers will be also the age of great poets.

The first of the great play-writers of Greece was Æschylus, and he fought with all his strength at Marathon. In the age of Pericles lived two other great tragic play-writers, Sophocles and Euripides, and their plays, which students read today with the greatest admiration, were then played before the Athenian people in their beautiful open-air theatre; and the people wept over them and gained new ideas from them, and went away full of joy and wonder at the beautiful things they had seen and heard. Sophocles had been a boy of sixteen at the time of the battle of Salamis, and he was chosen, because he was so beautiful and could play so well on the lyre, to lead the chorus of boys who took part in the thanksgiving ceremonies on the island of Salamis to celebrate the victory. Then, too, there was Aristophanes, a writer of comedies which made people laugh instead of weep.

SOCRATES

The age of Pericles was the time, too, when the great Greek thinkers and philosophers gave their teaching to the world. The first great Greek philosopher was Socrates. The most educated of the Greeks had begun to ask questions about the real meaning of the world and the

Socrates, the First Great Greek Philosopher (From a bust in British Museum).

things around them, but Socrates was the first who gave any real answer. He understood that the tales about the gods of Greece and of the other nations could not be true, and that there could only be one God. He might have been seen any day in the streets of Athens asking questions of boys and young men, who crowded round him to listen to his wise answers. When they gave foolish or thoughtless answers he laughed, and showed how necessary it is to think before we speak.

Socrates was a little ugly man with a flat, snub nose, but he was a very noble character. He would talk to any man he met, workmen as well as scholars, and he longed to help men to be good and truthful. He loved the town with its crowds and liveliness, and many of the people loved him. He dressed always in the poorest clothes and ate the simplest food, for he thought that these things did not matter. He cared only for knowledge and goodness. In the end he had a very sad death.

Some of the people at whom he had laughed were very angry with him. Others thought that it was very dangerous that their young men should be told that the old tales about the gods were not true. After the death of Pericles the Athenians, spoilt by success, had grown very changeable and restless. Socrates irritated them by insisting that goodness consisted in doing right, and that offerings to the gods were of no use without this. Thirty years after the death of Pericles, Socrates, now seventy years of age, was called before the judges, and put on trial for offences against the gods and the state. He was condemned to die, but did not seem in the least afraid. He even vexed the judges by joking on the subject. When they asked him to suggest what else the Athenians might do to him instead of putting him to death, he suggested that they should keep him in a certain hall in Athens, where men who had served the state were kept at the expense of the state. The judges indignantly passed sentence of death on the old philosopher, and he spent some time in prison before the time appointed for his death.

One of his followers told Socrates how sad he was because he was being put to death without deserving it. But Socrates replied, smiling, that it would have been much worse if he *had* deserved it. He declared that no real harm could happen to a good man in this life or the next. The Greeks used to give poison to a condemned man, and allow him to drink it himself at any moment he might choose. Socrates drank the hemlock with his friends around him, and when they broke out in cries and tears he begged them to be quiet and allow him to die in peace.

It was not many years before the Athenians were very sorry indeed for the way Socrates had been treated, and those who had caused his death were punished. The death of Socrates came when Athens had fallen far from her greatness in the days of Pericles. In the days of Pericles he was still held in great honor.

It was in wars against the other states of Greece that Athens lost her riches and her power. Pericles knew that a struggle with Sparta must come, and he did all he could to strengthen Athens for the fight. He built the famous 'Long Walls' from Athens down to the sea, reaching the coast at the Piræus, the port of Athens. No better plan could have been made for the safety of Athens. It would for the future be of little use for Sparta or any other state to besiege her by land, for food could always be brought in ships to the port, and then carried between the two Long Walls into the city. Twice in the early years of Pericles' rule Sparta had taken arms against Athens, but peace had been made.

It was not until two years before his death that the famous war between Sparta and Athens, known as the Peloponnesian War, broke out. The policy of Pericles had prepared Athens for the struggle, but she was weakened by jealousies among the members of the Confederacy of Delos, whom she had treated so proudly and so unjustly. Other causes helped to make Sparta win; and the later history of Athens, in its sadness and gloom, serves to throw into contrast her wonderful activity and prosperity in the age of Pericles.

CHAPTER V—THE GREEK COLONIES IN THE WEST

Before continuing the history of the Greeks in Greece proper, it will be well to take a glance at what was happening to the Greek colonies farther west. It will be remembered that about the same time that Greeks had gone forth from Greece proper to make settlements on the coast of Asia Minor, others had sailed westward and made colonies in Sicily and the south of Italy. The Greeks loved to live in cities, and when possible near the sea, and so most of these towns were on the coast. Sicily and Southern Italy became known as Greater Greece, and the settlers never forgot that they were Greeks. They set up temples to the gods of their country, and lived much as they had done at home.

Some of these Greek colonies in Greater Greece were much richer than the Greek cities at home. So luxurious were the people of Sybaris, a town in South Italy, that even today we call a person who loves pleasure more than anything else a 'Sybarite.' A colony which went out from Sybaris itself was called Croton, and became famous for its clever doctors. Pythagoras, a famous philosopher, belonged to Croton. The Sybarites and Crotonians always hated each other, and finally the Crotonians destroyed Sybaris completely in war; for these Greek states abroad were like those at home, always fighting with each other. Another colony famous for its luxury, although it was founded by men from Sparta, who must have been brought up in the strictest way, was Tarentum, on the gulf of the same name.

There were many Greek settlements in Sicily, the chief being Syracuse, founded by people from Corinth. Another great Greek settlement in Sicily was Agrigentum, which is remembered by its tyrant, Phalaris. He was a tyrant in our sense of the word as well as the Greek. He is said to have burnt his enemies alive inside a bull made of brass. After some years the people turned on him, and put him to death with terrible torture.

The Greeks in Sicily and Italy had changes of government very like the states in Greece proper. Some became aristocracies, some democracies, but they always remained city states, and were too jealous of one another ever to unite under one government. The people of Agrigentum built temples almost as beautiful as those of Athens, and their ruins are still to be seen.

The Ruins of the Temple of the Greek Colony at Agrigentum in Sicily. *Wherever the Greeks settled they always erected temples, generally like the beautiful one of which the ruins are shown in this picture.*

The most westerly of all the Greek settlements was Marsilia, in the south of France, now called Marseilles.

THE STRUGGLE WITH CARTHAGE

It was a curious fact that at the same time that Greece proper was engaged in its life-and-death struggle with Persia, the Greeks of the west were also threatened by a great power. This was Carthage, a settlement made on the north of Africa long before by the Phœnicians in the days of their greatness. Phœnicia had long ceased to be a great power but Carthage had grown rich, and had herself sent out colonies. She had also won for herself much land along the north of Africa, partly consisting of other smaller Phœnician settlements, and partly to the native people, called the Libyans, with whom the Carthaginians mixed freely. The Libyans, however, had no part in the government, which was, in fact, in the hands of a few Carthaginian nobles. It was an aristocracy of the narrowest sort. The Carthaginians were rich and fond of pleasure, though the men who were actually ruling the state at any time lived plainly, and would not touch wine, thinking that a ruler should keep his brain clear and his wits sharp.

The Greeks and Carthaginians in the Western Mediterranean soon became very jealous of each other. There was a third state, higher up in Italy, Rome, which in the end was to conquer both, but her turn had not yet come. There were many small fights between the Carthaginians and Greeks, especially in Sicily, in the west of which the Carthaginians had made several settlements. The Greeks tried in the early part of the fifth century B.C. to push the Carthaginians out of Sicily altogether, but they did not manage it; and the Carthaginians in their turn chose the time when Xerxes was attacking Greece proper to make a determined attack on the Greeks in Sicily. They chose this time because they were afraid that otherwise the Greeks at home would come to the help of their colonies.

The Carthaginians made up their minds to send a great army, under Hamilcar, a brave soldier, who was a Carthaginian on his father's side and a Syracusan Greek on his mother's. Under his command were three thousand ships carrying an enormous army. It was an army much like that of Xerxes, awkward and unwieldy, too large because of the different peoples which went to make it up. There were Carthaginians and men from their colonies, the native Libyans, and some Greeks from states which were enemies of Himera, and the other Greek states of Sicily which were to be attacked. A storm destroyed many of the ships on their way across to Panormus (now Palermo), where Hamilcar landed his men and marched on Himera.

A great battle was fought, which the Greeks won, partly by a clever trick and partly by their better fighting. It was said that a hundred and fifty thousand men of the army of Carthage lay dead upon the field. Hamilcar watched the fight all day, burning a great fire of sacrifice to his gods, which may have been a sacrifice of human beings, for the Carthaginians had this dreadful practice. At sunset, seeing that defeat was certain, he threw himself into the fire and died, rather than return home to tell of his misfortune. All of the ships which had been drawn up upon the beach were burnt by the Greeks, and of the twenty which had not been drawn up, and so sailed away, only one returned to Carthage to tell the sad tale; for again a storm rose, and the others were destroyed.

The Greeks raised a monument in honor of Hamilcar, although he was their enemy, and the Carthaginians, although they were not usually grateful to their heroes, honored his memory for many years.

The soldiers who remained alive out of the army of Carthage were made slaves by the people of Agrigentum.

It was afterwards told that the battle of Himera was fought on the same day as the great sea-fight of Salamis. It was at any rate about the same time, and so the Greeks triumphed against their enemies in both east and west.

For seventy years after the battle of Himera the Carthaginians left the Greeks alone. If they had won Sicily, the Carthaginians might have won the south of Italy too. As it was, time was given for Rome to grow and extend its power there. The Greeks and Carthaginians were to have many a desperate struggle yet in Sicily; but by that time the Greek power had become as nothing compared to that of Rome, and it was to Rome that the fall of Carthage was in the end due.

Chapter VI—The Peloponnesian War

The history of this war, which lasted with periods of peace nearly thirty years, is perhaps of more importance in the history of Greece than in the history of the world. In it the power and greatness of Athens were brought to an end. It is just possible but not probable that if Athens had won she would have conquered the rest of Greece, and a great Athenian empire might have been formed. If this had been so, Athens would have had an even greater influence on later history than she has had. But it was not to be, and there is no real reason to believe that Athens, even if she had been victorious, would have set up such an empire. Still, the story of the war is interesting and important.

Ever since the Persian War, and especially under the rule of Pericles, Athens had irritated the other Greek states. She had made conquests on land, but these had been soon taken from her. But she clung to her empire, for such the Confederacy of Delos had become. The Persian power no longer threatened Greece, and had definitely set free even the Greek colonies in Asia Minor, but still Athens collected contributions from all the islands in the Ægean. The money was no longer kept at Delos, but was sent to Athens, and much of it was spent on the buildings there and on the amusement of the people.

Athens interfered also in the government of the other states of the confederacy whenever trouble arose, and set up democratic governments like their own. All important law cases had to be heard in Athens. When Samos, a large island which clung to its independence, refused to allow its quarrel with Miletus to be settled by Athens, the Athenians attacked her, destroyed all her walls of defence, took away her fleet, and made her pay the costs of the war. The Athenians kept sixty boats always in the Ægean Sea, as though she was afraid of a rebellion. For years a great struggle between Sparta and Athens had been expected. With Sparta necessarily went the whole of the Peloponnesian League, of which she was the chief member. The third greatest state in Greece was Corinth, which was a sea-power nearly as strong as Athens.

It was with Corinth that Athens first quarrelled, but Sparta took the opportunity of calling a meeting to discuss a war with Athens. Messages were sent threatening war if the Athenians would not send Pericles away. This, of course, they would not do; but they might have sent peaceful messages back but for a speech which Pericles himself made to the people. He was a great speaker, and when he pointed out that the war was sure to come some day, and that the Athenians were quite strong enough to face their enemies, they made up their minds to fight, and to fight as Pericles should tell them.

So in the year 431 B.C. the great struggle between the two greatest states in Greece began. On the side of the Spartans were nearly all the Greeks of the peninsula, though Sparta's old enemy, Argos in the Peloponnesus, refused to join, and Platæa, the faithful little ally of Athens, fought once more on her side. The war began with an attack on Platæa by the people of Thebes. Three hundred Thebans got into Platæa, and kept the people shut up in their houses. But the Platæans broke down the inside walls of their houses, and so were able to talk to each other. They arranged an attack on the Thebans, and a terrible fight took place. The Platæans killed many Thebans, and many others were driven into a large building where grain was kept. Other Thebans came up to the walls to help them; but the Platæans got them to go away, and then, in spite of their promises, killed every Theban left in the town. So angry were the people of Thebes that they sent another great army to attack Platæa, and the Athenians, although they were vexed that the Platæans had broken their word, had to send an army to protect them from the Thebans.

Then the Spartans marched into Attica itself. Pericles thought that the Athenians would have little chance on land against the great army of Sparta, so he collected all the people of Attica within the Long Walls, for he knew that they could get plenty of food by sea.

The people of Attica hated to leave their farms and vineyards to be destroyed by the enemy, but there was nothing else to do. The cattle were sent to the island of Eubœa, and the people lived in huts and tents put up in haste in the empty space between the Long Walls. Then Pericles sent ships round to harass the people on the coasts of the Peloponnesus. The great Spartan army, once it had laid waste all the country round Athens, could do nothing more to harm the Athenians. Only a few bands of horsemen went out to hamper them. So

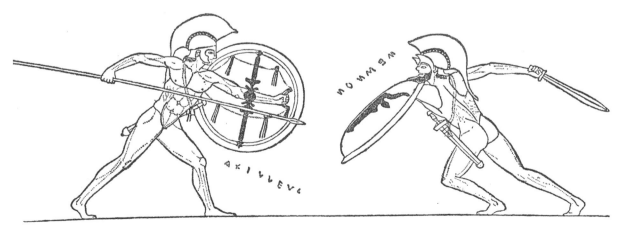

Two Greek Soldiers of the Fifth Century B.C. (*From an ancient vase painting representing the fight of Achilles and Agamemnon, whose names are written in Greek beside each figure*).

the first year of the war ended. There was a great funeral service in memory of those who had been killed; and Pericles made a noble speech, assuring the Athenians that the severity of Sparta could never make men so noble as the freedom of Athens, and begging them not to grieve too much over the dead, but to be ready to die in their turn if need were.

The next year things happened in much the same way. In the spring (for ancient peoples never fought in the winter) a great Spartan army ravaged Attica again. The people of the countryside again took refuge between the Long Walls; but a terrible misfortune fell upon the Athenians. A dreadful sickness called the plague broke out in the Piræus. It came to Europe from the East, and had broken out in Egypt and also in Italy. It must have been brought by some ship to the Piræus, and it spread quickly among the people crowded unhealthily together between the Long Walls. The people suffered terribly, and hundreds died, without any one to bury them. Pericles himself fell ill, but got better.

On all sides people began to grumble against him, as though their misfortunes were through his fault. A leather-seller called Cleon, a vulgar and ignorant man, tried to have the rule of Athens taken from him, but Pericles kept it till his death, which came shortly afterwards.

In the next year the Spartans took revenge on the little city of Platæa. All its men were killed, its women and children sold as slaves, and the city itself destroyed.

After the death of Pericles power in Athens fell to Cleon the leather-seller. He was very violent, and determined to remain at war, although many in Athens would have wished for peace. Just after his death, and after ten years of cruel and foolish warfare, a peace was at last made between Sparta and Athens. It lasted seven years, though it was made for fifty. Life in Athens had quite changed, and so had the spirit of the people. Socrates was still there, a relic of the great age of Pericles, but the new generation was changeable and fickle.

ALCIBIADES

Even when the fifty years' peace was signed, the best-known man in Athens was Alcibiades, a man thirty years old. His wayward character, his cleverness and courage, and his faults seem to be signs of the change which had come upon the Athenians. Alcibiades was a young relation of Pericles, and he was a pupil of Socrates, but he was not wise and serious like them. Knowing, as did Socrates, that the belief in the gods was not true, he merely laughed at them, whereas Socrates had taught men to look to higher things than these, and to do good even if they no longer honored the gods. Alcibiades was what is called

The Wayward Alcibiades (*From a bust in the Louvre*).

irresponsible. He would do anything which came into his head at any moment. He often drank too much wine, and went noisily about the town with his companions. Yet it was to such a man as this that the Athenians now gave their trust. They mistook cleverness for wisdom.

At the first Olympic games after the fifty years' peace was signed, it was thought that Athens would not be able to send any people to take part. But Alcibiades was there offering sacrifices in beautiful golden bowls, and with seven four-horsed chariots to run in the races. Twice he was crowned as victor with the crown of wild olive. All the time Alcibiades was anxious that Athens should fight again with Sparta, and war did in fact soon break out again.

The Athenians at this time showed the greatest cruelty towards any member of the Confederacy of Delos which dared to rebel against her unjust empire. The Island of Melos, which rebelled, was conquered, and every man there was put to death, the women and children being sold into slavery.

Shortly after this the Athenians were induced by Alcibiades to send a great fleet and army to Sicily, where the colonies of Sparta were at war with other states. The Athenian expedition went to help a city called Egesta against another called Selinus. The people of Egesta had promised to pay the expenses of the expedition, and Alcibiades had persuaded the Athenians to agree. Nicias, another statesman in Athens, persuaded the people to send messengers to see if the people of Egesta were really as rich as they said. It was said afterwards that they showed the Athenian messengers plates and cups which were only gilded over, and pretended they were made of gold. The Athenians were deceived, and the expedition went off under Nicias and Alcibiades.

But the morning it sailed, the Athenians were shocked to find that all the busts of their god Hermes, which stood on little square pedestals at the street corners, had been thrown over and broken during the night. They came to the conclusion that this had been done by Alcibiades as a joke. It was nothing to him, because he did not believe in the gods, but to those who did it seemed a terrible sacrilege. Afterwards it was thought that perhaps Alcibiades had not done this thing after all, but he had done worse things against the gods. So messengers were sent after him to bring him back a prisoner in his own ship, but instead he sailed away to Sparta, and offered his services to the bitter enemy of his country.

The Sicilian expedition was a complete failure, for Alcibiades told to the Spartans all the plans of the Athenians, and persuaded them to send an army to fight against the Athenians in Sicily. He was full of anger against the men of his own state, and when he heard that sentence of death had been passed upon him, he declared, 'I will show them one day that I am still alive.'

The leadership of the Athenians in Sicily was left to Nicias, who had very little heart for it. Alcibiades had wished all the other Greek colonies in Sicily to join with the Athenians in an attack on the Spartan colonies, especially Syracuse, but most of them refused, and the Athenians were left practically alone. A great battle was fought in the immense harbor at

Syracuse. The Athenians had many more ships than the Syracusans, but the Syracusans had placed theirs right across the mouth of the harbor, and the two hundred Athenian ships were hemmed in. All but sixty were destroyed, and the men who could escape joined the Athenian army on the shore. Nicias saw that they must give up the ships and try to escape by land to a part of the island where the people were friendly.

It was a terrible march, and the sick and wounded had to be left to die. Nicias, who had hated the whole thing, now showed how brave he was. Although he was very ill and tired, he went about among the men trying to cheer them. At one place the army had to march through a narrow pass between high rocks which the Syracusans fortified. For two days the Athenians fought, and then had to give up and choose another direction. They were short of food and water. At another place they caught sight of a river flowing in a deep hollow, and they were so thirsty that the whole army rushed forward to drink. Those in front were pushed down into the water, while those behind fell upon them, and were either crushed or pierced by the spears of the fallen. A Spartan army fell upon them while they were in this miserable state.

At last Nicias gave himself up with his army, begging that mercy should be shown to the ten thousand men' who remained out of the forty thousand who had begun this terrible march. He promised that the Athenians would pay the Syracusans, all that they had spent on the war. But the same cruelty was now shown as has been noticed in the later wars in Greece proper. The Athenians who thus gave themselves up were put in stone quarries, and left in hunger and cold. Nicias and the other Athenian leader, Demosthenes, were to be put to death, but preferred to kill themselves.

So ended in miserable defeat this expedition, planned in all light-heartedness by Alcibiades, and it was largely he who, by helping the Spartans, had ruined it. Meanwhile at home Sparta was still destroying and burning in the Plain of Attica.

The Athenians were terribly distressed when they heard the sad fate of the Sicilian expedition. The loss of the ships was very bad for their navy, but they bravely set to work to build more. But the struggle was too severe. Nearly all the members of the Confederacy of Delos rebelled, and all the money of the League, so long stored up in Athens, was spent in fighting them. In Athens itself the people had not even enough food. The Persians once more began to fight against their old enemy Athens, and joined with Sparta in helping the revolt of the Athenian colonies in Asia Minor. Alcibiades had helped too in this rebellion, but the Spartans were beginning to grow tired of him. He had deceived one of their kings, and his liveliness of character prevented them from really liking him. At last they decided that he should die, but Alcibiades then joined the friends of Athens, and fought against the colonies whom he had encouraged to rebel. In the end he won several battles, and then went back to Athens, was forgiven, and even welcomed. His manner was as attractive to the Athenians as it was unpleasant to the Spartans, and all his terrible treachery was forgotten.

THE RUIN OF ATHENS

Alcibiades was a fine leader, but it was impossible to save Athens. She was ruined on sea and on land. Alcibiades was made head of the fleet, but he left it for a time under another leader. During this time it was attacked and defeated by the Spartan fleet, which was now bigger than that of Athens. Alcibiades was ordered back to Athens to give an account of his conduct, but he was afraid to go, and fled into Thrace. The Spartans soon afterwards won another great victory at sea, and took nearly the whole of the Athenian fleet prisoner.

Athens now gave up all hope, and after a terrible siege of four months she was forced to give in to Sparta, who made terribly hard conditions for peace. The Athenians had to destroy the long walls and all their docks and their port at the Piræus. They were to keep only twelve ships out of their once mighty fleet. They were not to attempt to gain power again over the members of the Confederacy of Delos, and indeed were not to have any possessions outside Attica. They must help Sparta for the future against all her enemies. The work of destruction of the long walls and the Piræus was done by Spartan workmen, to the sound of music and rejoicing, and with every mark of insult to the Athenians.

So ended the Peloponnesian war, which had made Greece miserable for nearly thirty years. It was one of the most foolish and most useless wars in history. The Athens of Pericles was gone for ever, and though the Athenians were still remarkable for their artists and scholars, there was never another chance of their taking the lead among the Greeks.

Alcibiades fled once more after the fall of Athens to the Persians, but the Spartans persuaded them to kill him. They set fire to his house, and when he ran out his enemies let fly a shower of arrows at him, and so killed him. His story is one of the strangest told of the great men of Greece. His cleverness and beauty do not make up for his selfishness and deceit. He was one of the chief causes of his city's downfall, though probably, if he had been allowed to lead the army in Sicily instead of being called back for punishment, he would have led it to victory. But he was hardly great enough to have conquered the Spartans, and even if he had done so he could never have made a great Greek empire with Athens at its head. Probably no one could have done this, though we cannot help wishing that it had been done, so that the learning and cleverness of the Athenians might have had an even greater influence on the world than they have had. As it was, Alcibiades, whom many of the Athenians had petted and admired, helped more than any other man to ruin the greatness of Athens.

Chapter VII—The Last Days of Greek Independence

It might have seemed that now there was nothing to prevent Sparta uniting all the states of Greece in one empire. But this was not to be. The Spartans were hardly broad enough in the way they looked at things, and the Greek states were growing more and more jealous of each other. In a short time, when Thebes grew as powerful as Sparta, Athens was glad to join with Sparta against Thebes, a city which she had always hated because of its tyranny over her old friend Platæa. As time went on too, the Greeks nearly everywhere gave themselves up more and more to pleasure. Yet just at the end of the Peloponnesian war, some of them showed that they could still fight as well as in the days of Marathon and Thermopylæ. The Spartans had during the war been friendly with various Persian princes, and now Cyrus, the brother of the Persian King Artaxerxes, asked permission of Sparta to collect an army in Greece, to help him in an expedition. He did not tell what the expedition was for, and many Greeks, who had been fighting at home and had nothing to do, joined him. In all there were thirteen thousand, and at their head was the Spartan Clearchus.

Xenophon's Great March

Among them was Xenophon, an Athenian and a pupil of Socrates. Cyrus led them with a great army of his own into the very center of the Persian empire, to Babylonia, to fight against Artaxerxes, kill him, and make himself king. The Greeks were surprised and angry when they found what he was doing, but they fought bravely, and chased the Persians opposed to them. But Cyrus himself was killed instead of his brother, and his army ran away. The Greeks were left alone, more than one thousand miles from home, with enemies all round them. The Persians were afraid of them, for they saw that a small army of Greeks was still more than equal to a large army of Persians. Artaxerxes sent one of his officers who pretended to be their friend, and offered to show them the way back to Greece. He got them safely out of Babylonia, and then asked their generals and captains to a meeting in his tent. Here men rushed upon them and killed them, and the army of ten thousand was left without their chief leaders in a strange land.

Most of them were nearly in despair, but Xenophon spoke to the chief men left, reminding them of the great victories which Greece had won over Persia, and begging them to fight their way home. And so they did. They had to march all that one thousand miles through strange countries where savage tribes attacked them, but they fought with them, and took food and went on, and at last they came within sight of the sea, and the brave men who had suffered so much, and so cheerfully, gave a great cry of joy, for they knew they were now within easy reach of home.

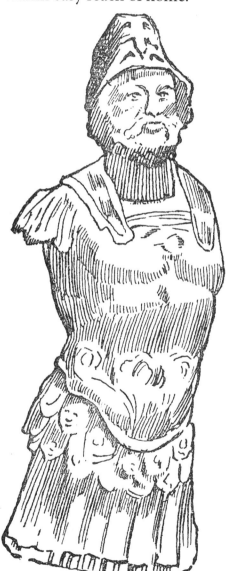

A Greek Soldier with a Corinthian Helmet (From a statuette in the Louvre).

Afterwards, when he was safe in Greece, Xenophon wrote down the story of all the adventures he had passed through in the 'Retreat of the Ten Thousand.' A curious fact about Xenophon is that, though he was so brave and clever, he never had any love for Athens, his own city. He even once fought for the Spartans against the Athenians, when Athens was helping Thebes in a fight with Sparta.

The Spartans sent an army under one of their kings to fight the Persians in Asia Minor, and she also sent out a fine fleet, but Agesilaus, the king, was called back to fight Thebes, and Athens who had joined her. Athens had built her long walls again in spite of Sparta. Agesilaus defeated the army of Thebes and Athens, but meanwhile his fleet was destroyed by the Persians, with an Athenian to lead them, and Sparta gave up the idea of becoming a great sea-power. She also made peace with the Great King, who was left free once more to take as his own the Greek colonies in Asia Minor.

Sparta had set up in many cities of Greece a government like her own, and in Thebes among others. Two of the citizens who hated this government had been sent into exile, but they made up their minds to upset the government. They dressed themselves as hunters, and with their dogs came back to their city, and to their houses, without any one guessing who they were. Some of their friends gave a feast to the two governors, who ruled like the two kings in Sparta, and the exiles again dressed themselves up, this time as women, and went into the room where the rulers were eating. They were taken by surprise, and easily killed by the pretended women.

So the enemies of Sparta came into power. Athens sent help to Thebes, and the Thebans found a splendid leader in Epaminondas, one of the greatest heroes of Greek history. He was a splendid soldier, and a very noble character. He had not taken any part in killing the rulers set up by Sparta. He was clever too, and had studied philosophy, and in some ways was very like Pericles. As soon as the Thebans had become free themselves, they helped the other cities which Sparta had conquered to set themselves free. Epaminondas won a great victory over the Spartans, at Leuctra. In the battle Epaminondas used a quite new way of attacking the enemies' lines, and he is considered one of the world's great generals. Seven hundred Spartans were killed, and only three hundred Thebans, but Sparta pretended not to care, and forbade any public show of sorrow.

EPAMINONDAS, THE HERO OF THEBES

The Thebans were now the chief people in Greece, but the other cities soon became as jealous of them as of Sparta, and the Spartans took advantage of this to make another attack on Thebes. Another great battle was fought at Mantinea. For a long time it seemed doubtful which of the splendid armies would win, but at last Epaminondas led a picked band of his best men in a determined dash on the enemy. The Spartan leader was wounded, and the Thebans won the battle, for soon afterwards the Spartans sent to ask permission to bury their dead, which meant that they owned that they were defeated.

But Epaminondas too was wounded to death. A javelin, a sharp weapon with a pointed head of iron and a handle of wood, stuck in his breast. The wooden part broke off, and the doctors said that as soon as the head should be pulled out of his breast, the brave leader must die. But Epaminondas did not care at all so long as the victory was won. After his death peace was made, and for a short time no one Greek state tried to conquer the others. Even if he had lived, Epaminondas would never have been able to join all the Greeks together. He was like Alcibiades in that, a great soldier but not a very clever statesman. So Thebes, like Sparta and Athens, fell once more to the level of the other states. But there was a country to the north of Greece, which was not properly Greek, but which succeeded for a time where the Greeks had failed, and joined them together for a while, though against their will.

Chapter VIII—Greece and Macedonia

To the North of Greece proper lay a country which the Greeks called Macedonia. Its people were not pure Greeks, but some Greeks had probably mixed with them and married among them in early times. The Macedonian kings declared that they themselves belonged to an old Greek family belonging to the same group of Greeks as the Spartans. Certainly the kings and people of Macedonia had some of the best qualities of both Greeks and Barbarians. They were splendid fighters, and though the people were rough and uneducated, the kings had some idea of Greek learning and philosophy. Philip of Macedon, who was king at the time when Sparta and Thebes were fighting, had been, as a boy, for three years in Thebes. He had learned a great deal about Greece, and probably he then first got the idea of how easy it would be for a really strong power to conquer it. When he got back to his own country there was a great deal of quarrelling in the royal family as to who should be king, but Philip made himself king.

Macedonia had already a good army, but Philip made up his mind to make it even better. There were some fierce tribes in some parts of the country, and these he marched against and put in order. Macedonia was of course bigger than any of the Greek states, and Philip was able to get together an immense and splendid army.

Demosthenes, a Great Athenian Speaker

As soon as he felt strong enough, he began to take for himself some of the Greek colonies on the coast near Macedonia. Several of those belonged to Athens, but the Athenians did not try to prevent it. There was one statesman, however, in Athens, who grew passionately angry against Philip. This was Demosthenes, a very splendid speaker. He told the Athenians over and over again that this barbarian king of the North would soon try to conquer all Greece, if Athens and the other Greek states would not join to fight him in time. Philip gradually began to interfere in the new quarrels among the Greek states, and especially he helped to defend the temple of Apollo at Delphi, which had been attacked by the Phocians.

He called himself a Greek and got some of the Greeks to say that Macedonia was a Greek state. He talked, too, very often of leading an army of all the Greek states (including Macedonia), with himself at its head, to fight the Persians as in the great days of Greece.

All the time Demosthenes was warning the Athenians against Philip. So bitterly did he hate him that he said he would rather have the Persians themselves. Even today, when any one speaks very angrily for a long time against anybody, we call such a speech a 'Philippic,' in memory of the long speeches in which Demosthenes tried to stir up the Athenians against Philip.

At last it became plain that the things which Demosthenes said against Philip were true and that he really meant to conquer all Greece. At last the Thebans and Athenians joined and fought a great battle with Philip at Chæronœa. The Macedonian soldiers had always been brave, but before Philip had trained them they had had only shields made of wicker, and rusty swords. But Philip had taught them all that he had learned about fighting in Thebes, and the Greeks found that they had to fight against men who were stronger and better trained than themselves. Philip won a complete victory. He was very severe with the Thebans, but quite kind to the Athenians. He was now head of all Greece, but he did not live long to enjoy his power.

Philip was a strange mixture of Greek and Barbarian. He was of course brave and clever, and a great general. But he had some terrible faults. He was very fond of wine and often drank too much. When he was in this state he did and said very curious things. One day a woman came and asked him to settle a quarrel for her, and he settled it quite wrongly. The woman quietly said, 'I appeal.' 'To whom do you appeal?' asked the king. 'To Philip sober,' answered the woman. Philip saw that she was right, and now settled the quarrel quite differently. The saying 'To appeal from Philip drunk to Philip sober' is now a very common one.

Demosthenes, the Enemy of Philip of Macedon
(From a statue at Rome).

Philip had several wives, imitating in this the Eastern kings. This was not a Greek custom, and in it Philip showed the Barbarian side of his character. His first wife was Olympias, who was also half a Greek. The people said she was a witch, and she was certainly very passionate and sometimes seemed almost mad. She and Philip quarrelled terribly, and naturally she did not like his other wives. Philip and Olympias had a son called Alexander, who became king after his father, and is famous in history as Alexander the Great, Alexander took his mother's part in her quarrels, and was not very friendly with Philip.

It was during the rejoicings over the marriage of his daughter that Philip died, being killed by a young man who belonged to his bodyguard but thought that Philip had been unjust to him. During the marriage festival there was a procession to a theatre, where a play was to be held. Statues of the twelve great gods of Greece were carried in the procession, and behind them one of Philip himself, as though he too was a god. Then came the king, but just as he reached the door of the theatre the young man rushed forward and stuck a sword right through his body. Philip fell dead. The young man ran away, but tripped and fell and was killed by the king's friends. The Greeks rejoiced at Philip's death, but it did not free them from the Macedonians, for in Alexander they had to deal with a king as brave as his father and cleverer, and even more anxious for power. For the next few years the history of Greece must be told in connection with the wonderful story of Alexander the Great.

ALEXANDER THE GREAT

Alexander, the son of Philip of Macedon, was only twenty years old when his father died. Demosthenes told the people of Athens that when he had seen him a few years before he was a dull boy. Demosthenes thought that the power of Macedon was at an end, but he can have been only a very poor judge of character. Alexander was a fine, handsome boy with a beautiful fair skin, blue eyes, and golden hair. There is a bust of him in the Museum of the Louvre at Paris, which shows him with fine shapely features and a noble forehead. Some people said that he was not the son of Philip at all, but that the god Jupiter was his father.

Alexander had of course a remarkable father and mother; in him can be seen his mother's power of imagination, without her tendency to madness. He had his father's ambition, courage, and power of ruling in a much higher degree. He soon showed the Greek cities that they could not throw off the Macedonian power. The city of Thebes, which dared to rise up against him, was destroyed, all but one house, that which had formerly belonged to the poet Pindar; for Alexander, like his father, had great respect for the art and poetry of Greece. He was himself a pupil of Aristotle, the greatest of all the Athenian philosophers.

It is said that Alexander asked the Greeks in his army who were helping him against Thebes what should be done to that city, and it was by their advice that it was destroyed.

Alexander himself was not generally cruel, but among these Greeks were men from Platæa, which had been by this time built up again, and they advised the destruction of Thebes in revenge for the destruction of their own city years before.

But the conquest of Greece was only one part of Alexander's work. He did not see why a Greek, as he called himself, should not conquer Persia as Persia had long ago tried to conquer Greece. He got together an army of thirty-five thousand men, and marched with them across the Hellespont. When he was half-way across, he killed a bull as a sacrifice to the god and goddesses of the sea, and poured wine from a golden cup into the water. When his ship drew near to the land, he flung a spear into the earth as a sign that he meant to win the land for his own.

The Persian leader who was sent to fight Alexander advised that his army should fall back before the Greeks and destroy everything on the way, so that Alexander and his army would have been without food. But his good advice was not followed, and the Persian army waited for the Greeks to come up to them. In order to reach them the Greeks had to cross the river Granicus, which was very deep in some places. Alexander's chief captain advised him to wait until the next morning before crossing, but Alexander was too impatient. He said he would not he stopped by a little stream, and spurred his horse into the river. The whole army followed, and a great battle was fought on the other side. Alexander himself killed two of the Persian leaders and went into the very thickest of the fight. He would indeed have been killed but for the quickness of the captain of his bodyguard, named Clitus.

Alexander the Great (Bust in the Acropolis Museum in Athens).

One of the Persians was in the very act of bringing his sword down in a deadly blow on the head of Alexander, when Clitus swiftly cut off the hand which held the sword. Alexander won a great victory, and all Asia Minor submitted to him.

The men who had fought hardest on the Persian side were some Greek soldiers, who fought for money. When these were taken as prisoners, Alexander sent them home to work as slaves in Macedonia, for he said they were traitors to Greece. But he had the enemy's dead buried with all respect, like those of his own army who had been killed. He sent three hundred suits of armour, taken from the Persians, to be dedicated to the goddess Athene in the Acropolis of Athens, and had these words sent with them: 'From Alexander, son of Philip, and the Greeks (except the Lacedæmonians), out of the spoil of the foreigners inhabiting Asia.' The Lacedæmonians was another name for the Spartans. Alexander made an exception of them because they had refused to join in his expedition.

THE GORDIAN KNOT

At Gordium, one of the towns of Asia Minor which Alexander took, he was shown a chariot, said to belong to the man who had founded the city. It was tied up with cords which were fastened in a knot which, it was said, no one could undo. Alexander took his sword and solved the difficulty by cutting the cord across. It was said that the man who undid the knot should conquer the world.

A second great battle was fought next year at the river Issus. This time the Persian king was there. He was another Darius by name. The Persian army is said to have had six hundred thousand men in it, but it was one of the immense useless armies of unwilling soldiers which the Greeks had met and conquered so often. The dashing attack of Alexander scattered it, and Darius himself ran away. Alexander seized the Persian camp, and among others the mother, wife and daughter of Darius were taken prisoners. They were crying because they thought the king had been killed, but Alexander told them that he had got safely away, and so comforted them. Alexander was nearly always kind and polite to his enemies when they were in his power.

He next took all the coast of Syria and Phœnicia, but the old city of Tyre, though it would have submitted to him, refused to let him enter the city to sacrifice to one of its gods.

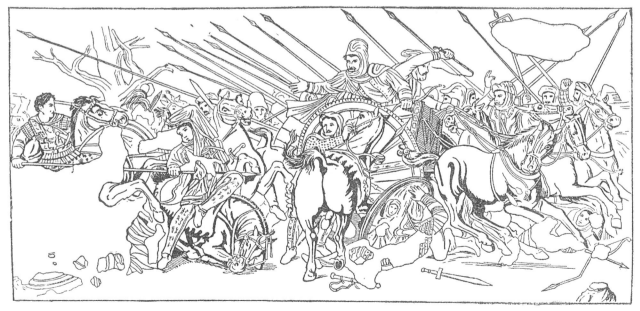

The Battle between Alexander and Darius at Issus (*From a wonderful picture in mosaic found at Pompeii, said to have been made from a painting by a Greek artist. It shows Darius turning to fly from the battlefield when he saw that he was defeated*).

Alexander the Great, the World Conqueror (*From the ancient statue in the Capitoline Museum at Rome*).

Alexander was terribly angry and besieged the city for seven months. He brought Phœnician ships to help him, and when at last Tyre had to give way, Alexander allowed his soldiers to kill most of the men in cold blood on the seashore. The women and children were sent into slavery. Alexander was terribly angry when his pride was offended, as it had been in this case. He sacrificed at the shrine, but there was little to be proud of in this victory.

Darius was not a very strong or brave king. He was now thoroughly frightened, and sent word to Alexander that he would give up to him all the land west of the river Euphrates if he would only let him live in peace beyond that river. But even such an immense empire could not satisfy Alexander. His chief captain Parmenio said to him, 'If I were Alexander I should agree to this rather than rush into further dangers.' 'And so should I,' replied Alexander, 'if I were Parmenio.'

But he was not. He was full of imagination, and seems to have thought it possible to join the East and West in one great empire. It was not possible, for, as can be seen through all history, the people of the East are quite different from those of the West. They have a quite different way of thinking about things. But Alexander did come nearer than anybody to joining the two.

At the town of Gaza Alexander again met with resistance, and he treated it with the same cruelty as Tyre. It is said that he went to Jerusalem and prayed in the temple. The Jews welcomed him, for they had suffered much under Persian rule, and they showed him the place in the Book of Daniel which says that a Greek would conquer the Persians. Afterwards when Alexander built the city of Alexandria, called after himself, he invited many Jews to settle there.

From Asia Minor Alexander marched into Egypt, which gave in to him immediately. It was on an island at the mouth of the Nile that he built Alexandria, which in time became the second greatest city in the world at the time when Rome was the greatest. From Egypt in the spring Alexander led his men right across Asia beyond the Euphrates through Mesopotamia, and across the Tigris, and there at last met the army of Darius. The battle was fought not very far from the town of Arbela, and is known as the battle of Arbela. Darius had had his army standing all night, for it was so large that he was afraid that if the soldiers lay down to sleep he would never get them into order again. The Macedonians had a good night's sleep and were quite fresh for the fight.

The army of Darius was rather different from the usual Persian armies. It had in it 50,000 paid Greek soldiers and men from wild tribes of the very East. There were elephants too which the Greek soldiers had never seen. Then again the land beyond the Euphrates had always been considered dangerous by the Greeks, and here they were beyond the Tigris as well. But Alexander's soldiers had the greatest trust in him and no one grumbled. The fight was fast and furious, but at last the Persian army fell into confusion, and Darius once more fled from the field. Alexander marched on to Babylon and then to the great Persian capital, Susa, and took it for his own.

At Susa Alexander, having, it is said, drunk too much wine, burnt down the royal palaces. In them were wonderful books full of the writings of the great Persian philosopher

Zoroaster and of the history of the Persian empire. These were lost for ever to the world, and many things written in these books can never now be known. Alexander was bitterly sorry afterwards, and indeed it was one of the worst acts of his life, and we find it hard to forgive him for it. He then marched after Darius, who was running away with Bersus, one of his relations.

For weeks Alexander followed him, and when at last Darius, who was worn out and weary of the struggle, knew that he would be caught, he told Bersus and his friends that he would give himself up to Alexander. But Bersus was an ambitious man, and as he knew that with Darius as a prisoner Alexander would be surer than ever of keeping Persia for his own, he turned and stuck his sword in Darius and killed him, and then fled on. Darius was found dying by one of Alexander's soldiers, and he begged him to thank Alexander for being so kind to his wife and daughter. Alexander buried Darius with all honor in the old tomb of the Persian kings.

Alexander in India

In four years Alexander had won for himself the great empire of Persia. But he was not yet satisfied. He stayed only to make things orderly and safe, and then marched through mountain passes into the great unknown continent of India. He conquered the land now known as the Punjab, and had a famous struggle with a prince called Porus.

Porus was almost a giant. He had an enormous elephant on which he used to ride into battle. When its master could no longer fight, the elephant would lie gently down, let him slide from its back, and pull the arrows from its body with its trunk. Porus was defeated and taken prisoner. Alexander asked him how he wished to be treated. He quietly answered, 'Like a king.' Alexander was so pleased with the answer that he gave Porus his kingdom back, and even some more land to make it larger. But of course Porus had to own that Alexander was over him.

Alexander, too, had a faithful animal which he loved very much. This was his horse Bucephalus, which he had ridden for many years. Alexander always tried to save it from too much work or any pain, but he always rode it in battle. It was wounded in the battle, and died soon afterwards. Alexander built a city on the spot where it was buried, and called it Bucephalia after the horse.

Alexander would probably have wished to add all India to his empire, but at last his army began to rebel, and would not follow him any farther. He led them back through the passes of North-West India, and across Asia once more to Susa, and from there to Babylon. Here he fell suddenly ill of a fever and died. He was only forty-two years old. In the ten years that he had been in Asia, he had won contests such as no man has done before or since. We can only imagine what he would have done had he lived longer.

He was one of the greatest men who ever lived. Besides being a wonderful soldier and leader of men, he was generally kind and he admired noble things. Of course he was sometimes cruel, and when really angry he was quite as savage and uncivilized as any of his enemies. It is dreadful to think that he killed in anger his great friend Clitus, who had saved his life at the battle of Granicus. In anger he was more Barbarian than Greek. But he lived in a savage time, and we must remember that the Greeks, who had been civilized for hundreds of years, were almost equally cruel. With all his faults, the name of Alexander the Great and the story of his life will always remain to fill men with wonder.

THE END OF ALEXANDER'S EMPIRE

As soon as Alexander was dead his great empire broke up, and his generals made themselves kings of different parts of it. Some of these rulers very soon lost much of their Greek character, and became very much like the people they ruled. In time most of them were conquered by the Roman people, who soon after this became a great conquering nation.

The cities which Alexander had built, and the colonies of Greek soldiers which he had left everywhere, taught the Eastern people something of Greek civilization. Alexandria became almost a second Athens, famous for its learning and its philosophy. Macedonia became a kingdom, and after many quarrels the family of one of his generals, Antigonus, got the kingship, and it remained in the family for more than a hundred years, when Macedonia was conquered by Rome and made part of the Roman empire.

After the death of Alexander the Greeks tried to free themselves from the power of Macedonia, but the Macedonian ruler marched against them and made them give in. Demosthenes, who had spent so many years in the struggle against the kingdom which he hated so much, and had hoped that now at last the Greeks would be free, now poisoned himself in despair.

After about fifty years some of the smaller states of Greece, which had never before taken much part in her history, joined together into leagues, and for the first time there was something like equality between the states of Greece. These smaller states were content to be equal with each other, and did not try to conquer other states like Sparta and Athens and the great states of earlier times. But they could never make Greece really great again, and even now there were jealousies. At last Sparta, who had always been ready to join with the enemies of Greece when she was angry and jealous, called in the Romans against the Achæan League, with which she was quarrelling. The Romans came and settled the quarrel by making Greece a province of her empire. This was in the year 146 B.C. The history of the next few hundred years is the history of this wonderful Roman people which had grown up from a city-state in the middle of Italy into a great nation, and then into an empire, the greatest the world has ever known. We must turn back more than six hundred years to tell the tale of the Roman people from the beginning.

Chapter IX—The Rise of Rome

The Romans, in a way, show us a world very much like that which we know today. There are no such things as city-states now as there were in Greece; but the great empires and nations of today are built very much as the Roman empire was built. The Greeks had never formed a great empire because they were not able to join together for any time. From the very beginning the Romans were very different. The history of the seven kings of Rome is a story of battles and struggles against various enemies, but the result is always much the same. Conquerors or conquered, they join with their foes, so that while the Roman race was at first Latin, we find some of their kings Sabines and others Etruscans.

The Romans show us another new thing. The Greeks had been in love with art and beauty and freedom. It would be wrong to say that the Romans did not like these things, but a Roman liked strength and usefulness and order much more. The Romans gave the laws to the world, so that even now when men study the laws of almost any country they must study a great deal that is Roman law. Everything in the Roman Empire was done by rule. Every one went about his business for a certain time and did it by certain rules. And the Romans introduced a new spirit into the world. The Greeks always thought 'what is really the best thing?' The Roman way of looking at things was 'what is the best and easiest thing I can do now?' It might not be, it probably would not be, on most occasions the really best thing; but it was the thing an ordinary practical man would do.

It was this spirit which helped Rome to rule in time over most of the known world. The Roman was a man of business, and he did just the best thing to settle any question at the moment. In time Romans were ruling over such different peoples as the British, the Egyptians, the French, and the Greeks, and many others with great success.

In each case the Roman Governor set about things in an orderly way. He had men to help him who each did his separate task, and so all the business of the country was gone through. Roman soldiers would be there at first, but by and by soldiers who belonged to the country would be taught to take their part in the army. Great roads would be built, roads which were made so strong that we can still follow them in England today. Courts where people could go and obtain what was owing to them would be set up, and the people would be taught useful arts. Wherever the Romans went some trace of them remains to this day. Many English towns, such as Chester, Lancaster, Winchester, etc., have earned their names from the Roman name for a camp, *castra*. And not only in the words but in roads and buildings, such as bridges, are their traces to be seen.

It is time now to look back at the story of the beginnings of this country which soon took its place as the seat of the chief rulers of the world. In shape Italy is like a human leg, with the island of Sicily standing near the toes. It is like a leg in another way: it has a hard center running throughout its length. The Apennines, as the mountain ridge is called, do not run through the exact center of Italy. They run to the east, forming in this way a rocky coast there, while the land on the west slopes gradually from them to the sea. It is important to remember this, for it explains the reason why the Greeks never invaded much of Italy. The land nearest to Greece was this same rocky eastern shore of Italy, on which it was not easy to make harbors for ships. And so the Greeks, with their eyes on trading, never pushed their way much beyond the southern heel of Italy and the south-west fringe of the coast; for farther north than Naples, where the Greeks settled, there were no good harbors.

About the center of the western side of Italy there is a river called the Tiber, and this naturally acted as a line dividing the people on the north from those on the south. On the north lived a race which is one of the oldest in the world. They were called the Etruscans. Where the Etruscans originally came from is not certainly known, but it is thought that they grew out of two distinct peoples, one that came from the north and the other which came very little later to Italy and crossed the Apennines from Lydia. The Etruscans were a highly civilized people. We read of a league which they made of twelve cities, not always the same, but cities which were great and important enough to be able to add something to the general defence. The cities were chiefly what we should call country towns, which had grown great from the crops, trees and cattle produced on the land about them. They were not only towns on the sea-coast, though some of them were, and they had good laws and some of the love of color which Rome borrowed from them. The Etruscans who lived in them were great fighters and made the Greeks and the people of Carthage fear them.

Though they were by trade a farming people, in their markets might be found the traders of all the world. The Greek and Phœnician merchants came there bringing their gold and silver and ivory and bronze. Some of these precious metals were no doubt dug from their own mines, but the greater part found its way into the land through the hands of traders, and the Etruscans, who did not know how to make beautiful things themselves, sold their metals, cattle and crops for such things as Egyptian vases and Phœnician cups. They were a people who loved luxury. Their slaves were beautifully dressed, and at their meals splendidly embroidered tablecloths and fine cups and plates of gold and silver were used. They were good flute-players, and flutes, harps and trumpets were played while they worked. They loved music and dancing, hunting and the watching of fights in which strong men fought between themselves and against beasts.

About three hundred years after the Etruscans settled down we find four great races grouped about the Tiber: to the north and west the Etruscans, to the east and north-east the Umbrians, a little farther south the Samnites, and to the south the Latins. These last three peoples belonged to the great Aryan race, and they were found already settled when the Etruscans pushed their way over the Apennines. The Latins were

An Ancient Etruscan Painting: Making a Sacrifice at an Altar (A tomb painting from Cære, now in the Louvre).

settled south in the plains of the Tiber, and from them it earned its name, Latium. Many different races ruled Rome at different times, but it was the Latin language that the people of Rome spoke from the beginning. The plain of Latium had also, like the land where the Etruscans lived, many cities—of some of them we know a little; and several have been made famous by the stories of old. Lavinium and Alba Longa are the best known, and the latter, which was about twelve miles south-east of Rome, will be mentioned again.

THE STORY OF ROMULUS AND REMUS

History can tell us very little of the beginning of Rome. The name 'Rome' is thought to mean 'river.' And as the city stands on the bank of the Tiber this seems probable; but it is quite uncertain. There is a very old story which connects the founding of Rome with twin brothers, Romulus and Remus. The story says that they were grandsons of the King Numitor, who ruled over Alba Longa. Numitor's brother took the throne and ordered the baby grandsons of Numitor to be put into a basket and thrown into the Tiber. The waters in the river ran very high at the time, but when they sank lower the basket was left standing in the Roman marshes, and the children were fed by a wolf as if they had been its own babies. Afterwards they were found by a shepherd on the Palatine Hill, and were from that time brought up with his children. Sturdy and strong they grew up, and became in time leaders of a band of brave shepherds. In one of their numerous fights they came to know who their grandfather was, and then they fought for him, and set him upon his throne once more. They thought it would be a good thing to build a city in the place where they had grown up; but the brothers now quarrelled and Remus was killed. Romulus then built his city upon the Palatine Hill.

This story has been told in many different ways. Sometimes the father of Romulus and Remus is the god Mars, sometimes he is only 'a stranger.' The wolf who fed the babies is also in some of the stories a woman. There are other stories, too, which tell of the history of the Latin people and the towns of Latium many hundreds of years before. But they are only stories, with so much that we know is untrue, although it is very interesting, that it is wiser not to tell them again.

All we know for certain is that some shepherds from Alba Longa built the city of Rome on the square-shaped Palatine Hill, which looks down on the river, probably as a fortress or strong place to prevent the Etruscans coming farther south. But it was built long before the time at which the first king is said to have lived. Romulus was probably a leader of the people, and he is supposed to have built the city in the year 753 B.C. This date is one of the most important in all history. It begins Roman history, and the years have ever been reckoned from it even to this day.

Very early in the history of Rome we find it already strongly defended against its enemies, and with wise rulers for its government. The people were composed of three classes: Patricians, who are thought to have been descended from the Sabines, a branch of the Umbrian race; the Clients, who depended upon the Patricians in some way; and the Plebeians, who were people the Romans had conquered, or who had come to Rome for protection against some enemy. The Patricians alone, at first, could have a share in the government, be fully protected by the laws and take part in the Roman religion. The Clients, some of whom were slaves, were people who wished to have the protection of the laws and be Roman citizens, and they were able to have these by choosing a Patrician as a 'patron,' who could represent them in any business with other citizens. The patron and Clients had very serious duties to each other. The Plebeians were at first people who were almost as free and fully protected by the laws as the Patricians, but they did not need to have a patron. Of course, it was not long before these three classes became really two: the Patricians and the Plebeians, the Clients becoming really a part of the Plebeian class.

Although we do not know much certainly of the reign of Romulus, we do know it must have been a very troubled time. The stories tell of fierce battles with the peoples who dwelt about the Palatine Hill, and all we know of early Rome shows us that, though the language of its people was Latin, the divisions, laws and customs were largely those of other people. An old story tells of battles with the Sabines, and, as we have seen, the real ruling people of Rome were of the Sabine race, showing that they must have been readily accepted as brothers by the Latins. The divisions of the people were, on the other hand, Etruscan.

The Patricians, who it must be remembered were the real Roman people, for they alone had full rights under the laws, were divided into three tribes; the tribes again were each divided into ten parts called Curiæ. There were, therefore, thirty Curiæ, and these had each its separate religious ceremonies, festivals, priests and chapels, together chose the king and settled questions about when people should be put to death. The Curiæ were again divided into families, not families like those we speak of today, but more like those of the Israelites, which include a man and all his descendants and relatives.

A hundred of the older men formed a body called the Senate and helped the king to rule. The number became greater when the first Romans joined with the Sabine people. All these divisions lasted, though changed in different ways, for hundreds of years, the Patricians being the rulers, the Senate assisting the chief ruler, and the Curiæ or wards choosing the ruler. The king was not like our kings. He was not only the head man among the people, but he was the chief man in the religious ceremonies, offering the sacrifices and consulting the gods, and he actually sat in the courts saying what was right and wrong, punishing the evil-doers and protecting the weak. The state was looked upon as a great home, and it therefore had a hall and hearth. On the hearth devoted women called Vestal Virgins kept ever alight a sacred fire, which an old story said had been brought years before from Troy.

The time during which the first four kings of Rome reigned was nearly a hundred and fifty years, and during this time many important things happened. Rome was continually growing, and when King Ancus died nearly the whole of the seven hills upon which Rome is built had been taken into the city which had started upon one. The religion of the people had become more fixed. Alba Longa had been conquered and destroyed, though its people became Romans, a bridge had been built over the river to a fortress—a building strongly defended against the enemy—and a colony, Ostia, had been founded at the mouth of the river Tiber.

The fifth king of Rome was an Etruscan, and under his rule and that of the two Etruscans after him Rome begins to have some of the look of the city which is known to later history. Two other hills were taken into the city, and the seven hills were now surrounded with a great high wall. Vast buildings begin to rise, such as the huge temple on the Capitoline Hill. Great drains and sewers were built to carry away the stagnant water which lay in the low places, a circus was laid out, and fights like those which the Etruscans loved to watch were arranged. But the Etruscan kings, the Tarquins as they are sometimes called, because Tarquin was the name of the first and last, gave more than this to Rome. They gave her above all a great position in Italy.

From the earliest times the small city-states of Latium, like those among the Etruscans, would join together to form a league. Alba Longa had long ago been the head of one of these leagues of thirty cities. In the league which existed at this time the Tarquins gave Rome a leading position, and it is probable for the first time brought the city into contact with the Greeks. The Tarquins were proud men and great fighters, and when they had won a victory they would come back to the city very gaily, wearing beautiful dresses and driving in carriages drawn by numbers of white horses. This was the beginning of what became a famous Roman custom. Every great Roman soldier who had won a battle looked on it as his reward to enter Rome in triumph, and these triumphs were sometimes almost as pictur-

An Etruscan Soldier from the 3rd Century B.C.

esque and fine to look upon as a Lord Mayor's show today. Sometimes the leaders of the enemy were dragged along in the procession; at one time it was thought a great thing to have a number of elephants walking together, and once the soldier entered the city between a long line of elephants holding lighted torches. The people came to like these triumphs, for they could see the great soldier and the strange sights and shout 'Hail, Commander' as loudly as they liked.

These Tarquin kings had not been lawfully chosen as the Roman laws ordered. So far as we can see, they must have been invaders who seized Rome; but they did great things for the growing city. They did not care much about the liberty of the Romans, and the last of them, Tarquin the Proud, came in this way to be driven from the city. The kings before them had been simple and, on the whole, good rulers. The Tarquins brought to Rome the luxury their people loved. They also increased the number of the senators, and the new senators were chosen from the states conquered by Rome. They changed the way the army was chosen, though this made the old Roman families very angry. Tarquin the Proud was certainly a bad king, but nothing we know of him really tells us the reason why the Romans for hundreds of years afterwards hated the very name of king. He made the Romans feared by all the Latin states around. And when he ceased to be king the Roman power for a time became much smaller. But when his son insulted one of the noblest Romen women, Lucretia, the Romans said that Tarquin should rule no longer, that neither he nor any of his relations should be allowed to enter Rome, and that they would never have another king.

Tarquin was not in Rome at the time. He was away fighting one of his many battles; but he did not mean to give up being king without a struggle. The battles which followed showed that although the Tarquin kings had made Rome so powerful, the people had the courage and strength to defend themselves if they wished. The people of two other towns joined Tarquin in his first battle, and all marched out to the borders of the city of Rome. But here the Romans met them and defeated the great army. The next battle, a year later, was one in which Tarquin was helped by all the Etruscans under the prince, Lars Porsena. It is this battle about which the story of Horatius is told.

THE STORY OF HORATIUS

The Etruscan army had marched so near to Rome that only a wooden bridge separated them from the city. It is said that the Roman soldier Horatius kept all the enemy from crossing the bridge until his friends had broken down the bridge behind him, when he jumped into the river and swam safely back. Certainly many Roman soldiers must have fought bravely that day, but the story does not prevent us from realizing that Rome was so thoroughly beaten by the Etruscans that she had to give up all her possessions on the north bank of the Tiber, and had to promise to make no more fighting weapons of iron. This last condition she did not keep to very long. A third battle was fought against the Latins, this time led by Mamilius, son-in-law of Tarquin, but the Romans were once more the winners, and Tarquin ran away to a place called Curiæ, where he died.

There were to be no more kings, and so the Romans chose two chief men to take their place. It was thought that when there were two, neither could be so strong as to cause the people so much trouble as the kings. The new rulers were called consuls, and later on we find that each consul had certain powers which made it impossible for one of them to be very powerful without the other. Most of the great Romans whose names we know during the next five hundred years were consuls. The kings of Rome, so far as we can discover, had reigned about two hundred and fifty years. Very few things are sure in these years; but at the end we know there existed a Roman city, strongly built, with some great and beautiful buildings, with wise laws, and a people brave, orderly and free. The Rome which we hear of afterwards is one that is almost continually growing in power, and it is the Rome which has made the world like it is today.

Chapter X—Rome and the Celts

The Etruscan people seem to have been at the highest point in their history when the last of the Tarquins was put off the Roman throne. They had been able to seize and hold the rulership of the city for a sufficient time for three kings to reign, and even when Tarquin the Proud had been forbidden to enter Rome ever again, we have seen how the great prince, Lars Porsena, was able to make the Romans do just what he wished. It could not have been easy for the brave Roman people to give up all the land they had won on the north side of the Tiber. Still less easy was it to promise never to use iron swords and spears again. But the Romans did not seem to look on their agreement as being very binding, and about a hundred years after they had been so shamefully defeated they had almost completely and for ever put an end to the power of the Etruscans.

The long struggle between the Romans and the Etruscans was really a struggle between Rome and the strong Etruscan town Veii. Sometimes they agreed to fight no more for some time. This happened on one occasion for over thirty years, and on another for about sixteen years. But when the time for which they had agreed to be at peace came to an end, each side commenced to carry on the war as vigorously as before.

Rome was all this time becoming more powerful. It made agreements with the strong cities and peoples near by that each would help the other both to defend themselves and to make war upon an enemy. And enemies increased as the Roman power grew; but these other towns kept their promise, and so Rome was protected from many of her enemies. It is just as well that this was so; for Rome was defeated by Veii, not once but very many times. On one occasion, however, when she had made peace with Veii, Rome regained the city Fidenæ and the land which Lars Porsena had made her give up thirty years before. Yet, although this might seem to be a great victory, it was not long before the people of Fidenæ rebelled, killed several Romans, and joined the king of Veii. This king was quickly killed by the Romans, and the city of Fidenæ was taken once again. Can it be wondered that, when the peace they had agreed upon after the last battle was ended, the Romans made up their minds to conquer the people of Veii once for all? It was almost exactly a hundred years since Lars Porsena had conquered the Romans.

Rome's First Conquest

Now to take Veii was quite a new idea in the Roman history. This was the first time the Romans had ever set out to conquer a foreign state. It was the first time, too, that the army ever went out for so long a time and did not return until it had done what it went to do. The long hot Italian summer faded into autumn, autumn passed into winter, and spring came again not once but perhaps ten times, and found the Roman army still shutting in the great city. For it is said that it was ten years before the people of Veii gave in. There were no great guns, as there are now, to knock down the walls, and the city was very strong. It was built on the top of a flat hill; and round each side but one there was a deep valley, a ravine as it is called. On the fourth side the people had built a great wall and dug a deep ditch, so that the town was like a small island, only it could not have been reached by boats. At length after ten long years the city was taken and destroyed in the year 396 by the brave general called Camillus.

The Romans could never have taken so strong a city if they had not been helped by their friends, and if the people of Veii had not been deserted by theirs. The reason why the Etruscans did not help their own people who lived in Veii we shall see in a moment. It must have been a very serious reason, for when Veii was conquered several other Etruscan towns had to agree to leave Rome in peace. In this way the Romans in conquering Veii had really conquered the southern part of the Etruscan people.

The Strong City of Veii Before It Was Taken by the Romans in 396 B.C. (From a drawing made by Canina, a famous Italian scholar, after studying all the remains of the city).

THE EARLY CELTS

The reason why their friends had not come to their help is that they were themselves fighting against an enemy who were now first being heard of in the civilized world. Many of the boys and girls who read this book are probably related to this new enemy. For it was the Celts, who are the forefathers of the French, Welsh and Irish. They were then, as now, very brave; and although in some ways they seem to have been just the same as they are at present, in some others—less important—they were very different.

From this time we find them marching about almost everywhere, gay, brave, careless, not caring for work but loving struggles and battles. They had found their way from their first home in the east to the far west, to France and even to the British Isles, and, in fact, it was in France they made their headquarters. But they never settled anywhere very long, and for the next four hundred years they were dreaded by every nation until the great Cæsar after years of war made them powerless. Other people have become soldiers to defend their country against the enemy or to increase their power. The Celts were soldiers just because they loved it. They were big men with rough shaggy hair and bearded faces; they often wore fine clothing and broad gold bands round their necks. When they were horse-soldiers they made fine cavalry; but when they fought on foot they were almost impossible to resist. So daring and careless were they, that they went into a battle bareheaded; and they did not throw spears like the Romans. They merely rushed straight at the enemy, and with the long sword, dagger or lance cut about them, protecting themselves by a big shield.

It was this people who changed the Roman fortunes in so remarkable a way, by helping them to conquer Veii by fighting against the Etruscans in the North. They did so in an even more extraordinary way, too, as we shall see.

Five years after Veii had been destroyed a band of Celts who had crossed the Alps and settled for a short time on the north-east coast of Italy suddenly made up their minds to cross the Apennine mountains, and they tried to seize the great Etruscan town, Clusium. It was the prince of Clusium who had long before conquered Rome; but now when the Etruscans found the Celtic soldiers at the gates of their city they sent to Rome to ask for help. The Romans saw that this meant a long struggle far from their home, and so they would not agree to help the people of Clusium. But they sent messengers to tell the Celts to go away. Now all people have agreed to leave such messengers, ambassadors as they are sometimes called, free, and the messengers themselves are, of course, bound not to fight against the people who trust them in this way. But the Roman messengers fought with some men of Clusium against the Celts, and this made them very angry indeed. They asked the Romans to send back to them the messengers who had behaved so deceitfully; but the Romans would not.

The Celtic army at Clusium then at once set out for Rome. It was a very large army for those days, about seventy thousand men; and they were men who did daring things as if they were quite ordinary. Clusium was about eighty-five miles north of Rome, and before the Romans had time to decide how to defend the city the Celts had crossed the Tiber and had arrived at a stream called the Allia, only about twelve miles from the city. It was only at this point that the Romans seem to have realized their danger, and an army of forty thousand men tried to stop the Celts.

The brave Camillus was not in the battle on this day; and so the strong Roman legions went out with very little thought to meet the terrible enemy whom they despised as barbarians. But the sudden rushes of the Celts soon put the Romans in disorder, drove them back, huddled them together, and at last drove them away from the battlefield so filled with fear that they actually left their homes behind and ran for safety to the north of the Tiber.

THE BURNING OF ROME

The Celts apparently did not think very much of their victory. They waited for three days and then marched into Rome. The gates were open and the streets empty. There were not sufficient soldiers to defend the city, but several had gone to the Capitol, which formed a fortified castle, and had got together large stores of provisions. The Roman women and children had been sent away across the Tiber; but the soldiers inside the Capitol were besieged for nearly seven months. The Celts, who, when they had entered the city, found many of the noblest old men sitting at the doors of their houses in their dresses for ceremonies, had at first left them alone; but finally they could not resist killing them. Then they stole anything they fancied, and at last burned the city. Still the Capitol held out. The rock on which it was built was steep. But it was only saved, on one occasion, by the cackling of the sacred geese, which warned the wearied soldiers one dark night when they had fallen asleep. At length news came to the Celtic general that his homeland was being besieged, and so he was glad to accept a sum of money to leave Rome.

So Rome was free once more. The soldiers and women and children returned, and there were some who were so frightened that they wished to leave the city altogether; but the brave soldier Camillus persuaded them to stay and build the city again. So very rapidly and with little order houses and streets sprang up, and it was owing to this that Roman consuls in later times had to pass laws to see that carts and carriages did not cause constant stoppages in these narrow, inconvenient streets.

It was a terrible thing for Rome to be burnt; but it affected its history very little except in one way. All the records of Roman history were burnt in the city fire, and it is owing to this that it is very difficult to say what is the true story of Rome before then. The year 390 B.C., therefore, marks the time from which we begin to know more certainly how the city of Rome fared in its growth from a tiny shepherds' town to the chief city of the world. In no other way did the burning of Rome produce any effect which is worth remembering.

Chapter XI—Rome Mistress of Italy

The burning of Rome was not the last Italy heard of the Celts. They had invaded Italy before, and for many years afterwards they continued to make sudden marches against different cities where they thought they could find things to steal. The distances they marched would be wonderful even now for a large army; but for these days when there were no trains and no way to carry their baggage except on horseback they must have been extraordinary. Twenty years after the burning of Rome Camillus defeated them at Alba. A few years later another Roman general marched out against them; but the Celts seem to have learned to fear their enemies, for they marched past them towards the South. They were again defeated by the Romans a few years afterwards; but in spite of this we find this extraordinary people only eight years later calmly settling down for the winter at Alba. They enjoyed themselves in their own way by sudden marches on various cities, where they took everything of value, and then returned to the Alban hill. But the next year the son of the brave Camillus, who was now dead, led a great army against them and made them go away.

There is a wise saying of an old Roman that manliness, upon which every Roman prided himself, grows in opposition, that is to say, when a man has to struggle hard he will probably become manly. If a nation knows it is in danger of being attacked by an enemy it must make it watchful, and this is another thing which the Romans liked, watchfulness. One result, then, of these constant troubles with the Celts, and there were troubles from other peoples too, was to make the Romans ever stronger and more manly. We must remember this, for it helps to explain why the city of Rome became mistress of Italy rather than any other of the cities. Of course, Rome had a very strong position. It was too far from the coast to be attacked by ships of war. It was in the center of Italy, and so could march north or south with equal ease, and thus meet one of its enemies at a time, instead of having them all marching against it at once. And also it was strongly built on hills. The Celts had taken it very easily; but it would have been very different if the Roman soldiers had stayed to defend the walls.

We have seen that by the time the Celts took Rome the Etruscan power had been almost completely crushed. This does not mean that the Etruscan cities could fight no more, or that there were not still some of them which, being far from Rome, still remained free. But while the Etruscans had been so strong long ago that they had put Rome to shame after Tarquin the Proud had been put off the throne, now the best they could hope for was to gain a victory for a moment over a small band of the Romans. When the great Roman army marched against them they were beaten.

Some years before the son of Camillus drove the Celts from the Alban hill the whole of South Etruria, the country of the Etruscans, was Roman, with Roman fortresses on its boundaries and Roman people living in its towns. But a little later the Etruscans, who became more and more angry as they saw the Roman power creeping always farther into their country, rebelled. Three of the great Etruscan towns sent their soldiers against the Roman army, and when they had taken some men in the battle, they cut them to pieces in the market-place. This horrible act was soon punished, for in the year that the Celts settled on the Alban hill the Romans took from one of these cities, Cære, half of its land and put the city under Rome. The other towns were forced to say they would do nothing against Rome for a long time. The Etruscan power sank lower and lower: the Celts were taking part of what had been their land in the North, and the Etruscan rulers of the cities which were free ruled so badly that the lower people fought against them, and the rulers asked the Romans to help them. They did; but the cities were not free any longer afterwards.

THE GROWTH OF ROMAN POWER

All this time the Romans were growing in power in the South too, so that by the time that she was really mistress of Etruria she was mistress of all Italy. But this was at the cost of many battles. The Latins did not at all like the Roman position in the Latin League. We have seen that it seemed a very fair agreement; but it really came to mean that Rome used all the strength of the Latin cities as if it was her own. The Romans even took care to keep the Latin cities under them, for when they made an agreement with Carthage for the Latins, the Carthaginians promised not to fight against the Latin cities if they remained friendly to Rome, and if any of them rebelled it would put them again under Rome.

This was very bitter to the cities of Latium, but so many of them had attempted to rebel against Rome, between the burning of the city and the year of this agreement, and each had been conquered with so little difficulty, that it is hardly to be wondered at that they did not rebel at once again. But the ill-feeling was there, and apparently the Romans knew it. Before, however, the Latins attempted to fight against Rome, that city went to war with a very powerful race of hillmen, who lived to the south of Rome, in part of the high land which runs through the heart of Italy.

Many years before bands of these hillmen had poured down into the plain of Campania, south of Latium. They seized the large and important towns Capua, which had before belonged to the

A Samnite Warrior (From a painting on an ancient vase in the Louvre).

Etruscans, and Cumæ, which was a Greek settlement. These Samnites, Campanians as we may call them, settled down in the new country, and very soon became less hardy and brave than their relatives who still lived in the hills. But the hillmen came down again and again, and the Campanians began to fear them so much that at last they sent to the Romans to ask for help. The Romans compelled the Samnites to make peace.

Whether they would have been so content to make peace we do not know, if they had not feared a rebellion of the Latin cities. The storm quickly burst. The Campanians, jealous of the Roman power, which they had been so glad to call upon when they were in danger, joined the Latin cities, and the position of the Roman army seemed almost hopeless. They had gone South to help the Campanians, and now the armies of the Latin cities stood between them and home. The Latins, on their side, seemed to feel that, if they were ever to be free, this was their only chance.

At the terrible battles of Mount Vesuvius and Trifanum the great army of the Latins and Campanians was thoroughly beaten, and in the next two years the Roman army completely conquered all the towns that still held out. The league of Latin cities came to an end forever.

These victories made Rome mistress of the plains of Latium and Campania. In some cases Rome made agreement with the separate cities, but other towns had a far different fate. The walls were pulled down, and the inhabitants were sent away from their homes. Or they were made into colonies, and these were dotted about over the country so as to protect Rome against the attacks of her enemies.

The colonies were really very often fortresses, and they could be used to gather Roman armies together. Thus Fregellae, the name of a colony on the road called the Latin Way, was on the river Liris, and therefore would protect an army wishing to cross it on the way to Campania. This colony would be like a Roman sword between Latium and the Campanians. The Roman army could march swiftly down this road, and be quite sure that food and all that was necessary would be ready for them in the colony.

We can easily see from the wise way Rome did its work that there must have been many great and wise men in the city, and if the acts of the Romans sometimes seem very cruel, we must remember that they thought, as the cities around them very clearly thought also, that against such wild and savage fighters as the Celts and hillmen not Rome alone or any one city could be successful, but only Rome with the armies of the Italian cities faithfully helping them. So the battles in Latium continued until the last resistance was finally broken down, when Privernum was taken and its leader was executed in Rome.

Only a few years after this, war broke out once more with the Samnites. The hillmen had objected to the Romans making colonies on the very borders of their land, but they had not sufficient wisdom to object strongly enough and at the right time. The Romans had therefore made themselves very strong in Latium before the second struggle broke out. The story of this war is not very interesting, but the Romans suffered one shameful defeat in it which we must mention. At first, however, they were everywhere victorious, so much so that the Samnites even grew so frightened that they asked the Romans to be at peace. The Romans refused, and now the Samnites fought even more vigorously, as men will when they have nothing to hope.

Misled by false news, the Romans were led to march through a place which was shut in on both sides by high hills. The entrance to this place was very narrow indeed, and so was the outlet from it. It seemed very terrible and mysterious as the army marched quickly through, but they were thoroughly frightened when they found at the outlet a great barrier with hundreds of Samnite soldiers behind it. Quickly they marched back, only to find that the entrance had been stopped in the same way. On the hill-tops, on both sides, they now saw the Samnite soldiers. They could not move backward or forward. They could not fight as they had been used to. And so they were compelled to give in.

This was bad enough, but it was not all. The Samnites made the Roman generals promise to destroy the strong town Fregellae and another colony, and to make a league with the Samnites. Then the Samnites made the disgraced Roman soldiers put their weapons on the ground, and go 'under the yoke,' *i.e.* creep under a spear which rested upon two other spears stuck upright in the ground. This was the most shameful thing that could happen to any soldier, for it meant that he who went under the yoke owned that the others were completely his master.

The conquered generals had promised to do what the Samnites had asked, and so had been allowed to go back to Rome with the army. But when they told the Romans what they had agreed to do, the Romans were very angry and refused to do these things. This was, of course, very dishonorable, for if the generals had not agreed they would not have been allowed to go home.

But the Romans thought that they could not give up all that they had won just because two of their generals had fallen into a trap. They prepared to go to war again. A new Roman army was formed quickly, and the Samnites were defeated, and themselves made to pass under the yoke. The Romans must have enjoyed paying the Samnites back for the shame they had made them suffer.

The battle was at Luceria, over the Apennine mountains, in the south-west of Italy, and the town was made into a fortress to protect the Roman power there. Other victories followed, and so the Samnites, by trapping the Romans, had not destroyed the power of Rome as they thought, they had simply made it more powerful still. For now she had a strong colony to the east of the country of the Samnites. A great Roman road, at this time, was built to Capua. It was the famous Appian Way. Good roads joining far-off colonies, colonies in strong towns in a district which had been made Roman, these were the chief ways in which more and more of Italy fell into the power of Rome.

When the war with the Samnites was over at length, after twenty years, it might have been thought that the Romans would have been finally acknowledged as rulers of Italy, especially as their wisdom in peace was even greater than their courage and skill in war. For the Romans very seldom were cruel to their enemies. They generally offered to let them enjoy some of the privileges of being a Roman citizen, if they promised to help their conquerors and to be faithful to them. Now, after the war with the Samnites more fortresses were built, and more of those strong straight roads to carry the Roman armies swiftly from one to another.

A view on the Appian Way as it is today.

Yet the Samnites could not easily give up their freedom and acknowledge the Romans their masters, and this is what those strong towns up and down Italy meant. They were really chains. Whenever and wherever the Samnites wished to leave their hill country, they found a strong Roman colony in their way. The Etruscans had recently rebelled against the Romans, and now they made up their minds to try once more, but this time they intended to join with the Samnites. The Romans found another enemy marching against them. The result of this was that the Romans had to fight armies in the far South of Italy, in Campania, and in Etruria. But although there were times when it looked as if the future mistress of the world would be destroyed, Rome came out of this terrible war victorious once more. Again colonies were settled over the conquered country, one being far south on the Appian Way, and no fewer than twenty thousand colonists were sent there.

In this way the South was made Roman, the two large states in the South of Italy, Apulia and Lucania, being put under her. She was not so strong that wars could not arise again; but, with the exception of the struggle with the Greeks in Italy (which must be told in the next chapter), almost the whole of Italy had now been conquered by Rome. She had fought for several hundred years, but now, in the year 290 B.C., when strong towns in almost every part of the country reminded men of the Roman power, she was practically mistress of the whole of Italy.

The practical orderly spirit of the Romans had made itself felt. The clever men in the city, ruling while their brothers fought in the distant wars, or wisely deciding what to do in the many difficult questions that arose—with whom they should make friends, whom they should treat mildly, whom they should punish harshly—had really made Rome the great city she was.

The Romans had not the imagination of the Celts, nor the artistic feeling and curiosity into the reasons of things which marked the Greeks, but they had a strong practical common sense, a wisdom which was more valuable than either in fitting them to rule over many peoples. Now this strong young nation is to be brought face to face with the old and splendid Greek race. Perhaps one might regret that the Romans won if it were not that, by that fact, much of the beauty and splendor of ancient Greece has been preserved for all time, for peoples in the most distant ages to enjoy and grow better through them.

Chapter XII—Rome and Carthage

Last of all the peoples in the South of Italy whom the Romans fought and conquered were the Greeks. For a long time the Romans left them alone, for they guessed that the Greek cities of Italy would ask help from other Greeks in Greece proper or some of the Greek colonies. This is what actually happened. One of the chief Greek towns in South Italy was Tarentum. It was built by men from Sparta in the days when so many Greeks sailed away from Greece proper and settled in Italy. It was a large and beautiful town, but for many years before it actually quarrelled with Rome it had been ruled very badly. It was not like Sparta, an aristocracy, but was a democracy of the worst sort. The people had no idea of keeping their tempers and acting wisely. When they were angry they would do anything to take revenge on their enemies, and never thought whether it was just or not. They were very jealous of the Romans, and afraid that they would conquer them as they had conquered the other peoples of Italy.

Pyrrhus, King of Epirus (*From a statue at Rome*).

But instead of going to war in a straightforward way with Rome, the people of Tarentum did a very mean and wrong thing. A Roman fleet had sailed into their harbor, and was lying there peacefully. The people of Tarentum rushed suddenly upon the ships. The Romans were taken by surprise, and five of the ships were easily taken by the Tarentines. The men on them were either killed or sold into slavery. Then the people of Tarentum, frightened of Rome, sent across the Adriatic Sea to the little kingdom of Epirus to ask its king, who was a Greek and a relation of Alexander the Great, to come and help them against Rome. Pyrrhus was the name of this king, and he was so handsome and brave, and such a fine soldier, that it has often been said that he was nearly as wonderful a man as Alexander the Great. But this is not quite true. He was a fine soldier, and could win battles, but he had not the imagination to make much use of them. He would win at all costs, but often lost so many men that winning did not seem of any use. Even now we speak of a victory or a success of any kind which is not of much use to the winner as a 'Pyrrhic Victory.'

THE FIRST FIGHT BETWEEN GREEKS AND ROMANS

Pyrrhus in his little kingdom of Epirus, which was really under the Macedonian power, was glad of the chance of going over the sea to fight for the people of Tarentum. He collected an army, and he took with him some elephants, and crossed the sea to Tarentum. Near the town he fought with a Roman army under one of the consuls. The Romans had never seen elephants before, and partly because of the strangeness of an army like that of Pyrrhus, they were defeated. It was the first time that a Roman army had fought against Greek soldiers, and the Greeks won. But it was only an accidental victory, and the Romans were much too used to winning and too sure of their own strength to think much of it. When Pyrrhus sent a messenger to the Senate to try to arrange conditions of peace, one of the Senators, Appius Claudius, who was old and blind, persuaded the Senate to send a message back to Pyrrhus, telling him proudly that the Romans never talked of peace with foreign soldiers on her land.

So next year another battle was fought, and again it was a 'Pyrrhic Victory,' and Pyrrhus then left Italy and crossed to Sicily, where the Greek colonies were fighting once more with the Carthaginians. He helped the Greek cities there, but as he himself seemed to treat them as a conqueror, they turned against him, and so he went back to Italy. Once more he fought against the Romans, but this time he was defeated and went back to Greece. Three years afterwards he was killed in a fight, after taking part in several of the struggles which were still going on among the Greek states.

After his departure from Italy, Tarentum soon became an 'ally' of Rome, which sounded as though she was still free, but she had to pull down her walls and join Rome in her battles if she was asked to do so. In a short time Rome had conquered the whole of South Italy. She soon began to think about conquering the island of Sicily too. This island is so near to Italy that it would be very dangerous for the Italian state if it belonged to anyone else.

At the time when Rome had won all the South of Italy, and began to think about conquering Sicily, the island was still divided between the colonies of Carthage and those of Greece. For seventy years after the Greeks had won the great victory of Himera over the Carthaginians under Hamilcar, there had been peace between the two peoples in Sicily. But the Carthaginians had never forgotten Hamilcar. Seventy years after his death a quarrel broke out between two Greek towns in Sicily. One of them asked the help of the

Carthaginians, and Carthage gladly sent help over to fight against the town of Selinus. The chief ruler in Carthage was Hannibal, the grandson of Hamilcar. He was very pleased at the idea of fighting the Greeks in Sicily, and winning, as he hoped, a great victory. He himself collected a great army from Africa and Spain, for the South of Spain had been conquered by Carthage, and crossed over to Sicily. With his great army he destroyed Selinus, killed thousands of its people, and then marched on to Himera to take revenge for the defeat of his grandfather seventy years before. Again he won a great victory, and destroyed Himera. His soldiers murdered the people in the streets until Hannibal gave the order to stop. But the people who had not been killed immediately were treated even worse. They were taken to the place where Hamilcar had last been seen and there killed as a sacrifice.

The Carthaginians, in spite of their wealth and power, were never really civilized. They offered sacrifices of men and women and even children to their gods. Hannibal now went home to Carthage, but four years afterwards was persuaded to go again to Sicily. This time he besieged the town of Agrigentum, even pulling up gravestones outside the town for his men to stand on when they threw their weapons into the city. But the plague broke out among his soldiers.

Hannibal thought this was a punishment from the gods for his having touched the graves of the dead, and he immediately offered a sacrifice of a child, hoping that the gods would forgive him. But he fell ill himself and died, and in the fights which followed the Greeks won. For one hundred and fifty years after this the Greeks and Carthaginians were at war in Sicily, though sometimes peace was made for some years. Then at last Rome was ready to interfere and take Sicily for herself.

In any case it was certain that now that Rome had become so strong she would have a struggle with Carthage, the only other great power in the West, to see which should become in the end the greater power. The struggle began over Sicily, but after the island was won by the Romans, it went on for more than a hundred years until Rome had won all her lands from Carthage, and completely destroyed that proud city itself.

A town in Sicily called Messana (and which is now named Messina) had been taken by some rough soldiers from the South of Italy. They were really robbers and had no right to the town. The people in the country near were very much afraid of them, and Hiero, the ruler of the great Greek colony in Sicily called Syracuse, made up his mind to fight against Messana and drive the robbers out. The robbers asked help of Rome and of Carthage. The Romans knew that they ought to help Hiero, who was their ally, but they were so afraid of Carthage getting power in Messana that they said they would help the robbers there instead. But some of the robbers let Carthaginian soldiers into Messana. These fought against the Roman soldiers, and so the great struggle began.

Rome's First Ships

The Carthaginians were so great by sea that the Romans knew that it was on the sea they must fight if they were to win. But so far Rome had never had a fleet. The Romans knew nothing either about building big ships. The only ships they had were the old-fashioned Greek boats with three rows of oars. The Greeks and Etruscans in Italy did know something about shipbuilding, and as these people were now really part of the Roman state, the Romans got them to help them to build new ships. A Carthaginian ship which was wrecked and washed up on the coast of Italy was examined and copied. A whole forest of trees was cut down, and a fleet of a hundred ships was made.

But the Romans did not yet know anything about managing ships, and for many years after this many of their ships were wrecked in storms because the sailors did not know what to do when danger or difficulty came. But they fought against the ships of Carthage, and won great victories. They managed to do this by fighting at sea much as they would have done on land. Each Roman ship had a kind of bridge with a great sharp hook at the end, and when a Carthaginian ship came near, the bridge was let down over its side, the hook caught it and held it fast, and then the Romans swarmed over the bridge on to the enemy's ship, and there fought a hand-to-hand fight.

In the first sea-fight between Rome and Carthage fifty Carthaginian ships were destroyed. Then the Carthaginians would fight no more, and the Romans sailed proudly home carrying the brass figureheads of their enemy's ships, which they fastened to a pillar which was put up in the Forum, the great market-place at Rome, in memory of Rome's first victory on the sea. Many more ships were built after this, and in a later battle we know that there were at least three hundred ships on each side. After several years of fighting at sea and in Sicily, the Romans made up their minds to land two great armies in the north of Africa, and fight Carthage at home. After another great victory at sea the armies landed. The Carthaginians then sent messengers to discuss conditions of peace. But the Romans said they must not only give up to them the islands of Sardinia and Sicily, but they must also destroy their own fleet, and send ships to help the Roman fleet when required.

The Carthaginians were naturally very angry at such a request, and determined to fight the matter out. The Romans were so confident that they called one of the armies back to Italy. The other was left under a brave commander called Regulus. He had a large army, but the Carthaginians got together a still larger one, and they had large numbers of horse-soldiers. Regulus might have got horse-soldiers for himself from some tribes which were in rebellion against Carthage, but he did not, and when the fighting took place the Romans were defeated. Regulus was taken prisoner, and later killed. A story is told, and it may be true, that he was sent to Rome with messages for the Senate, but he had promised to give himself up again to the Carthaginians if the conditions of peace which the Carthaginians offered were not agreed to by the Romans. It is told that Regulus himself persuaded the Senate to say 'No' to these conditions, for the people of Carthage were now, in their turn, asking too much. So Regulus kept his word, and went back to be killed.

After this, too, the Romans were very unfortunate in their fights with the Carthaginians on the sea. The fighting went on for years. Altogether the 'First Punic War,' as it was called, lasted seventeen years. In the end peace was made, and Carthage agreed to give up Sicily, and the small islands near it. Soon afterwards, when Carthage was having a great deal of trouble with some of the paid soldiers who had rebelled against her, the Romans suddenly seized Sardinia and Corsica too. At the time the Carthaginians could not do anything, but Hamilcar, their ruler who had made the peace with Rome, was now filled with a deadly hatred. He devoted the rest of his life to revenge.

He saw that he would have a better chance of getting together an army of splendid soldiers if he went over to Spain. The people of Carthage were rather tired of the struggle with Rome, and could not understand Hamilcar's feeling of deadly hatred for her. They were quite pleased when he proposed to go to Spain, and devote himself to getting together an army there. There were already many Carthaginian colonies in that country, and Hamilcar conquered more and more of the land until there was a large new kingdom there. He drilled the Spaniards, and made them into fine soldiers. For years he did this, content to prepare his revenge and leave it to others to carry out. When his little boy was only nine years of age he told him solemnly all the wrongs which Rome had done to Carthage, and the boy swore an oath to avenge his country when he had grown to be a man.

Hannibal (From the Louvre).

Hannibal the Great

The boy, whose name was Hannibal, grew up to be one of the greatest soldiers who have ever lived. After his father's death, when he himself was a young man of twenty-six, he fought against Rome; and though Rome was now a great nation, and Carthage was fast going to ruin, he almost won in the fight by his immense cleverness and courage. But he made two mistakes. He thought that the people of Italy whom the Romans had conquered would be glad to join him in fighting them, but this was not so, for the Italians had by this time settled down happily under Roman rule. He thought, too, that the people of Carthage would be anxious to help, but again this was not the case.

By this time the Roman people had learned all about ships and shipping. They had a great navy, and so when the moment came for Hannibal to attack them he chose to do it by land. He made up his mind to lead a great army out of Spain into Italy across the Alps. It was early Spring when the army began its march, and in the mountain passes the weather was bitterly cold. The men who guarded them went back to their homes at night, and so Hannibal chose to lead his army across in the darkness. Nearly all his horses and elephants carrying the baggage slipped down the steep precipices and were killed. Before the Alps were crossed, half of the men of his great army were dead, either through falling from the rocks or overcome by the terrible cold. The other half arrived in the plain of North Italy, tired out, but still full of courage and ready to fight. Hannibal was suffering from a terrible soreness of the eyes, through the great cold, and one eye became blind.

The Romans did not know anything of Hannibal's plans until he had nearly reached the Alps. Then they sent an army to Spain to prevent him getting any more men or food from there, and for ten years Hannibal had to depend on what he could get in Italy. For he stayed altogether fifteen years in that country fighting desperately, and always hoping for the help from Carthage, which came at last, but too late. He marched from the North to the South of Italy, winning three great battles, for he was a splendid general, and when he actually got the Romans to fight, he often won. At the battle of Cannæ, it is said that eighty thousand Romans were killed, and that Hannibal sent ten thousand gold rings to Carthage, taken from the fingers of the dead Roman nobles, to show how great had been his victory. It was a dreadful misfortune, but the Roman people and Senate never lost heart for a moment. New soldiers were enlisted, and the defences of Rome itself were made stronger. Hannibal was never able to take Rome itself, and for years he remained in the South of Italy, hoping for help from his brother in Spain and from the people in Carthage.

At the same time Scipio, a brave young Roman general, was fighting the Carthaginians in Spain, and took for Rome their capital there, the great town called New Carthage. Hannibal's brother had been left to rule in Spain, but Hannibal was always hoping that he would be able to come with a new army to help him in Italy. At last he came, but was met by a Roman army in the North of Italy. His army was destroyed, and he himself killed. The first that Hannibal heard of it was when the head of his brother was suddenly thrown into his camp. It was a terrible warning, and Hannibal, full of grief and horror, cried, 'I see the doom of Carthage.'

The Romans, too, felt that this was a turning point in the struggle. They went nearly mad with joy, crowding to their temples to praise their gods. The women, dressed in their most beautiful clothes, took their children with them to join in the thanksgiving. Hannibal still waited sadly in the South of Italy, until he was called back to defend Carthage itself. Scipio had left Spain, where he had won all the lands belonging to the Carthaginians, and had taken

Scipio Africanus (From a museum at Rome, of the brilliant young general who was called 'Africanus' because of his victorious campaigns against Carthage).

an army into North Africa. The Carthaginians begged Hannibal to come back and defend them, and so after fifteen years in Italy he sailed away to his own country again. It is said that he cried as he looked back on the Italian shore, for he knew that he would never now have the thing which he had spent his life to win.

At Zama, near Carthage, he fought against Scipio and lost. At last Hannibal gave up all hope. He himself advised the people of Carthage to make peace with Rome. He knew that there was now no hope that Carthage should be greater than Rome. Hannibal must have been all the more sad when he remembered that his long and bitter struggle with Rome would make the Roman people harder in their conditions of peace.

These were, indeed, terribly hard for Carthage. She had to give up her navy, except a few warships. Five hundred of the ships were burnt by the Romans, under the eyes of the people of Carthage, just outside the harbor. All her land in Spain was now to belong to Rome, and each year for fifty years she must pay a large sum of money to Rome to make up to the Romans for the expenses of the war. The Carthaginians had to give up all their prisoners too, and though they were allowed to keep their own laws, they were to fight against the enemies of Rome when she asked them, and so they could hardly be called free from this time. Carthage had, indeed, hardly made good use of her wealth and power, but it is impossible not to feel sorry for her fall. So ended the Punic Wars. Later we shall see how Carthage dared once more to rise up against Rome, and how she was burnt to the ground. Hannibal was dead before this.

For some time after he had made peace with Rome he stayed in Carthage, and did all he could to bring order and prosperity to the city. He found that when the affairs of the city were properly managed, the money could be paid each year to Rome, and yet less need be taken from the people in taxes. But some of the people said that Hannibal only wanted to make them rich, so that he could make them fight Rome again. They even told the Romans that he was plotting with their enemies, and messengers were sent from Rome to Carthage asking that Hannibal should be given up to the Romans. But he had made up his mind to escape, and sail away to another land.

He was afraid that the people in the ships in the harbor of Carthage would stop him, so he invited all the captains to a great feast, and begged them first to lend him the sails of their ships to make an enormous tent in which the feast should be held. This they did, and when they were all rejoicing and making merry, he slipped away to his ship, and even when it was known that he had gone, it was many hours before the ships could be got ready to follow him.

He fought for some years on the side of first one enemy of Rome and then another, but these were the days when the Romans were winning in all their battles, and at last Prusias, King of Bithynia, whom he was helping, agreed to give him up to the Romans. But Hannibal preferred to kill himself rather than be given into the hands of his life-long enemy. When he knew that all the doors of his house were guarded by soldiers ready to take him if he should come out, he drank poison, and so died. His life-story is very wonderful and strange, but it was a pity that so clever a statesman and so brave a soldier should have given his whole life to a hopeless revenge.

Chapter XIII—Rome and the East

The battle of Zama and the peace with Carthage in the year 202 B.C. made it quite clear that no other power could become as great as Rome in the West of Europe. She now had for her own practically all Italy, Sicily, Corsica, Sardinia, the Carthaginian lands in Spain which stretched over a great space in the North and another in the South. Carthage and the North of Africa were allied with her and must fight against any enemy of the Roman people if asked to do so.

It was almost certain that Rome would, when she found herself so strong, try to conquer more land in Western Europe. But immediately after the peace with Hannibal she naturally turned her attention to the East of Europe, where the states were fighting among themselves, and no one state was strong enough to conquer the others.

We saw how after the death of Alexander the Great his empire was divided into many kingdoms, some of which were governed by Greek rulers and others not. More than a hundred years had passed since the death of Alexander when the people of Rome turned their attention to the East. The Macedonian kings since Alexander had always kept their rule over the greater part of Greece, though some of the towns on the coast had set themselves free; but in the days of Philip V, King of Macedon, some of the Greek cities joined together in leagues to try to free Greece from Macedonian rule. At this Philip V sent help to Hannibal in his fight with Rome, the Romans sent help to a league which was struggling against Philip, and when peace was made with Carthage and Rome had less to trouble her in the West, she sent an army to fight against Philip in earnest. He was defeated in the great battle of Cynoscephalae, and so ended the Macedonian rule over Greece.

The Romans were always very full of admiration for the greatness and beauty of Greece. They were so practical themselves and had so little of the natural gift for art and beauty that they were filled with a kind of wonder at the beautiful things which had been done and written by the Greeks in the past. It

Philip V of Macedon (*A Macedonian coin*).

was partly this, and partly perhaps for other reasons, that Rome having freed Greece from the Macedonians declared that she would leave her free to govern herself. This proclamation was cried aloud at the Isthmian games at Corinth, when as usual a great crowd of people from all parts of Greece had met together for the festival.

The people were full of joy at the good news, and it was said afterwards that they broke out into a great cry of gladness which could be heard on the seashore miles away. The Greeks to show their gratitude set free many Roman prisoners who had been taken by Hannibal and sold to them as slaves. But the old weakness of the Greeks was to bring them after all before long under the rule of Rome. The states were still always quarrelling among themselves, and it was natural that Rome should interfere, and in the end make up her mind to rule Greece herself.

Meanwhile she had to deal with other people in the East. Antiochus, King of Syria, was anxious to gain power in Egypt and the Egyptians had asked for help from Rome. Antiochus was a friend, too, of Philip V of Macedon, but had not been able to help him against Rome. As soon as the Romans had left Greece one of the leagues asked Antiochus to help them to fight against Rome. Antiochus was anxious to win some of the lands which Philip of Macedon had lost, but he was defeated first in Greece and then in Asia Minor. He had to give up most of his lands and pay a large sum of money to the Romans.

After this the whole of Asia Minor belonged to Rome. Philip V of Macedon was still full of anger against the Romans and was always planning and plotting to win Greece again for Macedonia. But he could do nothing. When he died, his son Perseus became king, and he was even more anxious than his father to take his revenge on Rome. At last the Romans sent an army to fight against him and he was completely defeated. Perseus was taken prisoner to Italy, where he died some years later, and Macedonia now also belonged to Rome.

Perseus, Son of Philip V (A Macedonian coin).

It was the custom for the Roman generals who won great battles to have a triumphal procession through the streets of Rome on their return. The triumph of Æmilius Paulus, the general who had defeated Perseus, was most magnificent. It lasted three days, and the Romans, dressed in the white robes which they always wore on days of festival, crowded to see it. On the first day two hundred and fifty wagons went in procession, filled up with beautiful Greek statues and pictures which the conquerors had brought from Macedonia.

On the second day wagons carried great piles of beautiful polished armor and swords and other weapons, taken from the bodies of the Macedonian soldiers who had been killed, and great piles too of silver cups and bowls, also taken from the conquered. On the third day the triumph was most magnificent, but even the Roman people felt how sad it was, for behind a number of young Roman men leading great oxen, decorated with flowers and ribbons, to be killed in sacrifice, there followed all the gold cups and plates taken from Perseus himself.

Behind this was his chariot carrying the armor and the crown which he would never wear again. Then came the three children of Perseus surrounded by their teachers and servants, who held out their hands to the crowd as though asking for pity. Paulus in his splendid chariot came last, but in front of him walked Perseus clothed in black, looking down at the ground and seeming so heartbroken that all the people were sorry for him.

THE END OF GREEK FREEDOM

Perseus was the last civilized king against whom Rome fought. After this her Empire grew larger and larger, but after the fall of Greece it was against barbarous, or at least only half-civilized, people that she had to fight. For years before the conquest of Macedonia the Greek states had been quarrelling among themselves and complaining about each other to Rome, who often interfered to put things right. But after the conquest of Macedonia the Romans became harder towards Greece. Some Greeks had been glad when Perseus fought against Rome, and one thousand of the noblest of these people were carried off to Rome and kept prisoners there for seventeen years. At last, when one of the leagues tried to force Sparta to join them in spite of Rome forbidding them to do so, war broke out. The Romans of course won, and Corinth, a city which had been especially bold in the rebellion, was by order of the Romans burnt to the ground, and at last Greece was made into a Roman province and governed by a Roman governor.

It was in the year 146 B.C. that Corinth was burnt and the freedom of Greece lost forever. The beautiful statues and works of art of which Corinth was full were sent off to Rome. It is said that the Roman commander who sent them off told the owners of the ships that if any were broken they would have to be replaced by others of the same value. He was a rough soldier and did not understand that these things could never be replaced, for only the great Greek artists of a time gone by could make them. But the more educated Romans did understand this, and from this time onwards they were constantly learning about and imitating the art and literature of Greece, and it is through the Romans that we today have learnt so much from the old Greek civilization.

In the same year in which Corinth was burnt the Romans destroyed Carthage too. They had long wished to do so. There was one man in the Senate named Cato who ended every speech he made for several years with the words: 'Delenda est Carthago' — 'Carthage must be destroyed.' It will be remembered how by the peace made with Hannibal it was decided that Carthage might never again fight an enemy without permission from the Romans.

The king of Numidia, a country close to Carthage, was very friendly with the Romans, but always annoying Carthage. Rome would never give the Carthaginians permission to fight against him, but at last they could stand it no longer and did so. Immediately the Romans made up their minds to punish them. The Carthaginians were told that they must destroy their own city, but they said they would not. They shut their gates against the Roman army which was sent against them.

For three years they stood a terrible siege. There was an immense wall all round the city, and inside the women joined with the men making javelins and other weapons to fling at the Romans. When the horse hair which was required for certain weapons ran short, the women cut off their own long hair to take its place. The Carthaginians fought like lions. Sometimes a band of soldiers would come out to the walls and scatter the Romans, but in the end the Romans were able to prevent any food going into the city, and later broke in. There was fighting for three days in the narrow streets. Houses were burnt and women and children were buried in the ruins. The town was completely destroyed and the Romans cursed the ruins.

So ended the Third Punic War—the last traces of a great empire and of a people who with all their faults had done wonderful things on sea and land before the Romans were ever heard of.

Rome had now power over practically all the lands round the Mediterranean Sea except Egypt. She soon finished the conquest of Spain and the South of Gaul, which is now called France. Most of these lands were already Roman provinces governed by Roman governors, and those which were not immediately made into provinces very soon became so. It will be interesting to see what changes all these victories had made in the Romans themselves.

CHAPTER XIV—LAST DAYS OF THE ROMAN REPUBLIC

Great changes had come over the Roman people during the time they had been conquering the lands round the Mediterranean Sea. In the old days the Romans had lived very simply, and every member of a family did exactly what the father said. The Roman women had been very serious and very noble. Even now it is considered a great compliment to say that a woman is like an old Roman matron. But when the Romans began to fight farther from home the fathers of families were often away for a long time, and the old family life disappeared.

In the old days, too, the Roman people had lived very simply, but as some of them grew richer they began to live very differently. Some of the women cared for nothing but amusing themselves, and dressed themselves in fine clothes and wore a great deal of jewelry. Some of them left their children to be looked after altogether by slaves. The boys in rich houses were given lessons by slaves brought from Greece. Often these were not very good men, and though they taught the boys to read and write and to understand the wonderful writings of the Greeks, they did not teach them how important it is to be good and truthful and unselfish as the Roman fathers had taught their children in the old days. Of course there were some exceptions, and we shall hear about two noble Romans who had a splendid mother who brought them up in the good old way.

The fact that some people grew very rich while others became very poor was another great change from the days when every Roman had a little land of his own and none was either very rich or very poor. Now the rich people all over Italy bought great quantities of land, and the poorer Italians gave up their lands; some went into the towns and others to the wars, and many soldiers when they came home from the wars had nothing to live on. The rich new landowners had many foreign slaves who could take care of the sheep and cattle on the lands, and who were often treated very much like animals themselves. They were often driven to their work with a master standing over them all day, and then locked up at night, great numbers together, for fear they should escape. Land which had been used by the farmers in the old days to grow corn was now left to feed the sheep, and the corn was brought in from other countries.

So Italy soon began to have three classes of men—the rich landowners, the poor Italians, and a number of slaves, many of whom were in the greatest misery. Sometimes the slaves in one part of the country or another would rise up and attack their masters, but they were always put down, and it was a long time before anyone thought of doing anything for them.

A Fragment of a Sarcophogus Decpicting Some Roman Senators (*National Museum of Rome*).

Then, too, the government of Rome had changed by degrees. It was now the Senate which really settled everything, and the people no longer had any power. The people were supposed to choose the consuls and other rulers, but as no ruler held power except for a short number of years, and as the consuls were nearly always away fighting, the Senate soon got all real power. The Senators belonged to just a few families among the rich people, and though they knew all about fighting they had no idea how to make things better for the poor people and slaves, and did not even think about it.

Then, again, in all the lands under the rule of the Romans only those people who were Roman 'citizens' were really safe, and could get protection for their lives and their property from the government. Long after this we shall see how St. Paul, because he was a Roman citizen, got the right to be taken to Rome to be judged by the ruler there. There were many of the Italian 'allies' who thought that as they had helped Rome in her wars they should have the same rights as her 'citizens.' It was a long time before the Senate would grant this.

Such was the state of things in Rome in the last hundred and thirty years B.C. But during this time some Romans began to see that there must be a great change in Italy and in the Roman state. One great man after another appeared to try to put things right. It is the time in which the greatest men in Roman history lived, and at the end of this hundred years the greatest of them all did at last put things right. We shall see now who these men were, and what they did.

Many of them belonged to the same rich families as the Senators, but were different from them in understanding something about the troubles of the other people.

TWO NOBLE ROMANS

The first of these great Romans were two brothers— Tiberius and Gaius Gracchus. They belonged to a noble family in Rome, but their father died when they were quite young. Their mother was a noble Roman matron of the old sort. She was beautiful, and many nobles asked her to marry them, and so did at least one king, but she always said 'No,' for she wanted to give herself up altogether to taking care of her boys.

When other Roman matrons would show her their beautiful ornaments and jewelry she would smile, and show them her sons, saying that *they* were *her* jewels. Tiberius was nine years older than Gaius. Their mother had them taught by Greeks in the new Roman way, but she herself taught them to be good and kind and to think of others more than themselves. They grew up splendid men, and lived and died for their country.

Tiberius became a soldier, and fought in Africa and Spain, while Gaius was still having lessons at home. But he was not content like other soldiers to fight and win for Rome. He saw the misery all over Italy, and he saw, too, how the soldiers who came back from the wars had no land on which to grow things as in the old days of Rome, and how they stayed in the town, where the people were becoming poorer and more ignorant and rougher every day.

The Consuls, or chief rulers of Rome, had always been Patricians, and had not always thought enough of the happiness of the Plebeians, as the people who were not nobles were called. At one time the Plebeians had threatened to leave Rome and set up a new city for themselves; but it was then agreed that they should have magistrates of their own, called Tribunes of the People, to see that no wrong should be done to the people by the other rulers. Tiberius Gracchus was one of these magistrates.

Tiberius became a Tribune of the People. He tried to get a law passed to take some of the land away from the rich people and to give it to the soldiers back from the wars, so that they could become farmers and live happy and useful lives in the country. The rich people were very angry, and they got the other tribune (for there were always two) to 'veto' the law, that is, to say he was against it. In the old days if a tribune vetoed a law in this way that was an end of it, but Tiberius saw that the Roman government had become very bad indeed.

Instead of the old Roman people, farmers and soldiers, who used to choose the tribunes, here was now a crowd of rough people spending their days lying about the streets of the city. Tiberius thought that tribunes chosen by such people did not matter much. He knew that his law was good, and he tried to force the Senate to do what he wanted. Those lands which really belonged to the state were indeed taken away from the rich men, and men were appointed to arrange how they should be given out to the poorer people.

But before this was done Tiberius Gracchus was murdered in the streets of Rome by a crowd of angry and terrible people, who had been told by his enemies that he was really trying to make himself king. The name of king had been hated by the Romans ever since the early days, when the last of the Tarquins had been chased from the city.

A few years afterwards Gaius Gracchus began over again the work his brother had tried to do, and began it in a wiser and better way. Gaius was an even finer man than his brother. He was as full of pity for the people and as eager to make them happy, but he had learned from his brother's mistakes that it would not do to go against the Roman government. So he did his best to make that government better. For a long time, although the land had been taken from the rich people it was not divided among the others, and many of the rich men hoped it would never be given up. But Gaius Gracchus became tribune, and at once began to try to settle about the giving out of the land.

As he knew the Senate was against him, he tried to put new men into it, but the old Senators would not have them. He also wanted to give the Italians in all parts of Italy the rights of Roman citizens. This would have been a very good thing, but it made the people of Rome very angry, and Gracchus tried to please them and make them agree with his plans by doing another thing which was not very wise.

We have seen how rough and ignorant the people of Rome had become. Gains thought he could get them to agree to his plans by giving them very cheap food, and so they were allowed to buy corn and bread from the state for less money than it cost the state to buy it. When the people in the country round about Rome knew this they too crowded into the towns, and there were soon more rough and idle people than ever there. For years after this every Roman ruler had to try to please the people by giving them cheap bread. In the end they did not pay anything at all, but demanded as their right 'panem and circenses,' bread and circuses, for in the end the rulers had to give them free amusements as well as free bread.

The people of Rome liked Gaius Gracchus for his own sake too. He was a splendid speaker, and when he made speeches he would walk restlessly up and down speaking in a quick eager way which the people liked. But his enemies were too many for him, and the Senate set up another tribune who promised the people even better things than Gracchus had given them. He was chased like Tiberius through the streets of Rome, and when he saw that he was to be killed, he told a faithful slave to kill him. The slave did so, and then killed himself. His body was found beside his master's. So both these noble sons of a noble mother died in the attempt to make their country happier and better.

Free Distribution of Bread in Rome
(Enlarged from a design on a coin. The Emperor is enthroned on the left supervising the distribution, while the patron goddess of Rome approves by her presence).

The Gracchi were only the first of a great number of men who were to give their lives in the attempt. Although the Senate had overcome the two Gracchi, they themselves were never again so much respected by the people. Their government became worse and worse. In the conquered countries the Roman governors often ruled very badly, although things had been made better by Gaius Gracchus. He had passed a law by which governors were to be tried at home if the people they governed accused them of having taken money from them wrongfully, but though this law did some good it could not altogether put things right. Sometimes these governors even took money from the enemies of Rome.

Another very bad thing for Rome was that the soldiers had become very different from the soldiers of Rome's early days, and were now very hard to manage. As a matter of

The Roman Forum and Comitium after 44 B.C. (From the book The Roman Forum: a topographical study By Francis Morgan Nichols, 1877).

The Roman Forum As It Looks Today

fact, the only thing which could save Rome and bring order into her vast Empire was that some strong man who could manage both the soldiers and the state should seize power. Over and over again in this hundred years it seemed that this man had come; but there was always something weak or wanting in the character of each, until in the end the great Julius Cæsar, one of the greatest men of all time, rose to do the work. It is true that he was killed as his task was finished, but Augustus who came after him had the way made ready for him.

But in the days just after the death of Gaius Gracchus there were two men, great soldiers, who tried to put things right. These were Caius Marius, a young man who was born and brought up as a peasant, but who rose to be one of Rome's greatest soldiers and statesmen, and Lucius Cornelius Sulla, a man of noble birth and very rich.

Caius Marius

The two men were very different. Marius was rough but honest. He had very little education, but he was a splendid soldier, and he was anxious to make the lives of the people happier and better. He hated the rich and noble men who often lived very bad lives and cared only to make themselves richer, while the people of Italy and in all the provinces of the Roman Empire were growing more and more unhappy.

Sulla was an example of the things Marius hated so much. He was well educated, and knew a great deal about Greek art and literature; but he did not make good use of his knowledge. He gave himself over to pleasures of the worst sort.

He was horrible to look at. Naturally he was not very healthy, as he lived so irregularly, sitting up drinking and feasting through the night. He had blue eyes, but they had a curious stare, and his face was covered with ugly spots. A Greek jester spoke of Sulla as 'a mulberry sprinkled over with meal.'

Marius fought in a war with Jugurtha, the ruler of Numidia in North Africa. Jugurtha had tried to make his country, which had been an ally of Rome ever since the days of Hannibal, now independent of Rome. The first man sent to fight him had been bought off, and Jugurtha is said to have spoken contemptuously of Rome as 'a city for sale, ready to fall into the hands of the first bidder.' The way in which a small country like Numidia was able to defy Rome shows how bad things had become. It was Marius who in the end conquered Numidia and forced Jugurtha to give himself up to the Romans.

Sulla was fighting under Marius at the time, and he and his friends said that it was he who had captured Jugurtha. Sulla had a ring made with a picture on it of Jugurtha giving himself up to him. However, Marius was allowed a splendid triumph on his return to Rome, in which Jugurtha walked as a prisoner before he was dropped down into the terrible Mamertine prison, which was really a damp pit with water at the bottom. There he was left to starve to death, for the Romans had no mercy for an enemy like this.

The Barbarians Against Rome

Meanwhile new dangers from new peoples were threatening Rome. There was a fresh movement among the 'barbarian' peoples of Central Europe. Here some Celts and many Teutons, both people of the great Aryan race to which the Greeks and Romans belonged, were beginning to move West and South in search of new lands and new homes. At one time it seemed that they might conquer Rome itself. Many Roman armies were sent across the Alps to fight them, and prevent them crossing into Italy. There were now regular passes across the Alps into Italy, and the march was not difficult, as in the days of Hannibal.

The Roman armies were destroyed time after time by the barbarians, until Marius led an army into Gaul, and won a great victory over the barbarians there. When he got back to Rome he heard that another great barbarian army had crossed into the North-East of Italy. He marched against this too, and won another great victory. He saved Italy from the barbarians, and after this it was the Romans who went against the barbarians and won lands from them, so adding new provinces to the Empire.

For five years, one after another, Marius was elected consul, although he was away from Rome fighting. This was a new thing, and it showed how the people were beginning to feel that the man who ruled the soldiers was the really important person in the state.

By this time, of course, Marius had put order into the army. There was no longer any question of the soldiers disobeying their officers, and they all adored Marius. They were no longer men who became soldiers for a short time and then went back to their homes, as in the early days of Rome, but they stayed with the army for many years, and they would do anything their general told them, obeying him rather than the state. Marius had not much idea of how to make things better in Italy itself, but both he and Sulla did their best in fighting against the Italians, who suddenly demanded those rights of Roman citizenship which they had wanted for years.

As the Romans still refused to give these to them, they said they would have nothing more to do with Rome. The Italians, except the Romans, were to form a separate state with a new capital called Italica. They also made up their minds to destroy Rome. Marius and Sulla easily prevented this, but in the end the Italians won their right to citizenship, though only those could vote who could and would go to Rome to do so.

In a few years, however, the citizenship was really given to all Italian freemen, and so the whole of Italy became the real center of the Roman Empire. In the end this made things much better for Rome and Italy, but things could never be really right until the strong man should come who could settle Rome's troubles once for all.

Marius and Sulla were becoming more and more jealous of each other every day. Marius was now growing old, and when Mithridates the Great, king of Pontus in Asia Minor, began to attack the Roman allies in Asia Minor, it was Sulla who was appointed to lead an army against him. Marius was very jealous, and tried to please the Italians by some new laws, and so get them to give him the leadership of the war instead of Sulla. But Sulla marched with an army against Rome, and Marius had to run away. He was caught and put in prison, and was even condemned to die, but the slave who was to kill him would not do it, and the judges let Marius go.

He fled to Africa, and then Sulla went off with his army to the East. But as soon as he had gone, one of the consuls named Cinna tried to get together a number of men to vote that Marius should be called back in spite of the Senate. On the day of voting fighting broke out, and thousands were killed in the streets of Rome. Then Marius came back with an army, joined Cinna, and together they killed without mercy every man, sick or poor, who had been against Marius. Then the two named themselves consuls without any election, but Marius died in a few days. The people were glad in spite of all that Marius had done for them in his early days, for they were full of horror at the terrible bloodshed which he and Cinna had caused.

Sulla meanwhile had put things right in the East, and now sent word that he was coming back, and would take vengeance on the people who had murdered his friends. Cinna meant to fight against him, but was killed by his own soldiers. The Samnians and other Italians joined the enemies of Sulla, for it was the popular party of Marius and Cinna which had given them the rights of Roman citizens. Sulla came back and won victories everywhere. The Samnians marched to take Rome, but he defeated them also, and the eight thousand whom he captured were not even kept as slaves, but were killed on the Campus Martius.

DAYS OF BLOODSHED

Sulla was determined to get rid of the whole popular party. He drew up long lists of the richest and most important men on that side, and had them hunted out and killed. These lists were put up in the Forum, and the people crowded to read them. No one knew what name might next appear. The near relations of Marius were first on the list. Sulla had had himself made Dictator, the first for over a hundred years. He added new men to the Senate, and passed laws giving it all power in the state. The tribunes and the popular assemblies which had done so much for the Romans in the past had no longer any real power.

With all power in his own hands Sulla showed no shame in taking his revenge. The body of Marius was taken from his grave and thrown into the river Anio. New lists were drawn up one after another, and often they had in them the names of men who were not really enemies of Sulla, but whose lands or money he wanted for himself. It was now that the young Julius Cæsar showed something of what he was to be later. Marius had married an aunt of Julius Cæsar, although he himself was but a peasant, and she belonged to one of the oldest noble families of Rome. Julius Cæsar in his turn was married to Cornelia, the daughter of Cinna. So he was related to both the great leaders of the popular party.

Sulla ordered him to leave his wife, but Julius Cæsar loved Cornelia dearly, and he said he would not, although he knew that Sulla might kill him as he had killed so many other people. However, this did not happen, for his friends protected him. Sulla let him off, though he said that Cæsar would one day ruin the nobles, for he was 'more than a Marius.'

But for a time Cæsar kept quiet, and Sulla had things all his own way. When he had made the Senate quite strong he gave up his power, and went to live in his country house near Rome. He called the people of Rome together to tell them that he was going to give up his power, and he had great quantities of food given out to the poor, so that they might feast in his honor. There was so much food that some had to be thrown away. He then sent away the soldiers who had guarded him as ruler, and walked through the streets of the city, although he knew that there were many people who hated him, and he might be killed at any moment.

The people were too surprised to attack him, and he went off to live his curious life in his own way, drinking and feasting night after night for weeks, and then suddenly giving up all his time to hard study and reading. When he died in a few years his body was given a splendid funeral by the Senate. He had ordered that his body should be burnt, for he was afraid that some enemy might treat it later as he had treated the body of Marius. Some of the Romans preferred to be buried, and others cremated or burned, but the family of Sulla had previously always been buried.

Sulla is one of Rome's great men, but there is very little to like or admire in him. He fought for the Senate and the noble families to which he belonged, but he was a bad, selfish and proud man, and though he brought some kind of order into the state, he did it with a terrible cruelty that was quite unnecessary.

Sulla had only been able to settle Roman affairs for a time. So long as he lived no one dared to go against the government of the Senate, which he had tried to make strong, but when he died a change was at once felt. The Senate soon found that its powers were taken from it in the same way as before by the strong men who ruled the army.

THE GREAT JULIUS CÆSAR

One of these was Gneuis Pompeius Magnus, or as he was afterwards called, Pompeius the Great. Another was the great Julius Cæsar. Each of these did great things for Rome, and in the end there was a great jealousy and struggle between them as there had been between Sulla and Marius.

Both men were fine soldiers. Julius Cæsar was of course one of the finest generals who have ever lived. Both were handsome men. Pompeius was six years older than Cæsar. Both were born about one hundred years B.C. From the first Cæsar shows himself a stronger man than Pompeius. For when Sulla told them both to give up their wives Pompeius did so, but

Pompeius the Great. Marble bust on display in Chateau de Vaux-le-Vicomte, France.

Cæsar refused. At first Pompeius took the part of the Senate, but later he went over to the popular party, and the people almost adored him.

Cæsar from the first took the people's part. He also was much loved, and in time the people forgot Pompeius, and thought only of Cæsar. Cæsar was a tall handsome man with dark hair and black eyes, which lit up his pale, rather thin, face. He looked above all things very noble and distinguished. His family, which was one of the oldest in Rome, was said to be descended from the goddess Venus.

Cæsar always thought a great deal about dress, and he wore his girdle round his tunic in a loose way which was the fashion among the noble young men of his day. When he was quite a young man, Cæsar took part in the pleasures and feastings for which the Roman nobles were being so much blamed at the time. But he was never really frivolous. He seems to have done these things more in a spirit of mischief than anything else. He always meant to do great things and he did them.

For some time after the death of Sulla, Cæsar was content to help Pompeius to gain power in the state. But the great statesmen of the time had to be great soldiers too, and soon Pompeius had to leave Rome to fight her enemies far away.

Rome was then being threatened by three sets of enemies. The Mediterranean Sea was full of pirate ships which often took for themselves the ships carrying corn to Italy. Sometimes, too, they would attack a ship, and take as prisoners any rich men they found on it, and refuse to let them go until their friends paid large sums of money in ransom.

Cæsar was once taken prisoner in this way by the pirates. He spent his time reading to them some speeches which he had composed. At the same time he told them that he would kill them when he got the chance. And so he did. When his ransom was paid and he was free, he fitted out a ship and went against these same pirates, captured them, and killed them every one.

Pompeius determined to chase the pirates from the sea, so he got ready a great fleet of ships, and went out to fight them. He divided his ships into thirteen sets, and sent them out to different parts of the Mediterranean. After some fierce fighting the sea was quite cleared of the pirates, and Pompeius came back to Rome in triumph.

Pompeius helped, too, in putting down the famous 'Gladiators' Revolt.' This broke out a few years after the death of Sulla. Pompeius was in Spain, and it was Crassus, the richest man in Rome, who put down the revolt, but Pompeius came back in time to help at the end. The gladiators in Rome had been at first prisoners taken in war. They had been made to fight until one or other was killed.

At first these 'shows' only happened at funerals, but later on they became the greatest amusement of the Roman people. The strongest prisoners and slaves were chosen, and trained in 'schools' to be used merely to amuse the people. In every fight one or other of the gladiators fighting must be killed, and the stronger the men and the more desperate the fight the better pleased the people were.

No wonder the gladiators were miserable, and now at last two hundred of them from a big 'school' at Capua tried to escape. Eighty did get away, and they chose for their leader a big barbarian from Thrace called Spartacus. He was a brave and wise man. Other slaves joined him, and there were risings all over Italy. But in the end Spartacus was killed, and six thousand of his followers were crucified along the Appian Way, the great street leading out of Rome into the plain of Campania. The rising of the gladiators is but another example of the disorder and unhappiness in Italy at this time.

But in the Far East another enemy had to be faced. Mithridates of Pontus had been defeated by Sulla, and his soldiers chased out of Greece and the other parts of the Roman Empire which he had attacked. But he was now giving trouble again, and was being helped by Tigranes, the king of Armenia, who had even conquered Syria and Judaea. It was not for some years that the Senate sent out an army against them, and when they did so, though it conquered Mithridates, who fled to Tigranes in Armenia, the soldiers would not obey their commander. Pompeius now went out and soon conquered both kings. Mithridates died, and his kingdom was joined to Bithynia, and the two became a Roman province.

Tigranes was driven back into Armenia, and Syria became another Roman province. From this time the land in Asia as far as the Euphrates belonged to Rome either directly as provinces or as kingdoms governed by kings dependent on the Romans.

When Pompeius got back to Rome after being away four years he was granted a triumph. Great slabs of bronze were carried before him on which were engraved the story of the great things he had done in the East, how he had conquered kingdoms, set up new cities and captured eight hundred ships, and made treaties which it was hoped would give peace to the Roman Empire in the East at last. In the procession walked three hundred princes of the East whom Pompeius had brought back as prisoners. But in spite of all this the people were not so glad to see Pompeius as he had expected them to be.

Cæsar was now first favorite with them. Another trouble to Pompeius was that the Senate refused to agree to the settlements he had made in the East. This was foolish, for Pompeius had done things very well, but the Senate was growing ever weaker and more foolish. However, Cæsar agreed to help Pompeius, who was married to his daughter Julia, whom Cæsar loved very dearly for her own sake and that of her mother Cornelia. The two great men agreed to join with a third, a very rich man named Crassus, to take the government into their own hands.

The Senate was too weak to prevent this. Cæsar got the people to approve Pompeius's doings in the East. He himself became consul for one year, and then got himself made governor of the Roman provinces in the South of France, or Gaul as the country was then called. Cæsar's chief reason for wanting this was his wish to drive off the barbarian tribes, which were now ever threatening to swarm over into the Roman Empire itself.

A tribe from the country which is now called Switzerland was pressing towards the Roman province of Trans-Alpine Gaul (the part of France on the other side of the Alps from Italy, which belonged to Rome. That part on the side of the Alps nearer to Italy was called Cis-Alpine Gaul).

Cæsar immediately led his army against them and conquered them, and this was but the beginning of wars which lasted nine years, and in which Cæsar conquered all the land which we now call France and Belgium and part of Germany across the Rhine, and added them to the Roman Empire.

The story of these wonderful wars was written down by Cæsar himself very simply, and without any sign of pride. The books he wrote are called the 'Commentaries on the Gallic War,' and the story is so simple and yet in such good and pure Latin that it is one of the first writings to be given to boys and girls to read when they are beginning to study the Latin language.

The story is very exciting of how Cæsar fought with his legions, and especially his favorite Tenth Legion, against great hordes of 'barbarians,' who in spite of their bravery were in no way equal to the splendidly trained Roman soldiers with their splendid arms and weapons. If anyone could have conquered Cæsar it was the heroic leader of the Gauls named Vercengetorix. But in the end he was captured and taken to Rome to be led in triumph, and then killed.

It was while he was conquering Gaul that Cæsar crossed over to Britain in the year 55 B.C. The Britons had somehow heard of his coming, and their soldiers with their blue eyes and fair hair, and their bodies painted all over with blue, were ready to meet him. The sea was not deep enough for the ships to sail right to the shore, so the Romans had to wade to the land. We are told that they did not like this, and some of them held hack, but the standard-hearer of the Tenth Legion dashed into the water, and called to the soldiers to follow him unless they wanted to see their standard taken by the Britons.

This would have been a great disgrace. So the Romans fought their way to the shore, but they did not stay long in Britain. Next year they came again, and this time had some real hard fights with the Britons. The Romans won, but again sailed away, taking only a few British prisoners to show the people at Rome that Britain was conquered. But this was not really true, for it was a hundred years before the Romans came again, and began really to conquer Britain as a province of their empire.

It has often been asked why Cæsar was so anxious to win Gaul for Rome. There must have been many reasons. He was anxious to do great things because he felt that he alone could do them. It is said that when he was quite a young man he was one day reading the story of Alexander the Great and suddenly burst into tears. Someone asked him why he was weeping, and he answered that it was because Alexander had conquered many nations when he was his age and he as yet had done nothing great. Perhaps, too, Cæsar was anxious to show the Roman people that he could do even greater things than Pompeius.

Even during the years he was in Gaul, he would come down to the South to consult with Pompeius and Crassus about the affairs of Rome or to meet Senators who came to show him honor, for the Senate was becoming more and more afraid of the great soldier and statesman of the time. Crassus went off to the East, hoping to do great things there and so make himself seem equal to Cæsar, but he died, and then there were only Pompeius and Cæsar left to fight for power in Rome. Julia, the wife of Pompeius, died too, and so he felt less bound to Cæsar than before, and he was dreadfully jealous of him.

Julius Cæsar (Sixteenth century imitation of First century original.)

When Cæsar's work in Gaul was done the time had come for him to return to Rome, and he offered himself as consul for the next year. Some of the Senators, and especially Cato, a descendant of the Cato who had hated Hannibal so much, were dreadfully afraid of his return. They were afraid that he would do away altogether with the old Roman government, the Senate, and consuls, and tribunes, and all the things which had become useless, since, as we have seen, it was the great generals like Pompeius and Cæsar who really ruled the state.

But there was one great difference between Pompeius and Cæsar. Pompeius never quite made up his mind to do away with the Senate, whereas Cæsar, they knew, would have no pity for it, but would try to give good government in his own way.

These men did all they could to prevent Cæsar being consul, but when he saw this he led his army into Italy, saying as he crossed the little river Rubicon which divided Gaul from Italy, 'Alea jacta est,' 'the die is cast,' as though he was playing a game of dice and had taken the throw, and so knew he could never turn back. Both this expression and to 'cross the Rubicon' have become proverbs.

When the Senate and his enemies heard that Cæsar was marching upon Rome they fled in terror, and when Cæsar arrived there was no form of government left. The people, however, made him Dictator. He knew that Pompeius, who had fled to the East, could get together a great army there, and that he already had one in Spain.

So Cæsar did not stay long in Rome, but went off to Spain to conquer the army of Pompeius there. He conquered them and then let them go free, for Cæsar was not cruel when fighting against his countrymen, though he had not shown much mercy to the Gauls. Then he hastened after Pompeius to the East, where he defeated him.

Pompeius, now feeling very tired and old, fled to Egypt, but as he stepped on shore his head was cut off by one of the generals of the king of Egypt. His body was thrown into the sea, but afterwards taken out and buried by a faithful slave.

Cæsar followed Pompeius to Egypt, and the head of his enemy, once his friend, was shown to him in triumph. But Cæsar was shocked and surprised and burst into tears at the sight. Cæsar stayed some months in Egypt, and it is said that this was because he had fallen in love with Cleopatra, the sister of the young Ptolemy, as the ruler of Egypt was called.

But he had work to do elsewhere, for in different parts of the Empire the friends of Pompeius were still ready to fight. But Cæsar conquered them all, and then went back to Rome as Dictator once more. He had already in the short time he had stayed in Rome tried to settle the affairs of the country and the Empire, and he now turned his attention altogether to this work. He had not many months to do it in. He did not try to make a new way of government, but he kept all power in his own hands.

In Rome he said that only a certain number of people, and these the very poor, should receive free bread. He made the number of slaves in Italy much smaller. He raised the number of Senators to nine hundred, and the Senate now had in it men from the middle as well as the higher class. But it could never again have any real power. Above all, Cæsar himself appointed the governors of the provinces of the Empire, and they had to account to him for their government. From the time of Cæsar until the great Roman Empire broke up the government remained in one man's hands and this man was the Emperor.

Cæsar himself was sometimes, but not always, called by the name of 'Imperator,' but after his day it became the regular name of the ruler. Several times attempts were made to crown him 'King,' but Cæsar knew that the name had been hated for centuries by the Romans, and he was afraid that they would turn against him, although they treated him almost as a god. He was careful to please the people, and had great festivals prepared for them at which gladiators would fight against each other in the theatre.

A Roman Legionary Soldier (From a carving on Trajan's Column).

Cæsar would be present, but only to please the people, for often he was quietly writing his letters and not looking at the performance at all. Once, when he was sitting at the games in his chair of gold, dressed in purple and with a golden wreath of bay leaves on his head, Antony, one of his friends, suddenly came up to him and placed a crown on his head. As he did so he said, 'The people give you this.' But Cæsar took the crown from his head and said in a loud voice so that every one could hear, 'I am not king; the king of the Romans is Jupiter,' and he sent the crown as an offering to the temple of Jupiter.

All the same there were many people who said that Cæsar was a tyrant. They wanted what they called 'liberty,' forgetting all the terrible things which had happened when the government of Rome had grown old and all the good things Cæsar had done for the state. So it was that even the friends to whom Cæsar had been most loving and kind had a certain feeling of enmity against him and joined in a plot to kill him.

THE DEATH OF CÆSAR

Among the great men of that time was Cicero, the great writer whose splendid speeches are often given to boys and girls to read when they have learnt enough Latin to read Cæsar easily. Cicero was not a great statesman, and never really knew which side to take, but although he too was sorry that the days of 'liberty' were over, he could not help seeing how much good Cæsar had done for Rome. He knew how many dangers threatened Cæsar, and at least once warned him in a splendid speech in the Senate to take care of his life, which was so valuable for the state.

Cæsar was naturally without fear. He had no patience to be always on his guard against danger, and made his wife and his best friends anxious because in the end he went about without the guard of soldiers which he had had at first. Of course he could not guess that even some of his friends had joined with his enemies in a plot to kill him. He was warned by an old man who was supposed to be able to tell things which were going to happen to 'beware of the ides of March,' that is of the 15th March, the very day he died.

The night before, his wife Calpurnia could not sleep, being full of strange dreams and fears. In the morning she begged him not to go to the Senate-house, but he would not stay at home. As he stood that day in the Senate without sword or weapon, a number of men pressed round him as though they were going to ask him some favor, when suddenly he saw that they were going to strike him with their swords. There was no chance for him, but he was going to try to fight when he caught sight of Decimus Brutus, a man who had fought against him for Pompeius, but who had since been his friend. Cæsar had treated him like a son, and the shock of seeing him among his enemies was very terrible. He said three words, 'Et tu, Brute!' 'You also, Brutus!' and then seeing that he must die he drew his toga over his face and fell at the feet of the statue of Pompeius which he had had put in the Senate-house.

There as he lay they stabbed him to death, and then stole away while the news went through Rome that the 'tyrant' was dead. There was one man, Marcus Antonius, who did justice to Cæsar's memory. He was not so much the friend of Cæsar as ambitious for himself, and he hoped that by showing the people how cruel and mean the men were who had killed Cæsar, he would be able to get the power of the state into his own hands.

A few days later the body of Cæsar was carried into the Forum to be publicly burned, and there Antonius, who was a splendid speaker, made the people weep with the story of Cæsar's wrongs. He told them, too, how Cæsar had left all his gardens and some of his money to the people. He asked them not to be angry with the murderers, but he showed them Cæsar's blood-stained clothes, and pointing to the holes in them said the names of those who had struck the blows. The people became almost mad with anger and sorrow, and old soldiers threw their armor and women their ornaments and jewels into the funeral fire.

Marcus Antonius became the hero of the moment. He was named Dictator, and war broke out between his party and those of Cæsar's murderers. But there was another man anxious to avenge Cæsar's murder who was to show himself greater than Antonius. This was the young Octavius, the nephew of Cæsar. Cæsar had adopted him as his son and left him most of his money. It is almost certain that he meant him to rule the Roman Empire after him, and so he did. Octavius became Emperor of Rome and was called Augustus. From his time there was never again a chance of the old Senatorial government coming back. Julius Cæsar had made the Empire and Augustus inherited it.

Chapter XV—Early Days of the Roman Empire

The way in which the young Octavius took up Cæsar's position, and began to act at once as though he had a claim to be Emperor, shows how strong Cæsar had already made his position.

Octavius was a very handsome young man. There is still a bust of him in the British Museum in London, which shows that he had the features of Julius Cæsar, but with a much softer and younger look. He showed himself a great man in the way in which he took up Cæsar's work. Antonius did his best to keep him from seeming too important to the people, and for a time Octavius had to divide the Empire with him. The murderers of Cæsar and their party were hunted out, and hundreds of them killed. Octavius was far less merciful than Cæsar to his countrymen.

But when this was done the jealousy between Octavius and Antonius showed itself plainly. Antonius, thinking all was safe, gave himself up to pleasure. In Egypt he met Cleopatra, who had charmed Cæsar some years before. But Antonius fell so much in love with her that he could not leave her, even when he knew Octavius was coming to fight him. He spent his days with Cleopatra, who sailed in the Eastern Mediterranean in a ship coated with gold, and with purple sails and oars of silver. When at last Antonius and Cleopatra did prepare a fleet to fight with that of Octavius it was easily conquered, and the two fled back to Alexandria, Cleopatra's home. Octavius followed them, and Antonius in despair killed himself.

When Cleopatra heard that Octavius meant to take her back to Rome to lead her in triumph through the streets, she too tried to kill herself. But Octavius was very anxious to show her in his triumph, and she was not allowed to have any weapon. She managed, however, to get a basket of beautiful ripe figs sent to her. This seemed quite harmless, and she was allowed to have them. But underneath them was an asp, a kind of small snake. Cleopatra knew that if it bit her she would surely die, and when the time came she put it on her bare arm and so killed herself. Two of her women slaves, who were their mistress's favorites, killed themselves too. Octavius now made Egypt a Roman province.

THE ROMAN EMPIRE UNDER AUGUSTUS

153

Roman Empire under Augustus

THE FIRST ROMAN EMPEROR

When he got back to Rome there was no longer any one to take his empire from him. It was

Sardonyx Cameo Portrait of the Emperor Augustus (British Museum).

now that he was first called Augustus, and under him now for the first time for years there was peace in all parts of the great Empire. Augustus loved peace, and he loved learning and poetry too. He gathered scholars and poets round him. The greatest of all was the poet Virgil, who wrote the great poem called the Æneid, one of the most wonderful poems ever written. The people who lived in the days of Augustus, and the Emperor himself, were full of admiration for the great history of Rome. It was the Emperor who asked the poet to write a long poem on the beginnings of its greatness. The Æneid tells the story of the adventures of Æneas, who the Romans believed was the son of the goddess Venus and Anchises and the ancestor of Julius Cæsar and Augustus.

Augustus, like Cæsar, was head of the state and head of the army. The great Empire, divided into provinces, was ruled by governors appointed by him, and every Roman citizen could appeal to the Emperor. Julius Cæsar had given the rights of Roman citizens to some of the people of Gaul, and later they were given to specially favored cities throughout the Empire.

The great roads which the Romans knew so well how to build had already begun to stretch out across the Empire. The Roman legions were always marching along these roads. Colonies of Romans were sent to distant provinces, and messengers were constantly going to and from Rome and the provinces to let the Emperor know what was happening in all parts of the Empire.

Roman civilization spread through the Empire. Where there were already towns the life there became Roman, and in a country like Britain, where there were hardly any towns, the Romans built new ones. All the towns in England which have names ending with 'Chester' were built by the Romans. Chester is the later way of writing 'castra,' the Roman word for camp. London was already in existence when a hundred years after Cæsar's invasion the Romans came really to conquer Britain, but York was founded by the Romans.

When the Emperor Claudius sent soldiers to conquer Britain a hundred years after Cæsar's 'invasions,' the Britons fought fiercely, and it was many years before the whole of Britain was conquered. Everyone knows the story of Caractacus, the brave British chief who was taken prisoner to Rome, and spoke so bravely that the Emperor set him free. Everybody knows, too, the story of Boadicea, the British warrior queen, who fought as bravely as any man against the Romans, who had whipped her and insulted her daughters, and how, when she knew she could not win, she poisoned herself and her two daughters, and so escaped from the Romans whom she hated.

But Britain became a Roman province, and was covered over with the strong walls and the towns which the Romans knew so well how to build. In most of these towns set up by the Romans they built great baths and theatres so that they might live and amuse themselves as their countrymen did in Italy. Even though the world was growing more civilized, the old terrible fights between gladiators, or the hunting of wild beasts to death in the circus, were the chief amusements of the Romans, and they spread them all over the Empire.

For some hundreds of years nothing changed very much in the Empire except that sometimes bad emperors came after good ones, but even this did not make a very great difference except to the people in Rome, for there were now a great number of officers and servants who did the Emperor's work for him.

Painting of the Nativity, *in Sainte Madeleine Church, Strasbourg, Bas-Rhin, France. It was previously in the sacristy of Strasbourg's cathedral-probably XIXth century.*

It was while Augustus was still Emperor that Jesus Christ was born in the kingdom of Judæa ruled by King Herod, but dependent on Rome. At the time no one noticed it except a few poor shepherds and the wise men of the East. King Herod, who had been warned of the birth of a king, thought he was killed with the other babies of Judæa when he ordered all the boys under two years old to be killed.

But later men knew that this was the greatest thing that has ever happened in the world, and all the things which have happened since are counted from that date, so that the letters A.D., meaning 'Anno Domini' or 'the Year of Our Lord,' are used instead of B.C., which stand for 'Before Christ,' in giving dates after this time.

THE COMING OF CHRISTIANITY

When the Christian religion began to be preached by the Apostles, and those whom they taught about Our Lord, the fact that all parts of the Roman Empire were so united made it possible for the Faith to spread more quickly. It was along the great roads of the Empire that the preachers travelled, and it was chiefly in the towns that they stayed to convert and baptize the people.

St. Paul travelled on these roads in Asia Minor and Greece, preaching the gospel to Jews and Gentiles (as the Jews called those who were not Jews) too. Everyone knows how Paul had first been against the Christians and then had been converted, and how he understood much better than the other followers of Our Lord that the Gospel was to be preached to all nations and not only to the Jews.

St. Paul spent his life, as he tells us himself, in journeying from place to place telling about the teaching of Our Lord. In Athens and Corinth, which were still great cities, but where the people now lived bad lives, he made converts to Christianity. In Ephesus he was nearly killed by the crowd when he preached against their idolatrous worship of 'Diana of the Ephesians.' In the crowd were many men who lived by making images of the goddess, and they were angry for fear the people would no longer want these images.

At Jerusalem the Jews who were still against Our Lord complained that Paul brought Greeks into the synagogue. The Roman governor was told that he disturbed the peace, but Paul being a citizen of Tarsus, a place which had received the rights of Roman citizenship, 'appealed to Cæsar.' (The emperors who were still of Cæsar's family still kept this name.)

The emperor who was ruler after Augustus was his stepson Tiberius. Then came Claudius, and now Nero, the last emperor of this family, was ruling. St. Paul was taken to Rome, and though a prisoner he was allowed to preach. He was given a house in Rome, but always had to go about chained by one hand to the soldier who had charge of him.

The Cruel Emperor Nero

St. Paul was very unfortunate in coming to Rome during the reign of Nero, who was one of the cruellest and most terrible men who have ever lived. When he was a young boy he was bright and handsome, and a great favorite with the Roman people. He became Emperor when he was seventeen years old, and in the next year he poisoned his brother Britannicus for fear he might try to make himself Emperor in his place.

Later, when he wanted to marry a woman whom his mother Agrippina did not like, he made up his mind to kill his mother too. He presented her with a beautiful ship with sails of silk, but it was so made that when it got out to sea it would split in two. When his mother went on the ship Nero kissed her with every sign of love, although he hoped he was sending her to her death. She was nearly drowned, but was saved by some fishermen, and then Nero had her stabbed to death.

Nero spent his time in luxury and most terrible wickedness. He loved to hurt people. Suddenly, in the midst of all this, a great fire broke out in Rome, and almost the whole city was burned to the ground. People said that Nero had set the city on fire for his own amusement, and that while it burned he stood on one of the hills outside Rome and sang verses from Homer on the burning of Troy. The tale may be true, for Nero seemed quite mad at times.

But afterwards he grew frightened lest the people should turn against him, and so he said that it was the Christians, the people with the strange new religion, who had done this thing. And so he had the Christians of Rome hunted out from their quiet homes, where they lived good and holy lives, spending much of their time in prayer. Nero thought he would kill the Christians, and amuse the Roman people at the same time, so he had them tied to poles in the theatre, wrapped in cloths dipped in oil, and then set fire to them, so that they burned like living torches.

It was a dreadful sight, but Nero rode round the circus enjoying it, until at last even the Roman people, used as they were to terrible sights of bloodshed, begged that it might stop. Paul was not among the Christians who were burned, but both he and St. Peter were killed soon after. St. Paul, because he was a Roman citizen, was allowed the honorable death of being beheaded, while St. Peter was crucified like his Master.

But before long every one grew tired of Nero. He was terribly vain and thought himself a great artist and poet. He became terribly ugly through eating and drinking too much, and all near him trembled at his anger, for it might at any moment mean death for them. He preferred to stay at Naples rather than Rome, and it was here that he heard that the generals of the army had risen against him, and that the Senate had condemned him to die. The Senate of course had now no power, but it suited the leaders of the rebellion to make use of them. There was nothing for Nero to do but kill himself. For a long time he held the dagger to his throat, too frightened to strike the blow, but a faithful servant who saw that it was the easiest death for his master, gave his hand a sudden push, and so Nero died.

In the next year four emperors succeeded one another, being put forward by the different parts of the army. Vespasian, the last of the four, was followed by his son Titus, who is famous for his great siege of Jerusalem, which destroyed that great city and put an end to the life of the Jews as a nation. The Jews had always hated the Roman rule, partly because, although the Romans tried not to interfere with the Jewish religion, yet they could not help doing so to a certain extent. But it was a mad thing for the Jews to rebel.

Jerusalem was a wonderfully strong city with wall within wall, but Titus was determined to destroy it, and after a terrible siege the town and the temple were burnt to the ground. A million Jews were killed and a hundred thousand sold as slaves. After this the Jews were scattered all over the world, and have never since had a country of their own.

It was in the time of Titus, too, that the great cities of Pompeii and Herculaneum, two of the richest towns of Italy, were destroyed, but in another way. Pompeii stood at the foot of Mount Vesuvius, and was like a smaller Rome with baths and theatres and many shops. The Romans used to go there to make holiday. Suddenly, with very little warning, the volcano became active, the earth shook, and then the burning lava poured out from the mountain and buried the cities. Some people got away, but many were buried under the lava. Some years ago men began to dig out the buried cities, and found them very little different from what they were in Roman days. Even the bodies of the people may be seen preserved by the layer of lava poured over them and lying in the positions of fright in which they died.

Nero Crowned as Victor in the Greek Games (A bust in the Capitoline Museum in Rome).

After the death of Nero the Christians had been left alone for a time. As a rule the Romans did not interfere with the religion of the peoples they conquered. They set up temples to their own gods in the provinces, and very often the people worshipped them as well as their own. But the idea spread that the Christians were against the state, and then they would from time to time be asked to show honor to the gods of Rome as a proof that they were not. This they could not do, as they knew it was wrong to pretend to believe in these gods.

Some emperors left the Christians alone, and they went on quietly converting others, some rich and some poor, bringing happiness for the first time into the lives of slaves, who now found a religion which said that all people were equal in the sight of God. In days of persecution the Christians had to worship in secret. In Rome they made those underground passages which are now called the Catacombs, and which we can still visit and see the graves of some of the martyrs.

Soldiers of the Famous Prætorian Guard at Rome. *In the later days of the Roman Empire the man who could get the Prætorian Guard on his side was always able to make himself Emperor (From a bas-relief in the Louvre).*

For here the Christians of Rome buried their dead and held their services, especially in times of persecution. The bodies of the dead were placed on shelves opening into the wall, and a slab of stone or marble was then placed in front. Sometimes there is not any name or mark on these slabs, but often there is painted or cut the name of the person buried, and sometimes there are drawings or images such as the early Christians used. Sometimes there will be seen a palm, which may mean that the person buried there was a martyr. Often there is a fish, which was a sign much used by the early Christians.

Often little vases or bottles, which have in them a red liquid dried up, have been found. People used to think that this was the blood of the martyrs, but it is now thought that it was the red wine used by the priest in saying mass at the tombs. The story of these martyrs makes us understand better than anything else the great change which the Christian religion had made in the lives of people everywhere. While many of those who were not Christians, especially the rich people, still lived the terrible lives of which Nero's gives us the worst example, and while many of the poorer people who were not Christians led bad lives too, the Christians showed a beautiful example of love and peace and courage.

THE EARLY CHRISTIAN SAINTS AND MARTYRS

It was a time of great saints. We can only mention one or two of these saints. There was Saint Ignatius, Bishop of Antioch in Syria. Under the Emperor Trajan, an order was given that everybody in all the provinces should make a sacrifice to the gods in honor of his having conquered and added Dacia, a new province across the Danube, to the Empire. When the Christians of Antioch refused to do this, Trajan ordered that their bishop should be brought before him. He hoped to persuade him to worship the gods, but Ignatius refused and was sent to Rome. Here he was taken into the Coliseum, the great theatre where the Roman games were held, and there he was torn to pieces before all the people and eaten by two hungry lions who were let loose upon him.

Yet Trajan was not a bad man. Indeed, he was the first of five emperors who ruled from 96 A.D. to 180 A.D., and were called the Good Emperors. One of these, the great Marcus Aurelius, was so good and wise that in some ways he was almost a saint. He wrote a book of 'Thoughts' which is read and considered very wonderful even now. But he did not understand the Christians, and the persecution went on under him also. It was under him that St. Cecilia, the patron saint of music, was put to death. She was a noble lady of Rome or Sicily who had become a Christian, and persuaded her husband to do so too. It is said that the executioner who was to behead her, seeing her so good and beautiful, trembled so much that he only wounded her, and she lay for three days before she died, singing all the time her praises to God. It was said afterwards that St. Cecilia was the first to invent playing on the organ, and in pictures she is generally seen with organ pipes in her hands.

A splendid church which was built in her honor may be seen in Rome today, and in it is a beautiful statue in white marble of the saint as she lay when the executioner had done his work.

After the death of Marcus Aurelius, his son, a very bad man, ruled for a few years, and was then murdered. After this came another long time during which one emperor after another was set up by the legions. One of the great things which the early emperors had done was to strengthen the frontiers or boundaries of the Empire to keep the 'barbarians' out. Even in Britain we can still see the wall which Hadrian built between England and Scotland to keep out the barbarous Picts and Scots.

A Triumph of Roman Architecture. The Pont du Gard, perhaps the finest aqueduct the Romans ever built. It carried water across the river Garden in France.

But in the third hundred years after Our Lord's birth the barbarians were becoming too strong and were beginning to burst over the frontiers. Emperor after emperor themselves led the soldiers against them, but it was of no use. The Emperor Diocletian chose another emperor to help him to govern, and two under-emperors who were called Cæsars. The Empire was for a time divided between these.

It was under Diocletian that the last and most terrible persecution of the Christians took place. While the barbarians threatened the Empire from outside it was felt that the Christians were a danger inside, and thousands everywhere, but especially in Rome, were flung to the lions. St. Agnes, the patron saint of young girls, died in this persecution. The story is that she was a Roman girl thirteen years old, and belonging to a noble family. A rich Roman who was not a Christian wanted her to marry his son, but she would not, and so he had her killed as a Christian. At first they tried to burn her, but the fire would not burn. So they took her outside the city and cut off her head.

One of the two 'Cæsars' whom Diocletian had chosen to help him was Constantine, who afterwards became head of the whole Empire, and was called Constantine the Great. He was a handsome man and a fine soldier.

Under him a wonderful thing happened for the Christians. Constantine was fighting in a battle against a man who wanted to take part of the Empire for himself, when he saw a great cross of fire in the sky, and across it was written the words 'Under this Standard thou shalt Conquer.' Constantine won the battle, and after that he said that the Christian religion should be the religion of the Roman people.

So the great fight was won. Henceforward the Christians could not only worship freely, but people were encouraged to join them. In a very short time the whole Empire was Christian. When the barbarians broke in and swarmed over the Empire this is what they found, and they in their turn became Christians too. It seemed as though the way was suddenly made clear very wonderfully for the spread of the Christian religion, but it was the quiet work and prayer and the noble deaths of the martyrs which had prepared the way.

CHAPTER XVI—THE BARBARIANS AND THE EMPIRE

For many years before the time of Constantine, the city of Rome was becoming less and less important in the Empire. The emperors often preferred to live somewhere else, and especially when Diocletian broke the Empire up under four rulers. Constantine liked the ways of the Eastern Empire better than the West, and he made up his mind to make for himself a new capital there. He chose for it Byzantium, an old Greek colony, beautifully situated on the shores of the sea of Bosphorus, and the bay called the Golden Horn. Byzantium was only a little city, but Constantine had houses and churches, theatres and baths built round about it, and made it into a 'new Rome.' The name of the city was changed into 'Constantinople,' or the city of Constantine, and so it is called to this day.

Rome, however, became important in another way. Its bishop was the chief bishop of the Christian church. He came to be called the Pope, and in time became much more powerful than any emperor or king. If the emperor had stayed in Rome, it would not have been so easy for the Pope to become so great, and this is one important result of Constantine choosing a new capital in the East.

Another important result was that it made it easier for the 'barbarians,' who, as we have seen, were ready to break into the Empire to do so. In a hundred years from Constantine's time, the Roman Empire had become an Eastern Empire only, and swarms of barbarians were settling down on the western part, ready to break it up into new nations, each under a different king.

Ever since the days of Cæsar and Augustus, the rulers of Rome had known that there was a great movement going on among the barbarian peoples. From time to time the emperors had found it necessary to drive some tribes back as they crossed into the Empire itself. Always they had had to keep a good watch on the frontiers, and in the end they allowed some of these peoples to settle down in the Roman provinces round the Danube, which was always the hardest frontier to keep safe. In time, too, the emperors began to take men from the peoples who had settled down to fight in the Roman army. This was a mistake, for when the time came for these soldiers to fight the barbarians they did not care to do so.

The chief among these barbarian peoples who were threatening Rome were the Goths, the Vandals, the Burgundians, and the Franks. They were all of the Teutonic race, to which the English who conquered Britain also belonged. They were big, fair men, seeming almost like giants to the Italians, and the other peoples already living in Spain, and France, and Africa, and all the lands of the western part of the Roman Empire.

Behind the Teutons there were other peoples belonging to the Slavonic race. These pushed the Teutons before them, but in the end settled down in the East of Europe. The people of the countries which are now called Hungary, Servia, and Bulgaria came from this race. They were smaller, darker, and more like the peoples of the East than the Teutons.

Constantine The Great. The first Christian Emperor (A painting by Jacopo Vignali).

Behind them again pushed a terrible people called the Huns. They were small savages, and came from the wildest parts of Central Asia. They were fierce and good fighters, but they could not keep together as well as the Teutons, or make use of a victory when they won it. In the end they were driven right out of Europe again. The moving about of all these peoples is now called the 'Wandering of the Nations.'

People have often wondered how it was that the great Roman Empire came to be over-run by the barbarian peoples. It has been said that it was because the people in the Roman Empire were weak and wicked, while the new peoples were brave and honest. But we must remember that now nearly all the people in the Empire had become Christians, and most of them lived good lives.

One reason, perhaps, was that the Empire was too big, and it was impossible for any but very clever rulers to rule it properly. We have already seen how it was, as it were, falling to pieces when it had to be divided among several rulers. Then again there were great numbers of the barbarians, and generally the armies which fought against them were much smaller, but quite as brave.

The people of the Empire, too, had not so much interest in fighting for the Empire as people today in fighting for their own countries. But the barbarians themselves saw that the Empire was not weak and bad, and were glad to learn many things from the people they conquered. One thing which they learned was the Christian religion, and all these peoples who settled down in the Empire became Christians in the end.

No sooner had Constantine made the whole Empire Christian, than the Christians began to quarrel among themselves. A priest of Egypt called Arius taught that Our Lord was not quite equal to God the Father, and a great many people believed this. His followers were called 'Arians,' and many of the barbarians as they were converted by Arians became Arians too. Constantine was very sorry to see the Christians quarrelling among themselves, and he called a great council, that is, a meeting of bishops from all parts of the Church, to discuss the question. They met at the town of Nicaea, some having travelled thousands of miles to be present.

This council of Nicaea, the first great council of the Church, said that Arius was wrong. One of those who spoke most against Arius at the council was a young priest called Athanasius, who came from Alexandria. After the council there were many people who still were Arians, and Athanasius spent his long life in preaching and writing against them. It was he who wrote the famous 'Athanasian Creed,' which is still read in the churches.

JULIAN THE APOSTATE

Athanasius was a saint, but he was only one of many who lived in the hundred years after the time when Constantine made the Empire Christian. There were Basil and Gregory, who were companions with the Emperor Julian when they were students in the schools of Athens. (For Athens was still a great place for learning.) Julian was a nephew of Constantine the Great, and afterwards became emperor himself. He is famous because he tried to destroy the Christian religion and make the Empire pagan again.

In spite of being a great friend of St. Basil and St. Gregory in his young days, Julian had never really believed in Christianity. When he was emperor he did all he could to hurt the Christians, though he did not persecute them like the emperors in the old days of paganism. He built again the pagan temples, and he would not let the Christians study the old writings of the Greeks and Romans. He said that if they did not believe in the gods, they should not read about them. He really hoped that the Christians would become ignorant and uneducated.

But Christianity was too strong for him, and it is said that on his deathbed he cried in anger 'Galilean' (meaning Our Lord), 'Thou hast conquered.' Meanwhile his two school companions had been living holy lives. Basil had become the head of a monastery in an eastern desert, spending his time in prayer, and work, and fasting with other holy men who joined him. He had wanted Gregory to go too, but he had become a priest, and then bishop of Cæsarea, and afterwards of Constantinople.

Another great saint of this time, and one of the four great 'doctors' of the Church, was St. Ambrose, archbishop of Milan. He, too, spent his life fighting the Arians. He was a very noble and charitable man. Once when the Goths carried off a great number of Christians (for all this time the barbarians were attacking the Empire) St. Ambrose sold all he could find, even the beautiful gold cups belonging to his church, to buy them back.

He showed how brave he was when once he refused to allow Theodosius the Emperor to go into his church. At least so the story goes. In any case, St. Ambrose wrote a letter reproving the emperor, and Theodosius in his turn did penance in the church. He had, indeed, done a very wrong thing, and the story shows how beside the great holiness of the saints of the time there was still a terrible amount of cruelty and bloodshed.

In the town of Thessalonica, one of the Emperor's officers had been killed by the people. The Emperor pretended that he was not angry, and invited the people of the town to see some games in the circus, and when they were all there Theodosius sent in his soldiers and killed them.

St. Ambrose wrote some beautiful Latin hymns which we can still read and sing, and one of the oldest churches in the world is the Church built in his honor at Milan.

In those days when on the death of an emperor several men often fought to be made emperor in his place, and when the barbarians were continually breaking in and fighting, many men fled to the desert to become monks and say their prayers in peace. One of the greatest men of this time who became a monk was St. Jerome, who put the Bible into Latin, for these

St. Ambrose (*A painting in the Vatican*).

old monks worked as well as prayed. He lived the last years of his life in a monastery which he made at Bethlehem, which he loved because Our Lord was born there.

St. Jerome is generally seen in pictures with the Bible, which he translated into Latin, which was the language which all scholars then read. He is sometimes seen too with a lion, and the story is that he once saw a lion with a thorn in its paw, and instead of being frightened St. Jerome took the thorn out and bandaged the paw. After that the lion followed the saint everywhere like a dog.

There were saints too like St. John 'Chrysostom,' or the 'golden-mouthed,' bishop of Antioch, and then of Constantinople, who won his name because of the beautiful way in which he spoke and preached to the people, and St. Simeon Stylites, who thought that the best thing to please God was to mortify himself, and who lived for years and then died on the top of a stone pillar stretching up into the sky in the Syrian desert.

But perhaps the greatest saint of all at that time was St. Augustine of Hippo, a town in North Africa. St. Augustine wrote himself, in a book called his *Confessions,* the story of his life. He tells how he was brought up tenderly by his mother Monica, a saint herself, and anxious that her son might grow into a good and holy man. But when he was a boy and a young man Augustine was not very good, and his mother wept often and bitterly over his sins.

But at Milan he met St. Ambrose, and listened to his sermons. He was suddenly filled with hatred for his past life, and changed it completely. He went back to Hippo, became a priest, and later bishop of Hippo. His writings were read then, and are read now by Christians everywhere. His greatest book, *De Civitate Dei,* or *The City of God,* was written at the time when a barbarian army had entered Rome itself, and he died when he was seventy-six years old, when a barbarian army had been besieging his city of Hippo for three months, and just in time to escape seeing it taken. For the barbarians were now spread all over the Western part of the Empire, and we must now turn to the story of their conquests.

The Emperor Theodosius the Great died in the year 395 A.D., and the Empire was divided between his sons Arcadius, who ruled the East, and Honorius, who ruled the West. It was now that the Visigoths or Western Goths who had settled in the provinces round the Danube first went forward into Italy itself.

They had as their leader a brave chief called Alaric, but they had to fight hard battles against Stilicho, the general of Honorius in Italy. He was a Vandal, one of those barbarians who had been taken into the Roman army, but he fought well for Rome. He defeated Alaric in three great battles, but the enemies of Stilicho persuaded the Emperor that he was a traitor, and Honorius allowed him to be put to death. Two years afterwards, in the year 410, Alaric led his victorious army into Rome itself. It was the first time since eight hundred years before, when the Gauls had burnt the city and marched away, that any enemy had got within the walls of Rome. The Romans tried to frighten him by telling him how great were their numbers, but he only answered, 'The thicker the hay the easier mown.' And when they asked him what he would leave them, he answered, 'Your lives.'

The Goths broke into the beautiful buildings of Rome, and took for themselves the treasures which the Romans had collected from all parts of the world in the days when they were winning their empire. Honorius, the Emperor of the West, was a weak and foolish young man. While the barbarians were pouring into Rome he was in the country looking after the hens which he kept and of which he was very fond. A messenger came to tell him that the end of Rome had come. Now Honorius had a hen to which he had given the name of 'Rome.' 'How can that be,' he said, 'when I have just been feeding her?' He seemed almost pleased to hear that it was his empire and not his hen that he had lost.

Alaric meant to keep Rome, but he could not help admiring the civilization which he saw everywhere in the Empire, and he said he would like to be appointed an officer in the service of the Empire. Many of the barbarian chiefs after Alaric did the same. This did not mean that they obeyed the Emperor, for they did not, but they liked to feel that they had a share in the greatness and civilization of the Empire.

About the same time as Alaric was conquering Italy the Vandals were overrunning Gaul and Spain, but three years after he had taken Rome Alaric died, and under their next ruler the Visigoths marched out of Italy, followed the Vandals into Gaul and Spain, and drove them out of those countries into Africa. It was while these Vandals were taking Africa for themselves that the siege of Hippo took place, during which St. Augustine died.

The Vandals were one of the roughest of these barbarian peoples, and they soon made the North of Africa, which ever since the days of Alexander had been a place of civilization and learning, almost savage again. Meanwhile, the Visigoths had made a kingdom stretching all over the South-West of France and the greater part of Spain, with its capital at the Roman town of Toulouse. It seemed almost as though the Visigoths might form a new empire in the West, but in the end they did not even hold together as a nation. They were Christians, but Arians, and it will be seen later that the barbarians who were Arians were nearly always conquered by those who were Christians proper. For one reason, the people whom they conquered were not as a rule Arians, and therefore disliked them more than if they had been of their own religion.

Another Teutonic people, the Franks, who became later a very great people indeed, now overran nearly all the North and central part of France. They were not yet Christians at all. The Burgundians made themselves a kingdom in the South-East of Gaul. So all the provinces of the West, except Italy itself, were now in the hands of the new peoples.

It was at this time that the Roman legions left the province of Britain. Britain was one of the latest provinces won by the Roman Empire, and in spite of the great Roman roads, which may still be seen in this country today, and the many towns and colonies which the Romans had set up, Britain does not seem to have become really Roman in its civilization like France and Spain, which had been so much longer under Roman rule. So that when the Angles and Saxons and Jutes, who were only other branches of the Teutonic race, came and conquered this country, while the Goths and Vandals and Franks were conquering the other provinces, these people learned very little of Roman life and civilization, and did not become Christians like the barbarian peoples who conquered the other provinces. They still went on worshipping their own gods—Woden the god of war, Thor the god of thunder, and many others—until monks were sent from Rome long after to teach them the true faith.

The reason that Italy was not conquered and kept by the barbarians was that the emperors were more anxious to keep it, and the barbarians were frightened by its past greatness. For many years after the other kingdoms were more or less settled, the barbarians and the followers of the emperor still struggled in Italy. Then there was the great power of the Pope growing there. Italy, in fact, was never joined as a nation under one king until the second half of the nineteenth century.

ATTILA THE HUN

About the year 433 A.D., Attila, a fierce chief, became king of the Huns, who were still living in the land north of the Danube to the east. There their king had built himself a wooden palace, and from there he led his great army of savages, each seated on a shaggy pony, right over Europe.

Attila, we are told, was a short, square man curiously shaped, with a large head, dark skin, eyes set deep back in his head, and with a flat nose, and very little hair. He was cunning and fierce, and like all the Huns he hated the civilization of the West. The people called him the 'Scourge of God.' He first attacked the Eastern Empire, destroying one city after another, until he got to the walls of Constantinople. The Emperor paid him a large sum of money, and gave him an enormous piece of land along the Danube before he would go away. But the next emperor refused to pay the tribute, and Attila then decided to attack the Western Empire.

Ætius, the Roman General Who Defeated Attila (From a Byzantine carving in ivory).

He rode across Europe, destroying cities, and killing the people everywhere, until he was stopped at Orleans, where the soldiers were encouraged by the brave bishop Anianus to resist him. While he was here an army came up to fight him. It was the army of Theodoric; king of the Visigoths, joined with the army of the brave Roman general Ætius, who was trying to rule Italy for the weak and useless emperors, who now had their capital at Ravenna.

On the Plain of Chalons, not far from Orleans, Attila was completely defeated. The Visigothic king was killed, but Europe was saved. If Attila and his Huns had conquered Europe, the civilization which Rome had spread, and which the Teutonic races were learning, would have been lost, and Europe would have become savage again. Attila had to draw back from Gaul, but the next year he marched into Italy itself. Ætius marched after him, but was not in time to prevent many cities in the North of Italy from being destroyed.

Many of the people fled to the islands and lakes in the north of the Adriatic, and it was from the homes they built themselves there that the famous and beautiful city of Venice had its beginnings. The Emperor Valentinian sent messages to Attila, begging him to go away. With the messengers went the great Pope Leo, and it was said that Attila was much struck by the noble and beautiful face of the great Pope. But it was probably because his soldiers were tired and ill, and because he was offered a princess of the Emperor's family as one of his wives, and much money, that he agreed to go away. Fortunately the princess was saved from this fate, for Attila died shortly afterwards, after a feast to celebrate another of his marriages.

His sons were not so cunning and clever as Attila, and the Huns after this moved eastwards again, and practically disappear from history. Just as Stilicho had been put to death by the jealous and foolish Emperor Honorius, for whom he had done so much, so now the equally foolish Emperor Valentinian killed Ætius with his own hand.

Shortly after this Genseric, the fierce Arian king of the Vandals in Africa, sailed across to Italy and attacked Rome itself, carrying away many treasures, among them the golden table and the golden candlestick carried by Titus from the temple at Jerusalem, when he destroyed that city. The Western emperors at Ravenna were becoming weaker and weaker. They were often chosen by the general of the barbarian armies in Italy. The Eastern emperor was supposed to give his consent, but in the end this was never asked.

At last in 476 Odoacer the Herulian, a great barbarian general in Italy, made the last emperor of the West give up his throne. This emperor was a young boy, the son of another barbarian adventurer. He had been given the grand old names of Romulus, the founder of Rome, and Augustus, its first emperor. But he soon came to be called in mockery Romulus Augustulus, or the little Augustus. For a wonder Odoacer did not kill him, but let him live quietly in one of the Italian towns. He sent the emperor's crown and robe to the Emperor at Constantinople, telling him that the Roman Senate wished that the Western Empire should end, and declaring that they would honor the one emperor at Constantinople.

Of course this did not mean anything. Odoacer took the name of king, meaning to have Italy for his own. The giving up of the name of Roman emperor by the boy Romulus Augustulus in 476 A.D. is often spoken of as the moment when the Roman Empire in the West broke up, but we have seen that it had broken up long before, and that the barbarians had been fast taking the lands of the Western Empire, and making them their own for a hundred years before.

Chapter XVII—The New Nations

We have now reached the story of that time in history which is known as the 'Middle Ages.' We give it that name because in many ways it stands half-way between our own times and the Greek and Roman times of which we have been speaking. The first few hundred years of the Middle Ages are often called the 'Dark Ages,' because there was so much ignorance and bloodshed, and because though the Church did much to civilize the barbarians, yet the art and civilization of the Roman Empire disappeared, and though the barbarians were always learning from what remained, it was a long time before the new and wonderful civilization of the Middle Ages appeared.

The history of the early part of the Middle Ages in the West of Europe is the story of how the barbarian tribes settled down on the lands of the Roman Empire, how they fought between themselves, and how some won and some disappeared, how new nations appeared when the conquering barbarians married and mixed with the peoples they conquered, how all were Christian, how after a time of much ignorance, and disorder, and bloodshed, a new civilization grew up, which, if rougher in some ways than the Roman and Greek civilizations, yet was better than them, because it was Christian. The Eastern Empire, too, has a wonderful history of its own in the early Middle Ages, and we must now turn to the story.

Odoacer, the barbarian soldier, who had made Romulus Augustulus give up his name of emperor, and now called himself 'King of the Nations' in Italy, did not enjoy his position long. The famous Theodoric, king of the Ostrogoths or Eastern Goths, another group of that people who had been allowed to settle in the Roman provinces on the Danube, suddenly made up his mind to take Italy for his own. He was a fine soldier, and his family, known as the Amali, had ruled the Ostrogoths for many years. The Ostrogotlis had learned more from Rome than any other of the barbarians, and Theodoric had made up his mind that if he won Italy he would rule it in a wise and civilized way.

In the year 489 A.D., he led a great army into Italy, and made Odoacer give up his kingdom. Soon after Odoacer was murdered at a feast. Probably Theodoric had him killed, thinking it would be safer to have him out of the way. Even the best men of the time, at any rate soldiers like Theodoric, thought much less about killing people than we do now. But when he had won Italy, Theodoric did his best to rule it well. He tried to join the Goths and the Italians together to form a nation.

He ruled Italy for thirty years, having Goths for his soldiers and officers, but choosing the wisest and cleverest of the conquered Italians to help him to rule the country. He lived chiefly at Ravenna, for Rome was beginning to belong more and more to the Pope, who was growing more powerful as time went on. Theodoric built beautiful churches and a palace at Ravenna. He married members of his family into the families of the other barbarian kings, for he hoped to hand on his kingdom to his family, and knew that it would be stronger if it had the help of other royal families.

But Theodoric was an Arian, and like all the other barbarians who had become Arians, the Ostrogoths found that the conquered peoples would not mix with them. If Theodoric had been a Christian proper, he might have made a kingdom of Italy which would have lasted, but this was not to be. At the end of his reign, Theodoric had his friend Boëthius, one of the Italians whom he had had to help him to rule his kingdom, cruelly put to death, because he thought he was plotting to help the Eastern emperor to get Italy back again.

Boëthius was a very good and holy man, and had not done this thing. While he was in prison he quietly gave his time to writing a book, called *The Consolations of Philosophy*. When he was dead, Theodoric was sorry for what he had done, and it is said that it was partly through this that he himself fell ill and died soon after. Then the Eastern Emperor did try to win back Italy.

An Ancient Byzantine Picture of Theodoric's Palace at Ravenna (*From a mosaic in a Byzantine church at Ravenna*).

THE GREAT EMPEROR JUSTINIAN

The new Emperor Justinian was a very clever and great man. It is thought that he belonged to a Slavonic family, but took a Roman name, when he was adopted by his uncle, the Emperor Justin. Justinian was the greatest of all the Roman emperors in the East. He was ambitious, and was one of those strong men who are always working and yet are always healthy. He could do with very little sleep, and spent most of the night reading or writing. He often went for days without food, and yet always looked bright and well, and had a red color in his face. Justinian had to fight hard against the Persians who had risen up again as a great power, and were threatening all the Roman provinces in Asia Minor. He kept them back to the Euphrates, but wasted years in fighting them.

It would have been better if Justinian had given all his strength to the struggle with the Persians, but he could not bear to think that the Empire had lost Italy.

After the death of Theodoric, the Ostrogoth, Justinian sent a great general called Belisarius to conquer the Goths. The Gothic kings after Theodoric were not such great men, and in the end Justinian's generals won, but Italy did not remain long under the Eastern Emperor, for when Justinian and Belisarius died both in the same year, new barbarian peoples swarmed into Italy. The officer of the Eastern Empire remained at Ravenna, and was called the Exarch, but he never had any real power in Italy, and only helped to prevent that country becoming a nation like France and Spain and the other lands of the Western Roman Empire.

No sooner was Justinian dead than the Longobards, another Teutonic people who had been allowed to settle near the Danube, rushed down upon the North of Italy. They set up their capital at Pavia, and under the name of Lombards, which was the Italian way of saying it, they ruled North Italy for the next two hundred years. But all this time there were two other capitals in Italy, Rome under the Pope, and Ravenna under the Exarch, who still pretended that he was ruling all Italy for the Eastern Emperor.

Justinian had attacked the Vandal kingdom in North Africa, and he did win this back for the Eastern Empire, until it was taken by a new and terrible enemy whom we shall have to speak about later on. But the name of Justinian is famous for another work which he did, the results of which have lasted down to our own times. The barbarian peoples had laws of their own, but the Roman laws were much better, and most of the new nations when they settled down began to use these laws as well as their own.

Justinian had the Roman laws written down and clearly arranged. It was a great work, and we do not know how much of it Justinian himself did, but in any case it was his idea. All the nations of Western Europe except England lived by these laws all through the Middle Ages, and even England began to use some of them later on.

Meanwhile, the Visigoths in Gaul had been driven farther and farther south by that other Teutonic people which had at first settled only in the North of France. These were the

MAXIMIANVS.

Justinian the Great, Emperor and Law-giver of Byzantium, with his Court (From an ancient Byzantine mosaic in the Church of St. Vitale at Ravenna).

Franks. When they first took part of Gaul for their own, they were still pagans. They were much fiercer and less civilized than the Goths, whom they hated.

About the same time that the Ostrogoths were ruled by their great king, Theodoric, the Franks, too, had a great king called Clovis. He was the first great king of the Franks, and the only one for many years. He led his fierce soldiers against the Visigoths, and drove them before him out of Gaul into Spain, and then the whole of Gaul belonged to the Franks, and in time took the name France from them. The wife of Clovis was a Christian, and Clovis had made a promise to God that if he won a certain battle he would become a Christian too. He did so, and all his people did the same.

The Franks were Christians proper, and so had a much better chance of making friends with the conquered people than the Visigoths had had. In a very short time they settled down, and took the language and laws as well as the religion of the conquered people. We must remember that the Latin language remained in all the western provinces of the Empire, except in England. Though the conquerors were Teutonic, they gave up their own language, and spoke that of the people round them. Of course, some changes were made in the language; but Italian, Spanish, and French are only new forms of the beautiful Latin language which the Teutonic conquerors learned from the people they conquered.

The Visigoths were driven into Spain, until they in their turn were conquered by that same enemy which overran North Africa, and which for a time threatened all Western Europe. But before that time the Visigoths in Spain had been converted from Arianism to Christianity proper, and, like the Franks, married and mixed with the people they had conquered, so that the Spanish nation today, like the French, is descended from both peoples. In this they are very different from the English people, for as far as we can tell, the Angles and Saxons and Jutes drove most of the Britons out of England into Wales, except the few whom they kept as slaves, so that the English today are descended from these purely Teutonic peoples.

While the nations were settling down great changes were, of course, taking place. There was still much fighting and bloodshed. The Church and the bishops did what they could to civilize the people, but they were still very rough. Very few children went to school, and there was very little learning. The old Roman buildings fell into ruins, though their roads were still used everywhere. The great theatre, called the Coliseum at Rome, was used as a sort of quarry all through the Middle Ages, as the people of Rome carried off the stones to build their houses and churches.

THE EARLY MONKS

The new barbarian peoples knew nothing about art or building, and for the first few hundred years their churches were quite small and plain. During all this time monasteries were being set up all over Western Europe, and in these the best men of the time lived, and sometimes set up schools for boys. The monasteries were often set up in wild and lonely regions, but the monks worked hard and cultivated the land. Their houses became places of peace and prosperity, and served as an example to the people in those rough times. Many of these monasteries used the 'Rule of St. Benedict.' St. Benedict was an Italian monk, who wrote down the way of life, which he had found good for several monasteries which he had set up in Italy.

It was a very wonderful rule, and for many hundreds of years after, the monasteries, which spread all over the West of Europe, used it. St. Benedict wanted his monasteries to be like families, where all should work for the good of the others, and all obey the Abbot, the head monk, who was to be a sort of father to the others. The name 'Abbot' means 'Father.' The monks were called Benedictines, or as they wore a plain black habit or frock, they were later called the Black Monks of St. Benedict. It was one of these monks, St. Augustine, who came first to convert the English to Christianity, and he was sent by another Benedictine monk who had become Pope.

This was Saint Gregory the Great. Gregory was a boy belonging to a rich and noble family at Rome. He was very clever and handsome, and he was given a high position in the government of the city. But he gave it up to become a monk at the great monastery of St. Andrew at Rome, and later, when the Pope died, all the people begged that Gregory should be made Pope in his place. It was before he was Pope that one day, as he walked through the market-place at Rome, he saw some beautiful children standing there, with blue eyes and fair hair (very different from the Italian children round about). They were little slave children who had been taken prisoners in the wars in England, and were now being sold. For in those days prisoners were nearly always sold as slaves.

Gregory asked who these children were. He was told that they

Saint Gregory the Great (*A painting by Jacopo Vignali*).

were Angles. But he said they *looked* like angels, and as he knew that the English were still pagans he made up his mind to do all that he could to teach them the Christian religion. When he was Pope, he sent the monk Augustine with some others to teach the English the true religion. St. Augustine landed in Kent, because Ethelbert, the king of Kent, had married a Frankish princess who was already a Christian.

Ethelbert and all his people became Christians, and Augustine built a church at Canterbury. But there were many other kingdoms in England, for Britain was not conquered by one people like France or Spain, but by several tribes, and it was many years before all the little kingdoms were joined together to make one nation. One of the kingdoms, Mercia, in the middle of England, had a savage king called Penda, who hated the Christians, and fought against them for many years. In the end he was killed, but all the preaching and teaching had to be done over again. This time other monks, who were not Benedictines but came from Ireland, did the work.

Ireland had never been part of the Roman Empire. Its people were Celts, but they had been made Christians by the great St. Patrick, another Celt, who left his home in Britain to convert the Irish. Britain had, of course, become Christian under the Romans. About the time that St. Benedict was setting up his monasteries in Italy, other monasteries were growing up all over Ireland, and a great Irish monk, St. Columba, set out from his own country to teach Christianity to the people in Scotland. He built a great monastery on the Island of Iona, and it was from there that St. Aidan and other monks came into the North of England to help to make the people Christians.

The missionaries from Iona did not altogether agree with the missionaries from Rome. The Irish Church had been cut off from the other churches of the West through being so far away, and some differences had grown up. They kept Easter at a different time, for one thing. So Oswy, king of Northumbria, called a Synod or meeting of bishops and priests at Whitby in 664, and there it was decided that the Roman way of doing things should be taken, and from this time onwards the English Church was closely connected with the Popes. Later, another great man was sent from Rome to put order into the English Church. This was Theodore of Tarsus, who became the first Archbishop of Canterbury.

He set up bishops in different parts of England, all under the Archbishop of Canterbury, and when the English people were joined in this way by the Church, it became easier for them to join together as one nation. England, too, was soon covered over by monasteries, and her first historian, Bede, and her first poet, Caedmon, were both monks. In the eighth century, that is, between the years 700 and 800 A.D., English monks and nuns were going out in their turn to convert the heathen peoples of Germany, beyond the Rhine. The greatest of these English missionaries was St. Boniface, who spent the greater part of his life in the work. But we must now turn to tell the story of a new danger which was threatening Christianity and the civilization it was helping to make.

Chapter XVIII—The Beginnings of Mohammedanism

The land of Arabia, a square peninsula lying as it were on the corner between Asia and Africa, with the sea on three sides of it, and the desert on the fourth, had never been conquered by any of the big empires of the East or by Rome. It was a difficult land to get at, and it had not much to give to the conqueror.

The Arabs are a Semitic people, and related to the Jews. They have always lived much the same lives as they do today, being shepherds or merchants living in tents and carrying the things they had to sell to the coasts in caravans with long strings of camels. The Arabs were at one time worshippers of the stars, but knew that there was only one God. Later on they began to worship idols which they set, up in temples.

It was near one of these temples in the 'Holy City' of Mecca that the famous Mohammed lived as a boy. His father was dead, and the boy lived with an uncle who was a priest of the temple. Mohammed lived a quiet life near the temple, and as he grew up sometimes travelled with the caravans which went from Mecca to the sea-coast. There were many Jews in Arabia descended from some who had fled there when Titus destroyed Jerusalem.

It was perhaps from them that Mohammed got the idea that there was only one God, and that it was wrong to worship idols. But he thought that this was taught to him by God Himself, and that he was meant to preach a new religion. He used to have attacks of sickness and convulsions, in which he thought that God showed him wonderful things. He tried to write them down afterwards, and later they were made into a book called the Koran, which Mohammedans to this day believe to be a holy book like the Bible. Mohammed was married, and soon converted his wife and her relations to his religion.

His religion was that there was 'one God' and Mohammed was His prophet. At first the people of Mecca were very angry when he spoke against their idols, for the black stone called the Kaaba, which was built into the wall of their temple, was visited each year by numbers of pilgrims from all parts of Arabia, and this made the city rich. The story was that this stone was really the angel who had been told to look after Adam in the Garden of Eden, and that it had been changed into a stone as a punishment for neglecting its duties. Meanwhile, it was counting the kisses of the people who came to worship at the temple, and when it should be changed into an angel again at the last day it would give an account of them. So the people of Mecca did not like Mohammed's teaching at all, and Mohammed thought it best to run away.

His 'flight,' as the Mohammedans called it, was in the year 622 A.D., and they count that as their year 1 just as we do the year in which Christ was born. Mohammed fled to the city of Medina, and there a great number of followers joined him and listened to his preaching. There were so many of them that in a few years Mohammed led them to Mecca ready to fight and take the 'Holy City.' The people of Mecca had to give way, and after this the temple became the center of the new religion, 'Islam' as it was called.

Mecca was still a holy city and a place of pilgrimage, and people from all parts of Arabia still flocked to it. When Mohammed died all the people of Arabia were Mohammedans. One of Mohammed's followers became head of the new religion, and was called the Kaliph. And now suddenly the Arabs, who had always lived so quietly in their own land, were filled with a wish to spread their religion. The Kaliph led great armies to conquer other lands, and the people who were conquered were offered the choice of three things. They could become Mohammedans or pay tribute. If they refused these things they must die.

To the people of the East the Mohammedan religion often seemed good. It was better than the worship of idols, which was the religion of most of these people. But to Christians it seemed a terrible religion, and the Mohammedans terrible people.

When the Kaliph led his armies out of Arabia, he went first against the great Persian Empire. In a short time it was conquered by the Arabians, or Saracens as they were called, and they now ruled the land even past the Euphrates. Soon, too, they conquered Syria, which belonged to the Eastern Emperor. Then they turned to the North of Africa, took Egypt, where they destroyed Alexandria, and built the city which is now called Cairo. A Saracen fleet was built and sailed the Mediterranean, and soon the whole of North Africa was taken, and they crossed into Spain.

It seemed that this strange fierce people with their curious half-savage religion might go on to conquer the Empire in the East, and overthrow the new nations in the West. But this was not to be. The great Emperor of the East, Leo the Iconoclast, went out to fight them when they were attacking Constantinople

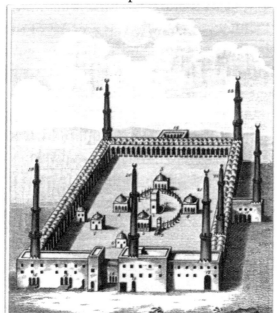

The Great Mohammedan Shrine at Mecca (From a drawing by James Duncan, 1830).

itself. He won a great victory in the year 718 A.D., and drove them out of Asia Minor. They did not attack the Eastern Empire again for many years.

This Emperor Leo was called the Iconoclast or Image-breaker because he took the part of some of the people in the Eastern Empire, who did not like the use of pictures or images of Christ and the saints. They thought that to use them was like idolatry. For a time the iconoclasts had their way, but soon the images were brought back.

Not many years after the Saracens had been driven back from the walls of Constantinople they had conquered the whole of Spain. The Visigoths were driven back into a corner of the North-West of Spain, and now the Saracens prepared to cross the Pyrenees and conquer the kingdom of the Franks. But they were defeated by the Frank Charles Martel at the battle of Tours in 782, and so driven back into Spain.

The Franks had become by this time the greatest people in the West of Europe. They were splendid fighters. Their soldiers went on foot, but were protected by mail shirts and shields. They stood close together, their shields making a sort of wall. Time after time the Arabs dashed themselves against it until they were tired out, and then for the first time the Franks moved, chasing the enemy across the Pyrenees, the mountains between France and Spain.

So the Arabs were held back in both East and West, but they kept Spain and Africa. All through the Middle Ages the Christians in Spain were fighting against the Arabs. Bit by bit the Spanish people, which was formed by the mixture of the races which lived in Spain under the Roman Empire and the Visigoths who had conquered them, drove the Arabs South, but it was not for seven hundred years that the last of the Moors, as the Spanish Arabs were called, were driven out of Spain into Africa.

The North of Africa, though it was conquered by other nations later, is quite Mohammedan in its people to this day. When the Saracens settled down in a country they often became very civilized, and the greatest scholars of the early Middle Ages belonged to this people. They studied the philosophy of the Greeks, and put together a philosophy of their own. They studied science too. We can best understand what the Arabian civilization was like by a study of their beautiful buildings, which may still be seen in the South of Spain. The most beautiful of all perhaps is the wonderful palace called the Alhambra, with its marble pillars and painted walls. The Moorish poets called it 'a pearl set in emeralds,' referring to its whiteness among green trees of the woods around.

Charles Martel, the great Frank soldier who drove the Arabs out of France at the battle of Tours, was not the king of the Franks. After the death of Clovis, the kings of his family who followed him were very weak and stupid. They left the government of the country very much to their officers, called the Mayors of the Palace.

This position was kept for a long time by one family, and handed down from father to son. They became a sort of royal family themselves, and certainly had all the power. The Franks by this time had conquered a great deal of the land to the East of the river Rhine, so that their kingdom was made up of the country which is now France, and also part of the

*Frankish Soldiers of
the Ninth Century*
(From an ancient
carving).

Country which is now Germany. They were always conquering, too, the German tribes further East, and it was while these conquests were going on that English monks, like St. Boniface, went among these people to make them Christians. As the Franks became more and more powerful they became more friendly with the bishop of Rome, who was now generally called the Pope, and who was head of all the churches in the West.

The Church in the East sometimes obeyed the Pope, too, but there were always quarrels between them, and in the end the Eastern Church became divided from the Western, and only the Western Church obeyed the Pope. This state of things has remained until now. The Russian and Greek Churches believe in very much the same things as the Catholic Church, but they will not have the Pope as their head. In the West, however, the Pope was growing more and more powerful. Kings and bishops from all the nations soon had to do what he told them.

When Charles Martel died he left his power to two sons, Carloman and Pepin. But Carloman chose to become a monk, and went off to Italy and became a Benedictine in St. Benedict's own great monastery at 'Monte Cassino.' So his brother, who was called Pepin the Short, was left to rule the Frank kingdom. Charles Martel had been king in everything but the name, and now Pepin took the name of king too.

He asked the Pope to help him in this, and the Pope, who was named Zacharias, did so. He said that it was only right that he who had the power of a king should have the name too. The king himself was a weak, stupid man, who lived in a kind of farm in the country with very few servants and no riches or magnificence. Pepin now told him that he must give up the throne, and to make things quite safe he made him become a monk.

Meanwhile, the Pope was having a great deal of trouble with the Lombard people in the North of Italy. They had given up their Arianism long before, but they had never really settled down and mixed with the Italians. They hated the Pope because they wanted Rome as their own. The Lombard king was threatening to attack Rome when the Pope asked Pepin to go to his help.

Pepin marched over the Alps, defeated the Lombards, took from them a large piece of land in the middle of Italy, which they had conquered from the Exarch of Ravenna, and gave it to the Pope. Before this the Pope had only had Rome, but this land with others which were added to it afterwards became a little kingdom by itself, ruled by the Pope and called the Papal States.

Once these States were taken in this way by the Pope, there was no chance of Italy becoming a nation under one king like England or France or Spain. The Lombards had to pay tribute to Pepin for their lands in the North of Italy. Some years afterwards Pepin died. He, too, divided his kingdom between two sons, Carloman and Charles, but Carloman soon died, and Charles became king of the Franks. He is one of the greatest men of the Middle Ages, and famous in history under the name of Charles the Great.

CHAPTER XIX—CHARLES THE GREAT AND THE HOLY ROMAN EMPIRE

Charles the Great is often called Charlemagne, which is a French way of saying his name, but it must be remembered that the Franks in his days were still more German than French, and soon Charles conquered so many lands that France was only a very small part of his empire.

Charles was not a little man like his father, Pepin the Short. Indeed, it was said after his death that he was seven feet high. He was very handsome, and very clever, and in a few years he won for himself an enormous empire.

The Lombards, under a new king, were worrying the Pope again, and Charles marched across the Alps to help him. The Lombards were conquered, Didier their king was forced to go into a monastery, and Charles the Great became king of the Lombards.

Then Charles turned against the Saxon tribes between the rivers Rhine and Elbe, and conquered them too. He made them all become Christians, and added their land to his empire, but it took thirty years of terrible wars to finish the conquest. Charles conquered also the terrible Avars, a people related to the Huns, and very like them. They had overrun the country of Bavaria, but Charles practically destroyed them, and added Bavaria to his empire, so that it now stretched right across the middle of Europe. He also crossed into Spain, and drove the Saracens south as far as the river Ebro.

There is a famous French poem, written in the Middle Ages, called the 'Chanson de Roland,' which tells a story of Charles's war against the Saracens in Spain. The story tells (but we are not sure how true it is) that Roland was the nephew of Charles, and fought with him against the Saracens. As they were crossing the Pyrenees back into France, Roland was at the very back of the army. Charles had gone on before, when suddenly a great army of Saracens appeared on a mountain-top between them.

Roland had only a few men, and his friends advised him to blow his horn and bring Charles back to help him. But he was too brave to do this, and made up his mind to fight the great Saracen army with his few men. He did so, and all day they fought, killing many

Saracens, but being nearly all killed themselves. At last Roland blew his horn, and Charles heard it far away, and wanted to turn back, but an enemy of Roland told him it was only the sound of the wind. Twice more Roland blew, but the last time it was when he was dying, and all his men were dead. Charles turned back to help him, but found him dead. He loved Roland dearly, and was almost heartbroken.

There was another enemy whom Charles dreaded more than any others. These were the terrible Northmen or Vikings from Norway and Sweden and Denmark. They were a Teutonic people too, and now when the Teutons in the rest of Europe had been settling down for hundreds of years they suddenly began to move, and for the next two hundred years were constantly attacking the countries of Western Europe. We shall see later how dreadfully these Northmen or Danes attacked the English. In Charles's time they were already attacking the Northern coasts of his empire, and after his death they conquered and settled down on parts of it.

Charles was a very good and holy man. He was anxious that all the people of his empire should be good Christians. He made good laws, and tried to keep order through all his empire. He was always a great friend of the Pope, and was called the 'Most Christian King,' and 'Defender of the Church.'

At last he received the highest title of all, that of Roman Emperor, which, as we have seen, had been given up more than three hundred years before. Charles had now an enormous empire, and perhaps he himself was anxious to have the name of Emperor. We do not know, but this is how he got it at last.

On Christmas Day in the year 800, the emperor was kneeling, saying his prayers before the Tomb of St. Peter in the church of St. Peter at Rome, when Pope Leo III suddenly placed a golden crown on his head, and all the people cheered and cried out the name of the Emperor. There was no Emperor of the East at that time, but an empress. However, Charles and the emperors in the West who came after them were never emperors in the old way. Sometimes they were powerful, and sometimes they were not. Later on in the Middle Ages there were terrible struggles between the 'Holy Roman Emperors,' as the Emperors of the West came to be called, and the Popes, as each wanted to be more powerful than the other.

Charles the Great (*By Agostino Cornacchini at St. Peter's Basilica, Vatican, Italy*).

It was a very difficult question to settle. The Emperor could only be crowned by the Pope, and yet when he was crowned the Pope had to bow before him.

The proud popes of the later Middle Ages would do no such thing. Some of the emperors expected the Pope to do just what they told him to, and so there were terrible struggles between them. But this was not so with Leo and Charles. They worked together for the good of the people and the good of the Church.

Charles lived to enjoy his empire until he was seventy years old, and was then buried sitting on a marble throne in a vault beneath the beautiful church he had built near his palace in the city of Aachen or Aix-la-chapelle. He had ruled so well and lived so simple a life that the people looked on him as almost a saint. When he was not fighting he gathered scholars around him in his palace. While he was at meals he would have someone reading or playing to him. He ate well, but drank very little, and cared nothing at all for luxury or magnificence. His whole life was given to the service of the Church and the people of the great empire he had built up. He has always been one of the great heroes of the Middle Ages.

Charles the Great died in the year 814, and his son Lewis the Pious became emperor after him. Lewis was a very good and holy man, and tried to rule the Empire well. But he was struggling during the whole of his reign with the people who wanted the Empire after him. At first he had three sons and one nephew, and he arranged for the Empire to be divided between them when he died, the first son to be emperor.

But his nephew, a young man named Bernard, wanted to have Italy for himself, even while his uncle was still alive. He rose in rebellion against Lewis, but was defeated, and by order of the Emperor he had his eyes put out, and soon afterwards died. This shows how cruel even a good man like Lewis could be in those days. Afterwards Lewis knelt humbly at the feet of the Pope and asked pardon for this sin. Later, Lewis married a second time and had another young son. His elder brothers did not want this boy to have any of the lands of the Empire, and when their father arranged a kingdom for him, they gathered an army to fight him.

Before the battle many of the Emperor's friends went over to fight on his sons' side against him, and afterwards the meeting-place was called the 'Field of Lies.' The Emperor was taken prisoner and shut up in a monastery. The sons tried to make him give up his throne, but he would not. After a time Lewis got free again and defeated his sons before he died, but it was a very sad ending. After his death, and after many quarrels between the sons, the great empire was broken up into three kingdoms, which were really France, Germany, and Italy with a small part of the South of France. This division did not last long. There were many more changes, but in the end France became a separate kingdom from Germany. Generally whichever king had Italy as part of his kingdom was called the Emperor. Sometimes there was no Emperor at all. Meanwhile great changes were taking place all over Western Europe.

Chapter XX—The Days of the Northmen

In the days after the death of Charles the Great, while his grandsons and their sons were fighting over his lands, the Northmen or Danes whom he had dreaded so much were sailing the seas and attacking the countries of the West in greater numbers than ever. They would sail up the mouths of rivers, attack the cities, carrying off all the best things from the houses and the richest treasures of the churches. Then they would sail away again.

In this way they sailed up the mouths of the French rivers and the rivers of the North of Germany. They came to England, too, and robbed and burned for many years. Then there came a time when these fierce men of the North came and conquered and did not go away again. They were great tall men, fierce and uncivilized, and still of course pagans. In fact, they were very much like the Franks and the Angles and Saxons who had overrun Gaul and Britain four hundred years before. In France the Northmen nearly took Paris for their people, but they were driven back by Count Robert the Strong.

The French kings, the descendants of Charles Martel and Pepin and Charles the Great, had become weak and stupid just as the family of Clovis had done. One of them who ruled both Germany and France for a time was called Charles the Fat, and he went mad before his death. Another of this family who was king of France was called Charles the Simple. A king like this was of no use against the fierce Northmen, but the Counts of Paris helped these weak kings just as the Mayors of the Palace had ruled for the family of Clovis.

Under Rolf or Rollo, a fierce chief, the Northmen were allowed to settle down in the land round Rouen, which they had seized and which became the Duchy of Normandy. Rolf was called 'Rolf the Ganger' or walker, because he always went on foot, as no horse was strong enough to carry him. The Northmen showed themselves very clever in learning the ways of the new countries they settled, and in Normandy especially showed themselves a brave and brilliant people. Meanwhile other Northmen, or Danes as they were generally called, had settled down in England.

THE GREAT KING ALFRED

When they began to attack England in earnest, the kings of Wessex had for the first time joined all the little kingdoms into which England had been so long divided into one kingdom. There were still kings of Northumbria and Mercia, but they were under the king of Wessex. When the Danes came, it was the king of Wessex who had to fight them. It was as king of Wessex that the great King Alfred fought the Danes and kept them from conquering the whole of England. After many years of fighting, Alfred made peace with the Danish King Guthrun, but even then he had to give up the whole of the East of England to the Danes.

King Alfred the Great *(Statue at Winchester, England).*

It was called the Danelaw and in it the Danes settled down, and lived at peace with the English just as the other Northmen had done in Normandy. Guthrun, the Danish king, had been baptized, and Alfred was his godfather. All the Danes of course became Christians like their king. Alfred was able to rule his own people in peace. In some ways he was very much like Charles the Great, but he was a better man in many ways, especially in his own private life.

Like Charles, he made good laws and tried to keep his people safe and happy. He himself wrote things in English which they might read. It was he who began the English Chronicle in which the history of England began to be written down for the first time. Like Charles, he set up schools and monasteries. He built ships, too, to keep England safe from any more attacks.

Alfred was the greatest of the early English kings. The kings who came after him tried to go on with his work, and in time they conquered the whole of England, even the part which had been given to the Danes. The last of these great kings was Edgar the Peaceful, and it is told of him how six under-kings rowed him up the river Dee to the church of St. John at Chester.

But after Edgar came the weak king 'Ethelred the Unready.' The Danes, who had now settled in kingdoms of their own in Norway, and Sweden, and Denmark, began to come again, and Ethelred, instead of fighting them, gave them money to go away. Then he did a very dreadful and foolish thing. He had many of the Danes who were already in England murdered on St. Brice's Day in the year 1002. The Danes from Denmark came to punish Ethelred, and he was driven out of the country. Danish kings now ruled England, the most famous being the great king Canute, who was almost a saint. But not many Danes came with him, and they did not alter the English ways of doing things or the English language.

After a time England got English kings again, the last of them being Edward the Confessor, who was a saint, but a weak king. After him, Earl Harold took the throne, but was killed by the Norman Duke William at the Battle of Hastings; so the Northmen again ruled England, but the story of William the Conqueror will come later on.

While the Northmen were attacking the West countries, the Magyars, a wild tribe like the Huns, were attacking Germany on the East and the Saracens were overrunning Sicily and Italy. One result of all this danger, and also of the disorder after the empire of Charles the Great was divided up, was the growth of what is called the Feudal System.

In the Feudal System, all the land of any country belongs to the king. He gives large pieces out to his nobles, who must do him 'homage' for them. They, in their turn give their lands out to other men, knights and others who become their 'men,' and have to do them homage and fight for them, just as they have to do homage to the king and fight for him. The poorest people of all under the Feudal System were 'serfs.'

Norman Soldiers Attacking a Castle by Sea

They were not exactly slaves. They lived on a small piece of land on which they could grow things for themselves, but they had also to work on the land of their lords. They could not be sold like slaves, but they were not free to go from one master to another, but had always to stay on the land and work for the lord who owned it. They could not do anything, such as getting married or sending their children to school, without permission from their lord. There were not many schools then, of course, but sometimes even the sons of serfs were chosen to go to the schools at the monasteries. Generally they would become monks, but this could only be with the permission of the lords.

In the days when enemies like the Danes were threatening the lands, it often seemed safer for free men to put themselves under the protection of some great lord who lived near. They would give their land up to the lord and receive it back as his 'man.' It was in this way that the Feudal System grew. Although the king was supposed to be at the head of all, for many years it was the great lords who had all the power. This was so in France and also in Germany, where some of the 'Counts' whom Charles the Great had set up to rule different parts of the country took the lands for themselves when he died.

In England when William the Conqueror came the Feudal System had begun to grow, chiefly through the power which the great nobles got during the weak rule of Edward the Confessor. All through the Early Middle Ages, when the great nobles everywhere were fighting against each other, the poor people suffered very much. The Church did all it could to make things better for them. When on their deathbeds, men were persuaded to set their serfs free. Feudalism was useful in the days when it first grew up, when the rich men fought for the poor against the enemies of both.

But it meant that every great lord was a soldier and in some ways a king. He could always call his knights to fight for him against some other lord, and the people were made miserable by the continual fighting. The Church tried to make things better by getting the great nobles to agree to a 'Truce of God.' This meant that they would stop fighting for some fixed time. It might be from Wednesday evening to Monday morning in each week, or from the beginning of Lent until after Easter. Or again the lords might be asked to promise that they would not attack priests, or merchants, or Jews, or women. It must have been a great relief to the people when the lords agreed to a 'Truce of God.'

In the Early Middle Ages every gentleman who was not a priest was a soldier, and many were called knights. Though they were often cruel to each other and to the poor people, the best of them were kind and good, especially to women. The Church tried to teach the knights to do what was right, and sometimes a knight

Making a Knight in the Middle Ages. *After he had spent the night in vigil in the church, the young knight had his sword buckled on by the king, while others invested him in spurs, shirt of mail, banner and shield (From a drawing by Matthew Paris, a famous English monk and historian about 1200).*

was given his sword and armor with the blessing of the Church. Often he had knelt through the whole of the night before praying in the church. The worst sides of feudalism were put down later on in the Middle Ages when the kings grew stronger, especially in England and France.

In France, Hugh Capet, the Count of Paris, became king in the year 987. At first he had very little more power than the duke of Normandy or the other great feudal lords in France with their strong castles and their armies ready to fight for them. But in time the French kings grew stronger and stronger, and were able to keep the great lords in order, and joined the whole of France into a strong and great kingdom.

THE END OF THE 'DARK AGES'

In Germany the descendants of Charles the Great were dead, and one of the dukes of the four great Duchies into which his German lands were divided became king of Germany. One of the greatest of these was Otto, son of Henry the Fowler of Saxony. It was he who, in the great battle of Lechfield, at last conquered the Magyars, who settled down and mixed with the people in Hungary, which now became a kingdom. The Magyars became Christians, and fifty years later had a saint for their king.

New kingdoms were being made all over the North and East, where at last the people were settling down as they had already done in the West. We have seen how the Danes had made the kingdoms of Norway, Sweden, and Denmark. The Slavonic kingdom of Poland was made in the tenth century. Then Northern pirates attacked the country we now call Russia, and mixed with the Slavonic tribes to form a great kingdom there. And all these new peoples became Christians in a very short time, for missionaries from East or West went to convert them. Russia was converted by the Eastern Church, to which it has belonged ever since. With the settlement of all these peoples one of the great dangers which had threatened the nations of the West all through the Early Middle Ages was over.

All this time Italy had been full of disorder. The North had been broken up among several dukes. The Popes ruled Rome and the middle of Italy, while the South was divided between the Greeks and Saracens. After the death of Charles the Great the Popes had seemed more powerful than ever.

Pope Nicholas I especially was very much like the Popes who came later in the Middle Ages, and who claimed power over kings and bishops alike. But by the time of the Emperor Otto the Great the Popes had become very weak and wicked, and Otto made up his mind to go into Italy and put all things right again. He first interfered in the North, where a great struggle was going on for the Lombard Crown. Otto went to the help of a young and beautiful woman, Adelaide of Burgundy, whose husband had died while he was trying to have himself made king. Adelaide was put in prison by one of his enemies. Otto now went into Italy, took the crown for himself, and being a widower himself he married Adelaide.

Cluny Abbey

Ten years later, in 963, when he had gone to Italy for a second time, he had himself crowned emperor by the Pope, John XII, who had begged for his help against his enemies. Otto was anxious to set up good Popes again, and did so. He was the friend of the monks of the new order of Cluny, which was doing its best to make the Church and the people better and holier. The monastery of Cluny in the middle of France had been set up by William the Pious, a French duke, and under its abbot Otto had been made very strict. Many of the Benedictine abbeys had by this time forgotten to do most of the things which they were told to do in the Rule of St. Benedict.

But the abbot of Cluny set up new monasteries, and got some of the old ones to join him. All the monasteries belonging to Cluny had to obey the abbot of Cluny. The old Benedictine monasteries had been quite independent of each other, so that if an abbot was not good or did not mind the rule there was no one to keep him in order. The monks of Cluny did not work in the fields like the Benedictine monks had done, but they had longer time for prayers and lived very simply.

The setting up of this new order of monks shows that there was a new feeling for religion growing up at the end of the 'Dark Ages.' The spread of the order helped to make the feeling stronger. In a short time the Church everywhere became stronger and better. The new Popes were quite different from the Popes before Otto the Great was crowned emperor. With the 'Cluniac Reform,' as it was called, a change seems to come over the times, and we find ourselves in the Middle Ages proper, with their great soldiers and saints, and wonderful churches, and castles, and schools, and monasteries. It is a time above all of wonderful adventure and romance, and we must now tell something of its story.

Chapter XXI—The Great Pope Hildebrand

The greatest time of the Middle Ages was the thirteenth century, that is, the time between the years 1200 and 1300 A.D. It was the time of great popes, and great kings and saints, but for two hundred years before this people had been becoming more civilized, and times were changing. These changes took place in all the countries of Western Europe, but perhaps they are more easily noticed in England.

In the year 1066 there happened in England a great thing which helped to bring these changes about. This was the Norman Conquest, when the great William, duke of Normandy, came over to England, and had himself crowned king of England. Edward the Confessor, the last real English king, had been brought up in Normandy, and loved the Norman people and the Norman ways. He was a very good man, a saint, in fact, and had a very gentle face and a long white beard. He was a friend of Duke William of Normandy, and promised that he should be king of England when Edward died, as he had not any children to reign after him.

Duke William was a tall dark man, with a handsome but stern face and strong like a giant. When the news came to him that Edward of England was dead he cried out, 'Then England is mine.' But the English had chosen for their king an English earl named Harold. He was a short fair man with a handsome face and smiling blue eyes. He had long fair hair hanging in curls to his shoulders, for that was how the young Englishmen wore their hair at that time. They had sometimes beards too, but the Normans had short hair and shaven faces.

When William heard that Harold had been chosen king of England he was very angry and made up his mind to come and take England from him. He was especially angry, because a short time before Harold had been wrecked on the coast of Normandy, and William had made him promise to help him in making himself king of England. If he had not made this promise William would not have let him go, so Harold promised; but he did not feel that he was bound to keep his promise, and now he had been chosen king himself. William got together a fleet and went over the sea to fight Harold. Harold was fighting another

Harold takes the oath to Duke William of Normandy, and thereafter returns to England.

Harold is offered the crown on the death of King Edward, and takes his seat upon the English throne.

At the Battle of Hastings against Duke William Harold receives an arrow in his eye, and pulling it out, dies.

Scenes in the life of Harold, the last Saxon King of England. *(From the famous Bayeux Tapestry woven with pictures of the Conquest of England, made probably by the sister of William the Conqueror.)*

enemy in the North of England when he heard that William with a great army of Norman soldiers was at Hastings in the South. He at once marched South, and the great battle of Hastings was fought.

Both sides fought splendidly, but the English were tired with their long march. At the end of the day only the soldiers of Harold's guard were left fighting around him beside his standard, where he had set it up at the top of the hill. Then at last William told his foot-soldiers to shoot high above the heads of the Englishmen so that the arrows might strike their heads and faces. An arrow pierced Harold's eye, and he fell at the foot of his standard. He was killed immediately and his friends with him, and so William won England for himself.

He had the body of Harold put under a heap of stones on the cliff at Hastings, but it was afterwards taken away and buried by the priests of the church of Holy Cross at Waltham which Harold had built. For Harold was a good man and brave.

THE NORMAN CONQUEST OF ENGLAND

William the Conqueror was a religious man too, and he made great changes in the church in England. The Archbishop of Canterbury, Stigand, had his church taken away from him, and a holy monk named Lanfranc from the Abbey of Bec in Normandy was made archbishop instead. He was very strict, and made all the priests in England live better and stricter lives. A great many Norman priests and monks came to England too, and did great good for the people. But there were other changes which made the English people very unhappy. Nearly all the great English nobles were killed, and their lands were given to William's Norman friends.

For two or three hundred years all the rich people in England were Normans and spoke French. A great many French words changed a little were added to the English language. The Normans had much finer manners than the English, whom they looked down on. But after a time the Normans began to mix with the English and learned their language, and in the end the Norman settlers and the English they had conquered became one people.

The Normans were much more civilized than the English, and they taught the English many things. They were great builders and built beautiful stone churches all over England, some of which remain to this day, for they were

Norman and Early English Arches Contrasted. *Above are round arches from the nave of Durham Cathedral, while the pointed arches below, from the choir of Canterbury Cathedral, show the first development of Norman to Early English style.*

very strong as well as beautiful. One way of telling a Norman church from those built in the later Middle Ages is that the arches of the Norman churches were round and later they were pointed. Great feudal castles, too, were built all over England, but William the Conqueror was one of the first kings in any country to keep the feudal lords in order. They dared not rebel against him, as the feudal lords in France and Germany were always rebelling against their kings. Nor would he let them fight among themselves and disturb the people.

William tried to rule the English people well, but he could be very cruel. When the English in the North of England rebelled against him he marched against them, and killed all the people, and burned every house and destroyed every living thing, so that for years the whole county of Yorkshire was as bare as a desert.

William the Conqueror when he came to England brought with him a banner sent to him with his blessing by the great Pope Gregory VII, who is generally called Hildebrand, and was one of the best and greatest of all the Popes. Since the days of the Emperor Otto there had been several popes. Sometimes the emperors had chosen them and sometimes they had not taken any notice of them. But when Hildebrand became Pope in 1073 the Emperor Henry III had got much power over the popes.

Hildebrand, who was a monk, was very anxious to make the Church better, but he did not think it was right that even a good emperor should be more powerful than the Pope. He thought, indeed, that the Pope should be the head of all Christian countries, and that kings and people should do what he told them. This was why he thought he had the right to take the kingdom of England from Harold and give it to William the Conqueror. But when William became king of England, although he was very good and helped the holy Lanfranc to make the Church better, he did not think he was bound to obey the Pope in every way.

Pope St. Gregory VII saying Mass (From Little Pictorial Lives of the Saints, 1878).

But with the emperors who thought themselves greater than the popes there were struggles for many years. The first great struggle between an emperor and a pope was between Hildebrand and the Emperor Henry IV. Hildebrand was a little man and rather fat. He stammered when he spoke, and he had a rather dull face except for his glittering eyes. He was not a great scholar, but he was a great ruler. His one idea was to make the world better, and he thought that only the Pope as head of the Church could do this.

All over Europe the feudal lords were fighting one another, and kings and princes were often not much better.

Hildebrand offended Henry IV when he said that bishops should not receive the ring or crozier (the crook which was always given to a bishop) from princes or nobles, but only from the Pope, or somebody in his place. In those days the bishops were really great nobles too, and received lands like the other great nobles. The kings thought that it was only right that as the lands came from them so should the ring and crozier to show that the king owned the bishop as feudal lord. So the Emperor Henry IV was very angry when Hildebrand forbade this.

Henry was a young man, tall and handsome. He had become king of Germany when he was only a boy six years old. His father Henry III had died then. Henry III was one of the greatest of the emperors, and in his time the different peoples who lived in Germany had been kept well in order, and the people of the North of Italy which still belonged to the emperor also. But while Henry IV was a boy disorder had come again. Henry belonged to the Swabian people in South Germany, and the Saxons of North Germany tried to break away from his rule. Henry was still having trouble with these people when the Pope gave his order about 'investiture,' as the giving of the ring and crozier to the bishops was called.

Henry sent an angry letter to the Pope, saying that he would not obey him in this, and telling him that he was 'no Pope but a false monk.' Hildebrand then declared that Henry should no longer be Emperor, and so war broke out between the two. But the Saxons again rose up against Henry, and the German nobles said that Henry must give in to the Pope. The Pope had excommunicated Henry, too, which means that he said he could not belong to the Church until he was forgiven.

At last Henry saw that he would have to ask pardon of the Pope. He was told that he must remain quietly at a place in Germany until absolution was sent by the Pope. Meanwhile he was almost an outcast with no honors shown to him as a king, and not even allowed to go to church. For many weeks he waited, and then could bear it no longer. He made up his mind to go over the Alps, although it was winter-time and very cold, and beg pardon from the Pope.

The Pope was at Canossa, and the story used to be told that outside the gate of the castle there Henry had to stand three days with bare feet in the snow until, at last, the Pope forgave him. In any case, we know that Henry had to beg hard for forgiveness, and it was three days before the Pope would agree. Even then he still said he had the right to take Henry's kingdom from him, and shortly afterwards the messengers whom the Pope had sent to Germany did choose another king. Henry fought against the new king, Rudolph of Swabia, and got the bishops of Germany and Italy who were friendly to him to elect a new Pope, who was called Clement III. So now there were two Popes and two emperors. Then Henry marched into Italy and into Rome, where Hildebrand shut himself up in the castle of St. Angelo. He sent for help to a great Norman prince, Robert Guiscard, who had conquered the South of Italy, and made it a kingdom for himself. The Saracens had had to give in to him, and at last the Greek Exarch of Ravenna had to give up that city.

From this time the Eastern Emperor had not had even one city in the West. At the same time that Robert Guiscard was winning South Italy his younger brother Roger conquered

Sicily, and ruled it till he died in 1101. His little son Roger ruled after him, and when he had grown to be a man, and his cousin, the son of Robert Guiscard, died, Roger II got South Italy too, and joined them together as one kingdom. Roger won more land still in South Italy, and among other places he won the beautiful city of Naples. Later, his kingdom was called the kingdom of Naples and Sicily. The Normans had always been very friendly to the Pope, and Robert Guiscard went to Gregory's help.

A Norman army marched to Rome, and instead of attacking Henry burned the city and killed many of the people and then marched away again. It was the third time in history that the great city had been attacked and burnt by enemies, but the Normans, who were of course Christians, did far more harm than the Gauls so long ago or the heathen Goth Alaric.

Hildebrand followed the Normans to Salerno, and there died soon afterwards. As he lay dying, he said 'I have loved God and hated iniquity. Therefore I die in exile.' And it was true. Hildebrand only behaved as he did to Henry because he was anxious to have good bishops, and so make the Church better. But he did not understand that it would have been much better to try to do this in some other way, by helping the Cluniac monks and the other new 'orders' of monks which were growing up.

For good men everywhere were, like Hildebrand himself, anxious for a new time, when men should be better, and there would be an end of bloodshed and misery, and all priests and peoples and kings, and nobles too, should join together to lead good and peaceful lives. Hildebrand did not understand that the kings and princes of Europe would never agree to hold their kingdoms from him. He made a great mistake, but all the same he was a very good and noble man, and one of the greatest of the popes.

The popes who came after Hildebrand were good men too, and the work he had begun went on. They were not so fierce as Hildebrand, yet Henry IV was never forgiven. His eldest son Conrad was encouraged to rebel against him, and when Conrad died his other son Henry did the same. He raised the Saxons in rebellion against his father, and was called king by the Pope.

Henry was growing old and tired. His life had been one long struggle. In his younger days he had not lived a very good life, but he had grown better as he grew older. His sons and many other people thought that it was not wrong to rebel against him because he was excommunicated, and therefore an outcast. Henry had struggled against his elder son, but when the younger turned against him he threw himself at his feet and begged that at any rate his sins should not be punished by his own child. He tried hard to get the Pope's forgiveness, but would not give up his kingdom.

And so at last he died, and was buried with his ancestors in the beautiful church at Liége, which he himself had built; but the bishop of Speyer ordered that his body should be taken up again, and for five years it was kept in a chapel at Speyer, and then at last buried in the cathedral there. But before Henry's death great things had been happening in Europe, which showed, even more than his sad life did, the great power of the popes.

Chapter XXII—The Crusades

It was in the days of Pope Paschal that the Emperor Henry IV died, but before him there had been the great Pope Urban II, and under him began the most wonderful thing that happened during the Middle Ages. This was the beginning of the crusades, when knights and soldiers from all the countries of Western Europe joined together and went to the East to fight the Mohammedans, and win back from them the Holy Sepulchre or Tomb of Our Lord, which they had taken.

At first all the countries conquered by the Arabs had been governed by one ruler, but afterwards there had been two Kaliphs, one in the East at Bagdad, the beautiful city on the Tigris which the Eastern Kaliph made his capital, and one in the West. Then after many years the Kaliphs began to lose power, and many Mohammedan kings made little kingdoms of their own, and forgot to obey the Kaliphs any more. Soon after the year 1000 some Turks from the middle of Asia poured in great numbers into the lands of the Mohammedans in Asia, and soon conquered them.

These Seljuk Turks, as they were called (because they told tales of a great heroic leader they once had whose name was Seljuk), were a very fierce people related to the terrible Huns who had tried to destroy Europe in the days of Attila. The Turks became Mohammedans, but were much fiercer than the Arabs had ever been. They conquered Palestine and Syria, and this was how they took the Holy Sepulchre from the Christians. Before this Jerusalem had belonged to the Mohammedans of Egypt, who had allowed the Christians to go to pray at the Holy Sepulchre.

In the Middle Ages people very often made long journeys or pilgrimages to pray at the graves of saints and martyrs, and pilgrims went in great numbers especially to the Holy Sepulchre of Christ at Jerusalem. But the fierce Seljuk Turks were very cruel to the pilgrims, and very disrespectful to the Holy Sepulchre. When the people in the West of Europe heard of these things they were very angry, and it was this which brought about the crusades.

The first crusade was in the year 1096, and for two hundred years after this, from time to time new crusades were preached and fought. The great preacher of the first crusade was a

Frenchman called Peter the Hermit. He was a priest who lived a very strict life, and about the year 1093 he made a pilgrimage to Jerusalem, and there saw how badly the Christian pilgrims were treated by the Turks. He came back to Europe and told Pope Urban II all about it, and asked his permission to preach to the people, and get the soldiers of Europe to go and save the Sepulchre from the Turks.

The Pope gave him permission, and Peter travelled all over Italy and France telling the people the things he had seen. He was a little man with a thin pale face, but bright eager eyes. He wore only a shirt, and a pilgrim's cloak, and he rode on a donkey, holding in his hand a cross. People gave him money and presents, but he gave it all to the poor again, and ate just enough to keep himself alive. The people grew very excited when he talked to them, and every man who made up his mind to go to the East to fight the Turks wore a badge in the shape of a red cross on the right shoulder, and he was called a crusader, or a soldier of the cross.

Peter the Hermit

The Pope himself went to a place in France called Clermont, and there he called a great meeting, called a council, of bishops and princes and nobles, to whom he talked about the crusade. He spoke to a great crowd of the poorer people too, asking all who could to join the crusade. The people shouted as he finished his speech, 'It is the will of God.' Great nobles and captains offered themselves for the crusade, and the soldiers chose which leader they would follow.

But before the real crusaders were ready to start, an impatient crowd set off to the Holy Land under Peter the

Hermit, and a captain called Walter the Penniless. They had no order, and they did much harm and destruction in the countries they passed through. They never reached even Constantinople, but were killed by fierce tribes in the East of Europe. Only Peter the Hermit lived to tell the tale. Meanwhile, on August 15th, 1096, the army of the First Crusade set out for the East. Among the great nobles who led their soldiers on this crusade was Robert, duke of Normandy, the eldest son of William the Conqueror. The Conqueror was now dead, but Robert had not been made king of England. He was duke of Normandy, and William the Red was king of England. But Robert was a soldier more than anything else, and had practically sold Normandy to William, to get money for the crusade.

Many of the princes and nobles were good and religious men, but many, too, went on crusade because they loved fighting and adventures. These were Norman nobles from the South of Italy, and French nobles like Raimond of Toulouse, and Godfrey de Bouillon, duke of Lower Lorraine.

GODFREY DE BOUILLON THE HERO OF THE CRUSADES

Godfrey was the real hero of the crusade. The crusaders marched through Germany and Hungary to the gates of Constantinople, where the Eastern Emperor wanted them to help him to win back some of his land, which the Turks had taken from him. But the crusaders were thinking of quite other things. For nine months they besieged the city of Antioch, but took it at last. Then they marched on to Jerusalem, and as they came in sight of the Holy City which they had come to win, the crusaders fell on their knees. Then they took off their armor, and walked with bare feet like pilgrims to the city. But it was a month before they could break their way in, and then the crusaders showed no mercy.

They were cruel enough in their wars with each other at home, but with the enemies of Christ they were more cruel still. The Mohammedans were cut down and killed in the streets, and the horses of the crusaders were up to their knees in blood as they went to the Holy Sepulchre. There the leaders prayed, with heads and feet bare, and Godfrey dressed in a robe of white linen.

The nobles had now to choose a king to rule over Palestine with his capital at Jerusalem. Robert of Normandy was chosen first, but he loved better to fight than to rule, and so refused. So Godfrey was chosen and agreed to do the work of a king, but he would not wear a crown, he said, 'in a city where his King had been crowned with thorns.' Then most of the knights and soldiers went home again, while Godfrey stayed to rule his kingdom, and so ended the First Crusade.

Godfrey de Bouillon died before a year was past, and his brother Baldwin became king of Jerusalem in his place. Godfrey and his friend Tancred were the greatest and best of the knights who fought in the Holy War. Many of the others were not good men, but the lives of men like Godfrey show us the better side of the times. Not very many knights remained in the East after the First Crusade, but new ones were always going out. Baldwin ruled Jerusalem for eighteen years, and after him his nephew, another Baldwin.

All this time there was fighting with the Mohammedans, but the kingdom of Jerusalem was well and strongly governed. But after the death of Baldwin II, when the counts of Anjou got the crown, things were different. One of these kings was a leper, and others were only children, and the feudal lords, among whom the land had been divided, became very disorderly.

Many of these lords had married women of the East, and lived in luxury which they learned from the Eastern peoples. Their children and their children's children forgot the ways of the West, and were very different from Godfrey and Tancred and the knights of the First Crusade. In fact, the defence of the Holy Sepulchre and the fighting against the Mohammedans was now chiefly done by some knights who really became monks. That is to say, they lived the lives of monks during times of peace, not marrying, but living together in a monastery and spending most of their time in prayer, while in time of war they lived as soldiers.

There were two 'orders' of these knights at Jerusalem. The knights of one order were called the Templars because they made their first monastery near the place where the great temple of Solomon had once been. The other was the Order of St. John, or the Hospitallers, who were so called because they set up a hotel or hospital where poor pilgrims to the Holy Sepulchre could eat and sleep.

In the year 1145, the Turks attacked the city of Edessa, in the North-East of the kingdom of Jerusalem. Edessa was ruled by one of those feudal knights who had given themselves up to pleasure, and he did not even try to save the town. But when the news came to Western Europe the Christians were very indignant, and so the Second Crusade was made ready. The man who did most to persuade princes and people to join this crusade was the great monk St. Bernard, who was the most important man of his time. The two chief leaders in the Sec-

Knights Templar

ond Crusade, which started for the East in 1146, were the Emperor Conrad and the French King Louis VII. But the Second Crusade was quite a failure, and Louis and Conrad soon came home again.

The kingdom of Jerusalem grew weaker and weaker, while the Turks grew stronger. At last there arose a great hero among the Turks called Saladin. In some ways, although he was a fierce Mohammedan and hated Christianity, Saladin was very like the best of the Christian knights. He was very fond of children and gentle to women. Though he was fierce in fighting, he was not cruel to his prisoners. His soldiers loved him and would do anything for him. The people of Western Europe were shocked to hear, in the year 1088, that Saladin had conquered the Christian kingdom and taken Jerusalem itself. It was this news which brought about the Third Crusade.

KING RICHARD OF THE LION HEART

The Third Crusade was almost as great as the First, though it did not win much in the end. The Emperor Frederick Barbarossa, or Frederick with the Red Beard, who was one of the greatest of the emperors, joined it. So did Philip Augustus, one of the greatest of the French kings, who had by this time become strong rulers, able to keep the French feudal lords in order. The great hero of the crusade, on the Christian side, was the king of England, Richard Coeur de Lion, or Richard of the Lion Heart as he was called, because he was so brave. Many dukes and nobles joined the crusade too.

Frederick Barbarossa had been crowned emperor when he was about thirty years old by Pope Adrian IV, the only Englishman who was ever a Pope. Adrian's name, before he became Pope, was Nicholas Breakspear. He had been a poor student at one time. Frederick was one of those emperors who thought that the Emperor should be above the Pope, and he nearly quarreled with Adrian by saying that he would not hold the Pope's stirrup to help him to get off his horse, but in the end he did it.

But later on the Pope and the Emperor had many quarrels. A great many important towns had grown up in the North of Italy, and some of these, especially Milan, did not want to be under the Emperor, who still kept the North of Italy as well as Germany. But Frederick took a great army into Italy and practically

Philip Augustus, King of France From 1180 to 1223 (From a statue, perhaps carved during his life-time, in a church founded by the king).

destroyed Milan. He quarreled, too, with the new Pope, Alexander III, and soon after his friends tried to set up another Pope, who was called the anti-pope. Once during the quarrel he marched to Rome, had the anti-pope set up in the palace of the popes, and got him to crown his wife Beatrix.

After many years the other cities joined together into a league called the Lombard League, and helped to build up Milan again. When the Emperor came again on one of his many visits from Germany to fight them there was a great battle. The men of Milan fought round a sacred car on which was a figure of Christ. The best soldiers had been picked out to defend the car, and they were called the Company of Death. This time the towns won, and the Emperor had to give them a great deal of freedom, though he still kept a sort of power over them.

Frederick then gave in to the Pope and was received again into the Church, for he had of course been excommunicated. In the great piazza or square in Venice he knelt at Pope Alexander's feet, and the Pope raised him up and gave him the kiss of peace. It was just one hundred years since Henry IV had asked forgiveness at Canossa. So again the Pope had won.

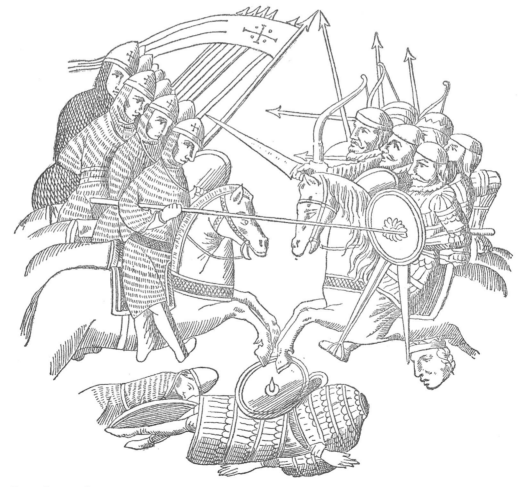

Crusaders and Saracens in Battle (*From a stained-glass window made early in the twelfth century*).

Frederick, then, had had a stormy life, and was an old man when he joined the Third Crusade. He led his great army by land while Philip and Richard took theirs by sea, but as the German army reached a stream just before crossing into Syria, the brave old Emperor was drowned. The river was flowing very quickly, but the Emperor spurred his horse into it, and was carried away and drowned. The people of Germany were full of sorrow, for he had ruled them well and they had loved him.

He was a very handsome man, with long yellow hair curling over his ears and with a long red beard, from which the Italians called him Barbarossa. He had a clear white skin and bright eyes and a merry smile. Long afterwards the German people looked back on his reign as a time of great peace and joy. They said, indeed, that he did not die, but was only sleeping, and would come one day to rule them again.

The other leaders stopped before the town of Acre, and besieged it for two years. There was fierce fighting, and Richard of the Lion Heart, who had come late, showed his great courage when, although he was ill, he had himself carried among the soldiers, so that he could give them orders in the fight. The Black Standard of Saladin waved proudly above the city, though Saladin was not there at the time. With Richard's help Acre was soon taken, and the crusaders were now free to march to Jerusalem. But Philip Augustus was anxious to get home again and give himself up to the work of making France stronger. Most of the French soldiers went home with their king.

Richard led the rest of the crusaders after this, and won many battles against Saladin, but he could not win Jerusalem, and at last he made peace with Saladin. The Christians had lost the kingdom which they had won in the First Crusade, but were allowed to keep a little land on the coast round Jaffa, and pilgrims in small numbers were to be allowed to visit the Holy Sepulchre. Before he turned homewards Richard was taken to the top of a hill, from which he could see the white buildings of Jerusalem glistening far off in the sunshine. But Richard put his shield before his face. He could not bear to look at the Holy City, which he had hoped to win again for the Christians.

For a hundred years after this there were other crusades, though not so great as the First and Third. But Jerusalem was never really won back, and is in the hands of the Mohammedans still. Richard started for home, but it was a long time before he reached England, for he had many adventures on the way. Saladin died the next year.

One reason why the Third Crusade was not a great success was that the leaders were jealous of each other. Although Richard was so brave and splendid a knight, he was not easy to get on with, for he wanted to have things all his own way. One of the leaders who had quarreled very bitterly with Richard was Leopold, duke of Austria. Richard had to pass through Leopold's country on his way home. He dressed himself up as a pilgrim, but someone found out who he was, and he was put in prison by the duke.

After a time Richard was given over to the new emperor, Henry VI, the son of Frederick Barbarossa. The Emperor kept him in prison for two years. A story is told that no one in

England really knew what had happened to Richard until his minstrel Blondel found out where he was. A story is told of how Blondel travelled from castle to castle all over Germany, and at last, as he rested outside the castle where Richard was shut up, he heard his master's voice singing an old French song. Blondel, in great excitement, sang a verse of the song, hoping that Richard would hear him, and he did. Richard was glad, for he knew that Blondel would go back to England and tell the English people of the troubles of their king. And so he did.

Richard's wicked brother John was looking after England and did not want the king to come back, but in the end he had to pay the ransom of a great sum of money which the Emperor asked for, and Richard was at last set free. He did not live long after he got back to England. For years after his time the Mohammedans told tales of his great courage and strength, and in Syria if an Arab's horse jumped or seemed frightened the Arab would say to it, 'Why! Do you think it is King Richard?'

King Richard and Saladin from a Vintage Engraving

At the same time that the Christians and Mohammedans were struggling in the East, a great struggle was going on too between the Christians and the Moors in Spain. We have seen that Spain was the only country in Western Europe, except the South of Italy, which was won by the Mohammedans. The Normans had conquered South Italy again, but for hundreds of years nearly all Spain belonged to the Moors. Charles the Great had, however, driven them as far South as the Ebro, and little Christian kingdoms had grown up there.

In time these began to grow stronger, and by degrees to push the Moors farther and farther South, so that by the end of the thirteenth century they only had a little strip of land in the South, and nearly all Spain was Christian again. The great hero in this struggle between the Moors and Christians in Spain was a man named Ruy Diaz, but who has always been called by the Spaniards the 'Cid,' which means the 'Lord.' He was born not many years after the year 1000, and spent his whole life in fighting.

The people of Spain tell that he always fought for the Christians, but other people have said that he sometimes fought for the Moors. At any rate he won many marvelous victories over the Moors, and he died still fighting them, when he was an old man, about the time of the First Crusade.

The Spaniards tell that their hero was kind and gentle as well as brave. Once, they say, as he was returning after a victory, which he had won over five Moorish kings, he saw a poor man suffering from the dreadful disease of leprosy, which so many people had in the Middle Ages. The leper was lying on the road begging for pity, but the Spanish knights passed him by, all except the Cid, who lifted him up and took him home on his horse, fed him and put him to sleep in his own bed. In the night the Cid awoke and the leper was no longer there, but a beautiful figure stood beside him and spoke to him, telling him that he was St. Lazarus and had only appeared to him as a leper, and he promised him that he should win in his battles against the Moors.

The Spaniards told, too, how when the Cid lay dying he heard that a great Moorish army from North Africa was coming to Spain. He told his soldiers that when he died they must not cry out or moan, so that the enemy would know what had happened, but they must dress him in his armor, put a sword in his hand and tie him sitting on his horse, and he would once more lead them to victory though he was dead. And so he did. His soldiers fought around their dead leader, and the Moors were defeated in a great battle. And after this the Christians went on conquering until the Moors were driven out of Spain.

Chapter XXIII—The Monks and the People in the Time of the Crusades

In the early days of the crusades, when the soldiers of the Cross were fighting in the East, many interesting things were happening among the people left at home.

We have seen that in all the countries of Western Europe there were people who were anxious to live better lives. New monasteries and convents were built where men and women who wanted to pray and live in peace could go. Especially in France this happened, partly perhaps because the feudal lords were so powerful in France, while the king had not yet got much power. Great new 'orders' of monks rose up, for sometimes a monk seeing the faults in the older monasteries would set up a new monastery with new rules by which to keep from these faults.

One of the greatest of these new orders was one founded by St. Bruno. At first Bruno was head of the school belonging to the cathedral at the French town called Rheims. In those days there were no schools except those belonging to cathedrals and monasteries, and as a rule only boys who were going to be priests or monks were taught to read and write. Bruno was very good and pious, and when the new archbishop of Rheims, who was named Manasses, did wrong things Bruno scolded him. But the archbishop was very angry, and Bruno had to go away from Rheims and hide for a long time.

Then when Manasses died the priests at the cathedral chose Bruno to be their archbishop, but the French king, Philip I, would not agree to this. Rheims was in that part of France where the French king had real power. Philip was a very wicked king, and Pope Hildebrand had told him so plainly, while later Pope Urban excommunicated him because he sent away his queen, Bertha, after he had been married to her for twenty years, and took another wife.

Naturally, Philip did not want an archbishop who was a saint like Bruno. However, Bruno did not mind at all, but went into a wild part of the country near a town called Grenoble and built there a new monastery. He made quite a new rule for his monks. Instead of doing everything together, like the earlier monks eating in a large room called the refectory, and sleeping in another large room called the dormitory, St. Bruno and his monks had each a little house of his own. Each monk lived and ate and slept in his own house, and only went with the other monks at those times when they prayed in the church. The monks never spoke, and lived the very strictest of lives.

The monastery which St. Bruno built near Grenoble was called the Grand Chartreuse. Afterwards, he went to Calabria in Italy, and built two more charterhouses, as monasteries of this order were called. The order was called the Carthusian order, and it soon spread over the countries of Western Europe. It never became less strict like many other orders. There is a Carthusian monastery in the South of England even now, where the monks live exactly the same kind of life that St. Bruno and his monks lived nine hundred years ago.

There were 'lay brothers' also in the order who did not spend so much time in saying prayers, but did the work of the monastery and grew things on the land. The monks of the Grand Chartreuse found out how to make a certain kind of wine which is called 'Chartreuse,' and nobody else has ever found out exactly how it is made.

There was another great order of monks which was begun about the same time as the Carthusians. This was the great 'Cistercian' order, which also began in France. A holy monk named Robert set up a Benedictine monastery at Moleme in the North of Burgundy. He tried to make his monks keep the Rule of St. Benedict properly, but they thought he was too strict and would not. So very sadly Robert left them with just a few of the monks and went to a lonely place called Citeaux in the South of France. He began another monastery there.

THE GREAT ST. BERNARD

At first there were only Robert and his few friends. One of these was named Stephen Harding, and was an Englishman. Afterwards he was made a saint. Soon people began to hear about the splendid lives which the monks of Citeaux lived, and one day there came to the monastery a young French nobleman named Bernard. He had with him thirty of his relations, and he begged that they might all become monks. This Bernard was the great St. Bernard who became the most important man of his time.

So many men came to be monks at Citeaux that the monastery would not hold them, and so little bands of monks were always going away to set up new monasteries in other places. St. Bernard himself did this, and became head of a monastery at Clairvaux. He is often called St. Bernard of Clairvaux. But all the monasteries of the Cistercian order were under the abbot of Citeaux, and he in his turn had to take the advice of the abbots of the four other chief monasteries of the order. One of these was Clairvaux.

The Cistercian monks gave up the black robe of the Benedictines and wore white habits. They are often called the 'White Monks,' though the Carthusians and some others of the new orders wore white too. The Cistercians always built their monasteries in wild country places far from the towns. For instance, when they came to England soon after the year 1100, they set up many of their monasteries in the wild districts of Yorkshire, and soon they turned these places into the most beautiful spots in the country. For the Cistercians were always very clever in growing things, and in many places, too, they covered the land with sheep. The wool of the sheep was sold to be made into cloth.

The Cistercians often became very rich, but they were very kind to the poor, and were not allowed to spend much money even on their churches. At first especially their churches were built very plainly, and were not allowed to have towers or spires, because these were not necessary. There were no silver or gold crosses in their churches, but only painted crosses made of wood.

But though the Cistercian monks lived such strict and quiet lives they soon spread all over Europe. St. Bernard was greater, indeed, than any pope, and the popes and bishops of the time were glad of his advice on all sorts of things. He lived a very strict life indeed, and ate so little food that after a time he became so weak that he was sick every time he took any

Mosaic Detail of the Cistercian Saint Bernard, Nunraw Abbey, Scotland.

food at all. But this did not prevent his praying and preaching. He travelled through France and Italy, preaching to the people who crowded to see and hear him. When once more an anti-pope was struggling with the real Pope, it was St. Bernard who got the anti-pope to give in, and so made peace in the Church.

St. Bernard was very severe with anybody who was against the Church in any way. In his time, when people were thinking more and more about religion, there were some men and women who began to believe things which the Church said were wrong. These people were called heretics, and were sometimes punished and even killed. St. Bernard had no mercy on such people, and was always anxious to have them punished, for he thought that they did much harm to the people by teaching them wrong things. There were many heretics in the South of France.

There was one man called Peter de Bruys who was a priest but had done something very wrong, and so was not allowed to live any longer as a priest. He wandered about the South of France preaching against the priests, and saying that what they taught was wrong. He made a great bonfire of crosses and statues, which he said it was wrong to use. But the people were so angry that they took him and burned him alive.

There was another man, too, named Peter Waldez, a rich merchant belonging to the French city of Lyons. He was excommunicated, but long after his death his followers wandered about France and Italy preaching against the Church. These heretics were sometimes called the Poor Men of Lyons. The chief heretics in the South of France were called the Albigenses, because Albi was one of their chief towns.

St. Bernard was full of sorrow and anger against the heretics, and he blamed it all on one man. This was the famous Abelard, whose life story is one of the saddest and strangest in all history. He was born in Brittany, and like St. Bernard himself, he belonged to a noble family. While he was still a young boy people saw that he was going to be very clever. In those days the schools were still joined to monasteries or cathedrals, but some of the schools had become more famous than others, and when the news spread that a good teacher was to be found at any particular place, scholars would crowd to his school.

Abelard when he was a young man went from one great school to another. Before he was twenty he was at the school belonging to the Cathedral of Notre Dame at Paris, listening to the lectures of a famous teacher called William of Champeaux. But Abelard soon showed himself much cleverer than his master. He asked questions which William could not answer, and soon the students left their old master, and followed Abelard from place to place. At last he set up his school on the Mont Ste Geneviève, the famous hill in Paris looking down on the cathedral.

Abelard's teaching was very clear. He said that people must not believe what they were told just because they were told, but that students should see the reasons of the things they believed. He said that the older teachers had not really tried to make things clear, but 'lighted a fire, not to give light, but to fill the house with smoke.' After a while William of

Champeaux found that he had no pupils at all, and so gave up teaching in disgust. Abelard was afterwards made a canon, as a priest belonging to a cathedral was called, of Notre Dame at Paris.

One of the older canons named Fulbert had a young niece living in his house. Her name was Heloïse, and she was very beautiful and very clever. She could read Latin, and even Greek, and Abelard used to help her in her studies. After a while Abelard and Heloïse loved each other very much, and in the end they were married to each other. Fulbert was very angry about it all, because a priest was forbidden to get married. He was still more angry when Heloïse told people that they were not married. She did this because she was afraid that it would do harm to Abelard if people knew that he had married her. In the end Heloïse became a nun, and Abelard fled away from the anger of her uncle to a monastery.

He left the monastery of St. Denis outside Paris, because he quarreled with the other monks. Even now that he was a much sadder and wiser man, he could not help teaching what he thought was the truth. He made the monks very angry by saying that some of the things they said about their patron saint, St. Denis, were not true but only old tales. He still gave lectures, and crowds followed him.

After a while he set up another monastery in a lonely spot, but left it again, and Heloïse then went with some nuns, and lived the rest of her life in this convent of the Paraclete, as it was called. She always loved Abelard, and wrote the most beautiful letters to him, which we may still read.

St. Bernard hated the teaching of Abelard, not so much for the things he said as for the independent spirit which he encouraged. To St. Bernard his questioning and arguing about the things which the Church taught seemed little better than the teaching of heretics like Peter de Bruys or the Poor Men of Lyons. At last St. Bernard got a council of bishops to meet at the town of Sens in France, and they said that Abelard's teaching was heresy.

Abelard appealed to the Pope, that is, he would not agree that he was wrong, and offered to go to Rome and let the Pope judge the case.

On his way he stopped at the monastery of Cluny, which then had for its abbot a great and good man called Peter the Venerable. Here Abelard became very ill, and Peter, although he was as devoted to the Church and its teaching as St. Bernard himself, was very gentle and kind to Abelard. Indeed, Abelard begged to be received as a monk of Cluny, and very soon afterwards he died. Heloïse asked that his body might be buried at her convent of the Paraclete, and so it was. Years afterwards, when she died an old woman, her body was buried beside that of the man she had loved all her life.

Afterwards, they were moved from place to place for different reasons, but now they rest in one grave in the great cemetery of Père Lachaise at Paris, and there visitors may see it any day.

Some of Abelard's pupils became the greatest teachers of the time, and were honored by the Church, for although they taught the same things as Abelard they taught in a different way. But one of Abelard's pupils, a man called Arnold of Brescia (a town in North Italy, where he was born), had a very sad ending indeed. He was a canon regular, that is to say, he belonged to a church where the canons lived like monks, although they did the work of ordinary priests.

Arnold was very discontented with the Church as it was. He said that priests should not have any money at all, but should live on what the people gave them. He said, too, that it was not right that the Pope should rule the city of Rome. It was quite right, he said, that the Pope should rule the whole Church in religious things, but in things of this world he should have no power. He went to Rome and got the people to rebel against the Pope and set up a government of their own. One Pope fled away from Rome altogether, and for a time Arnold of Brescia got his way.

But when the English Pope, Adrian IV had crowned Frederick Barbarossa, the Emperor took Arnold of Brescia prisoner and gave him up to the Pope. He was tried for heresy and found guilty. He was killed and his body was burnt. The ashes were thrown into the river Tiber for fear the people who had followed him and loved him should carry them away and keep them as relics of a saint. Two years before St. Bernard himself had died, he had called Arnold 'the armor-bearer of his master Goliath,' meaning Abelard.

St. Bernard was the greatest man of his age. His one fault was his severity to men like these, but this did not come from any cruelty, but because he was afraid of the harm they might do to the Church and the people. Naturally, St. Bernard was very gentle and tender. He wrote some beautiful hymns in Latin, which are still sung in the Catholic Church. They have been put into English and are sung in other churches too.

England after the Conquest

We have seen how English dukes and kings took part in the crusades. The English people, too, shared in all the changes which were going on in the other countries of Western Europe. Monks from the new orders came to England, and monasteries of Cistercians, Carthusians, and regular canons were spread all over England. England had her saints, too, in the twelfth century. The two greatest were St. Anselm and St. Thomas Becket. St. Anselm was a monk from that same abbey of Bec in Normandy from which William the Conqueror had brought Archbishop Lanfranc. Lanfranc died soon after the Conqueror's son, William Rufus or the Red, became king.

The Red King was not only strict like his father, but he was wicked and cruel. For a long time he would not have a new archbishop at all, but he became ill, and was then so frightened that God would punish him that he asked Anselm to be archbishop. Anselm was very gentle and good. When he was abbot of Bec, the other monks were not always pleased, for if he saw poor and hungry people he would give away all the food in the monastery, never troubling about the fact that there would be nothing left for himself and his monks to eat.

Anselm did not want to be archbishop of Canterbury. He knew that as soon as the Red King was well again, he would forget all about God, and would be cruel once more to the Church and the people, and he thought that he would never be strong enough to struggle with such a king. He said that it would never do for a 'poor sheep' like himself to be put to the plough with a 'wild bull' like Rufus, instead of the two strong oxen, William the Conqueror and Lanfranc, who had worked together so well to make the English Church better.

But the bishops made him give in, and almost carried him to the church to be made archbishop. Everything happened just as St. Anselm expected. When the Red King got well again he behaved just as badly as ever, and in the end St. Anselm fled away to France, and stayed there till the Red King died.

Then his brother, Henry I, who was called 'Beauclerc,' or 'the Scholar,' became king. He was a clever man and a good king, and he wrote and asked St. Anselm to come back, like a father, to his son Henry and the English people. He came, and together Henry and he did all they could to make the people and the priests better. Priests had been forbidden to get married, but in the days before the Norman Conquest nearly all priests had wives. But now this was strictly forbidden.

Henry himself and his wife, the Good Queen Maud, gave a great deal of money to set up new monasteries. The king and the archbishop had one quarrel about investitures, the thing which the Emperor and the Pope were quarrelling about at the same time.

In England it was soon settled. Bishops were to have the ring and crozier given to them by the archbishop, but were to do homage for their lands to the king. The struggle was settled between the Pope and the Emperor in the same way a few years later. Henry's only son was drowned as he was sailing from France to England in the 'White Ship.'

The prince had given the sailors a great deal of beer to drink in his honor, and the nobles and ladies had danced on the deck of the ship in the moonlight. But the sailors were not paying attention to their work, and though it was a beautifully still and clear night, they let the ship strike against a rock. It was wrecked, and every one was drowned, except one poor butcher, who clung on to a floating piece of wood. When Henry heard of the death of his son, he was broken-hearted, and people said that he never smiled again. He got the nobles to promise that they would have his daughter Matilda for queen when he died.

The English had never had a queen to rule them without a king before, and some of the nobles broke their promise, and crowned Henry's nephew, Stephen, king. Then for nearly twenty years Matilda and Stephen fought. Stephen was a weak man, and the nobles did just what they liked. They built strong castles all over England, and fought with each other.

The people lived in misery, and the monks who wrote their chronicles, the only books of history which there were in those days, give long and terrible stories of the sufferings of the poor people when the cruel nobles took all they had from them and prevented them from growing things on the land. It was the only time that the feudal lords had things their own way in England, and the people could understand what the French and German peoples suffered until strong kings saved them from the nobles. In the end it was settled that Matilda should give up her right to the crown, but that her son Henry should be king when Stephen died. And so it was.

Henry II was a strong king. He soon put an end to the disorders of feudalism, and made the nobles pull down most of the castles which they had built in the time of Stephen. He tried to bring order in the Church too, and it was this which brought about a great quarrel with Thomas Becket, who is now looked upon as one of England's greatest saints. Before William the Conqueror came to England, priests and other people had always been tried and punished for doing wrong things by the same judges. But William had said that the Church should have courts of its own and priests should be tried in them only. This had been done.

But the punishments in the Church courts were not so severe as in the other courts. In those days every one who could read was called a clerk and could say that he would be tried in the Church courts. Henry thought that this was bad, for clerks could even commit murder and only have the easy punishments given by the Church courts. So he wanted to have clerks tried first in the Church courts, and if they were found guilty he said that they should then be tried again in the ordinary courts and be punished just like other people. Becket, who was archbishop of Canterbury, said that this was not fair.

Becket had at first been Henry's chancellor, and had been so lively and fond of pleasure and so friendly with the king that Henry thought that if he made him archbishop he could have things all his own way in the Church. But he found out his mistake. Becket did not want to be archbishop, but once he had said 'Yes,' he made up his mind to live like a saint. He gave up all his old amusements and spent his life

Becket's Return to England in 1170, Sculpted Panel from the 15th Century

161

in work and prayer. When Henry tried to get him to agree to his new arrangements for the Church, there was a terrible quarrel, and Becket, like Anselm before him, fled over the seas to be safe and peaceful.

After six years he was allowed to come back. Henry was in France, and heard there that Becket had punished some of the bishops for doing certain things without his permission while he was away. Henry flew into a terrible fit of anger and said, 'Is there nobody who will rid me of this insolent priest?'

Four of his knights who heard him immediately went out, crossed the sea to England, and as the archbishop was in his cathedral just before vespers or evensong, they attacked him, knocked him down dead with his brains dashed out on the stone floor. When the monks of the cathedral took up his body to make it ready to be buried, they found that the archbishop wore under all his splendid robes a shirt made of prickly hair which he always wore to do penance for his sins. The people honored him as a saint, and later he was called a saint by the Church.

Henry was full of horror when he heard the news. He often had these terrible fits of anger and said things which he did not mean. When he got back to England he went to do penance at the archbishop's tomb in the cathedral. He felt that he had committed a great sin, and he must have remembered, too, that Thomas Becket had once been his dear friend. He knelt at the tomb, dressed only in a shirt. He got the monks to scourge him with a whip, and then knelt alone praying at the tomb during the whole night.

For hundreds of years after this pilgrims came in crowds to pray at the tomb of St. Thomas Becket, and it was soon covered with their offerings of gold and jewels and became the richest shrine in England. After this Henry did not dare to interfere with the Church courts, but in time the worst kinds of crime, whether by priests or people, came to be tried in the ordinary courts.

THE GREAT CHARTER

There was another struggle between an English king and the archbishop of Canterbury which is even more important than the story of Thomas Becket. After the death of Henry II, England was ruled by Richard of the Lion Heart, the great knight and crusader. He died soon, and his wicked brother John became king after him. John was a handsome man and clever, but he cared for no one but himself. He was very cruel, and once when a noble rebelled against him he starved the man's wife and child to death. He made the people pay great sums of money in taxes and spent it on his own pleasures. Another thing which made the English people very angry was that John let the French king win Normandy from him. This seemed a great disgrace, but after this the English kings thought more of England and less of Normandy and stayed more in England instead of always sailing over to France. John had a great quarrel with the Pope.

This Pope was Innocent III, the greatest since Hildebrand. There was a quarrel between the king and the monks of Canterbury about choosing an archbishop, and in the end the Pope chose one himself. This was a good priest named Stephen Langton. John said he would not have him for archbishop, and then the Pope put all England under an interdict. This meant that the churches were closed. There could not be any services. Babies could not be baptized, and men and women could not get married. All this seemed very dreadful to the people. For five years John would not let Stephen Langton come to England. Then the Pope said he should be king no longer. This terrified John, and he gave in. The interdict was taken off the country. John gave up his crown and took it back from a cardinal who took the place of the Pope.

Stephen Langton came and was made archbishop. He immediately began to help the nobles to force King John to rule better. They wrote down many things which the king was to promise to do, and these promises were afterwards called the Great Charter. The nobles got together an army and marched to meet the king at London, but he fled to Windsor. At last he saw that he must give in, and at a place nearby, called Runnymede, he signed the Great Charter. But he never meant to keep his promises.

When he had signed the Charter and the nobles had gone, he threw himself on the ground shrieking in anger. Afterwards he got Pope Innocent to set him free from his promise. Then the nobles said they would take Louis, the son of the French king, to be king of England instead of John. A French army came to England, but soon John died. He had been nearly drowned in crossing the Wash, and his crown and jewels were lost in the water with his other luggage. Afterwards he was ill, and made himself worse by eating fruit and drinking cider, and so died.

The nobles then joined together and made John's baby son, Henry, king. It is said that he was crowned with his mother's bracelet. There was much trouble sometimes after this, but after the Great Charter no English king ever dared again to treat the English people so badly, and it was chiefly Stephen Langton whom the English people had to thank for the signing of the Charter. So we see how in England, just as in the other countries of Europe at that time, the monks and priests took a leading part in history. In the century which followed we shall see great kings and soldiers and greater saints still.

King John signing Magna Charta.

CHAPTER XXIV—THE THIRTEENTH CENTURY

A Pope in the Thirteenth Century (From an old stained-glass window in the cathedral at Chartres).

AT the beginning of the thirteenth century, the Western Church was ruled by the greatest of all the popes, Innocent III. We have seen how Pope Innocent interfered in affairs in England. But in all the other countries of Europe it was the same. He was a very handsome and noble-looking man. He belonged to a noble Roman family, and became Pope when he was only thirty-seven years old, which was young for a pope. He lived a good life, and was very kind and gentle, though sometimes his fierce temper would break out.

He believed that the Pope should rule over all the world and that the kings should obey him, or if they did not, that he could take their kingdoms from them as he had threatened to do with John. Pope Innocent was the first Pope who was really able to do these things, and indeed he was the last, for no Pope after him was able to behave in this way. The kings and people were ready to obey the Pope in religious matters, but would not agree that he was over them in other things.

Yet Pope Innocent used his power well. King Philip Augustus of France was growing more and more powerful. It was he who won Normandy from King John, and he made the feudal lords obey him, so that France became a strong kingdom like England. But Philip Augustus was not a good man. He married a young Danish princess called Ingeborg, but the day after the marriage he sent her away, and said he would not have her any more for his wife. He then married another lady.

Pope Innocent was very angry, and sent word to the French king that he must take back his proper wife. Philip Augustus would not, and so France, like England, was put under an interdict. Then the

3. CHARTRES: KATHEDRALE. 1 : 400.

South elevation, Cathedrale Notre-Dame de Chartres, built in the 12th and 13th centuries. Drawing by G. Dehio and G. von Bezold.

king gave in, and soon after when the new wife died he took Ingeborg back, but it was twenty years before he behaved to her as though she was really his wife. All this time Innocent would not be friendly with the king, but after this they became great friends.

Innocent was very anxious that the crusades should go on, and so they did through all the thirteenth century, but though great men joined them, there was never any real success. One great result of the crusades was that there was much more trading between East and West, and in time the ships of Venice, the city which had grown up among the lagoons in the North of the Adriatic Sea, got most of this trade. Venice became rich and important. At the same time the Eastern Empire lost a great deal of its trade and was becoming weaker and weaker. Its emperors were weak and stupid men. Now, when in the year 1203 the Fourth Crusade was begun, it was arranged that the Venetian ships should carry the crusaders to the East. But instead of sailing to Palestine, the Venetians attacked Constantinople and made themselves master of it.

Constantinople was a most beautiful city, full of great buildings and statues and treasures, some of which belonged to the great days of the Roman Empire. The Venetians robbed the churches and other buildings, and sent back some of the greatest treasures to help to make their own beautiful city still more beautiful. Most of the North Italian cities were independent by this time. Venice was a republic and was ruled by a duke, the Doge, as he was called, chosen by the people.

Every year at the same date, the Doge, sitting on a throne in a beautiful ship, hung with scarlet and gold stuffs, sailed through the canals of Venice into the harbor. There the Doge dropped a golden ring into the water, saying, 'We wed thee, O Sea, in token of our true and eternal dominion over thee.' It was a blind old doge called Dandalo who led the Venetians against Constantinople on the Fourth Crusade. Pope Innocent was not pleased that the crusaders had attacked a Christian city instead of the Mohammedans, but he comforted himself, for the church of the Eastern Empire did not obey the Pope, and now for nearly sixty years Constantinople was ruled by princes from the West, just as the kingdom of Jerusalem had been. In the end, the Greeks won their empire back, but Crete and other islands belonged to the Venetians for hundreds of years.

Every year Venice grew richer and more beautiful. Marble palaces and churches were built along her canals, and even now, when the city is no longer great, visitors gliding in gondolas, as Venetian boats are called, along her canals are filled with wonder at their beauty. Pope Innocent was always trying to stir people up for a fresh crusade, and in his time people must have been talking continually about the Holy Land.

A Doge of Venice

THE CHILDREN'S CRUSADE

Frederick II and Innocent III, Cathedral in Koln, Germany

In the year 1212, at a time when no one seemed to be taking any notice of the Pope's requests, a young French shepherd boy called Stephen made up his mind to lead a crusade himself. He got together thousands of other young boys, and they marched south to Marseilles on the coast of France. Stephen promised those who followed him that he would lead them over the seas without wetting their feet. But most of these children, for they were only boys, were carried off by slave-dealers, and sold as slaves in Egypt.

About the same time a boy called Nicolas, from Cologne in Germany, got together an army of young boys, and led them into Italy, meaning to go on to the Holy Land, but no one knows what became of them. These expeditions were called the 'Children's Crusade,' and Pope Innocent said to the men whom he wanted to go to the Holy Land, 'The very children put us to shame.' At last a new crusade did start.

The Fifth Crusade had for its leader the Emperor Frederick II, who was one of the greatest men of the Middle Ages. He was the grandson of Frederick Barbarossa, and his father was the Emperor Henry VI. His father died while he was a baby, and his mother Constance died soon afterwards. She was a Norman, and from her he had the kingdom of Sicily.

While he was a boy, Pope Innocent looked after Frederick. He was brought up at Palermo, and he was a very clever and nice-looking boy. He learned all he could from the Greeks and Arabs of Sicily, and knew so much that people called him the 'Wonder of the World.' Pope Innocent died when Frederick was only twenty.

Although Frederick had been brought up by a pope, this did not prevent him from quarrelling with the popes who came after. Indeed, the quarrel between the Emperor and the popes was perhaps bitterer than ever under Frederick II. Frederick pretended to be a good Christian, but people said that he did not really believe the things which the Church taught. He made friends with the Arabs in Sicily and South Italy, and lived in great luxury as they did. He gathered scholars and poets together in his palace, and even studied the use of medicines. He had a great number of camels brought from the East, and the Sultan of Egypt sent him a present of an elephant, which people thought a very curious and wonderful animal. Very few people had ever seen such a thing, although four hundred years before Charles the Great had had one too.

The Pope after Innocent was called Honorius III. He had once been Frederick's teacher, and was always very gentle with him. But Frederick only made use of his friendship to please himself. He got the Pope to agree to his son becoming emperor after him, although he had promised that he would not make him emperor and king of Sicily too, as the Pope thought that this was too much power for one man. All during the time of Honorius, Frederick was promising to go on crusade, but he never did.

Then the new Pope, Gregory IX, at last lost patience, and excommunicated Frederick for not keeping his promise. Then at last Frederick led a great army to the East, and now the Pope was angry again, for he said that a man under sentence of excommunication should not dare to fight in the Holy War. There was practically no fighting, but Frederick made a ten years' peace with the Mohammedans, and Bethlehem, Nazareth, and Jerusalem were handed over to the Christians. Frederick crowned himself king of Jerusalem, but no priest could be got to go through the services of the Church for him.

Frederick then went back to Italy, where he found the Pope's armies in Apulia, part of his kingdom in South Italy. Frederick soon drove them out, and then at last peace was made between the Pope and the Emperor. Frederick cared much more for Italy than he did for Germany. In his kingdom in the South he made himself a despot. No one else had any power at all. But in Germany he let the great lords do what they liked, and although his father and grandfather had done a great deal to join the German states into one kingdom, Frederick let them become almost independent, and it was this which helped to keep Germany broken up for hundreds of years into little states, instead of being one nation like France or England.

Frederick's son Henry, who was to be emperor after him, rebelled against his father and was shut up in prison in Apulia. There he was to stay until he died, but he escaped, and, as he preferred to die rather than be caught and put in prison again, he drove his horse over a high precipice, and so killed himself.

Frederick had a long struggle, too, with the towns of Northern Italy, and won great victories over them, and he quarreled once more with the Pope. Frederick invited all kings and princes to join him in fighting against the Pope, for he said the Pope wanted to take all power from them, but the other kings took no notice. Pope Gregory in his turn said that Frederick was wicked in his life and a heretic in his beliefs, and tried to get the Germans to rebel against him. He even offered the Emperor's crown to the brother of King Louis IX of France, but the French nobles told the Pope that he could not give or take a king's crown,

A Great Gothic Building: The Cathedral at Rheims, Built in the 13th and 14th Centuries

except with the advice of a general council, that is, a meeting of bishops from different parts of the world.

Pope Gregory did try to get a council together at Rome. The ships of Genoa were to carry the bishops to the council, but Frederick had nearly all the greatest towns on the coast of Italy on his side; chief of them was Pisa. They got together a fleet, and captured the Genoese ships. The bishops were carried off to Naples, and were tormented with hunger and thirst and then thrown into prison. Frederick was even going to attack Rome when Pope Gregory died.

A new pope, Innocent IV, was just as bitter as Gregory, and the Emperor again threatened to attack Rome. Innocent fled to Lyons in the South of France, and there called a council, which said that Frederick should be Emperor no longer. King Louis of France tried to make peace, but the enemies were too bitter. Rebellion broke out against Frederick in different parts of Germany and Italy, and in these later years of his life he lost instead of winning battles. Frederick grew very unhappy, and began to look on every one as his enemy.

He thought that his faithful friend, Peter della Vigna, who had always served him well, had turned against him, and he had his eyes put out. He then dragged him with him, dressed in rags, wherever he went, until in the end Peter killed himself. Frederick's favorite son Enzio was taken prisoner by the people of Bologna, one of the North Italian cities which fought against him, and the Emperor was told that he was to be kept in prison all his life. Soon after Frederick became very ill and died. It was said that he made peace with the Church, and had himself dressed in the habit of a Cistercian monk, and so died peacefully and happily. Others said that he died cursing, and in the greatest misery, but probably this is not true.

Frederick II was the last of the great emperors who struggled against the great popes. When Frederick II died his son Conrad ruled as king in Germany. He sent his brother Manfred to rule Sicily for him. But the Pope was no more friendly to Conrad than he had been to Frederick. He offered Sicily to different people, among them Henry III of England, who gladly paid large sums of money to the Pope, who promised Sicily to Henry's second son, Edmund.

A crusade was preached against Conrad and fighting began, but before long the Emperor died, leaving a little son called Conradin. Manfred then fought and won Naples and Sicily for himself, but the Pope now offered the crown of Sicily to Charles of Anjou, the brother of King Louis IX of France. Charles led a great army against Manfred and killed him.

Conradin was now fifteen years old. He was a brave and handsome boy, and he made up his mind to march from Germany and win back the kingdom of the two Sicilies from Charles of Anjou. He took with him his dearest friend Frederick, Duke of Austria, and a small army, but he was taken prisoner, and he and his friend had their heads cut off by Charles's order.

Charles of Anjou was a cruel ruler, and the people of Sicily and South Italy hated him. They hated him, too, for his cruelty to Conradin. As Conradin was going to lay his head on the block, he had thrown down his glove (which was the way a knight invited another to fight), and had declared that the German people would wash out in French blood this insult to their king.

It was not very many years before the Sicilians themselves took a terrible revenge on their French rulers. A French soldier insulted a Sicilian girl on the street, and her lover stabbed him to the heart. It was the signal for an attack on all the French in the island. The massacre began as the church bells were ringing for vespers, and went on through the whole night. It was always afterwards spoken of as the Sicilian Vespers. Soon after Pedro of Aragon, the husband of Conradin's cousin, fought Charles and won Sicily from him. French rulers still governed Naples, but in a few years this, too, went to a Spanish ruler. Conradin was the last of the family of Frederick II.

After his death, the seven German princes who had the right of electing the Emperor, chose foreigners like Richard, duke of Cornwall, the brother of Henry III of England, or Alfonso the Wise, king of Castile. But at last they saw that they must elect a German prince, so that the Emperor could keep order between the states. But after Frederick's time these rulers were German kings and hardly interfered at all in Italy. The great towns of Northern Italy began each to conquer the smaller towns round them, and soon Venice, Milan and Florence was each the capital of a little Italian state.

St. Louis of France

King Louis IX of France, who had tried to make peace between the Pope and the Emperor, was very different from Frederick. He was a saint and a splendid king besides. He, too, had become king as a baby, when his father, Louis VIII, the son of Philip Augustus, died. His mother was a Spanish lady, Blanche of Castile. She was a very brave and determined woman, and when the feudal nobles, whom Philip Augustus had kept in order, tried to get their own way again she soon put down their rebellion. She looked well after her boy, and had him carefully taught and trained, so that he was not at all spoilt by being a king so soon.

He loved his prayers, and when he was grown up he would get up at midnight to go to matins in the church just as the monks did. His nobles, indeed, grumbled because they said he wasted so much time in prayer, but he reminded them that they wasted more time still in gambling and hunting.

But St. Louis was not sad or gloomy. He was always good-tempered and patient, and could not bear people to say unkind things about each other. He hated swearing or rough ways of speaking. Every day he brought a hundred poor people to eat at his table. For himself he took any food which was set before him, and always added water to his wine. He went to see sick people in their homes, and would wash the feet of beggars and even nursed lepers.

Yet St. Louis found plenty of time, too, to rule his country well. He was strong and healthy, taller by a head than any of his knights, finely shaped with bright eyes and long fair hair. He loved his children very much, and was a splendid husband and father. He kept France orderly and happy, and although he was strict with the feudal lords he never cheated them or used them roughly as his grandfather, Philip Augustus, had done. There was never a better king or a nobler knight than St. Louis of France.

St. Louis went twice on crusade. The first time was in the year 1248. Four years before the Christians had again lost Jerusalem, and this time they lost it forever. It was the Sultan of Egypt who had captured it, and it was against him that St. Louis led his army.

St. Louis was a brave soldier and a good leader, but the swampy lands of the mouth of the Nile were difficult to cross for soldiers who were not used to them. The heat was dreadful, and there was very little food. A plague broke out among the soldiers, and soon St. Louis was taken prisoner. His whole army laid down their arms, but nearly all were killed. Only St. Louis and the rich lords were kept alive and set free when a large ransom was paid.

Then St. Louis went on to the Holy Land, but he would not go to Jerusalem, for, like Richard of the Lion Heart, he could not bear to see the Holy City, when he knew that he could not win it back for the Christians. St. Louis brought back to France a crown of thorns, which was said to be that with which Our Lord was crowned, and the lance which pierced His side and the sponge which moistened His lips.

He built a beautiful little chapel in Paris in which these relics were kept. It was called the Sainte Chapelle, and may still be seen today. After St. Louis came back from the crusade he always wore quite plain woollen clothes in winter and robes of dark-colored silks in summer.

St. Louis, King of France, Crosses the Sea to the Holy Land *(From a thirteenth-century stained-glass window in the Abbey of St. Denis).*

The Christians still had Antioch and the other cities of the kingdom of Jerusalem, but they were always quarrelling among themselves. At last the Sultan of Egypt took Antioch too, and threatened Acre and the other cities. Once more St. Louis got ready to go on crusade, but he died on the way in the year 1270. His last words were, 'Jerusalem, Jerusalem.' His followers sadly carried his body back to France. Charles of Anjou, the cruel king of Sicily, was with St. Louis when he died at Tunis. Charles was only anxious to win something for himself from the crusade, and made peace when the ruler of Tunis promised to pay double of the tribute to the kings of Sicily which he was already paying.

Edward of England, the son of the English king Henry III and grandson of King John, sailed up to join the crusade, just as the treaty had been signed. He was very angry, and sailed on with his own thirteen ships to Acre. He stayed in the Holy Land a year, but once more Charles of Anjou arranged for peace with the Sultan of Egypt. The Sultan tried to have Edward secretly killed with a poisoned weapon, but he was wounded and not killed. His good wife Eleanor sucked the poison from the wound, and so saved his life.

THE END OF THE CRUSADES

Edward left the Holy Land to come back to be king of England when his father died. He was the last great Western prince who really went on crusade. A year or two later the Pope preached a great crusade, but died before it started, and the crusade was given up. In a few years more even the few places which remained of the kingdom of Jerusalem were taken by the Mohammedans, and only a few ruins remain today to tell the tale.

The crusades may seem to us to have failed altogether, but after all great things had been done in them, and though some of the men who joined them were selfish and ambitious, many others were very noble. It was a splendid thing that the kings and princes of Europe could agree to go together, and fight for their religion in far-off lands. It was a pity that they could not always agree, and that the journeys were not arranged better. If only the kingdom of Jerusalem had been kept in the hands of Christians, the Turks who have since conquered Greece and other parts of Eastern Europe, and ruled them very cruelly, might have been kept out of Europe altogether.

Edward of England, the last of the great crusaders, was called Edward I when he became king of England. There had been other kings named Edward, but not since the Norman Conquest, and it was from that time that the kings were now counted. But by the time Edward became king of England, the English and the Normans in England had become one people. Edward was an old English name, and Edward I was a real English king.

In his reign the English language began to be used in the courts of law. Before that French had been spoken there. Edward was a fine handsome man, like St. Louis, taller by a head than ordinary men. He was not a saint, but he was a very good man. Even when he was a boy, he had been very wise and sensible. His father, Henry III, the son of John, who was crowned king of England while still a baby, had not been a very good ruler. He was a good man, but not a wise king. He loved poetry and artistic things, and in those days the French people knew much more about these things than the English did. Henry filled his court with Frenchmen. Some of them were wicked and greedy men, and very cruel to the people.

At last a great English nobleman, called Earl Simon de Montfort, made up his mind to fight the king and make him send away the foreigners, and rule England properly. Earl Simon took the king prisoner, and the young Edward too, but after a time Edward got away, and he himself got together an army and fought against Earl Simon. A great battle was fought at Evesham in the South of England, and Earl Simon was killed. Then Henry was able to rule England again, but Edward told him that Earl Simon was quite right in wanting him to send the foreigners away, and so Henry ruled England with Edward's advice until he died, and when Edward became king he, too, remembered the lessons he had learnt from Earl Simon, and ruled England well and wisely. So although Earl Simon died in a struggle against his king, England ought to be very grateful to him, for he fought and died for the sake of his country.

One great thing Edward learned from Earl Simon. Ever since the Norman Conquest, the kings of England, when they asked advice at all, had called a meeting of the great nobles; but Simon de Montfort got each county to choose men to send to parliament, and told some of the chief towns to do so too, and so the ordinary people began to have a share in the government of the country. King Edward saw that this was a good thing, and so he did the same, and this is how our parliament really began.

Edward I was a very brave soldier. He was anxious to win Wales and Scotland, and join them to England. In his time Wales, whose people were descendants of the Britons who had been driven West by the English when they first came to this country, was ruled by princes of their own. Edward made the princes pay tribute to the English king, and afterwards when they rebelled, he conquered Wales, and it has belonged to England ever since.

He tried to do the same with Scotland, but Scottish heroes like Robert Bruce and William Wallace fought hard for their country, and all his life Edward was fighting to win Scotland, but never did. He died on his way with an army to Scotland, and he told his son, who became Edward II, to carry his body with him to battle, and never to bury it until Scotland had been won.

But Edward II was a weak and foolish king. He took no notice of his promise, and soon Scotland was quite free from England, and remained so for three hundred years longer, when a Scottish king became king of England too, and so joined the two countries. But in spite of his failures, Edward I was perhaps the greatest of our old English kings and one of the noblest knights of his time.

Chapter XXV—St. Dominic and St. Francis

We have already seen how full of great men the thirteenth century was». There were great popes like Pope Innocent III, great kings like St. Louis of France and Edward I of England, and great emperors like Frederick II.

But the greatest men of all in that wonderful time were two saints, St. Francis of Assisi and St. Dominic. Both these saints founded new orders which were different from the older orders of monks, and did work especially needed at the time. The stories of the two saints are very much alike and yet very different.

St. Francis was born in a little town called Assisi, among the hills in the middle of Italy. His real name was John Bernadone, but his father, who was a cloth-merchant, called him 'little Francis,' or the little Frenchman, and the boy kept the name when he grew up. In those days there were not, of course, any big shops like there are today. Merchants travelled from place to place selling their goods, and Pietro Bernadone, the father of St. Francis, travelled a great deal in France. Pietro gained a good deal of money, and the little Francis was always well dressed. He was a merry little boy with dark skin and laughing brown eyes, and he was always the leader in fun and mischief with the other boys of Assisi.

But as he grew up into a young man, he grew very serious indeed. It was a time when men were growing more religious, and Francis could think of nothing else. His father was very angry once when Francis, who was helping him with his business, sold a great deal of cloth, and gave the money to a priest to help him to build again his poor little chapel, which was falling into ruins.

Pietro now said he would have nothing more to do with him, and took him before the bishop of Assisi to have him disinherited, that is to say, that nothing he possessed should ever go to his son. Francis said that this only made him understand better than ever that he had no father except his Father in heaven. He took off his clothes, saying that he would have nothing at all which came from his father on earth.

The bishop gave Francis a cloak, and for the next few years Francis lived as a beggar in Assisi, nursing the sick and helping the poor. When he was a boy he had had a great horror of the terrible disease of leprosy, but now he made it his special duty to take care of the lepers.

There was a little old chapel in the flat land below the hills of Assisi. It was called the Chapel of St. Mary of the Angels. One day, when St. Francis was hearing Mass there, he suddenly thought of the words of our Lord in the Bible, which told the apostles to preach the gospel and to 'carry neither gold nor silver, nor money in their girdles, nor bag, nor two coats, nor sandals, nor staff.' It seemed to Francis that these words were spoken to him, and though he was not a priest he went up to Assisi and began to preach to the people. Other young men joined him, and when there were twelve of them altogether Francis said, 'Let us go to Rome and ask the blessing of the Pope.'

And so they did. With bare feet and dressed only in rough brown frocks, with a rope tied round the waist for girdles, they went to Rome, and Pope Innocent III blessed them and agreed to their way of living, and St. Francis went back happily to Assisi. Many of his old companions who had laughed at him, and thrown stones at him when he first began to live like a beggar, now followed him. It was very difficult not to love Francis, for he himself loved everybody and everything. His great wish was to live just as Our Lord had lived and to be as meek and gentle as possible.

Perhaps no one who has ever lived has been so nearly perfect as St. Francis was. He loved poverty for Christ's sake, and was never happier than when quite without food. No Franciscan, as the men who joined the new order were called, were allowed to carry money. They had to beg for food, and if no one gave it to them, then they must go without and be glad for Christ's sake.

Yet St. Francis was always joyful and even merry. He would sing as he tramped barefoot along the dusty roads of Italy, for soon the Franciscans began to go from place to place to preach. He said that poverty was his lady and his bride, and he loved her more than any man could love a wife. Franciscans were soon travelling in all the countries of Europe. They were called Friars Minor or 'Little Brothers.' Wherever they went they lived as St. Francis had taught them.

All over Western Europe now towns were growing up, and in most of them there were very poor people. It was in the poorest parts of the towns that the Franciscans built their houses and churches. At first these houses were very plain, although the thirteenth century was the time when the great Gothic churches, with their pointed arches and beautiful carvings and statues, were being built. After a time the Franciscans forgot some of the things St. Francis had told them, and built fine churches too, but not at first.

The Franciscans preached in plain simple language, so that the people could understand easily, and so they taught and comforted the people whom the ordinary priests had often left quite to themselves. The older orders of monks had often become very rich by this time, and also they had their monasteries chiefly in the country. The Franciscans travelled, too, into far-

St. Francis of Assisi Takes the 'Lady Poverty' to Be His Bride (*From the painting by Giotto in the Church of St. Francis at Assisi*).

off countries. St. Francis himself went to the Holy Land and preached on the way to the Sultan of Egypt.

Before the century was over, Franciscans travelled right across Asia and preached at the court of the 'Great Khan,' the ruler of a people called the Mongols.

St. Francis lived the last years of his life at Assisi, preaching and praying. His chief thought was of the terrible sufferings of Our Lord, and before he died, in some mysterious way, his own hands and feet and breast had on them wounds like those made by the nails and lance in the Body of Christ.

When St. Francis died, his body was buried at Assisi, and a great church was built above his tomb. On the walls there may still be seen wonderful paintings by Giotto, one of the earliest of the great Italian painters. In them we may see stories of the life of St. Francis, and there is one very beautiful picture which shows St. Francis taking the 'Lady Poverty' for his bride.

After the death of St. Francis the Franciscans still went on with their work, but in time they came to use money and to live very much like the older monks, though they always went on doing good work among the poor, and even in England today we may still find the friars of St. Francis doing the work which St. Francis and his companions did seven hundred years ago.

St. Dominic lived and did his work at the same time as St. Francis. He was a Spaniard, and belonged to a noble family of Castile. Very early he became a priest and a regular canon. While on a visit to the South of France, he made up his mind to spend his life in preaching against the heretics there, who were called the Albigensians. Although these people thought that they were much better than ordinary Christians, they taught some very dreadful things. They thought that everything about the body was bad, and that only the soul was good. They even thought it was a noble thing to starve oneself to death, or to kill babies and so free their souls from their bodies.

St. Dominic went about preaching better things to these heretics, and other young men joined him. They wore a white frock with a black cloak, and were soon called the Preaching Friars.

St. Dominic, like St. Francis, wished his friars to be poor, and for a long time they lived very much like the Franciscans. But their chief work was preaching against heresy. St. Dominic was very gentle like St. Francis. He would spend his nights on the stone floors of a church, only stopping in his prayers to go quietly to look at his friars as they lay sleeping, and to cover them up more warmly. He could not bear to see other people suffering, and would cry from pity.

He had a very noble and beautiful face, and his friars said that a heavenly light shone round his head. He had very beautiful hands. St. Dominic's preaching did not put an end to the heresy of the Albigensians, and in the end the Pope preached a great crusade against them. Simon de Montfort, the father of the great Earl Simon who fought against Henry III, led this crusade, and in the end the Albigensians were nearly all killed, and so their heresy died out. But St. Dominic himself did not take any part in the crusade. He trusted altogether to preaching the truth, and hated the idea of fighting. Both the Dominicans and Franciscans often preached in the open air, and great crowds of people would gather round to hear them.

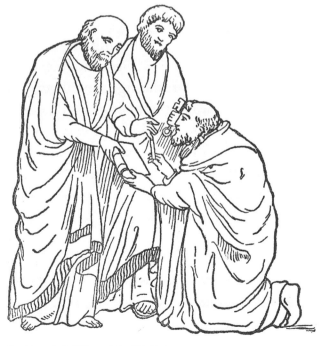

St. Dominic Blessed by St. Peter

The Black Friars, as the Dominicans were soon called because of their black cloaks, were always good scholars, and very soon they became the greatest teachers of philosophy and theology in all the countries of Europe. The schools, like that at Paris where Abelard had taught, had now been turned into universities. In the universities the teachers banded themselves together, and got privileges from kings or popes. There were soon universities in most of the great towns, where great teachers had taught in the twelfth century. Scholars and teachers from Paris had come to England, and set up schools at Oxford, which soon became a university too. Cambridge became a university soon after. In Italy and Spain, too, the universities spread.

Still, as in the old days, scholars flocked to the place where a great teacher of any subject could be found. At Paris or at Oxford there were not only French or English students, but many foreigners as well. It was not long before the Grey Friars, as the Franciscans were called, and the Black Friars too, were found teaching in the universities. The greatest philosopher and teacher of the thirteenth century was an Italian Dominican friar called Thomas of Aquino, and now generally called St. Thomas Aquinas. He wrote a very wonderful book on philosophy, and another on theology. He wrote, too, some wonderful and beautiful Latin hymns.

The Franciscans, too, were great hymn writers. An Italian Franciscan, St. Bonaventura, wrote a wonderful Latin hymn called the 'Dies Iras,' or the 'Day of Wrath,' which is still sung in Catholic churches today.

Another great Franciscan was an Englishman called Roger Bacon. The Franciscans studied the uses of herbs and medicines, to help them to cure sick people, and Roger Bacon was the first man in the Middle Ages who said that people should try to find out all about the world and things in it by making experiments, that is, doing things and seeing what would happen, instead of just believing the teaching which was passed on from one generation to another. Roger Bacon's way of studying science has been followed now for many years, but in his own time his teaching seemed very dangerous. He was even kept in prison for fourteen years, but was let out before he died.

There were nuns, too, belonging to both the new orders. The Franciscan nuns were called 'Poor Clares,' from the name of St. Clare, who was the first woman to follow St. Francis. She was only a girl of seventeen when she begged St. Francis to give her the habit or frock of a Franciscan. She belonged to a noble family of Assisi, and her father was very angry, but Clare was determined to lead the life she had chosen. Her sister Agnes and many of her friends and relations joined her, and they had their convent at the little church of San Damiano outside Assisi, which St. Francis had given his father's money to rebuild.

There St. Clare lived with her nuns dressed in rough frocks, like the Friars Minor with bare feet, and there she lived the strictest of lives. The 'Poor Clares' lived always in their convents, and gave up all their time to praying and working. There are many convents of Poor Clares still.

Then, too, people in the world who were married and had children, or for some other reason could not become monks and nuns, were joined to these orders and called 'Tertiaries.' They had to live as good lives as they possibly could, and say certain prayers, and when they died they had the privilege of being buried in the habit of a Franciscan or a Dominican, according to which order they belonged. So St. Dominic and St. Francis and their friars played a very important part in the lives of the people in the later Middle Ages.

THE GREAT POET DANTE

There was one other great man born in this century whose name is better known to people today than even those of St. Francis and St. Dominic. This was the great Italian poet, Dante. We have seen how the North Italian towns at last made themselves practically free from the Emperor's rule and governed themselves. Venice became a republic, governed by men chosen from a few noble families. Others, like Milan, soon fell into the hands of despots, and were ruled by one family, who passed on power from father to son for many years.

The beautiful city of Florence, on the river Arno, was at first a democracy. In nearly all these cities there were quarrels always going on between different sides. Sometimes one side would be for the Pope and the other for the Emperor, and long after the struggle between emperors and popes was over, the names of Ghibellines and Guelfs, as the supporters of the emperors and those of the popes were called, went on.

A little after the middle of the thirteenth century, there was born in one of the great families of Florence a little boy called Dante Alighieri. Dante grew up in the beautiful city of Florence, and loved it dearly. He tells us himself how, when he was a boy of nine, he met at a children's party a little girl just a little younger than himself. She was dressed in a simple frock of a beautiful red color, and from the moment he saw her the boy thought her the most beautiful thing on earth.

He always loved her, but though she grew to be a woman in Florence, he only met her again once or twice. She married another Florentine, and died before she was thirty years old, but Dante never forgot her, and he wrote about her afterwards in his wonderful poetry.

He himself married a Florentine lady, and had four children. He had an important place in the government of his city, but when he was thirty-five the party to which he did not belong got power in Florence, and Dante was banished from the city he loved so much. An order was given that if he came back he should be burnt to death. His wife stayed in Florence, but Dante spent the rest of his life wandering from city to city in Italy.

He was always welcomed and honored by the rulers of other cities, but he was always homesick for his own beloved Florence. At last he was told that he could go back if he apologized and paid a fine, but he said he would never go back unless he was to be received with honor. He spent his years of exile in writing poetry.

His great poem is called the *Divina Commedia* or the *Divine Comedy.* It was the first great poem of the Middle Ages written by a poet in his own language. Dante, like all the scholars of the time, had been trained in Latin, which was the language used by all scholars, and of course the language of the Church.

But Dante chose to write in his own beautiful Italian language. In the *Divine Comedy,* Dante described the life after death as it was imagined to be by the men of the Middle Ages. The great poem was divided into three parts, describing hell and the punishments of lost souls, purgatory and the sufferings of those good people who died before they were perfect, and heaven and the joy of good people freed from all stain of sin.

Dante described himself as passing in a vision or dream through all this, and it is Bea-

Statue of Beatrice consoling Dante, by Giovanni Battista Comolli, on the grounds of the Villa Melzi (Bellagio), on Lake Como, Italy.

trice, grave and beautiful, who leads him through the courts of heaven.

Everything which the great philosophers and theologians like St. Thomas Aquinas taught about God and religion is to be found described poetically in this wonderful poem. The language itself is very musical and beautiful, and everyone who really wants to understand the Middle Ages should read it through. Dante died at last in Ravenna, and was buried there.

In later years the Florentines would have given a great deal to have his body buried in his own city, but the people of Ravenna would not give it up. One of Dante's great dreams was that all Italy should be joined together as one nation, but that did not come until nearly five hundred years after his time.

Chapter XXVI—The Black Death

The men who lived in the fourteenth century were different in many ways from those of the thirteenth. It was not a time of great saints. The crusades were over. Sometimes a prince or noble would get ready to go on a new crusade, but never went. There were great kings in the fourteenth century, but they were not such splendid men as St. Louis of France or Edward I of England. The great popes, too, had passed away. They no longer quarreled with the emperors about ruling the whole world, for they soon found that they had no real power in ordinary matters over kings and princes, but only in matters of religion.

For seventy years, indeed, the popes lived at Avignon in the South of France instead of at Rome, and were very much under the power of the French kings. In 1294 Boniface VIII became Pope. He was full of the old ideas of Hildebrand and Innocent III about the greatness of the popes. He gave an order that in no country should priests pay any sort of tax to the state. Edward I of England, although he was a good and pious man, was very angry at this, and made the priests pay their taxes all the same. Philip the Fair of France, the grandson of St. Louis, was very angry too. But Boniface took no notice.

The next year he invited pilgrims to come from all parts of the world for a great feast in honor of the Apostles. People came in thousands and thousands, and Boniface was delighted. It took two men working all the time to shovel the offerings of money from the tomb of St. Peter.

Meanwhile the quarrel between the Pope and the French king went on. Philip declared that France was independent of the Pope; Boniface replied by threatening to take the French throne from Philip. At last Philip sent some of his servants to attack Boniface in his palace at Anagni, up in the mountains near Rome. These men burst into the palace, threatened the Pope, and kept him prisoner for three days. Then his Italian friends went to his help.

But Boniface had received a dreadful shock, and a few days after he died. He understood at last that the Pope was not all-powerful, and his heart was broken. Another Pope was elected, but died almost immediately. People said that he was poisoned by some figs sent to him by the servants of the French king. The next Pope was a Frenchman, and it was he who chose to set up his court at Avignon, a town in the South of France, but which had been given to the Pope.

For seventy years the popes were Frenchmen and lived at Avignon. The Italians and the people of the other countries of Europe did not like this, because it gave the French kings too much power over the popes. People mocked and said that the Pope was really a prisoner, and afterwards this time in the history of the popes was always called the Babylonish Captivity, a name taken from the seventy years during which the Jews had been kept captive in Babylon.

THE HUNDRED YEARS' WAR

It seemed a very strange thing to people in the fourteenth century to have the popes living at Avignon, when they had lived at Rome during so many hundreds of years. But many other strange things happened too, and there was a great deal of discontent and excitement. The English and French people began a great war with each other, which lasted altogether for a hundred years. Sometimes it would stop for a few years, but never for very many. It was called the 'Hundred Years' War.' It caused the greatest misery to the French people, and though for many years the English won most of the battles, it did them no good in the end.

The war was begun by Edward III of England, the grandson of Edward I. Edward was like his grandfather in many ways, but he was not such an earnest man. He was a great knight and a good soldier, but the knights of this time were very frivolous and luxurious. They wasted days and weeks in tournaments, and were very vain and extravagant in their dress. They loved fighting for its own sake. When his uncle the king of France died, Edward III said that he ought to be king because of his mother, who was the sister of the king. In France women could not inherit the crown, and in any case there were other women with a better right than Edward's mother. But Edward really wanted an excuse for fighting the French.

There were many reasons for the French and English disagreeing at the time. Ever since the days of Henry II, the English kings had had land in the South of France, and the French kings were always trying to win it from them. Then, too, the French and the English were both building more ships, and the sailors of the two nations often quarreled on the seas.

The first great fight of the Hundred Years' War was between the French and English fleets, and the English won. After this the English were always greater at sea than the French. Edward's way of fighting the French was to land in the north of the country, and march along burning every village he came to. If a French army faced him he would fight it, win a victory, march on, and then come home. But he never really made any use of his victories. Perhaps he knew that he had no real chance of winning France.

His greatest victory of all was at the battle of Crécy in 1847. This was won by the English archers, who fought on foot. These archers were men of the middle and poorer classes of Englishmen, and there were always a good many in Edward's armies. The French armies were chiefly made up of knights who fought on horseback. The archers were men from Genoa in Italy, who fought with old-fashioned 'crossbows,' while the English used the 'long bow.' When the English archers shot at the French horses and knights, these were immediately thrown into disorder. Often the ground was soft and swampy, and the horses could hardly get along.

As the years went on nearly all the fighting in France was done by Edward's eldest son, the Black Prince. He led great armies, burning and destroying, through the South of France, causing the greatest misery to the people. In 1356 he won the great battle of Poitiers, and took the French king prisoner. The prince waited on the king at table, and treated him with the greatest respect.

The knights of the fourteenth century were always careful about these things, yet they could be terribly cruel. The Black Prince himself burned the town of Limoges to the ground, and had all its people killed because they had offended him. King John was carried to England, but allowed to go back to France to try to collect his ransom; but France was miserably poor through the war, and he could not get enough money. So he went back to England again, and died a prisoner.

After the Battle of Crécy

In the year 1360 peace was made between England and France. The English king gave up his claim to the French throne, but was given the Duchy of Acquitaine, which covered nearly half of the South of France. For the next ten years there was peace. Edward III was now growing old, but the Black Prince died the year before him, in 1376. Before he died nearly all of Acquitaine had been won back by France.

Edward III had grown very weak and foolish in his old age. He had never been a very good man, and in his old age he gathered round him wicked men and women. One woman stole the rings from his fingers as he lay dying, and left the old king to die alone. It is hard to believe that this was the same king who had been so gay and merry a few years before. It was Edward III who set up the 'Order of the Garter.' It became the greatest honor to be made a Knight of the Garter, and it still is. Yet the beginnings of the Order were very peculiar. Once at a ball at the court of Edward III somebody picked up a garter, and Edward immediately said he would set up an Order of Knights, who should wear a garter on the left leg as their special badge.

It is sometimes said that Edward set up the Order of the Garter in honor of the taking of the French town of Calais by the English, at the beginning of the Hundred Years' War. The English had been besieging this town for many months, when at last it sent to ask for mercy from the king. Edward, who was very angry, said he would only let the people of Calais go free from punishment if they gave their city up, and also sent to him six of their chief men dressed only in shirts with ropes round their necks, and the keys of the city in their hands, and he would do what he liked with them. Six of the chief men of Calais offered to do this, and came before Edward and his Queen Philippa. But the good queen was full of pity for them, fell on her knees crying, and begged the king to let them go free, and so he did.

When Edward III died, his young grandson, the son of the Black Prince, became king of England. He was called Richard II. He was only a boy of sixteen when a great rebellion of the poor people of England broke out. It was called the Peasants' Revolt. The peasants in different parts of England rose in revolt against the rich owners of the land. Often they took scythes and other things with which they worked on the land for weapons. The peasants of Kent had for their leader a man called Wat Tyler. He persuaded them to march to London, so that they could tell the king their troubles. When they got to London the boy king rode to meet them, and promised to try to make things better for them. But Wat Tyler, who must have been a bad man, led his men into the city, and they burned houses and killed every servant of the king they could find.

The next day Richard rode out to meet them again. He was a tall, slim, handsome boy, and looked very brave and noble as he faced the peasants. Wat Tyler rode up to speak to the king, but he looked as though he was going to strike him, and the mayor of London, who was with the king, drew his dagger and stabbed him to the heart. He fell dead, and the mayor was afraid that the peasants would attack the king, but Richard rode bravely up to them, and talked to them, while the mayor rode off and brought some soldiers to protect

Methods of Warfare During the Hundred Years War. *An interesting picture in the splendidly illuminated MS. of Froissart's "Chronicles of England and France" in the British Museum. On the left, soldiers, protected by a wooden tower, shoot into the besieged city. Just below are two of the early kinds of cannon; they were very feeble, and sometimes did more damage to the men using them than to the enemy.*

the king. The peasants, now that their leader was dead, went back to their homes again. The thing that they had complained about was a tax which the king had tried to collect from them. They said they were too poor to pay it. They had other troubles too.

Three times during the fourteenth century a terrible plague of sickness called the Black Death had spread over the countries of Europe from the East. People died in hundreds. Half the people in England altogether died of it, and especially the poorer people. In those days there were not, of course, nearly so many people in any country as there are today. In the whole of England there were not as many people as there are now in London. After the Black Death the rich landowners found that there were not so many men as before to cut the corn and work on the land. Sometimes whole fields of corn had to be left to go bad because there were no laborers to cut it. Then the laborers seeing that, asked for more wages.

In the early days after the Norman Conquest, the laborers had not had money wages, but had had small pieces of land for themselves, and were bound to work several days each week on the land of their lord. They were serfs. But for many years the lords had been letting the serfs go free, and were paying wages to laborers. Now some of them wanted to make the laborers serfs again.

Altogether the lords, and the laborers too, were very discontented with the changes caused by the terrible Black Death, and it was really this which brought about the Peasants' Revolt. There were even some people who said, as people called socialists say now, that there should not be rich people and poor people, but that all should be equal. One man, who was a priest and named John Ball, went about the country saying—

'When Adam delved and Eve span
Who was then the gentleman?'

He was called the mad priest of Kent. Another of these preachers was called Jack Straw, and another Grindcob. They were all taken and hanged before the end of the Peasants' Revolt.

Some people said, too, that the peasants were encouraged by another priest, named John Wycliff, but he had not really anything to do with the revolt, except that he taught that priests should he poor, and that the Church in England was too rich, and sent out priests of this kind to preach to the people. John Wycliff was a teacher at Oxford, and a very clever man. Besides teaching that the Church should be poor, he said, too, that the bread and wine which the Church taught were changed into the Body and Blood of Christ in the Mass, were not really changed.

This was heresy, and Wycliff was taken before the archbishop of Canterbury to be examined on these things. He either denied that he had said them or explained them in some way to which the archbishop agreed, and so Wycliff went back safely to his church at Lutterworth, where he lived for some years saying Mass and working as a priest, and then died.

But for many years there were men who went on teaching these heresies of Wycliff. They were called Lollards, and some of them were burnt to death in the fifteenth century.

Agricultural Life in the Fourteenth Century (From a wonderful series of drawings made about 1340 in an English book of prayers called the Luttrell Psalter. In the first picture two men thresh corn with flails; in the second an old woman brings her corn to the miller to be ground; in the last laborers stack the sheaves of corn. The drawings show very clearly how farm people dressed in the fourteenth century).

After the Peasants' Revolt people settled down again, and as time went on the quarrel between the landowners and the laborers died out. By the end of the Middle Ages all the serfs in England were free, and all the men who worked on the landowners' farms were laborers who were paid with money,

In France, too, during the wars of Edward III, there had been much discontent among the peasants. When King John of France was a prisoner in England, a terrible rebellion of the peasants broke out, which was called the 'Jacquerie,' as 'Jacques' or 'James' was an ordinary peasant name in France. The soldiers, who had no more fighting to do after the battle of Poitiers, went about stealing from the people.

The nobles who had been taken prisoners by the English made the people on their lands pay a great deal of money towards their ransom, and the French peasants had suffered from the terrible Black Death too. The French parliament, which was called the States-General, had very little power in France, and now they tried to get more, thinking they could help to make things better for the people.

The dauphin, as the French king's eldest son was always called, made promises which he did not mean to keep, and one of the chief men in Paris, called Etienne Marcel, got the people of Paris to attack the nobles of the court. Marcel himself forced his way into the palace; and killed two of the greatest men of the court.

Then all over France the peasants rose. The feudal castles were burnt, and great numbers of the nobles and their wives were killed. The French peasants had always been much more badly treated by their lords than the English, and now they took a terrible revenge. The dauphin's wife and her ladies had shut themselves up in the town of Meaux, and an angry crowd of peasants were attacking it when they were attacked themselves by Gaston Phoebus, Count of Foix, and his friends. He fought heroically, and the serfs were scattered. After this they lost heart, and they were dreadfully punished, hunted down like wild beasts, and killed in thousands. The Jacquerie in France was a far more terrible thing than even the Peasants' Revolt in England.

THE FIRST GREAT ENGLISH POET

Yet though the story of the fourteenth century seems a sad one in many ways, it was the time when the first great English poet, Geoffrey Chaucer, lived and wrote. By this time there were French poets writing in French. In Italy Petrarch had followed in the steps of Dante, and written poems in the beautiful language of Tuscany, the part of Italy round Florence. Petrarch's best poems are his sonnets, in honor of Madonna Laura, a lady whom he loved, and who died of the plague in 1348.

In England, at the end of the thirteenth century, some of the chroniclers of the monasteries had begun to write in English instead of Latin. In the next century Wycliff wrote his opinions in English, and also translated part of the Bible into English. The poem called the 'Vision of Piers Plowman' was written in English too, but Chaucer wrote the best poetry of all.

He was born in London, and was the son of a wine-merchant. He himself had work at the court of Edward III and Richard II, and it was for the lords and ladies of the court that he wrote. But he wrote about what he saw around him, and his poetry, which is very musical and beautiful, is full of fun too. His chief work was the 'Canterbury Tales,' in which Chaucer described a number of pilgrims on their way to the tomb of St. Thomas Becket at Canterbury. He makes each of them tell a tale. By reading these poems we can get a true idea of what life in England was like in Chaucer's time, and at the same time enjoy the first beautiful poetry written in English.

Chapter XXVII—The End of the Middle Ages

After the popes had been at Avignon nearly sixty years, Pope Urban V made up his mind to go back to Rome. While the popes had been away, Rome had become very poor and miserable. The houses in the outer parts of the city were left empty, and the people crowded to the center of the town.

One or two of the great noble families got all power over the city until Rienzi, a young Roman, the son of a hotel keeper and a washerwoman, persuaded the people to try to set up again the old Roman republic. He really made himself head of the city, and sent messengers to the other Italian cities to ask them to put themselves under the leadership of Rome. Two princes in Germany were fighting as to which of them was really emperor. He ordered them to let him judge between them. At first the people admired Rienzi and treated him as a hero. He lived in the greatest luxury, and was full of wild plans. But at last the people turned against him, and an angry crowd surrounded his palace. He tried to escape, dressed like a poor man, but the people recognized him and killed him immediately.

After this there was still much misery and disorder, and the Romans were delighted when Pope Urban V came back to Rome. All the best people of the time were glad. The poet Petrarch, and St. Brigit of Sweden, and many others had begged the Pope to return to the city of St. Peter. But Urban V soon went back to Avignon. He was persuaded to do so by the French cardinals, who loved Avignon, where the popes had a splendid court and lived very magnificently; but at last, in the year 1377, Pope Gregory IX left Avignon and went back to Rome, where the popes have remained ever since.

The person who did most to persuade the Pope to go back was St. Catherine of Siena. Catherine was the youngest of the twenty-five children of a dyer who lived in Siena, one of the beautiful towns of North Italy. When she was only seven years old, Catherine made up her mind never to marry, but to give all her time and strength to religion. When she was only a young girl about seventeen, she became a Dominican tertiary, and for a time lived

St. Catherine of Siena *(A painting in the Dominican nuns' convent at Caleruega, Spain.)*

very quietly by herself. But when her father died she went back to take care of her mother, and ever afterwards she was surrounded by friends, whom she was always helping.

Great statesmen all over Europe took her advice, for she was very wise as well as good. She wrote the most beautiful letters in Italian which was just as beautiful as that written by Petrarch himself. St. Catherine wrote to persuade the Pope to go back to Rome, and went there herself to help to receive him. It was a very wonderful thing that the great men of the time took the advice of a woman.

Everywhere she went a little band of men and women, some of the cleverest and best of the time, went with her. And though St. Catherine was a strong and firm character there was nothing unwomanly about her. She was full of sorrow for other people's troubles. Once she spent the whole night with a young man who had committed a crime and was condemned to die. She consoled him like a mother, allowing him to rest his head on her breast, and soothing him and helping him to meet death bravely.

St. Catherine and all the Italians were delighted to have the Pope back in Rome, but new troubles soon arose. Gregory IX died, and the cardinals elected another Pope. But the French cardinals said they would not have him, and elected an anti-pope of their own. The Pope elected at Rome was, of course, the real Pope, but a great many people pretended to believe that the anti-pope was the true Pope. Everyone who was friendly to France did this, while the English, who were always the enemies of France, sided with the true Pope. At last the confusion was so great that it was agreed to call a general council, a meeting of bishops from all parts, to settle the question. This council met at Pisa, and chose a new Pope, but neither of the other Popes would give in, and so things were now worse than ever.

A few years afterwards the Emperor Sigismund called another council at Constance. At this council the real Pope resigned and the other two were deposed, and then at last the cardinals elected Pope Martin V. Everybody agreed to take him as Pope, and so the 'Great Schism,' as it was called, ended. But all this trouble and disorder had made people think less of the popes, and a new spirit arose of disrespect and criticism, which made it easier for the men in the next century who said that the Pope was not head even in religious things, as everyone in the Middle Ages believed.

Already there were men who refused to believe what the Church and the Pope taught. In the kingdom of Bohemia, in the east of Germany, there were men who were still teaching the things that Wycliff had taught in England. Like Wycliff, they were educated men, not ignorant people like the Albigensians and most of the heretics of the earlier Middle Ages.

They knew how to write and argue about their opinions, and so they were very dangerous

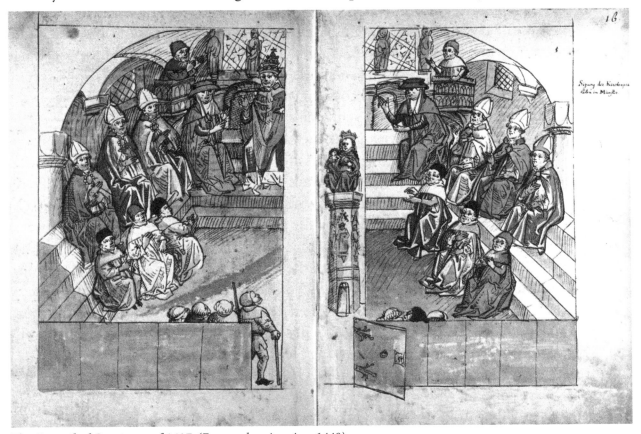

The Council of Constance of 1417 (*From a drawing circa 1440*).

to the Church. The chief of these new heretics in Bohemia was a teacher in the University of Prague, the capital of that country. His name was John Huss. The Council of Constance was anxious to bring order into the Church, as well as to settle the question about the popes, and John Huss was called before it to give an account of his teaching. The Emperor Sigismund gave him a safe-conduct, that is, a promise that he could come and go safely. But Sigismund broke his promise.

The council treated Huss in a very rough and angry manner. Things which he had written in his books were read out, and he was commanded to agree that they were heresies. But he would not. For a month Huss was kept in prison, while the bishops tried to persuade him to give in. Everyone knew that he was a good and holy man, but the council thought he should give in to the Church. At last, in spite of the Emperor's promise, they said he must die.

When he was tied to the stake with the wood piled up round him ready to burn, he was again begged to give in, but he answered that he had taught what he thought right and that he died joyfully. Then he was burnt and his ashes were thrown into the Rhine. His great friend, Jerome of Prague, was burnt soon afterwards.

But in Bohemia their followers still went on with their teaching. Even when Sigismund led a crusade against them, the Bohemians, under their leader John Zizka, fought desperately. Zizka was really a very terrible man in spite of his courage. He was blinded first in one eye and then in the other in two different battles. But he would get his officers to tell him all about the land where a battle was to be fought, and then would tell them how to arrange the army. But he was terribly cruel. His enemies told a tale of how once he fastened several priests up in barrels and then had them covered with tar and set on fire. When he heard the shrieks of the priests dying in dreadful agony he said, ' Listen to the bridal song.'

In the end, after Zizka's peace was made, the Hussites got their own way about most of the things for which they had fought. The Hussites always declared that they belonged to the Catholic Church, but they were in many ways very like the Protestants of the sixteenth century. In the Middle Ages no one had been sorry for heretics when they were burnt, but there were many people now who were sorry for John Huss and his friend, and this was a sign that things would soon change.

Meanwhile England and France had begun the second part of the Hundred Years' War. Richard II of England, the brave young king who had faced the peasants in the Peasants' Revolt, married a little French princess, and had made a truce with France. But Richard II ruled England badly in the end, and was deposed and probably murdered in prison by Henry, Duke of Hereford, who was called King Henry IV.

During Henry IV's reign two great parties began to quarrel in France, and while Henry IV was ill, his young son, who was also called Henry and afterwards became Henry V, sent help to the party of the duke of Burgundy, who were called the Burgundians, while the side they fought against were called the Armagnacs. Henry IV died soon afterwards. He had never been a happy king. It seemed as though he could never forget his cruelty to the handsome and unhappy Richard II. People had never really loved him, but his son Henry V was loved by everyone.

He was a very brave man and very religious. He seems to have believed that he really had a right to the crown of France, and at the very beginning of his reign he made up his mind to try to win it. The king of France at that time was mad. He was called Charles VI. His son, the dauphin, was friendly with the party of the Armagnacs, and the people of the South of France liked them best. But Paris and the North of France preferred the Burgundians.

In the year 1415 Henry V sailed with a great army to France. He marched through the north of the country, until he was faced by a great French army near the village of Agincourt. Here the famous battle of Agincourt was fought. All during the night before the battle, the French soldiers drank and played while the English slept or prayed. In the morning Henry stood before the army with his jeweled crown on top of his helmet and spoke to his soldiers. Then he knelt down before them all and prayed aloud for victory.

The English army still had many archers, while the French still went on using great numbers of horse-soldiers, as in the battles of the first part of the Hundred Years' War. King Henry put a long row of stakes in front of his army, wide enough apart for the archers to pass between. Then they went forward, and shot a great shower of arrows into the French army, and ran quickly back again. Then the French horsemen dashed forward, but could not pass between the stakes. Those at the back crowded on to the front lines. The horses sank into the soft ground and there was the greatest confusion, while the English archers killed hundreds of men and horses with shower after shower of arrows. Once again it was seen how the ordinary Englishmen could defeat the great feudal lords of France. After the victory Henry sailed back to England.

The people were so delighted and proud that at Dover they could not wait for the ships to come to the shore, but dashed into the sea as far as their waists to meet the king. In London the people went nearly mad with joy; all the church bells rang merrily as Henry rode to St. Paul's to give thanks for his victory. Soon Henry went back to France and won victory after victory, and at last in 1420 the French king and queen were persuaded to sign the Treaty of Troyes. Henry was to marry Katharine, their daughter, and he was to be king of France when the mad king died. The whole of the North of France agreed to this, but the dauphin would not give up his rights, and the South of France took his side. Henry was fighting on the river Loire when he died, at the age of thirty-five years.

The English people have always thought of him as a hero, but after all he had no right to France. His wife, Katharine, had had a baby son, who became king of England, and was called Henry VI. For many years his uncles went on fighting in France for him, but the English never fought so well when Henry V was dead.

St. Joan of Arc depicted on horseback in an illustration from a 1505 manuscript.

JOAN OF ARC

And now a very wonderful thing happened which saved France from the English. Three years before the battle of Agincourt there was born in the village of Domremy in France a little peasant girl named Joan. She was brought up like other little peasants to say her prayers and do her sewing, and help to look after her father's sheep,

But from the first Joan was not quite like other little girls. She was merry and good-tempered, but often, while the other village children were playing their games, Joan would go quietly away into the woods near her home, to say her prayers all by herself. All the time she was growing up she heard stories of the terrible sufferings of the French people through the dreadful wars with the English. Always she was full of pity, as she said, 'for the fair kingdom of France.'

Then while she was praying in the woods she thought she heard voices telling her to be very good, and that she had been chosen to save France from her enemies. Then she thought that St. Michael and St. Catherine appeared to her. Joan felt very frightened at the thought that a poor girl like her had to do these great things, but at last she made up her mind that she could not refuse. Very seriously she told her friends about her voices, and begged to be taken to the king. 'It was for this that I was born,' she said gently and rather sadly.

At last her uncle took her to the governor of a town near, and when he heard her story, it was settled that she should be taken to the king.

For eleven days she travelled to reach the court. The nobles had heard of her coming, and some of them were inclined to make fun of the poor peasant girl. The mad king was now dead, and it was the dauphin, who became Charles VII of France, who was now the rightful king of France.

Charles was plainly dressed, and stood among a little crowd of his courtiers as Joan went into the room where he was. There was nothing to show that he was king, but Joan went up to him at once, and fell on her knees before him, saying: 'I am sent to you by the King of Heaven to tell you that you shall be crowned king of France.' Even the mocking courtiers began to think that the 'Maid,' as she was soon called by everyone, had been really sent by God to save France.

The English were then besieging the great town of Orleans on the river Loire. If only they could take it, they thought they would be able to win the South of France, as well as the North, for the young Henry VI. The king said Joan could lead the army against the English. She was given a suit of white armor to wear, and a beautiful white horse to ride on, and she carried a beautiful white banner with the lilies of France embroidered on one side and the Face of God with angels kneeling before Him on the other.

The French soldiers were full of love and respect for Joan, and followed her gladly. When they reached Orleans nearly all the forts round the city had been taken by the English, but Joan soon won them back. She was wounded on the first day, but rode on just the same.

The French soldiers knew that she was a saint, but the English said she was a witch. They were frightened of her, and this made it easier for Joan to win. The English in the end fled away from Orleans, and the town was saved. Then Joan begged the dauphin to go with her to Rheims and be crowned, for in the cathedral there the French kings were always crowned. And so he did. Joan knelt in the cathedral full of happiness, for now that the king was crowned she knew her work was over. Her voices had told her to save Orleans, and to take the king to be crowned at Rheims. Now that this was done she was ready to go back and look after her father's sheep once more.

But the king would not let her, and his officers, who did not like Joan and hated that she should have the command of the army, did not want her to go either because she was too useful. They made her lead the armies against the English in the North of France, but she had no longer any belief that she was doing God's will. At last she was taken prisoner by the English, and was given up by them to the bishop of Rouen, who was a Frenchman but on the English side.

She was now told that she was to be tried for being a witch. She was taken time after time before the bishop with his court of priests. Time after time she was asked question after question about her voices. The bishop tried to make her say that they were from the devil and not from God, but Joan felt that this was not true. She was kept in prison, and grew very ill as the trial went on, but she always answered sensibly and wisely, and though the cunning bishop tried often to catch her in some mean way, she never once made any slip, always answering simply and to the point. Sometimes indeed her answers were so witty that they made the bishop seem very foolish.

At last, when she was very ill, Joan signed a paper agreeing that her voices were not from God, but afterwards she was sorry, and held to her word again. Then she was condemned to die, and was burnt as a witch in the market-place of Rouen. As she stood tied to the stake she said once more, 'Yes, my voices were from God,' and then, as the flames rose up around her, she bent her head, saying 'Jesus,' and died.

An English soldier standing near was heard to say, 'We are lost, for we have burned a saint.' The French people long after said that a white dove rose out of the ashes of the fire in which Joan of Arc was burned, and that it was the dove, peace, which she had brought to France.

For though Joan died in this terrible way her work went on. The French soldiers could never forget her, and the English, too, were always haunted by her memory. It was not long before the English were driven right out of France, and only the town of Calais remained to them of all they had won and lost in the Hundred Years' War.

Joan of Arc is now looked upon by the French, and other people too, as one of the greatest women who have ever lived. The Church has called her a saint, and in the market-place of Rouen, where she was burned, may be seen now the statue of the girl of seventeen who gave her life to save France.

In England, even before the French War was over, things were very miserable. Henry VI grew up to be a very weak man. It seemed as though he had almost inherited the madness of his grandfather, Charles VI of France. Henry was very religious and fond of learning, but he had no idea of how to govern the country. One of the great dukes, Richard, Duke of York, made up his mind to get the crown for himself. He fought against the king and shut him up in prison, and at last Henry said that Richard should rule England for him while he lived and be king when he died.

Margaret of Anjou, the king's wife, would not hear of this. She meant her son, the young Prince Edward, to be king after his father as was right. For years all the great nobles in England fought, some on the one side and some on the other. The wars were called the Wars of the Roses, because the Yorkists wore white roses and King Henry's side red. King Henry died miserably early in the struggle, and the poor little Prince Edward, whom Margaret had tried so hard to protect, was killed on a battlefield. Richard, Duke of York, was killed too, but his son Edward became king as Edward IV.

Nearly all the nobles of England had been killed in the Wars of the Roses, and King Edward IV was able to rule England more strongly that any king during the fifteenth century. Parliament, which still met, had grown very weak now that there were so few nobles to lead it. From the time that Edward IV became king, the kings of England were almost despots for some hundreds of years. Parliament met, but only to do what the king told it. Edward hardly ever called parliament together at all. But at the time this was quite a good thing for England. The people wanted peace after so many years of war abroad and at home. Even during the Wars of the Roses the middle classes in England had gone peacefully on with their business and trade. Towns were getting larger, and new ones were growing up. Things were growing more orderly than they had been in the Middle Ages.

When Edward IV died there was a short time of trouble. His two little sons, the elder of whom should have been king, were shut up in the Tower of London, and probably killed there by their uncle, who had himself made king and was called Richard III. But he did not reign long. The crown was taken from him by Henry, Earl of Richmond, who belonged to the family of Henry VI. He fought with Richard, who was killed in the battle of Bosworth Field, and was crowned on the field with the crown which rolled from the dead king's head.

The new king was called Henry VII. He was the first king of the great House of Tudor. He ruled England very much as Edward IV had done, and in his time the Middle Ages seem to come to an end in England. Great new changes were coming near, which seem to bring the beginnings of modern times.

In France, after the English had been driven out, the kings grew more powerful too. Charles VII, the dauphin whom Joan of Arc took to Rheims to be crowned, got an army together of the middle classes of Frenchmen, like the English armies, and no longer depended so much on the great lords. Charles VII became almost mad like his father before he died, but his son, Louis XI, went on with the struggle against the nobles.

He was a clever and cunning king, but not a good man. He tried hard to get the lands of some of the greatest French nobles for the crown, and even sometimes murdered people who stood in his way. He was naturally cruel, and it was said that he even shut up some of his enemies in iron cages, and kept them there for years. Louis had a long struggle, especially with Charles the Bold of Burgundy. In the end he won Burgundy for the French crown, but Flanders and the Low Countries, the lands to the North of France which are now called Holland and Belgium, and which also belonged to Charles the Bold, went to the Emperor Maximilian, who married Charles's daughter Mary. Louis XI left the French crown very strong and powerful for the kings who came after him, and in the next century the kings of France were despots like the Tudor kings of England. In France, too, this change seems to be the beginning of modern times.

The End of the Middle Ages: Two Knights about to Begin a Joust (*From a fourteenth-century manuscript*).

Chapter XXVIII—The Beginnings of Modern Times

Towards the end of the fifteenth century many changes took place which made immense differences in all the countries of Europe. It is often said that this time was really the end of the Middle Ages and the beginning of modern times, and in many ways this is true. Yet we must remember that the people of the sixteenth century were very different in many ways from the people we know today. All changes in history have taken place slowly.

Still the people of the sixteenth century were more like ourselves in their ways and thoughts than like the people of the Middle Ages.

In the later fifteenth century many things were happening to bring about this change. People were beginning to ask questions about all sorts of things which they had never thought of in the Middle Ages.

In Italy especially men were beginning to take a new interest in learning. Instead of studying chiefly theology and the writings of the philosophers of the Middle Ages, they began to take a new interest in the old Greek and Roman philosophers and poets.

In nearly all the city-states of Northern Italy some great family had seized power. In Florence, a great family of bankers called the Medici really ruled the city and the country round, which Florence had conquered.

All these great families, and the princes at their head, tried to make their courts famous for learning and poetry and art. The greater number of scholars and artists they could gather round them, the better pleased they were.

Ever since the time of Giotto, in the fourteenth century, there had been great painters in Italy, but it was at the end of the fifteenth century and the beginning of the sixteenth that the greatest Italian painters did their work.

All these new interests, which began in Italy and soon spread to the other countries of Europe, are described by one word, the 'Renaissance,' which means the 'new birth.' It seemed as though the minds of men, after a long time in which they obeyed and kept to certain ways of thinking, were now set free to think as they pleased.

The result of the Renaissance or the Revival of Learning, as it was sometimes called, was that the scholars and artists of the time began to despise the Middle Ages as savage and barbarous and to look back to the great days of Greece and Rome as times of the highest civilization. Sometimes these men forgot the terrible cruelties of the Greeks and Romans, and forgot too how much better the world had become in many ways during the Middle Ages.

The scholars of the Renaissance in Italy did not write very interesting things, because they were always trying to imitate the writings of the Greeks and Romans, so that in this time, although men were much more learned than in the Middle Ages, there were no great poets like Dante and Petrarch, the poets of the Middle Ages.

The Italian scholars were always pleased to find a Greek and learn his language from him, for though Latin was, of course, spoken by all scholars in the Middle Ages, very few knew Greek, and these Italians of the Renaissance were eager to read the writings of the great Greeks in their own language. Then something happened which brought great crowds of Greeks into Italy, ready to teach the Italians all they knew. This was the capture of Constantinople by the Turks in the year 1453, which is often said to have been the beginning of the Renaissance.

THE FALL OF CONSTANTINOPLE

For many years before this the Mohammedan lands of Western Asia had been conquered and overrun by a new branch of the Turks, called the Ottoman Turks. They then crossed into the East of Europe, and conquered land to the north of the Balkan Peninsula. Hungary and Poland were only saved by the desperate bravery of the Hungarian hero, John Hunyadi, whose son, Matthias Corvinus, became king of Hungary later. Since the days when the Venetians and other crusaders had taken Constantinople from the Greek Emperor, the Eastern Empire had been very miserable and weak. The Greeks had won back Constantinople, but never got back their former possessions. New kingdoms like Bulgaria now grew up out of land which had once belonged to the Empire.

In the Balkan Peninsula the Ottoman Turks had already won much land when they turned against Constantinople. The last emperor was named like the first, who had taken Byzantium for his capital, Constantine. He was a weak man, and his nobles had no idea of fighting. Yet they did their best to defend their city. Constantine begged for help from the Pope. There had been attempts during the century to join the Eastern and Western Churches again, but they had not been successful.

Now no one went to the help of the Greeks. A Christian had invented for the fierce Turkish sultan, who was called Mohammed II, a gun which could throw a cannon ball, weighing three hundred pounds, the length of a mile. The Greeks had nothing but the most old-fashioned weapons, and the nobles, who had spent their lives in luxury, were not strong enough even to wear the heavy armor which it was still the fashion to use. Mohammed, who was a terribly cruel man and lived a very wicked life, easily took the city.

Constantine, weak though he was, was too proud to be taken prisoner by his conqueror, and mixed with his soldiers so that no one might know that he was the Emperor, and so he died with the rest. Mohammed turned his soldiers loose for three days to rob and kill. Thousands of people were killed in the streets and churches. Many had taken shelter in the great church of Saint Sofia, but they, too, were killed. The church itself was afterwards changed into a mosque for the Mohammedans, though the other churches were left to the Christians. Many thousands of people were sold into slavery.

Constantinople has belonged to the Turks from that day to this. It was not long before they conquered the whole of the Balkan Peninsula, and not till more than three hundred years later did Greece

Mahmet II Enters Constantinople by Benjamin Constant, 1876. In 1453 the Turks captured Constantinople and the last Emperor of Byzantium met his heroic death.

win back her freedom. Other nations, like Bulgaria and Servia, are still fighting for theirs.

No sooner was Constantinople taken than scholars in hundreds, collecting the precious manuscripts which held the writings of the great Greeks, fled West, chiefly to Italy, where the princes and scholars of the Renaissance welcomed them. Above all were they welcomed in Florence, which was always the chief city of the Italian Renaissance.

It had great memories to look back to. Dante and Petrarch were both Florentines. The first Medici ruler of Florence, Cosmo de Medici, who was still ruling Florence when Constantinople was taken by the Greeks, was a great builder. He had for his architects Michelozzo and Brunellesco, two of the greatest artists of the time. It was Brunellesco who built the beautiful white marble cathedral of Our Lady of the Flowers at Florence.

The architects, like the scholars of the time, despised everything belonging to the Middle Ages, so Brunellesco did not build a Gothic cathedral. He studied the old Roman buildings and built in the same way as the old Roman architects, and his cupola or dome at Florence is one of the wonders of the world. The Italian cathedrals generally have a baptistery and a bell tower built quite separately from the cathedral. The baptistery at Florence has bronze doors covered with the most wonderful sculpture done by an artist called Ghiberti.

For the new sculpture of the Renaissance was quite different from that of the Middle Ages. The porches of the Gothic cathedrals were often covered with statues of the saints, but they were often stiff and lifeless, though very charming in their way. But the men of the Renaissance carved beautiful statues often nearly as beautiful as those of the great Greek sculptors. Especially in Florence were great sculptors to be found. Perhaps the best of all the early sculptors was Donatello, whose work may still be seen in some of the most beautiful marble tombs in the fine churches of Florence.

Later the sculpture of the great Florentine, Michael Angelo, was perhaps even more wonderful than that of the Greeks, just as beautiful in form and with more expression. Cosmo de Medici got Brunellesco to build other places for him besides the cathedral. He

Cosmo de Medici as One of the Wise Men (*From the painting of the Adoration of the Wise Men, by Sandro Botticelli, who included a portrait of his patron*).

built the Dominican convent of San Marco, on the walls of which may still be seen the wonderful pictures by one of the friars, Fra Angelico. Although Fra Angelico was a painter of the early Renaissance, he was quite different from the other painters of the time, and even from Giotto, who was so much earlier. The other painters tried to paint much more naturally than Fra Angelico. They painted religious subjects, too, but they made the figures like the people they saw around them. One of the painters whom Cosmo de Medici helped was Sandro Botticelli, and in his picture of the Adoration of the Magi, one of the wise men was a portrait of Cosmo himself.

But Fra Angelico had a gift of producing beautiful color, and his saints had faces of the most wonderful expression, although they were stiff and not well drawn. It is said that he would cry all the time he was painting a Crucifixion, which was one of his favorite subjects. His real name was John, but he was called 'Angelico' because of his goodness and sweetness of temper.

Cosmo de Medici was a good Christian, but many of the great men of the Renaissance turned against their religion and became, or pretended to become, pagans like the old Greeks and Romans, whom they admired so much.

Cosmo's grandson, Lorenzo the Magnificent, was one of these. He was the greatest of all the Italian princes who took part in the Renaissance. He himself wrote poetry, and was full of all the learning of the time. He had at his court the greatest scholars, painters, and sculptors. He collected all the beautiful old statues that he could find from different parts of Italy and placed them in the beautiful gardens round his palace. It was in these gardens and studying this sculpture that Michael Angelo took his first lessons.

When Lorenzo de Medici heard one morning a friend saying that he had been to church and heard Mass, he said; 'I have been better employed; I have been asleep and dreaming.'

But the popes of this time were as anxious as the other princes of Italy to help the men of the Renaissance. Pope Nicholas V, who was a scholar himself, had many of the Roman churches rebuilt, and sent for painters to come and paint their pictures on the walls. For in those days frescoes, or paintings of pictures on walls, were the chief way of decorating churches.

Fra Angelico died in Rome after doing some painting there. Pope Nicholas V collected five thousand manuscripts for the library of the Vatican, the palace of the popes at Rome.

The only way the Greeks and Romans had of making 'books' was writing with a pointed instrument on long rolls of parchment. A long book would fill many yards of parchment. These were rolled up and kept in jars or wooden boxes. In the days of the early Renaissance, the only way of spreading the writings of the Greeks was to copy the valuable manuscripts brought by the Greeks who had fled from Constantinople. But in the middle of the fifteenth century suddenly 'printing' was invented.

THE BEGINNING OF PRINTING

An Early Printer's Office (*From a sixteenth-century engraving*).

In the fourteenth century people had begun 'block' printing. A drawing would be made on a block of wood, and then all the wood which was not drawn on would be cut away. The letters or drawing was then smeared with oily ink, and pressed on to paper. In this way pictures and even books had been made, but it was in the fifteenth century that real printing was invented. Then someone in Germany or in Holland arranged letters cut out of metal which could be put together to form words, and then, when they were smeared with ink and many copies printed off, the letters could be put together again to form other words, and so on.

Most people think that it was a German called John Gutenberg, who lived at the town of Mainz, on the river Rhine, who invented this way of printing. One of the first books printed by Gutenberg was the Bible. It was a very beautiful book, for the early printing was beautifully clear. Soon Gutenberg's invention spread, and every big town, and even the larger monasteries in the countries of Western Europe, soon had their printing press. Before the end of the century there were over a thousand in Germany. German printers travelled into France, and Spain, and Italy, but soon these countries had their own printers too. Sometimes the trade would be passed on from father to son in one family. The family of the Aldi at Venice became very famous for their beautiful printing, and collectors of beautiful books now are very glad when they get an 'Aldine' edition.

The first printing press in England was set up in the sanctuary of Westminster Abbey some time about the year 1475, by a man called William Caxton. He had been a merchant, and lived for a long time at Bruges, and had gone to Cologne to learn the 'new art' from a printer there. The first book he printed was called the *Game and Play of the Chess,* but this was before he came back to England. In England he printed many books, and among others were *Chaucer's Works.*

The invention of printing was a very wonderful thing, and had very important results. Instead of one book being copied out with much labor by one man, many copies could be printed in less time by the press, though, of course, even the printing presses at first could not print books as quickly as we can have them done now.

At first people called printing the 'Holy Art,' or sometimes the 'Divine Art,' and in England no book could be printed without permission of the Church and the king's council. Of course it was still only the richer people or those who were going to be priests who could read, but later education spread, and the printing of books helped this. When people had books to read for themselves, they did not feel so dependent on the preachers of the Church as they had done in the Middle Ages, and this again encouraged the new free and independent feeling which so many men of the Renaissance had.

Another great discovery which gave people new thoughts and ideas about the world was that the earth was not standing still, as people in olden days and in the Middle Ages had believed. It had always been thought that the earth was the center of the universe, and that the sun, moon and stars whirled round her once in every twenty-four hours, and that this was what caused day and night. When the sun came round and shone opposite any particular place, that place had day, and when the sun had passed over, then it had night. But at the end of the fifteenth century there appeared a scholar who told people that this was not true, that it was the earth which was moving and not the sun.

This scholar was named Copernicus, and he was born in Poland. When he was a boy he loved mathematics and astronomy, the study of the stars, and when he was a young man he went to Rome to lecture there. But soon he went back to Poland, and spent years and years making instruments, and searching the sky night after night, hoping to find out the truth.

When he at last told people that the earth was moving faster than anything we know can ever move, and that it turns right round on its axis once in every twenty-four hours, and that this was what caused day and night, people laughed at him. Some people even thought it was wicked for Copernicus to say these things, and when his friends asked him to explain all these things in a book, these other people were very angry. But Copernicus wrote his book, and it was taken to be printed at Nuremberg, one of the chief places for printing in Germany.

People had become so excited and angry about the new teaching of Copernicus, that the printers had to work with a loaded gun beside them to protect themselves. Two of the scholar's friends stayed by day and night to protect the book. At last it was finished. But Copernicus lay dying. He was worn out with work and anxiety, but as he lay on his deathbed horsemen galloped up with copies of his book, and so he had the happiness of knowing before he died that nothing could now prevent the truth which he had found out being known to all the world. And so he died happy.

Since the time of Copernicus many new and wonderful discoveries have been made about the sun and the stars, but his was the greatest discovery of all.

While Copernicus had been, as it were, showing people a new heaven, great and wonderful discoveries had been made also about the earth itself, and great and brave men were able to show a new earth too.

Chapter XXIX—A New World

At the end of the fifteenth century there appeared a man who startled people as much as Copernicus with his new ideas about the stars. The thing which this man, the great Christopher Columbus, said was that the earth was round. People thought this very ridiculous, for could not any one see that the earth was flat, but Columbus only repeated: 'Sail to the West and you will find the East.'

This sounded like the words of a madman, but what Columbus meant was that if men could sail across the Atlantic they would come round to the other side of the continent of India. Of course everyone knows now that Columbus was right when he said the world was round, but to the people of that time it sounded foolish. Columbus himself was soon to sail across the Atlantic, the 'Sea of Darkness' as it was then called, and find land across it. He thought that it was India, and never knew before he died that it was really the great continent of America, which people up to that time had known nothing about. It was true that if Columbus had sailed round the coast of America and on he would have reached the coast of India.

Columbus was born in Genoa, one of the great seafaring towns of North Italy, but it was to the court of the king of Portugal that he went to tell his tale, and to ask for money and ships to help him to sail across the Atlantic to reach the East by going West.

The reason for this was that the sailors of Portugal had been making voyages of discovery all through the century, though none had ever ventured across the Atlantic.

Portugal was one of the Christian kingdoms which had been formed in the Spanish Peninsula during the long struggle between the Christians and the Saracens, which went on all through the Middle Ages. The little kingdom ran along the Western coast of the Peninsula, and its people naturally were very much interested in the sea.

At the beginning of the fifteenth century, one of the sons of King John of Portugal, called Prince Henry, had made up his mind to give his life to helping to find out something about the new lands which lay beyond those which the men of the Middle Ages had known. In the Middle Ages the Mediterranean Sea had been, as it were, the center of the world. The lands which had been won by the Roman Empire were thought to be the most Westerly part of the earth. Beyond them men thought that the Atlantic Ocean stretched across to the ends of the earth. To the East were the great stretches of Asia, and China had been reached by Franciscans who went to try to convert the Great Khan, the great ruler of the Mongol race, which had conquered so much of Asia in the thirteenth century.

The only men in the Middle Ages whom we know travelled for the love of discovery were three Venetians, Marco Polo and his father and uncle, who also travelled to the court of the Great Khan and lived there many years. Marco Polo wrote an account of all he had seen, but very few people took any notice of it, although they were ready to believe the wildest and most impossible tales about the East. Marco Polo's father and uncle had started off from Venice to trade at Constantinople the year that Marco was born. He was fifteen years old when they came back and told how they had crossed Asia, reached China and seen the court of the Great Khan. They were going back again, and the boy begged to go with them. He went, and the Great Khan was pleased to have him at his court. He learned the Chinese language and travelled into Persia, but always he went back to the court of the Great Khan.

After some years Marco and his father and uncle were anxious to go home again, but the Great Khan hated to let them go. But at last, after seventeen years, he did. When they arrived in Venice, dressed in strange clothes like the people of Asia, people would not believe them when they told them who they were. But Marco prepared a great feast to which they asked their friends, and he and his father and uncle appeared dressed in beautiful crimson satin robes.

Marco Polo Traveling. *Miniature from the Book "Travels of Marco Polo" ("Il milione"), originally published during Polo's lifetime (c. 1254 - January 8, 1324), but frequently reprinted and translated.*

When the banquet had begun they removed these clothes and put on others just as beautiful, while the first ones were cut up and divided among the servants. Then the old clothes in which they had come back from Asia were brought in and the seams were slit up. The most beautiful jewels fell out of them, and then at last their friends believed that it was really the Polos come back with great treasures from the East

But they were really the only men in the Middle Ages who seemed to have been anxious to visit strange lands. In the fifteenth century it was quite different. People became filled with a wish for discovery and adventure. It was part of the new spirit of the Renaissance. And this was how Prince Henry of Portugal gave up the pleasant life at his father's court and went to live on a lonely spot on the Southern coast of Portugal, so that he might give all his time to the study of seamanship.

The prince's motto was 'Desire to do well,' and he seems to have felt that this was the best way to carry it out. Up to that time the Northern deserts of Africa were all that were known of that continent, but Prince Henry sent out men and ships every year, and they sailed farther and farther South each time.

Before this people had believed that anyone who passed beyond a certain point on the coast of Africa would be changed from white to black. It had been thought, too, that that part of the world would be too hot for white men to live in. Some people said that there were great monsters there, and the sea was made of fire or at least of boiling water. But now it was seen that these old tales were ridiculous, and Prince Henry's sailors even landed on the coast of what is now called Guinea, and brought back gold dust which they found there.

They also brought back negroes as slaves for their prince, who was kind to them and taught them to be Christians; but this was the beginning of that dreadful slave trade in which the negroes for hundreds of years were carried off to work in far-off countries as slaves to white men.

One of the most daring sailors who sailed along the coast of Africa in Prince Henry's ships was a Venetian called Cadamosto, and he has written an account of his adventures. He tells how he sailed to Madeira, where Portuguese settlers were already living, on to the Canaries and then on to Cape Blanco or the White Cape, and then farther South still to the mouth of the river Senegal, where the negroes thought at first that the ships were birds and then that they must be great fishes. They thought, too, that it was very funny to see white men, and they tried to wash the white off.

Cadamosto sailed on past Cape Verde, which was the farthest point yet reached by the Portuguese. He could not understand why the Pole Star seemed to be so low in the sky as he went farther South, and when he got back he told Prince Henry about it, and also how he had seen a new and brilliant group of stars which we now know to be the Southern Cross. He did not know that the world was round, and that these changes in the position of the stars were caused by his moving over the curved surface of the earth.

Prince Henry died in 1460, but the work he had begun went on. In a few years the Portuguese had crossed the Equator and had landed near the mouth of the river Congo. The black king of Congo received them with great honor. He sat without any clothes at all on a throne of ivory. He wore copper bracelets on his arms and a horse's tail hanging from his shoulder. He became a Christian, and sent his children to Portugal to be educated.

At last, after some years, a brave sailor called Bartholomew Diaz, one of a family of sailors who had been for long in Prince Henry's service, sailed right round the South of Africa, passed the Cape of Good Hope and into Algoa Bay. Diaz would have liked to sail much farther, but his men were weary and impatient, and he had to sail for Rome. He told the king of Portugal about the great storm they had had to face as they passed the Cape, and he wanted to call it the Cape of Storms; but the king thought that the Cape of Good Hope would be a much better name, and so it has been called to this day.

The king of Portugal had called the Cape the Cape of Good Hope because he hoped that round it a new way would be found to India, and new trade with that land would begin between West and East.

Ten years after he sent out four ships under one of his noblemen called Vasco da Gama to try to reach India in this way. The ships sailed South, and were nearly wrecked in trying to pass the Cape of Good Hope. The sailors wanted to turn back, but their commander was very stern and grave. They were going on, he said, whatever happened, and so they did. They sailed joyfully into a calm sea on the other side of the Cape.

But another storm came, and again the men wished to turn back, but their leader was determined to push on. He worked as hard as any of his men in managing the ships against the storm. They passed the island of Santa Cruz near Algoa Bay, and saw the cross which Diaz had set up, for this was how the Portuguese showed that they had taken possession of the land in the name of then-king.

At last, on Christmas Day, they sailed into the mouth of a great river which they called the River of Mercy, to show their gratitude for the time of peace and rest they were to enjoy there. But this name has not remained as most of the beautiful names which the Portuguese, and after them the Spaniards, gave to the lands they discovered, and because they found it on the birthday or natal day of Our Lord they called it Natal. It is now called the Zambesi River. From here they sailed up the East coast, and a friendly king gave them a pilot to lead them across the sea to India.

It was twenty-three days before they reached Calicut. Here the natives received them gladly, hoping they had brought gold, silver, corals and scarlet cloth, for which they were ready to give them cinnamon, cloves, ginger, and many spices in return. These natives did not belong to the Aryan race like the people of Northern India, but were smaller and darker, and rather like negroes. The Portuguese had not brought so much as the king of Calicut had hoped, but they sailed home again very content and landed in Portugal nearly three years after the time they had sailed away. There was great rejoicing in Portugal and in Europe, except indeed in Venice.

The Venetians were sad, for it was they who up to now had received the rich silks and spices of India, and sold them in Europe. Arabs and Moors had carried these things to Ormuz, a town on the Persian Gulf; caravans had carried them across Asia Minor to the Venetian ships on the coast, or they were carried in ships to the Isthmus of Suez, and then in caravans to Cairo and in ships again down the Nile to Alexandria, where again Venetian ships were ready to receive them.

But now the way by sea would be much simpler, and besides the Portuguese took care to prevent things going in the old way, and so Venice was ruined. The days of her greatness were over. She has remained ever since beautiful but sad. Strangers crowd to see her beautiful churches and palaces, both Gothic and Renaissance, and her wonderful pictures, for Venice was only second to Florence in the part she took in the Renaissance. But she could never again be the proud and busy city she had been in the days when she was queen of trade between East and West.

When another expedition arrived in Calicut the king killed many of the men, and when the news reached Portugal, Vasco da Gama set out once more to take vengeance on him. His ships sailed, carrying banners and crosses, but the leader had no idea of Christian forgiveness. When he reached India he captured eight hundred peaceful merchants, cut off their hands and ears and noses, piled them up in a ship to which he set fire and sent it drifting to the shore. This was to be a lesson to the king of Calicut.

Then the king sent ships to fight the Portuguese, but they were clumsy ships, and the Portuguese easily fought them and killed still more men. Then they left a little colony of Portuguese on the coast near, and sailed back to tell their king what they had done. Vasco da Gama went once more to India some years later and died there. Another Portuguese named Albuquerque set up a colony at the town of Goa to the North of Calicut, and it became the great trading city of the Portuguese in India. It was called Golden Goa because of the great riches which were carried from it in ships to Portugal. No one but the Portuguese were allowed to trade with India.

On the South of Africa, Algoa was so called because ships going to Goa stopped there, and on their way back they stopped at Delagoa, which means 'From Goa,' and so got its name. The story of how the Portuguese sailed round the coast of Africa and across to India is, indeed, very wonderful, but after all they did the work gradually. One man followed where another led, and when they left Africa to sail bravely across to India they knew that land was there if only they persevered to reach it. But the story of the brave Columbus, the red-haired sailor with the blue eyes, who stood gravely before the king of Portugal and told him that the world was round, and begged for money and ships with which to sail across the Atlantic to the other side of India, is more wonderful and romantic still.

Chapter XXX—Christopher Columbus

Christopher Columbus was only fourteen years old when he first went to sea. His father was a weaver at Genoa and wanted his son to be a weaver too, but Christopher loved the sea passionately, and in the end his father let him be a sailor instead. Columbus learned all he could about the sea and ships, and he came to this conclusion, which seemed so strange to the people of his time, that the world was round.

When he was twenty-eight years old he went to Lisbon, the capital of Portugal, to learn what he could there, and it was six years after this that he went to the court to get help from the king who had done so much for sailors and ships.

The king listened as Columbus gave his reasons for believing that at the other side of the Atlantic land would be found. He told how pieces of wood, carved in strange ways, had been carried to the shores of Europe by the west wind. This, he said, showed that in land to the west of the Atlantic there were men who had carved this wood. He told them, too, how once the dead bodies of two men, quite different from any Europeans, had been found, and how on the West coast of Ireland strange plants grew up, whose seeds must have been carried by the wind from some country much warmer than Ireland.

The councilors of the king persuaded him not to trust Columbus, and got him to send off some ships to sail some distance west on the Atlantic, to see if they really did come to any signs of land. The ships were caught in a storm and soon came back, but when Columbus heard of this he felt that he had been insulted and would have nothing more to do with the Portuguese. Columbus himself was always very polite to other people.

He now went to the king and queen of Spain, the famous Ferdinand and Isabella. Ferdinand had been king of Aragon and Isabella queen of Castile when they married each other. Aragon and Castile were the two great Christian states formed besides Portugal in the struggle with the Moors. When Ferdinand and Isabella married, their two kingdoms together covered nearly the whole of Spain.

Both Ferdinand and Isabella were people of strong character and clever. They made up their minds to drive the Saracen rulers right out of Spain. There was only the little kingdom of Granada left to the Moors, and against this Ferdinand fought. He led his armies himself, while Isabella looked after the government of his country and her own. Granada was taken, and the Moorish ruler sadly gave up his kingdom and went to Africa, and so at last Spain, after a struggle of hundreds of years, became a united country like France or England. The Moors who remained in Spain were allowed to follow their own religion, but two centuries afterwards they were driven out of Spain altogether.

It was then to this great king and queen that Columbus went to tell his tale when he was insulted by the Portuguese.

But the king and queen were busy in these years fighting the Moors, and it was not until the year 1491 that Columbus was allowed to see them in their camp near Granada. They also thought his ideas were mad, and he left them sadly. But some of his friends persuaded Queen Isabella to help him, and when she began to understand how splendid a thing this might be, she declared she would sell all her jewels, if it were necessary, to help him.

In the same year that Granada fell Columbus started out in a Spanish ship on his strange voyage. He had received the title of Admiral, and his ship was called the *Santa Maria.* Two other ships went too, the *Niña* and the *Pinta.* The sailors were very frightened. It had been

Christopher Columbus, Arrives in America. *(Repository: Library of Congress Prints and Photographs Division Washington, D.C. 20540 USA)*

very hard to get anyone to go. Even as they left the shore many of them wept, and when they had passed the Canary Islands and were out of sight of land altogether they even spoke to each other of rebelling. Some said that it would be best to throw the mad admiral into the sea and sail back to Spain.

Columbus knew all this, but he remained quiet and brave, as he always was. He had learned to bear disappointment in all these weary years while he had been waiting for help in his great plan. He spoke to the men and tried to make them interested, like himself, in the voyage. After a while even the sailors began to see that land was near. Birds which belonged to the land were seen and heard round the ship; there was plenty of floating seaweed, which must have come from some shore; and best proof of all, there was a branch of a tree with red berries on it.

At last one night Columbus saw a light, and the next day they landed on a beautiful island covered with grass and with many trees. In the evening before, when the men knew that at last they were close to land, the sailors of the *Pinta* had struck up the great Latin hymn of thanksgiving called the 'Te Deum.'

There were dark-skinned natives watching Columbus as he planted the flag of Spain on the shore, set up a large cross and took possession of the island in the name of the king of Spain. The island which Columbus had discovered was one of the Bahama Islands in the West Indies off the coast of America. So Columbus, without knowing it, had discovered America, that great new continent to

Columbus's Ship (From a woodcut of 1493, supposed to have been made after a drawing by Columbus himself).

which in after years so many thousands of people from Europe, especially from England, were to swarm. The discovery of this little island by Columbus was the greatest thing that has happened in modern history.

But Columbus himself only knew that he had come round to land on the other side of the great sea which people had thought reached to the end of the world.

Columbus sailed to one island after another, always looking for the gold and spices which he wanted to take home from India to the king and queen. The *Santa Maria* struck on a rock off the Island of Hayti, and was wrecked. Columbus and his sailors went on board the *Niña*.

It was not big enough to hold them all, and so a little colony was left behind on the island, while Columbus, with two ships left, started back for Spain.

On the way great storms arose, and the *Pinta* went down with all its men. Columbus was in despair because he thought his ship would be wrecked too, and no one would ever know in Spain that he had really found land on the other side of the Atlantic. So he wrote on parchment an account of all his adventures, wrapped it up in a waxed cloth so that water could not get through to spoil it, and put it in a barrel, hoping that it would be washed up on to the coast of Europe.

But he got safely back to Spain after all. As he sailed into the mouth of the Tagus, Bartholomew Diaz, the other great explorer, went on board to talk to Columbus. Then Columbus went to Seville, the capital of Spain, and people crowded to see him riding past with the parrots and bright-colored birds which he had brought back, and with six natives who had come back with him too.

From Seville he went on to Barcelona, where he was received with great joy by the king and queen. Three times more Columbus sailed to the West Indies, and once he reached South America, from whence he brought back beautiful pearls.

A Spanish town called Isabella was set up in the Island of Hayti, and it was ruled by the brother of Columbus. From his third voyage Columbus was brought home a prisoner in chains. The king and queen had heard that he had been unjust to the settlers and cruel to the natives, but this was not true. When Columbus, now a white-haired old man, weary and worn, threw himself weeping at her feet, Isabella knew that he had been misjudged.

Once more he was given ships and sailors, and so set out on his fourth voyage. When he got back the queen was dead, and in a few years Columbus died too, very poor and friendless at the last in spite of the great work he had done. He died at the beginning of the sixteenth century, a time in which the great results of his discovery were to be seen. This century and the next had many splendid and heroic sailors, but none so great as Columbus.

Chapter XXXI—The Reformation

At the end of the Middle Ages, when so many new things were happening and so many discoveries were being made, some people began to have new ideas about the Church and religion too, and in time this led to the great religious change which was known as the Reformation.

Just as poets, and painters, and sculptors were stirred up with new ideas about beauty, so other men as great, or greater in their own way, were full of new ideas about goodness. They were anxious to make people more truly religious, and to do good in the Church. Most of these reformers were scholars too.

At the end of the Middle Ages, though many people were still very good, there was not any very great holiness in the Church. It was not a time of great saints like the twelfth or thirteenth century. There were no great new orders of monks, and though the monasteries of the old orders were spread over every country of Europe, the monks were often not nearly so strict as they had been in the early days of their orders. A few monasteries like those of the Carthusians in England were just as strict as ever, and there the monks lived just as St. Bruno had taught them to so many years before. But in some of the monasteries the monks lived quite wicked lives. Even in the better monasteries many of the monks did not know very much.

The reformers thought that people could pray and serve God better if they were better educated. They wanted to have Greek taught in the schools and universities. Some of the people who hated changes were very much against this 'new learning' of the Renaissance, and thought that the 'old learning' was quite enough. Sometimes at Oxford and Cambridge the students would actually fight among themselves about this question. Those who wanted Greek to be taught were called in fun the 'Greeks,' while those who wanted the 'old learning' were called the 'Trojans,' in memory of the battles of the Greeks and Trojans in the early history of the Greeks.

One of the first and greatest of the reformers in England was Sir Thomas More. He was the son of a lawyer, and was born in Milk Street, London, and went to St. Anthony's school

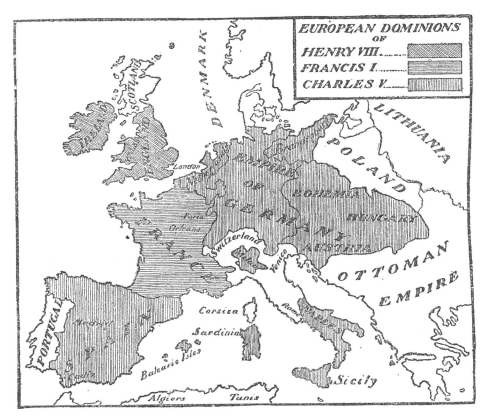

Map of Europe, Showing the Possessions of Henry, Francis, and Charles

in Threadneedle Street. While he was still a young boy he became a page in the house of Cardinal Morton, the archbishop of Canterbury. In those days the sons of gentlemen often became pages in the house of some great man, so as to learn perfect manners. Already More was very clever and witty, and the cardinal and his friends guessed that he would one day be a great man.

When he was older More was sent to the university at Oxford, and there he met some of the greatest men of his time. The chief of them was a priest called John Colet, who was one of the first people in England to study Greek. He gave lectures at Oxford on the New Testament, the part of the Bible which tells us about the Life of Our Lord. It was written first in Greek, but in the Middle Ages when hardly anyone knew Greek it had only been read in Latin, the great language of the Church. John Colet became a priest of St. Paul's Cathedral in London, and he set up a school for boys, who were taught the new learning, and brought up to be very good and religious men. Dean Colet, as he was called, was very fond of these boys, and we may still read a beautiful letter of his to them, in which he begs them to pray for him, saying 'Lift up your little white hands to God for me.'

Thomas More loved John Colet very dearly, although Colet was older than he. He had, too, another great friend called Erasmus, who was about the same age as himself. Erasmus was the cleverest man of his time. He was a priest, but the only thing he really cared for was learning. He belonged to the Low Countries, as the countries which are now Holland and Belgium were then called, but he travelled about from one country to another always studying and writing. He was very witty, and people roared with laughter when they read his books. He made fun of all the old ways and the people of the 'old learning,' and especially of those monks and people who were against the new ideas.

Colet and Erasmus and More were all good Catholics. They never thought of disobeying the Church, or saying that the Church's teaching was wrong. But there were other reformers who were quite different, and who rebelled against the Church. These were the first Protestants, and it was they who began the Reformation.

MARTIN LUTHER, THE FIRST GREAT PROTESTANT REFORMER

The first and greatest of all the Protestant reformers was Martin Luther. He was the son of a German peasant called Hans Luther, who was quite poor when Martin was a little boy, but became richer later on. Martin's family were all good people in their way, and his mother taught him to say his prayers, and to sing the beautiful German hymns which the people then sang.

But they were terribly strict and severe, and even his mother would beat him terribly for a little fault. Once he ran away from home after his father had punished him cruelly, and even when he was brought back he found it very hard to forgive his father. It was perhaps because of his sad childhood that Luther grew up into rather a sad young man, always worrying about his sins, and hardly able to believe that God would forgive them.

He was sent to school as a 'poor scholar,' and was fed and taught without paying, but sang in the choirs of the churches to which the schools belonged. Later on he went to the town of Erfurt, and there became an Augustinian friar. The Augustinians were one of the orders of friars which were set up soon after the Dominicans and Franciscans.

Martin Luther studied hard, especially the Bible, but he did not care much for Greek or the 'new learning.' After a time he was sent to lecture on theology at the new university of Wittenberg, which had been set up by the ruler of Saxony, who was one of the 'Electors' who had the right to choose the emperor.

This elector was called Frederick the Wise. At this time Germany was still made up of many little states, each ruled by its own prince, but with the Emperor over all. At Wittenberg, Luther began to preach, and people crowded to hear him, because of the simple yet strong way in which he spoke to them.

At this time there were things going on in the Church which Erasmus and the other reformers did not like, but which Luther made up his mind to fight against.

The Catholic Church taught that even after people had had their sins forgiven, there might still be punishment for them, which they would have to suffer in Purgatory when they died. But the Church said, too, that this punishment could be made less, or taken away altogether, if people said certain prayers or did good works for this reason. Sometimes 'indulgences,' or the letting off from punishment, were promised to people who would do certain things.

Unfortunately the poor people who were not educated sometimes thought that they could really buy forgiveness for their sins. They did not really understand what indulgences were. Just at the time when Luther was preaching at Wittenberg, a Dominican called John Tetzel was going about Germany, with the news that a great indulgence would be granted to anyone who gave money to help in the building of the church of St. Peter's at Rome, which the popes had got the great architect Bramante to plan for them and which was now half built. It was a magnificent building of great size, stretching out in the form of a cross, with a wonderful dome over the part where the arms of the cross met.

It was a good work to help to build this wonderful church, but Luther and other people were shocked at the way Tetzel spoke to the people about indulgences. It seemed to them that he was trying to sell forgiveness of sins, and was telling lies to the people just to get money for the Pope.

Some of the German people were already beginning to have much less respect for the popes than they had had in the Middle Ages. Some of the popes in the second part of the fifteenth century had lived very dreadful lives indeed. Even Pope Leo X, the Pope for whom John Tetzel was preaching the indulgences, did not care for many things except pleasure, although he was not a wicked man.

So when Luther began to preach against indulgences, and to say that it was wrong of the Pope to allow them to be preached as they were, there were already many people who were ready to listen to him.

Generally the preacher of an indulgence was received with great joy at each place to which he came. As he drew near to a place the priests and people would go out in a procession to meet him with lighted candles and banners. The message from the Pope giving permission for the indulgence was carried on a cloth of gold and velvet. The church bells were set ringing, and the preacher of the indulgence was taken to the chief church, where he could tell the people all about the indulgence.

To Luther, and to his Elector too, this all seemed just like a great auction sale. Frederick the Wise

Martin Luther *(From a painting by his friend, Lucas Oranach, 1529).*

A Great Church of the Renaissance: St. Peter's, Rome, for the Building of Which Tetzel's Indulgences Were Sold.

would not allow Tetzel to preach his indulgence in Saxony, but some of his people went to the nearest place in other states where they could get the indulgence. Some of them crowded back to Wittenberg with the papers on which the description of the indulgence was written to show Luther.

They were very much disappointed when he told them that the indulgences were no good to them at all, and that no pope or bishop could do the thing that they promised when they gave indulgences. He preached against them to the people, and at last he wrote down on a paper ninety-five reasons for not believing in indulgences, and nailed them to the door of the Castle Church at Wittenberg. Copies of this paper were printed off as quickly as the university printing press could do them, and in a short time they were spread all over Germany.

Everybody was very much excited. Soon afterwards Pope Leo sent a message to Luther that he must go to Rome and give an account of what he had done, but the Elector persuaded the Pope to allow Luther to be tried by the Pope's messenger, or Legate as he was called, in Germany.

When Luther stood before the cardinal Legate at the town of Augsburg, he was told that he must immediately say that the things he had said against indulgences were not true, but he declared he would never do that. He felt that he had spoken what he thought was the truth, and he could not now say differently. So he went back home, and the cardinal went back to the Pope to tell him how the German peasant monk had defied him.

For two years the question was not settled, and then the Pope sent a message to Luther telling him that he was excommunicated, and no longer belonged to the Church. But by this time Luther had begun not to believe any longer that the Pope ought to be head of the Church. At first he had certainly not meant to rebel against the Pope, but as the struggle went on, he grew more and more angry with the terrible anger he had inherited from his father, and in the end he made up his mind to rebel against the Pope and to get as many people as he could to follow him.

He showed how little he cared for the Pope when he got a great bonfire lighted outside the walls of Wittenberg, and burnt the Pope's message there before all the people. As the flames rose up, Luther's friends gave a great shout.

This was the beginning of Protestantism, by which half the people of Europe broke away from the Pope and set up religions of their own. It was the greatest change in history since the coming of Christianity into Europe, and it is very strange to remember that it was the preaching of one German peasant which brought it about. Still the Reformation would never have come if people had not already begun to get used to many new ideas which were brought to them by the Renaissance.

As time went on, Luther said that many other things which the Church taught were not true. He said that there were not seven sacraments, but only three, and later on he said there were only two. Many people listened eagerly to his teaching.

All the friars of his monastery at Wittenberg gave up their monastic life and went out to live in the world again. Many of them got married, as Luther himself did. He now hated monks and monasteries and nearly everything belonging to the Catholic Church. He wrote many books against the Pope.

In those days people who disagreed about any subject thought nothing of calling each other dreadful names in their books, and Luther was even more violent than the other people of his time in this way.

Luther told the people that there was really no need of priests, that people could save their souls only by really believing in Jesus Christ. He told them, too, that it was not true, as the Church taught, that in the mass the bread and wine which the priest consecrated were changed into the Body and Blood of Christ, which were received by the people who went to communion, but still he said that Christ was really present in the Sacrament. Above all, he told the people that they should read for themselves the words of Our Lord in the New Testament, and he himself translated the Bible into German, so that the people might read it for themselves.

Many of the German princes were pleased with Luther's teaching, because they were able to take the money and lands of the monasteries which were broken up.

The Emperor Charles V was against the Protestants, but in the end he had to agree that each prince should settle the religion of his state for himself. About half the states, chiefly those in the North, became Protestant, while the other half remained Catholic. One half of

Saxony, under Duke George, was Catholic, while the other half, under Luther's friend, the Elector Frederick, became Protestant.

There was a great deal of discontent and unhappiness at the time in Germany, and all these changes made the people ready to rebel. The towns, many of which became Protestant, were rich because the early sixteenth century was a time in which trade was growing, but in the country the poorer gentlemen who were called the Knights were growing poorer. Now they thought that they could become Protestants, fight against the rich Catholic princes, and especially the bishops who ruled over some of the German states. They fought what was known as the Knights' War, but they were defeated.

Then the peasants in Germany rose in revolt, but they were put down also. Thousands of people were killed, and there was terrible misery in the country. Many of these people said they were doing what Luther had taught them, but he would not have anything to do with them. Once he had started the Reformation he really left it to itself and did not become a leader who could give commands to the people like other reformers did, but settled down to his writing at Wittenberg. He said, in fact, that the people should take the religion given to them by their princes, and this is what soon happened in Germany, so that there were almost as many kinds of Protestantism as there were Protestant states.

THE GREAT KINGS OF THE RENAISSANCE

Charles V, who became Emperor the year after Luther had begun his fight against indulgences, was a young man. He belonged to the family of the Hapsburgs, who were the rulers of Austria. It had now become the custom for these rulers to be elected emperor. But the young Emperor Charles V had many other lands to rule over too. From his grandmother he had the Low Countries and the Free County of Burgundy, that part of Burgundy which had not been won by the kings of France. From his mother, Joanna the Mad, the daughter of Ferdinand and Isabella, he had inherited Spain and all the Spanish possessions, which were very great.

Soon after he was made Emperor, Charles gave up Austria and the kingdoms of Hungary and Bohemia to his brother Ferdinand, but still he had an immense empire. If only Charles could have governed Germany strongly, he would soon have been the strongest king in Europe; but it was very difficult to govern Germany, and the Reformation, which divided the princes still more against each other, made it more so. There were other kings who were watching Charles carefully for fear he should be too strong.

France was now a strong and united nation under another young king, Francis I. England had almost forgotten the Wars of the Roses, and was becoming a strong and important country under its second Tudor king, Henry VIII, who was also a young man at this time.

King Henry VIII Meeting the French King Francis at the Famous Field of the Cloth of Gold (*From a 16th century painting on wood at Hampton Court Palace*).

Both Francis I and Henry VIII were handsome men at this time, though they both became very ugly through too much self-indulgence as they grew older. They were both clever, but vain. They were both self-willed too, and got things very much their own way in the countries they ruled. In England the parliament was hardly ever called now to give advice, and when it was it did very much what the king told it to.

Charles V and Francis I were enemies from the beginning, and they were each anxious to get Henry VIII's help in fighting the other. It was to talk over this question that Henry met Francis in the North of France, when both kings dressed themselves and their servants so magnificently that the meeting was ever afterwards called the 'Field of the Cloth of Gold.' In spite of this, Henry afterwards helped Charles in his battles against the French king. A great deal of the fighting was done in Italy, for both Francis and Charles said that certain parts of Italy ought to belong to them.

Although the greater Italian states were rich, and the palaces of their Renaissance princes very beautiful, they were weak just because there were so many of them. They were jealous of one another, and could not all join against enemies like Francis or Charles. Instead, when they quarreled among themselves, some prince was sure to ask help from France or Germany, although they were sorry for it afterwards when they saw the misery which the foreign soldiers brought to Italy.

In one of the quarrels between Francis and Charles, the Pope, Clement VII, took the part of the French. The Emperor, though he was such a good Catholic, let his army march against Rome. Many of his soldiers were followers of Luther, and hated everything belonging to the old Church. They made a terrible attack on Rome, burning and killing and robbing, turning priests and nuns, children and old people, into the streets, and torturing them with the greatest cruelty. The Pope shut himself up in the castle of St. Angelo, but at last got the terrible foreign soldiers to go away by promising to pay a great deal of money to the Emperor. Rome never seemed quite so great and beautiful again, after the terrible destruction of this time. It happened in the year 1527.

Indeed, this seemed to be the end of the greatest time of the Renaissance. A sort of sadness came to Italy with these terrible wars. There were nearly always foreigners fighting over some part of her land, and there was no longer the great joyfulness which seemed to fill Italy in the days of the Renaissance. The great Michael Angelo lived and worked on far into the sixteenth century, but he was the last of the really great artists, and there is a sadness in his work. The artists who came after imitated the earlier painters and sculptors, and were not nearly so great.

All through the early years of the sixteenth century, the Protestants were preaching and teaching not only in Germany but in the other countries of Europe. We must see what happened to them, and which countries became Protestant and which remained Catholic.

THE REFORMATION IN ENGLAND

Henry VIII on his Throne (A painting by Holbein, who was court painter to Henry).

In England at first people took very little notice of the new German reformers, but neither did they take much notice of the Catholic reformers like Colet and Sir Thomas More, who wanted to make the Church better but would not rebel. This made some of the young scholars from Oxford and Cambridge feel inclined to follow Luther and his friends. Some of them went over to Germany to listen to the teaching of the reformers there, and then in a few years came back Protestants, and anxious to make all England Protestant too.

King Henry VIII was a clever man, and he was proud of the fact that he knew as much about religion and theology as most priests. When Martin Luther taught that there were only two sacraments. Baptism and the Holy Eucharist, Henry wrote a book against him, trying to prove that there were seven sacraments just as the Church taught. Pope Leo X was so pleased with this book, that he said that Henry should be called 'Defender of the Faith,' and all English kings and queens have kept this title ever since, although most of them have been Protestant. The letters 'F. D.' after the name of the king or queen are always still to be seen on English money.

The early Protestant reformers were always anxious to print the Bible in the language of their own country, so that all the people might read it for themselves. They thought that the people could learn much more from the Bible than from any Church. One of the young Protestant reformers, who had been to Germany and come back, translated the New Testament into English and had it printed, but the king had all the copies that could be found burnt before all the people at St. Paul's Cross in London.

Sir Thomas More

Sir Thomas More wrote against Tyndale, and Tyndale thought it would be safer to flee away to the Low Countries. For according to the law, heretics were to be burned to death. We shall see how, a little later, hundreds and thousands of both Catholics and Protestants were killed for believing in their religions. It was not for many years that people learnt toleration, that is, to allow people to believe what they liked.

Meanwhile the rulers of the Protestant states killed the Catholics, and the rulers of the Catholic states killed the Protestants, and there was terrible misery everywhere.

Although Henry VIII was so strong a Catholic at first, it was not many years before England became Protestant. When he found that the Pope would not give him something he wanted, Henry turned against him and began to believe like Luther, or pretended to believe, that the Pope had no right to be head of the Church.

The thing which Henry wanted was a divorce from his wife, the good queen, Catharine of Aragon. Catharine was a Spanish princess, who had been married to Henry many years when he first began to think of a divorce. She had only one child, the little Princess Mary, and Henry would have liked to have a son to be king after him. He said that he thought that there was no blessing on his marriage because Catharine had been married first to Henry's brother, who had died in a few months while he was still quite a boy. The Church did not allow a woman to marry the brother of her dead husband, but the Pope had given permission for the marriage of Henry and Catharine.

Now, Henry wanted the Pope to say that there had not really been any marriage, so that he could send Catharine away and marry again. But the Pope would not. Henry's chief adviser was the great Cardinal Wolsey. He had done everything he could to please the king. Indeed, he said afterwards as he lay dying that he wished he had served God as well as he had served the king. But when he could not get the Pope to give him the divorce, Henry turned against the cardinal and sent him away from the court. Afterwards, when the cardinal was at York, Henry sent for him to go to London to be tried for treason, which meant plotting against the king. Henry must have known that this was not true. Wolsey was very ill when the message reached him, and he died on the journey.

It was a very terrible thing about King Henry VIII that he was never grateful to anybody, but turned against his best friends as soon as they were no longer useful to him.

Henry then said that the Pope really had no right to judge in cases which came up in England, and he got Cranmer, archbishop of Canterbury, to give him the divorce. Queen Catharine was sent away, and Henry married a young and pretty lady of the court called Anne Boleyn. Soon afterwards he got the parliament to declare that he was 'Supreme Head on earth of the Church of England,' and that anyone who would not agree to this was guilty of treason and should be put to death. So in quite a different way from the German states which followed Luther, England became Protestant too.

Most of the English people changed their religion with the king, but many of the best people would not. The monks of the Carthusian monastery in London were asked to take the oath of supremacy, that is, to swear to take the king as head of the Church, but many of them would not, and so they were put to death in a very terrible way. Then Sir Thomas More, who had been Chancellor of England, but had given up his post, and Fisher, bishop of Rochester, who had preached against the king's doings, were sent for to go before Archbishop Cranmer at his palace at Lambeth. There they were to swear to agree that the children of the new queen had a right to have their father's crown after his death. A little daughter, who was afterwards Queen Elizabeth, had been born.

More and Fisher were also asked to take the oath of supremacy. They would not do this, though they were both quite ready to swear to be faithful to Henry and to the children of Anne Boleyn. The king might have been pleased with this, but Anne was very spiteful against More and Fisher and persuaded the king to have them put to death. So they both had their heads cut off.

It is said that More joked even on the scaffold. He was a very brave man. He had lived a splendid life, and he was not afraid to die. His beard had grown while he was in prison, and as he laid his head on the block, he put it to one side saying: 'Pity *that* should be cut: *it* has not committed treason.'

Yet at the same time King Henry did not like the Protestant teaching any more than before. Before the death of the Carthusians and of More and Fisher, for their clinging to the Pope, Protestant reformers had already been burnt for teaching the new doctrines.

The first who died for Protestantism in England was a Cambridge man called Thomas Bilney. He was a simple, gentle person and his friends called him 'Little Bilney,' but Henry

How a Town Was Besieged in the Sixteenth Century (*From a very old painting of the siege of Boulogne by Henry VIII in 1544. Cannon, protected, by great barrels, and archers attacked the town at the same time; but in those early days of gunpowder the arrows probably did nearly as much damage to the citizens as the cannon-balls*).

was very angry because he taught, like Luther, the people could save their souls through Faith alone. Before the end of his reign Henry had had many people, both Catholics and Protestants, killed for their faith. He would not let the people keep their Catholic religion, but he would not let them become too Protestant.

John Forest, a friar and a friend of Queen Catharine, was burnt in a fire made of a wooden image of a saint brought from Wales. For Henry was against the use of images, and had them destroyed wherever he could.

He got rid, too, of all the monasteries all over England. The monks and nuns were turned out and their property was taken by the king. Sometimes the beautiful churches and buildings of the monasteries were given to the king's friends. Many of them fell into ruin. Some of the monks who gave in easily were given money by the king. Others were turned out with nothing to live on. Some were put to death.

The poor people whom the monks had fed and clothed now became poorer still, and many people were angry that the monks should be treated so badly. In the North of England the people rose in a rebellion which was called the Pilgrimage of Grace, but it was easily put down. The new lords who got the monks' lands were often not so kind to the people who lived on the land as the monks had been, and there was a great deal of misery among the country people by the end of Henry's reign.

When Henry died his son Edward, who was only a boy, became king. He was fond of the Protestants, and during his short reign England became much more Protestant. But Edward VI did not live long.

After him his sister Mary, the daughter of Queen Catharine of Aragon, became queen. Edward had been the son of Henry's third wife, for Anne Boleyn had had her head cut off because the king said she was not faithful to him. Henry had six wives altogether, and another besides Anne Boleyn had her head cut off.

Queen Mary made England Catholic again, though she could not get the people who had the monks' lands to give them up again. Most of the people seemed to be quite pleased to become Catholic once more, but the people who really believed in Protestantism would

King Edward

not. So Queen Mary had them burnt. Although she was a good queen, she thought it was her duty to do this.

Among others Archbishop Cranmer, the great archbishop who had helped Henry VIII so much, was burnt too. He had been very frightened in prison, and had signed a paper saying that he did not believe in the Protestant religion, but when he knew he was to be burnt all the same he was sorry he had done this, and when he was tied to the stake to be burnt he plunged his hand into the flames, saying that his hand should be burnt first because he had done this wrong thing with it.

Queen Mary did not live long. She died broken-hearted at the way she was left alone by her husband, the great King Philip of Spain, who had married her because he wanted the English people to help him in his wars. They would not help him, and as he did not really love Mary he left her and stayed at home in Spain.

When Queen Mary died, Elizabeth, the daughter of Henry VIII and Anne Boleyn, became queen, and England became Protestant once more. This time it was really Protestant, and all through Elizabeth's long reign, which was a very great and glorious reign in many ways, the Catholics were hunted out. Priests who were found in England hiding so that they could say mass for the Catholics were put to a very terrible death, while all Catholics had to pay great fines for not going to church, and even the Catholic noblemen and gentlemen became very poor. Many of them sent their sons to Catholic countries to be educated, although this, too, was forbidden.

Yet Elizabeth also was against the people who were too Protestant. She punished the Puritans, as the people were called who at the end of her reign were trying to do away with the ceremonies which made the English Church seem to them too Catholic. Some Puritans who wrote books about these things had their hands cut or their ears slit. Some were even put to death. For Elizabeth was in many things very like her father, Henry VIII, and she was determined that the people should do things just as she told them.

Queen Elizabeth and Mary Queen of Scots

Scotland became Protestant too, although its beautiful young queen, Mary Queen of Scots, was a Catholic. Mary had been brought up in France, and had been married to the young French king, Francis II., but he had died and she came back to Scotland soon after Elizabeth became queen of England. But the Protestant Scottish nobles turned against her, and the great Protestant preacher John Knox preached against her, calling her terrible names.

Mary Queen of Scots (*From a portrait by a famous French painter named Clouet. painted when the queen was in mourning as a widow*).

Mary did some foolish things which gave her enemies the chance of doing her harm. She was shut up in the castle of Lochleven, but was helped by a young page to escape. The Catholic nobles helped her to fight her enemies, but she lost the battle and fled into England, hoping that Elizabeth would help her.

But Elizabeth had always been very jealous of Mary because of her beauty. Mary Queen of Scots had very beautiful golden-brown hair and a fair complexion. She had lovely brown eyes, and was very graceful and charming. Elizabeth who was very vain, was not nearly so beautiful, and this was one reason for which she had always disliked Mary. For nineteen years she kept her shut up in prison.

The English Catholics thought that Mary had a better right to the throne of England than Elizabeth, and some of them plotted to kill Elizabeth and make Mary queen of England. The plot was found out, and the plotters were put to death. Elizabeth said that Mary had known about it all, and had her put on trial and in the end put to death.

When Queen Mary, dressed in crimson, walked on to the platform in the great hall at the Palace of Fotheringay, where she was to be killed, she was an old woman. Her golden hair had become white in the long years she had been in prison. But she was still beautiful, and she died very bravely, comforting the women who were with her and who were crying.

John Knox and the Scottish Protestants were not Lutherans. They were followers of the great French reformer John Calvin. King Francis I began to persecute the Protestant reformers as soon as they appeared in France, and when he died the kings who came after him did the same, and France always remained Catholic. But there were always some Protestants in France, although later on, as we shall see, the Protestants suffered more terribly there than in any other country.

John Calvin was one of the early French Protestants, but he fled away to Switzerland and there became one of the greatest Protestant leaders. Switzerland became almost altogether Protestant, though a few of its cantons, as its divisions were called, remained Catholic. The city of Geneva, which had been before governed by a bishop, gave itself up to Calvin, and he governed it in his own way. Protestants from all over Europe travelled to Geneva to hear his teaching.

He taught very different things from Luther. He did not believe at all that Christ was present in the Holy Eucharist. He taught, too, that men had no free will, that is, that people cannot really choose whether they will be good or bad, and that even before a person is born he or she is destined to go to heaven or hell after their death.

This seems a very terrible teaching, and it might seem that the people who believed it might think it would not

John Calvin. One of the greatest Protestant Reformers.

really matter how they behaved. But this was not so. Still the Calvinists were often rather sad and gloomy people, and there was not much joy in their religion. But they loved it dearly, and fought for it with their lives.

The French Protestants were Calvinists, and so were the Protestants in the Low Countries. In both places they were terribly persecuted. The year before Francis I died, three thousand Protestants were killed in Provence in the South of France. The South was always the Protestant part of France, just as it was the part where there had been most heresy in the Middle Ages. In spite of persecution, the Protestant religion grew strong in the South of France. The great nobles there became Protestant, and were always ready to fight their Catholic king.

So strong did the Protestants become, that they were able to fight hard battles against the Catholics, and during the second half of the sixteenth century there were the most terrible civil wars, in which Frenchmen fought against Frenchmen because of their differences in religion.

The chief ruler in France in the second part of the sixteenth century was Catherine de Medici, one of the Medici family which ruled in Florence. She was married to Henry II, who was king of France after Francis I. While her husband was alive she had very little power in France, but when he died she ruled the country for her sons, who were very delicate, and died one after the other.

It was the eldest, Francis II, who was the husband of Mary Queen of Scots, and it was when he died that Mary went back to Scotland.

Catherine loved power above all things. Just like many Italian princes of that time, she would do anything to keep it. She seemed never to think whether a thing was good or bad to do, but only whether it would help her to keep power.

It was this which led her to make a most terrible attack on the Protestants of France.

At first she tried to keep the Catholics and Protestants fairly equal in power, and she invited the Admiral Coligny to the court. He was the chief Protestant nobleman in France. Catherine's son, Charles IX, a young boy, was king at this time. But Catherine soon saw that her son had taken a great liking for the brave old admiral, and she began to be afraid that Coligny would get power over the boy and her own power would grow less.

She had arranged, too, that her daughter, Margaret, should marry another Protestant, the handsome young King Henry of Navarre. The French part of the kingdom of Navarre is on the borders of France and Spain. The wedding was to be a very splendid one. It was in the summer of the year 1572. Even the Catholics of Paris could not help liking the young Henry with his pleasant ways and his charming smile.

On the wedding day he was dressed in pale yellow satin, ornamented with silver and pearls, and there was a wonderful procession of bishops and cardinals and knights. For three days there was feasting and gaiety in Paris, but the Queen Mother got a man to shoot at the admiral in the streets, hoping to kill him. The shot did not kill the admiral, but blew off one of his fingers. No one knew who had given the order, but the Huguenots, as the

French Protestants were called, were very angry, and Charles was full of anxiety. But his mother told him that the Protestants must be killed, and especially the admiral.

The poor boy hated the idea, but he was very weak and used to doing what his mother ordered. At last he cried out that if the admiral was to be killed then all the Huguenots in France should die too, so that there would be none left to reproach him.

Catherine was only too pleased at this idea. She gave secret orders that the Huguenots throughout France should be killed. The thing was to be done suddenly and quietly one summer night, and so it was. In Paris and all over France the Huguenots were suddenly attacked and killed in thousands.

Admiral Coligny was thrown by a servant from a window and fell dead in the street below. The massacre took place on the night before the Feast of St. Bartholomew, and was ever afterwards called the Massacre of St. Bartholomew. Henry of Navarre was not killed because he was the queen's son-in-law.

All the Protestants in Europe were full of surprise and anger at this terrible massacre. The young king, Charles IX, could never forget it himself. He died two years afterwards, full of horror still at the memory of it. Catherine's favorite son then became king as Henry III. He was killed in 1589, a few months after the death of his mother, who kept power to the last.

All during this time there were still miserable struggles between the Catholics and Protestants. A new and better time came when Henry III died, and after some years of fighting the handsome king of Navarre became king of France. He was called Henry IV, and he was one of the best kings France had ever had. He became a Catholic, because he saw that if he did not the Catholics of France would never have him as king. But he was never very serious about religion, and the story is told that when someone spoke to him about changing so easily, he laughed and said that Paris was 'well worth a mass.'

But Henry would not have any more persecution of the Protestants. They were now allowed to set up churches, and pray in their own way in certain towns. Indeed, it was through his kindness to the Huguenots that Henry IV died after a very short reign, and before he had time to make France into the greatest state of Europe, as he would have done if he had lived.

Henry was going to start in two days' time for a great war with Germany, when he was stabbed to the heart in the streets of Paris by a man named Ravaillac, who thought that he was not a good Catholic. It will be interesting to see what had been happening to the Protestants in other countries ruled by Catholic kings.

CHAPTER XXXII—THE COUNTER-REFORMATION

We have seen how, even before the Protestant reformers rebelled against the Church, Catholic reformers like Erasmus and Colet and More had tried to make the Church better. People had read their books and laughed at the witty and clever things in those of Erasmus and More; but there was no reform, and the Church and the people did not become more religious and better educated as the reformers had hoped, though there were always some people who were hoping for better things.

But when first Luther and then other Protestant reformers rose in rebellion against the Church, at last the Pope and the Catholics were startled. People began to think more seriously about religion. Many people were sad when they saw how the old teaching and ways of the Church were attacked by the reformers. This led to a new time in the life of the Church, a time when religion spread once more among the people, and new religious orders and great saints arose once more in the Church.

The changes at this time are called the 'Counter-Reformation,' which means the movement against the Reformation.

In this wonderful Counter-Reformation against Protestantism many countries were kept from being Protestant, and some which had become Protestant were even won back. It was the rise of this great eagerness and new love for the old Church which led to the great struggle between Catholics and Protestants during the second half of the sixteenth century and on to the seventeenth. In the end it was chiefly the Southern people who remained Catholic.

There were never more than a very few Protestants in Italy and Spain, and it was in these countries that the Counter-Reformation began. After many years of struggle nearly all South Germany was Catholic, and the Northern parts Protestant. Countries where the Slavs had settled, like Hungary and Poland, were Catholic. The Northern nations, Norway, Sweden and Denmark, were Protestant. We have already seen how England and Scotland became Protestant, while Ireland, which had been conquered by England, was always Catholic.

St. Ignatius of Loyola. This statue is in St Walburge's, a former Jesuit church, in Preston, Lancashire. Photo credit, Brother Lawrence Lew, O.P.

It was in Catholic countries under Protestant rulers and Protestant countries under Catholic rulers, that the bitterest struggles between the Reformation and the Counter-Reformation took place.

The great new religious order of the Counter-Reformation was the Society of Jesus. Those who belonged to it soon came to be called Jesuits. The man who starred it was St. Ignatius Loyola. Ignatius was a Spaniard and the son of a noble house. When he was a boy he was a page at the court of King Ferdinand of Aragon. He afterwards became a soldier, but was wounded in battle and made lame for life.

While he lay in bed, ill from his wound, Ignatius asked for some books to be brought to him. He wanted stories of knights and ladies such as he had read before and loved. But someone gave him instead the *Lives of the Saints.* He began to read them without much interest, for though he was a good Catholic he had not before thought very much about religion. But now all of a sudden it seemed to be the only thing worth living for.

Ignatius felt that he too could try to be a saint, and if he could no longer be a soldier of the king he could be what was much better—a soldier of Christ and a knight of Our Lady. Ignatius had always been very brave. When his leg was first hurt the bone had been joined badly, and the doctors had to break it and set it again. Ignatius bore it without a cry, just clenching his hands tightly. Now, when he changed his life altogether, he made up his mind to suffer bravely for the sake of Christ. At first he thought he would go and fight in the Holy Land, like the crusaders of the Middle Ages, and he did make a pilgrimage there.

But then the thought came to him that he might do far better work by fighting against Protestantism in Europe. He was not very well-educated, as he had been trained to be a soldier, and so, though he was a grown man, he went to several universities and studied beside young boys quite simply and humbly.

At the university of Paris several young men joined him, among them another Spaniard who became the great St. Francis Xavier.

They made up their minds to form a society, and in the end they got the Pope to allow them to do so. Many men joined the Society of Jesus, and Ignatius was head of all. He was called the general, and everyone in the society had to obey him, just as soldiers obey their generals without any question. It was this wonderful obedience which made the Society of Jesus different from any other religious order. The general knew that he had only to give an order, and any member of the society would obey whatever it might be. And the only reason for the setting up of the society was to work for the Pope.

In a short time the Jesuits spread into every country of Europe, and the Pope knew that he had in them a great army to help on the work of the Counter-Reformation. No Jesuit ever thought of himself, but always of the society. He was taught to do this from the first day he joined it.

St. Ignatius wrote a wonderful book called the *Spiritual Exercises*. The exercises were thoughts and meditations about God and religion, and every novice, as the young men who were being trained to be Jesuits were called, went into retreat for four weeks when he joined the society. That is to say, he did not speak to his companions, but gave up his time to prayer, and went right through the *Spiritual Exercises*.

The Jesuits set up many schools for boys, and trained their pupils to feel about the Church and Pope just as they did themselves. Jesuits travelled into far-off countries like India and Japan and the newly discovered America, giving their whole lives to teaching the Catholic religion.

Some Jesuits were always to be found in England under Elizabeth, although they knew that they would certainly be put to death if they were found, as many of them were. After St. Ignatius died his work went on, and the Jesuits today are still governed by a general whom all must obey like soldiers.

As there had been so much questioning about the Church's teaching, a great council was called at the city of Trent, in the North of Italy, to lay down once more the teaching of the Church. It met in the year 1545, and with interruptions went on until 1563.

The emperor, Charles V, and some of the Catholics hoped that the council would make some sort of agreement with the Protestants, and so perhaps get them back to the Church again, but the greater number of the Catholics, and especially the Jesuits, would not hear of this. Charles V was dead before the great Council of Trent came to an end, but he already saw that there was no hope of the Catholics and Protestants coming to an agreement. The council made the teaching of the Church plainer than ever, and made it plain, too, that no one who had any other opinions could remain in the Church.

THE STRUGGLE BETWEEN SPAIN AND THE NETHERLANDS

Among the strictest Catholics of the Counter-Reformation was King Philip II of Spain. He was the son of the Emperor Charles V, who in the year 1555, tired out and old before his time, gave up all his empire and went to live quietly in Spain. He did not become a monk, but he lived near a monastery and joined the monks in their long prayers. He did not live long. Charles's brother, Ferdinand, became emperor after him, but his son Philip became king of Spain and ruler of the Low Countries.

Philip was a young man with fair hair and a broad forehead and blue eyes like his father, Charles V, but he was not like his father in other ways. Charles had always been wise and fairly tolerant, and had treated the Protestants much better than any of the other Catholic rulers.

But Philip was quite different. He was absolute ruler of Spain. No one but the king had any power there, and he was determined to rule the Low Countries in just the same way. He

Philip II of Spain and the Netherlands (A portrait by the great painter Rubens).

hated the Protestants, and as there were many Protestants in the Low Countries, a terrible struggle broke out between them and Spain.

There were seventeen provinces altogether in the Low Countries, or the Netherlands as they were called. Each had its own ways and its own government, but they were all joined under one ruler, and this ruler was now the king of Spain. The people of the different provinces belonged to different races. There were Dutchmen in the North, many of whom were fishermen. The land was very low indeed there, and great walls or dykes were built to keep the sea from covering it.

There is a story of how a little boy was once going to his home at night when he saw that there was a hole in a dyke and the water was pouring in. He was afraid that if he went on to tell anybody the water would have time to flood the land, so he bravely pushed his arm through the hole. It was just big enough to stop it, and there he stayed all night in the cold and dark, until in the morning some workmen passing to their work found him. The hole was mended and the land was saved through the courage of the boy.

In the South and East the people were Flemish and Dutch. There were many cities and much trade. Very early the Protestant reformers had spread their teaching among the Netherlanders, and even Charles V had put many of the people to death, for he could do there what he did not dare to do in Germany. Yet Charles was really a Fleming and liked the people of the Netherlands, while Philip was a thorough Spaniard,

As soon as he became king, Philip sailed away to Spain, and left his sister Margaret to rule the Netherlands. But he left orders, too, that the Protestants should be rooted out of the land. 'I shall not rest,' he said, 'while there is one man left believing in the teaching of Martin Luther.'

He sent men called Inquisitors to find out which people were Protestants and to have them burnt to death. In Spain itself the Inquisition had been set up. It was in the hands of Dominicans, and it showed no mercy to Protestants. The story of the terrors of the Inquisition spread all over Europe, and made the Protestant countries like England hate Spain more than ever.

Not only the Protestants in the Netherlands, but the Catholics too were angry against Philip. They were ready to fight not only for their religion but also for freedom. Even Margaret, though she was a Catholic, sent word to Philip by the Catholic Count Egmont that he was making a mistake in his rule of the Low Countries. But he took no notice. Then two-hundred nobles carried a petition to Margaret at the court of Brussels, and when it was read to her she said nothing, but tears ran down her face. A story is told that someone standing near her said, 'Surely your Highness is not afraid of these Beggars.'

The name 'Beggars' stuck to the Protestants, and became their watchword. Still Philip took no notice. Then the news came that he was sending the great duke of Alva to govern the Netherlands. Everyone had heard of him, and knew that he would have no mercy. 'I have tamed men of iron,' he said; 'shall I not easily crush these men of butter?' He was to find that here again he had men of iron to deal with. Alva arrived with a great Spanish army. He had kept them in order while they marched, but in the Netherlands they were allowed to treat the people in the most terrible way.

The first thing Alva did was to put the two Catholic counts Egmont and Horn, who had stood up for the freedom of their country, in prison. He pretended to be friendly to them and asked them to his house at Brussels. When they were there, they were seized and carried off as prisoners to the castle of Ghent. After being there a year they were brought before the 'Council of Blood,' as the people called the judges whom Alva had set up to try the Protestants. They were condemned to die, and even the Spanish soldiers cried when they saw them led to the scaffold in the great square at Brussels. They walked bravely to their death, Count Egmont dressed in red, with a short cloak of black and gold over his shoulder. He prayed as he walked.

Alva wished to frighten the people by these things, but he only made them hate him. Margaret, who had now gone away from the Netherlands, had said that he would 'make the very name of Spaniard hateful to the people.' And so he did.

Hundreds of people besides the two counts were condemned to death by the Council of Blood, but the 'Beggars' only grew more determined than ever. They now had for their leader William of Orange. Orange was a little district in the South-East of France, but William had lands in the Netherlands, and Germany too, and was much more German than French. William's father was a Lutheran, but Charles V had had the boy brought up as a Catholic at his court. He was fond of him, and when he resigned his crown to Philip, in the great court of his palace at Brussels, the Emperor leaned on the shoulder of William, who was then a young man of twenty-two.

William fought for Charles in his wars with France, and he was one of the men who made the Treaty with France which ended the wars. He was very careful not to say anything too much at this time, for fear the French would take advantage of some slip of the tongue, and ever afterwards he was called 'William the Silent,' but he was not at all a quiet man. He was always very eager for what he thought was right, and was a great speaker. He used fine language, and could easily persuade the people who heard him to do what he wanted.

When Philip became king, William the Silent was made ruler over Holland and some other of the provinces of the North. But he never liked Philip, and he joined the counts of Egmont and Horn against him. Soon afterwards William became a Protestant, first a Lutheran and then a Calvinist, and from this time he led the Protestants in their struggle with Philip. William had left the Netherlands and gone to his lands in Germany before Alva came, but his eldest son, Philip William, a boy studying at the university of Louvain, was seized by the Spaniards and carried off to Spain. There he was brought up by Philip as an enemy to his father.

Many of the 'Beggars' had begun almost to live on the sea. The Netherlanders were always very much at home on the sea, and they now began to revenge themselves by attacking the Spanish ships, and taking their treasures.

Suddenly, on the 1st of April in the year 1572, some of the 'Beggars' ships sailed into the mouth of the river Meuse, and attacked the town of Brill. A ferryman saw them coming, and told the Spaniards and the people in the town, which was under the rule of Alva. The ferryman stated that perhaps there were five thousand, although he knew that there were not more than three hundred. Then all the people fled away from Brill, and the 'Beggars' took it for their own. It was the beginning of a great change.

All over the Northern provinces the people rose against the Spaniards, and took William the Silent to rule over them. The duke of Alva was terribly angry, but the Netherlanders were full of joy, and the people sang in the streets

'On April Fools' Day
Duke Alva's spectacles were stolen away.'

The name Brill means 'spectacles' in Dutch, and the rhyme was a pun on the name of the town.

The Protestants had to fight many a hard battle still against the Spaniards. In the first winter the Spaniards were surprised to see the Dutchmen skating over the frozen waters to fight them, but the Spaniards ordered skates too, and soon learned to use them. The beautiful city of Haarlem was besieged for seven months, but had to give way at last. Still thousands of Spaniards had lost their lives in taking it. Then began the siege of the town of Leyden, which lasted for a year. The people in it were dying of starvation, but still they would not give way.

Then William the Silent, 'Father William,' as the Dutch lovingly called him, thought of a way to save it. He had holes made in the dykes, and the water flowed in on the land. The people went into their ships. 'Better a drowned land than a lost land,' said William. The Spaniards laughed, for they thought the water would never rise as high as Leyden, but it did. The Spaniards fled away, and the 'Beggars' sailed up in their ships to save the people of Leyden, and to give them food and comfort.

For many years yet the struggle between Spain and the Netherlands went on. The duke of Alva went back to Spain, but Philip sent his own half-brother, the brave Don John of Austria, to take his place. One thing which prevented the Netherlanders from conquering the Spaniards was that the Provinces would not really join themselves together, as William advised them. He himself had no wish to be ruler, and was quite ready to set up a republic. But the Southern Provinces, which were Catholic, did not like this. There were many nobles there, and they did not like the idea of a republic.

The Spaniards Capture Antwerp in their Long Struggle with the Dutch. *This was one of many tragedies in the long fight of the Dutch people for freedom from Spanish tyranny. The Spaniards were the finest soldiers in Europe in the sixteenth century, and the stubborn resistance of the 'clumsy' Dutch so infuriated them that when they captured Antwerp they took so mad and merciless a revenge that it has always been known as the 'Spanish Fury.' (From a sixteenth-century engraving).*

In the end William lived the last part of his life very quietly in the North. He had spent nearly all his money for his country, and at last he was to give his life too. Philip had declared William an outlaw and a traitor, and offered a reward of a great deal of money to anyone who should rid the world of such a pest.

A Spaniard shot at William in the streets of Antwerp, but though the ball went in by his right ear and out through his left cheek he was not killed, but his wife died from the shock. Though William knew that he was always in danger, he could not bear to have himself guarded all the time, and at last he was shot down by a Frenchman in his own house at Delft. The people, and even the children, wept at the news, but William had after all won freedom for his country.

It was not long before the Spaniards had to give the Netherlands their freedom, for Philip had great battles to fight in other places. Great English soldiers crossed the sea to fight for the Netherlands against Spain, and so at last in 1609 the seven Northern Provinces became independent of Spain. The ten Provinces of the South remained under the government of the daughter of the Spanish king and her husband, but they, too, had won the liberties for which they had fought. The Northern Provinces are now the little Protestant kingdom of Holland, and the Southern Provinces the little Catholic kingdom of Belgium.

So ended one of the bitterest struggles between the Reformation and the Counter-Reformation.

Chapter XXXIII—England and Spain

In the year 1558, Mary Tudor, the sad daughter of Queen Catharine of Aragon, had died, and her half-sister, Elizabeth, the daughter of Henry VIII and Anne Boleyn, had become queen of England. She was only twenty-five years old then and she ruled England until she was seventy. Mary Tudor had said that when she died two names would be found written on her heart, those of 'Philip' and 'Calais'—Philip, the Spanish husband whom she loved, and who had left her lonely, and Calais, the only place which England had kept in France, and which had been taken again by the French when Philip got the English to help him in his wars against France.

Elizabeth, One of the Greatest of English Sovereigns (*A painting by George Gower*).

Now Philip Would have liked to marry Queen Elizabeth and so keep the help of England, but though Elizabeth never meant to marry him, she did not say 'No' at once. She never really meant to marry anybody. She was very vain, and loved to think that men admired her, although they never did fall in love with her, as people did with Mary Queen of Scots, of whom Elizabeth was so jealous.

But all through her reign Elizabeth pretended that she was going to marry first one foreign prince and then another. She did this to keep other countries friendly to England when she needed them, for with all her faults

Elizabeth loved England, and was wonderfully clever in keeping her country safe and strong at a very difficult time.

When Elizabeth came to the throne, England was not one of the greatest countries in Europe, but it was the greatest of all when she died. There were sad sides to her reign, such as the persecution of the Catholics and the Puritans, but in other ways it was a 'golden' age. England became the greatest power on the seas, and the people were full of joy and interest in life. There was a kind of late Renaissance in England when the Italian Renaissance was really ending. Great poets arose in England at this time. There was Edmund Spenser, who wrote the great poem called the Faerie Queene in honor of Elizabeth, and there was Sir Philip Sidney, who wrote beautiful sonnets.

Sidney was a brave soldier as well as a poet, and one of the noblest men of his time. He was killed while he was fighting for the Protestants of the Low Countries against Spain. A story is told of how when Sidney lay wounded on the battlefield he was very thirsty, and water was brought to him to drink. But he saw a poor soldier, who was lying near also wounded, look longingly at the water, and he told the person who was offering him the water to give it to the poor soldier instead, saying: 'He needs it more than I do.' There was, too, the greatest poet England, and perhaps the world, has ever known, William Shakespeare. Before the end of the reign he was writing his wonderful plays, and they were being acted in London.

It was a time, too, of great English sailors and soldiers and adventurers. It was no longer Italians like Columbus who were the leaders of discovery, but Englishmen like Sir Francis Drake and Sir Walter Raleigh.

It was partly this new love of adventure and the determination to be the greatest of all on the seas, that led to the terrible hatred between the English and the Spaniards in Elizabeth's reign. It was partly, too, the question of religion. By this time Englishmen loved their new religion and hated Catholicism, and they hated Spain because she was the most Catholic power of all.

All through Elizabeth's reign the English people were longing for war with Spain, but it was many years before Elizabeth would allow it. She waited until she felt that England was strong enough to conquer.

Yet long before the war began English sailors were attacking the great Spanish ships, or galleons as they were called, which were always sailing home to Spain laden with gold and silver and other treasure from the rich mines of the great continent of South America. For nearly the whole of South America belonged to Spain.

This is how it had happened. After Columbus had found lands across the Atlantic other discoverers followed him. In the year 1497, an Italian, John Cabot, with his son Sebastian, sailed out of Bristol harbor in a ship given to him by King Henry VII of England. He discovered the land which is now called Newfoundland, and in other voyages he came upon Labrador. But always he thought, like Columbus, that it was some part of China.

It was another Italian, called Amerigo Vespucci, who first declared that he believed the new land to be another continent altogether, and that another great ocean separated it from China.

He had sailed to the Northern coast of what was afterwards called South America. And so although it was through the genius of Columbus that the great new continent was discovered, it was called America after Amerigo Vespucci, who first guessed that it was not China.

But though it was Italians who made the first discoveries in America, it was Spain which had helped them, and soon Spaniards began to be most eager in the search, especially when it was found that the gold and silver and treasure which Columbus had searched for and never found in the North were really to be had in the South.

It was a Spaniard named Bilbao who was the first European to look upon the great ocean at the other side of America. Bilbao was one of the many Spaniards who left Spain and went to live at Hayti, the colony set up by Columbus. But Bilbao was not a good farmer, and he was soon in debt. It was a rule that no one could leave Hayti without paying his debts, but one day Bilbao hid himself in a barrel on a ship which was to sail away from Hayti. He crawled out when the ship was well out to sea, and so he got away. But the ship was wrecked on the coast of the Isthmus of Darien, now called Panama, the narrow piece of land joining North and South America. Bilbao found that there were many rich villages of natives near.

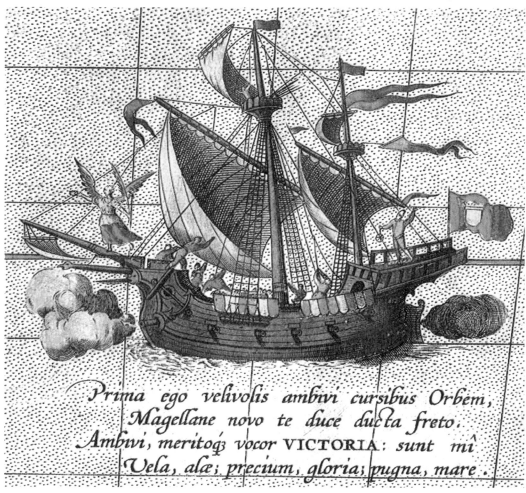

Detail from a Map of Ortelius: Magellan's Ship, Victoria

The discoverers called all the different peoples in America Indians, but they were not at all like the people of India, and they were very different, too, from one another. In the North the chief race were a red-skinned people, who were called the Red Indians. They were not exactly savages, though they lived very simply. In the South the people were darker, but were quite different from the negroes whom Prince Henry's explorers had found in Africa.

In some parts of South America these Indians were civilized, and had built great cities, but it was not a very high civilization. In some ways they lived rather in the same way as the Persians in the days of Xerxes or Darius. They made a great show of gold and precious stones, but they had never found out how to use iron, and were not, of course, nearly so civilized as the peoples of Europe. But it was not these more civilized peoples whom Bilbao saw, though he was told about them. Bilbao made up his mind to climb the high mountains which divided the isthmus. And so he did. From the top he saw the great ocean to the West. He and his companions sang the Te Deum, the great hymn of joy, and set up a cross, taking possession of the sea for the king of Spain.

It was a Portuguese, Magellan, who shortly afterwards sailed in Spanish ships right round the South of South America, and into the great sea beyond which he called the Pacific Ocean. Then, too, he sailed right across that ocean for over ninety days until, nearly dead with starvation, he and his men reached the Islands of the Philippines, as they were called later, after Philip II.

Everywhere these discoverers went they tried to make the natives Christians, and got them to pay tribute to the great king of Spain. But one native prince in the Philippines refused to do this, and Magellan was killed in a fight with him. Many of his men were killed too and others had died of starvation, and so it was only a few in the *Victoria,* one of the five ships which had set out on the voyage, who came again to Spain. They had suffered terribly, but they had done one of the most wonderful things men have ever done upon the seas. They were the first to sail right round the world. The straits to the South of South America were called after Magellan, the greatest explorer after Columbus that the world has ever had.

SPAIN'S CONQUESTS IN AMERICA

It was not long before the Spanish took for themselves two of the richest and most civilized parts of the new continent, Mexico, the land just to the North of the Isthmus of Panama, and Peru to the South of it. Mexico was conquered by a Spanish gentleman called Fernando Cortes. He landed on the spot which was afterwards called Vera Cruz, or the True Cross, and was surprised to see natives in fine cotton clothes and ornaments of gold coming down to meet them. These men could draw and sketch, for they immediately began making drawings of the Spaniards and their ships, which they called 'water houses.' These drawings they carried away to their king, Montezuma.

He was a very splendid king and lived in a very magnificent way in his chief town of Mexico. He never walked when the people could see him, but was carried by noblemen.

Hernan Fernando Cortes

In his palace when he walked, rich tapestries were laid down before him. He never used the same cup or dish twice. He agreed to see the Spaniards, but would not listen to their story of Christ or become a Christian. Cortes really took him prisoner, and the Spaniards, thinking the Mexicans were going to attack them, attacked them first, and a fight broke out. Cortes made Montezuma appear at one of the high windows of his palace and tell his people to stop fighting. But the people were angry and threw stones at him. He was hurt and broken-hearted, and died a few days after.

Cortes had to go away, but he brought back from Spain more ships and men, and laid siege to Mexico. It was a terrible siege, but the young king, Montezuma's nephew, would not give in. At last the city was taken, and the young king thought that he would be killed, but Cortes treated him with great respect, telling him that the Spaniards knew how to respect courage even in an enemy. But Mexico now belonged to Spain, and another beautiful city was built on the ruins of the old.

It was Pizarro, a very different man from Cortes, who conquered Peru. Peru was the most civilized part of all America, and the richest. Its kings were called the Incas. They had a great army, but did not know anything about guns or swords, Pizarro with a few men easily conquered them. He had to march miles and miles to reach the capital of Peru, and to cross a great range of mountains. He was very brave, but very cruel.

The Inca refused to become Christian, and was taken prisoner. He made a mark on the wall of the room in which he was shut, and told Pizarro he would give him the room full of gold to that height. Pizarro took the gold, but soon afterwards had the king killed, and now Peru, too, belonged to Spain. In the city of Cuzco, the capital of Peru, wonderful treasures were found. There were figures made of gold and floors made of silver. The Spaniards sent great ship loads home to Spain, and it was these ships which were so often attacked and taken by the English sailors.

At last the Spaniards found that it was safer to send several ships home together, and so they used to gather together in the mouth of the La Plata river in the South-East of South America, and sail off together at regular times. A number of ships sailing like this came to be called the 'Plate Fleet.'

The English and French ships soon began to sail to South America to take their part in its trade, but the Spaniards forbade this. English sailors who were caught were carried off to Spain, and dreadful stories were told of how they were tortured by the Inquisition. All this made the sailors of the two nations very bitter, and this is how there came to be endless struggles on the seas long before Elizabeth and Philip began the war between the two nations.

One of the greatest sailors of Queen Elizabeth's time was Francis Drake. He was a Devonshire man, like many of the best sailors of the time. He was one of those who had most often attacked the Spaniards on the sea and carried off their treasure. His relation, John Hawkins, was another of these Devonshire men. It was he who started the cruel slave trade, carrying off negroes from Africa in ship loads to America, where the Spaniards were glad to buy them.

For the native Indians were not fit for hard work, and were fast dying off, as certain natives always seem to do when more civilized people take their lands. This dreadful slave trade went on for many years. When Englishmen had settled in North America, they too bought slaves to work for them. The negroes are a strong race, and there are thousands and thousands of them in America today. They are free now, but this is how they came to America.

Francis Drake sailed round the world after attacking the Spanish treasure ships on the coast of South America. It took him three years to do it, and he had to put down rebellion among his men, as so many of these early leaders had to do. It was his friend, Thomas Doughty, who led the rebellion, and Drake had his head cut off, although he loved him. For he knew that only so could he keep himself and his ship safe. When, after three years, Drake landed in England, Elizabeth went herself to Plymouth, and knighted him on the deck of his ship, the Golden Hind, which she ordered to be kept in memory of the voyage, and people felt that now, at last, England was as great as Spain on the seas. She was soon to be much greater.

King Philip took it as a great insult that Elizabeth should honor the man who had taken Spanish treasure. He was more angry still at the execution of Mary Queen

Sir Francis Drake

of Scots in 1587. He said, too, that now he was the real king of England because the Catholics did not really think that Elizabeth had a right to the throne, because Queen Catherine was still alive when Anne Boleyn married Henry VIII.

Philip had already been getting together a great fleet to fight England, and in April 1587, two months after Mary Stewart's death, Drake sailed into the harbor at Cadiz, and set fire to thirty ships of the fleet which was lying ready there. He boasted afterwards that he had 'inged the king of Spain's beard this time,' and he wanted to do the same over and over again, so that the Spanish fleet would never be able to attack England. But Elizabeth was afraid that while the English fleet was away the Spaniards might suddenly attack England in another direction, and land a great army.

The Spanish armies were very fine, and they had had many years of training in the wars in the Netherlands. The help given by Englishmen to the Netherlands was another thing which had made Philip angry. So, in the spring of 1588, Philip had a great fleet ready to attack England. Some of the Spaniards boasted that it was so strong that it could never be conquered, and called it the 'Invincible Armada.' But one great mistake that the Spaniards made was to build great ships, chiefly to carry large numbers of soldiers. They did not understand that the ships themselves should be easy to move and difficult to attack. Their ships rose high out of the water, and their great sides could be easily pierced with bullets from ships lying lower, as the English ships did.

THE DEFEAT OF THE ARMADA

The English ships had more sailors and better ones than the Spanish, which were crammed with soldiers, for they meant really to land their men and fight on land. Still the Spanish Armada was a fine sight as it sailed into the English Channel. The admiral of the English fleet was playing the old English game of bowls with his captains, when the news came that the Spaniards were sailing into the Channel. Drake was anxious that everyone should keep cool, and a story tells that he said carelessly, 'There is plenty of time to finish the game and beat the Spaniards too.'

For a week the two fleets fought in the Channel, the English driving the Spaniards before them towards Calais. The English were careful never to get too near the Spanish ships, but would sail just near enough to pierce them with their shots, and then sail quickly away again. The Spanish shots passed over the top of the English ships, and the great army of Spanish soldiers were useless. At the end of the week the Spaniards had lost three of their biggest ships and thousands of their men. Powder and shot ran short on both sides, but the English could get more from the shore, while the Spaniards could not.

An English Ship in the Armada Fight (*From a tapestry woven in commemoration of the great victory*).

At last the Spaniards anchored off the coast of France, but the English sent fire-ships in among them, and destroyed many more ships. The others put out to sea again. More ships had come to the help of the English, and now, at last, the two fleets fought a great battle. Again the English won. The wind was with them, and they were able, when they liked, to sail against it, because they knew how to manage their ships, which the Spaniards did not.

At last the Spaniards made up their minds to sail round Scotland, and so back to Spain, but a great storm broke out, and many of the ships were wrecked on the coasts of Ireland. Not half of the ships of the great Armada got back to Spain again. It was partly bad management and partly bad luck which caused this great misfortune to Spain.

Philip tried to comfort the commander of his fleet by telling him that he had sent him to fight against men, and not against the wind. Elizabeth had medals made in memory of the victory, and on them were the words 'God blew with His wind, and they were scattered.'

The defeat of the Invincible Armada was indeed the end of Spain's greatness. Her fleets still carried home great loads of gold, but the English often captured them, and it was not long before the command of the seas was divided between the two great enemies against whom Spain had fought so bitterly, the Dutch and the English.

Later, these two were to fight each other for the mastery also. The English sailors would have liked Elizabeth to go on fighting Spain, until the power of that country was quite destroyed. But Elizabeth was wiser than this. She knew that it would be a mistake to make Spain too weak, because Spain could help her in preventing France becoming too strong. Elizabeth kept in mind what came to be called the 'Balance of Power,' which means that no country may be allowed to become too strong and so conquer the other countries of Europe. Twice since Elizabeth's time it has seemed that France might conquer all Europe, and the 'Balance of Power' be upset. Elizabeth was wise to see the danger, and this was why she would not fight too hard against Spain in the last years of her reign.

We cannot help being glad that Englishmen won in the struggle with Spain, but still we must remember that the Spaniards had proved themselves to be a wonderful people. They had led the way in the marvellous discoveries of the new times, and proved themselves over and over again thoroughly brave men. If their great time was soon over, and they sank to a low place among the nations of Europe, still it had been a very brilliant time indeed.

Just as in other countries great writers have appeared when the nation has been doing great things, so Spam's greatest writer, Cervantes, lived and wrote in the second half of the sixteenth century. His great book was the romantic novel called *Don Quixote*. It is one of the world's great books. Children enjoy it because it is full of fun and adventure, and grown-up people because it pictures for us the many different kinds of people who lived in Spain in the sixteenth century, just as Chaucer's writings show us the people who lived in England in the fourteenth century. The work of Cervantes, and the colonies she still has in South America, remain to remind us of the heroic days of Spain.

Chapter XXXIV—The Seventeenth Century

The seventeenth century was different in many ways from the sixteenth. Things were settling down. Religious questions were still very important, but other things became still more so. Yet one more great war of religion was fought in the first half of the seventeenth century. It was the great struggle between the Reformation and the Counter-Reformation in Germany. It began in 1618 and ended in 1648, and is always called the Thirty Years' War.

The emperor at the time was Ferdinand of Styria, who had been a pupil of the Jesuits, and was as eager a Catholic as Philip of Spain had been. He was anxious to make as many of the German states as possible Catholic again. The little Protestant kingdom of Bohemia generally elected as its king the prince who was going to be the emperor, and it elected Ferdinand in this way. But when the Bohemians saw that Ferdinand was going to be hard on the Protestants, they said they would not have him for their king, and chose instead Frederick, the Elector Palatine, the ruler of one of the German states called the Palatinate. Frederick had married the daughter of James I of England, who had become king of England when Elizabeth died in 1603.

James was the son of Mary Queen of Scots, but had been brought up as a Protestant. Frederick naturally thought that James would help him, but James always took a long time to make up his mind about anything. He was a clever man in some ways and proud of his learning, but he never really understood other men. He was always so long in making up his mind how to act towards other countries that people despised and laughed at him. Someone said that he was the 'wisest fool in Christendom.' He was the only one of the Stewarts who was not good-looking. His curious loose limbs and weak face gave a good idea of his character.

Frederick was driven from Bohemia, and even from his own Palatinate, before James had made up his mind to help him, and when he did send help it was of little use. James was full of an idea that countries should not fight with each other about religion, and he was anxious to show how tolerant he was by marrying his son to a Spanish princess. Then his thought that Spain would help him against the Catholic emperor, but all this was nonsense. The Spanish king would never marry his daughter to a Protestant prince, though he did not say so immediately to James.

Meanwhile, the struggle between Ferdinand and Frederick had become a fight between the Emperor and the Protestant princes of the empire. It was the last great war of religion, and one of the most terrible that have ever been. For thirty years the Germans suffered in the most terrible way, and at the end of the war half of all the people had been killed.

A great soldier called Wallenstein was the chief general on the Emperor's side. He did not really care very much about religion, but he wanted to give the Emperor real power over all Germany, and this frightened the Protestant princes very much, for till this time they had been like little kings in their own states. Wallenstein's soldiers loved him and were proud of him.

He won many victories, and the Protestants were almost in despair when the great Protestant king of Sweden, Gustavus Adolphus, crossed with an army into Germany to help the Protestants. The king of Sweden was afraid that if the Emperor got real power over the Northern states of Germany, as far as the Baltic, he would then threaten Sweden. Gustavus Adolphus was a very earnest Protestant too. When he landed in Germany the Protestants crowded to follow him. At first he was victorious everywhere. He encouraged his men by telling them that a good Christian could never be a bad soldier.

At first he did not fight against Wallenstein but against another general named Tilly. But at last he met Wallenstein at the great battle of Lutzen. Even here the Swedes were really victorious, but towards the end of the battle a thick fog covered the armies, and in the darkness Gustavus Adolphus, 'the Lion of the North,' was killed.

He had said 'Good-bye' to his people before he left Sweden, holding his little daughter Christina, who was only three years old, in his arms. She was now queen of Sweden, but when she grew up she became a Catholic and so gave up her crown. She lived most of her time in Italy, and was one of the cleverest women of her time.

In a little over a year after the battle of Lutzen, Wallenstein was murdered. He had always wanted to have things very much his own way, and the Emperor was afraid that he might even turn against him, and as the general could make the soldiers do anything he wished, this would have been very dangerous. So Wallenstein was declared a traitor, and soon after some men, hoping to please the Emperor for whom he had done so much, murdered him.

A Soldier of the Thirty Years War

After this the war went on for many years. The French, under the great Cardinal Richelieu, helped the Protestants, although of course France was a Catholic country. He did this to keep Germany weak, for in the seventeenth century there were only a few statesmen like Gustavus Adolphus who were really fighting for religion. The others made it an excuse to bring about things that they wanted. At last, when peace was made by the Treaty of Westphalia in 1648, things were not altered very much. The Northern states remained Protestant and the Southern states Catholic. The son of the Elector Frederick, who was now dead, got half of his Palatinate back, but Bohemia remained to the Emperor.

After this the Emperor had less power than ever in the empire. He became really the ruler of Austria with Hungary and Bohemia, the countries which still belong to the emperor of Austria. The little states of the North and West of Germany remained separate until two hundred years later the ruler of one of them, Prussia, which had grown stronger and stronger, won the rule of the others and so began the German empire of today.

In the seventeenth century all the rulers in the countries of Europe were really absolute. That is to say, neither the people nor the nobles had any power, but had to do just what the kings ordered. In many countries, in the Middle Ages, there had been the beginning of parliaments, in which the people had power to help in the government of their country. But only in England had this power grown. In England, too, parliament had lost much of its power under the absolute rule of the Tudor kings. Still, parliaments did meet, and even the Tudor kings pretended at least to take the advice of parliament, though really the parliaments passed any laws which the king ordered them to.

But towards the end of Queen Elizabeth's reign, the parliament several times sent very plain messages to the Queen. They complained of the way in which she gave some of her favorites 'monopolies,' that is, the right to trade in certain things. When a 'monopoly' was granted no other person could sell that thing, and the favorite could charge almost any price he liked. This was very hard on the people, but when parliament complained Elizabeth was wise enough to give way.

But when James I came to the throne troubles began between the king and parliament, and when his son Charles I became king a real struggle began, which ended in the 'Great Civil War.'

THE GREAT CIVIL WAR IN ENGLAND

Charles I became king of England in the year 1625. He was a handsome man and very good and religious. He married a Catholic princess, Henrietta Maria of France, and he always loved her and his children very much. Charles was almost a saint in some ways, but he was not a wise king. He could never understand that parliament had a right to help in the government of the country. He saw how other kings ruled absolutely, and he could not understand why the English king should not do the same.

Parliament first really began to quarrel with the king about religion. Archbishop Laud of Canterbury was a great friend of Charles. He wanted to make the English Church very much more like the Catholic Church than it had grown to be. He was fond of ceremonies, and he had the Communion table railed off like an altar at the east end of the churches. He said that the sign of the Cross should be used for baptizing babies.

The Puritans in the Church hated these things, which seemed to them 'Popish.' There were many Puritan gentlemen in the House of Commons, and they complained about these things in an act called the Petition of Right. Charles had to give his consent to the Petition, but he soon sent the parliament away, and for eleven years did without. But the king required money. Generally he had got it through 'grants' made by the parliament, but now he had to get it in some other ways. He began to gather taxes which had not been used for hundreds of years, especially one called 'Ship Money,' but even then he could not get enough.

The Scots, too, rose in rebellion, because Archbishop Laud had tried to force them to have a new prayer-book which was very like the English prayer-book read in their churches. Scotland was now joined to England, but had a separate parliament. The Scots were much more Protestant than the English, and they hated the new prayer-book.

On the first Sunday it was to be read in the churches, a servant woman called Jenny Geddes threw a stool at the head of the preacher in St. Giles's Cathedral, Edinburgh, and the people had to be turned out before the service could be read. When the Scots rebelled and an army marched into England, Charles had not enough money to fight them, and in the end he had to give way about the prayer-book. He had to call parliament again, and in 1640 the 'Long Parliament' met.

It was so called because it did not really come to an end for twenty years, though the friends of the king left it, and it suffered many other changes. The Puritans were now very angry against the king, and tried to take all power out of his hands. They tried, too, to get rid of bishops altogether from the English Church, and make it much more like the Calvinistic Churches of Scotland or Geneva. This made many gentlemen leave the parliament and take the king's part. The Earl of Strafford, Charles's friend and chief servant, had his head cut off. Archbishop Laud was put in prison, and in the end his head was cut off too.

At last, in 1642, the Great Civil War began. Nearly all the great lords were on the side of the king, though some fought against him. Charles had splendid horse soldiers to fight for him under his brave nephew. Prince Rupert. At first the two sides were equal, but later Oliver Cromwell, a Puritan gentleman, got together a splendid army of foot soldiers. He drilled them splendidly, and would have no drinking or swearing. They had to be what he called 'godly men.' They came to be called Cromwell's ' Ironsides.'

In the end Cromwell won. The king was taken prisoner, and had his head cut off' in front of the people at Whitehall. It was chiefly Cromwell who was determined that the 'man

The WARRANT to Collonel FRANCIS HACKER &c. for BEHEADING of K. CHARLES the First

The Execution of Charles I in Whitehall, 30th January 1649 *(From an engraving published in 1649).*

Charles Stuart,' as he called him, must be got rid of in this way. Many people looked on Charles as a martyr, and he died very nobly and bravely, after saying good-bye to some of his children.

On the morning he was to be executed, he put on an extra shirt, saying with a smile that he did not wish to tremble with the cold, for fear his enemies might think that he was shaking with fear.

His eldest son Charles escaped to France after many adventures, and for eleven years Cromwell and the parliament tried to govern England. Cromwell tried to set up a republic, but he could never get a parliament to suit him, and all the time he was really ruling like an absolute king. There were no more bishops, and the Puritans had things all their own way.

Cromwell was a very earnest Protestant. He thought all the time that he was doing God's work. He had many wise plans for the government of England, but many of the people felt that he was really more of a tyrant than Charles I had been. When he died his son was made

'Lord Protector,' but England was tired of the new ways, and a message was sent to Prince Charles, asking him to come back and govern the country.

There was great rejoicing when King Charles II rode into London, on the 29th May 1660. The bishops were brought back, and there began a very merry time in the history of England.

After the Restoration, as the return of Charles was called, the Puritans had a very hard time, although Charles the 'Merry Monarch' had promised to give them 'liberty of conscience.' He could not have been kind to them, even if he had wished, for the new parliaments, full of love for the king, and angry at the memory of the sorrows of his father, were determined to have their revenge. The bodies of Cromwell and two of his friends were taken from their graves in Westminster Abbey and hanged on the scaffold. They were buried again, but of course not in the Abbey.

King Charles II by Adriaen Hanneman

Charles II was always very careful not to interfere with the rights of parliament, and so England was the one country whose government left some power to the people. Later, when the peoples of other countries rose up and fought for power, they imitated the English government, so that our parliament is often called the 'Mother of Parliaments.'

The Puritans could no longer preach, or teach, or meet together for prayers or services. Those who did so were thrown into prison.

One of the most remarkable men who was put into prison at this time was John Bunyan, the son of a Bedford tinker. He was a very good and religious young man, but he tortured himself over his sins, the worst of which were dancing on the village green or ringing the church bells. To the Puritans nearly every amusement was a sin, and Bunyan thought himself very wicked because he loved these things. But in the end he gave them up and became a preacher. He was put in prison after the Restoration, and in Bedford Jail he wrote the wonderful book called the *Pilgrims Progress,* which tells the story of how a man named Christian travelled to the Celestial City, and all he suffered on the way. But it is really the story of any soul which is struggling to get rid of sin and find peace.

John Bunyan was not an educated man, but he wrote simple and beautiful English, and his book is still read by everyone today. John Bunyan was the great Puritan prose writer, but the Puritans had their great poet too. This was the blind poet, John Milton, whose greatest work was a wonderful long poem called *Paradise Lost.*

But many Puritans fled over seas to a land where some who believed as they did had already made their homes. It will be interesting to hear something of their story.

CHAPTER XXXV—THE PILGRIM FATHERS

When the English Puritans found that they could not worship God peacefully in their own way at home, many of them made up their minds to sail away to America, and make new homes for themselves there, and so be free to worship as they pleased.

The colonization of North America by the English had already begun. It had been very difficult indeed. The first man who had tried to set up a colony there was Sir Humphrey Gilbert, who took men and ships to Newfoundland, but everything went wrong and soon the men begged to be taken home. It was the stormy time of the year, and the smaller of the two ships, which were all that were left, was really not fit to cross the sea at such a time. But Sir Humphrey sailed in this. One night the ship went down in a storm, but the men on the other ship told how they saw Sir Humphrey sitting calmly with his Bible in his hands comforting his men as the ship went down.

The next attempt was made by Sir Humphrey Gilbert's brother-in-law. Sir Walter Raleigh, one of the cleverest and handsomest of the courtiers of Queen Elizabeth, and a great favorite of the Queen until the last years of her reign, when he fell into disgrace.

But while he was still in her favor, he sent out two ships to find a spot on the coast of North America suitable for a colony. The captains sailed like Columbus to the West Indies, and then along the coast to a place a hundred miles north. It was a beautiful spot with forests filled with birds, and grapes growing in the open air. When the captains came back and told Raleigh about it, he said that his new colony should be called Virginia after Elizabeth, the virgin queen.

Raleigh did not go himself to his colony though he had been on voyages before to America. It is often said that it was Sir Walter Raleigh who brought the potato plant to Ireland and first smoked tobacco in England, but it was probably Sir John Hawkins who did both these things, though Sir Walter was a great smoker too.

But these first colonists in Virginia did not want to work hard. They were always dreaming of gold, and gold was not to be found in North America so easily as in the South. So one day when Sir Francis Drake sailed up with food and men for the colony, the colonists begged to be taken home. Raleigh did not despair, but sent out more colonists, this time with women to make the homes comfortable. A baby was born in Virginia, and was called Virginia too, but these colonists soon came back also.

Raleigh did not try again. He spent the last years of his life as a prisoner in the Tower of London. It had been said that he had plotted against King James I when he first came to England, and he was condemned to death, but kept in prison instead. While there he wrote in very fine English part of the *History of the World,* but it was never finished.

Raleigh was always dreaming of his old adventures. Men in those days told of a wonderful city full of gold in Guiana in South America. They called it El Dorado. Raleigh begged King James to give him ships to go to find this city and bring back gold. James allowed him to go, but said he must not go near the land of the Spaniards. He must have known that this was ridiculous, but he was pretending to be friendly with Spain. Sir Walter went, but fell ill on the way.

When he reached the mouth of the great river Orinoco, he sent his young son Walter on with some of the men up the river to find the mine; but the Spaniards attacked them and 'little Wat,' as Sir Walter fondly called his son, was killed. No gold was found, and Raleigh came back broken-hearted to England. The Spaniards complained to James, and though he would have been only too pleased to forgive him if he had brought home the gold, James, to please the Spaniards, said he should have his head cut off after all. And so he had.

He died like the brave man he was, and though he had not been a great favorite with the people in the last years of his life, everyone was sorry for him, and felt that the English king had not been just to the man who had loved England so much.

The First English Settlement in Virginia (From a drawing by an artist who -went with Raleigh's expedition to Virginia in1558).

Raleigh had said, 'I shall yet live to see Virginia an English nation,' and before his death new attempts were being made to found a real colony that would last in Virginia.

During Elizabeth's time great riches had come to England, and the richer people and the people of the middle class had begun to live much more comfortably. New and bigger houses were built, and windows of glass, which had been very uncommon, now became quite common. Even Erasmus, who was used to the great poverty of many students at the foreign universities, had complained of the dirtiness of the floors in English houses, and the Spaniards at Queen Mary's court had said that the English had their houses 'built of sticks and dirt,' though they ate like kings. In Elizabeth's time chimneys were put into the houses, and there was more air and chance of the people being healthy. Carpets were used instead of the old floor coverings of rushes, which had often been very dirty.

In the Middle Ages people had slept with logs of wood for their pillows, except the very rich people, but in Elizabeth's time even poor people had bolsters or pillows, and the rich used feather beds, though these were thought great treasures. Instead of the old wooden plates, people now began to have silver or pewter, and glasses to drink from.

But while the rich grew richer, the poor grew poorer. This had been so ever since the destruction of the monasteries by King Henry VIII, though there were other causes for it. At the end of Elizabeth's reign the first 'Poor Law' was passed, which made the people of each town or village pay 'rates' to buy food for the poor people who could not earn their living.

It was partly this perhaps which made Englishmen leave England, and try to earn their living in America. At the beginning of James I's reign, another little band of Englishmen, one hundred and forty altogether, sailed in three ships to try once more to make a colony in Virginia. A poet wished them good luck,

> 'To get the pearl and gold,
> And Ours to hold Virginia,
> Earth's only Paradise.'

But again it was this wish for gold which nearly ruined the new colony. They landed at the mouth of the Chesapeake river, and they called the town which they built Jamestown after King James I. Only a few of the men were used to work, and the same thing happened as before. There was not much food, and the men began to die. The Indians, too, attacked them.

John Smith, the First Great English Colonist

At last a young man named John Smith, a very strong and determined person, made himself the leader or captain. He defended the town against the Indians, and led little groups of men in hunting expeditions to bring back food. He was once taken prisoner by the Indians, and led away to their king. His head was laid on a stone, and the Indians were just going to kill him with great wooden weapons when a little Indian girl called Pocahontas, the daughter of the king, rushed forward and put her head on his. So the king let him off, and he was taken back to his colony.

At last, through his great courage and the way he managed his men, the colony began to do well. He made every one work six hours a day, and he made a rule that anyone who swore should have a can of cold water poured down his sleeve. This made the men laugh very much. It was now seen that work was the secret of success. Hundreds more men with their wives and children went out to the colony, and so Virginia was the first successful English colony. It soon set up its own little parliament called the House of Burgesses.

It was not a Puritan colony, but kept the religion of the English Church and used the prayer-book. Soon the land was divided into large estates. Younger sons of English gentlemen went out and became 'planters.' The thing they grew chiefly was tobacco. Many negroes were bought to work on the plantations.

There were some poor white people too, and some were even used as slaves, but there were not many of them and generally they were allowed to go free. They did not require much to keep them in such a mild country, and lived idly and happily enough.

The second great English colony in North America had a very different beginning. It was a Puritan colony. When James I came to England, the Puritans, who had been persecuted under Elizabeth, hoped that they would now be well treated by a king who had been brought up in Scotland. But James was quite tired of the Scottish religion, which did not show enough respect to kings. He was never tired of saying that 'no bishop' meant 'no king.' The Puritans were very disappointed, and soon after the beginning of James's reign the people of a church at Scrooby in Nottinghamshire made up their minds to go to Holland, where they would be free to worship as they chose.

But after twelve years they decided to go to America, and so crossed over to England again, and went on board a ship called the *Mayflower* and another smaller ship, and so sailed off men, women, and little children, with all they possessed, to find a home in a new and strange land for the sake of their religion.

They meant to land in Virginia, but after a voyage of sixty-four days, during which they were very crowded together and miserable, they reached land far North of Virginia and they made their new colony there.

The men built a new town called 'Plymouth,' while the women and children stayed on the ships. After a terrible winter, the *Mayflower* was ready to sail back to England, but not one of the colonists wanted to go back with her.

As time went on, new settlers joined the colony, and Plymouth became the chief town of the great colony of Massachusetts, a name which was taken from the Indians. The memory of the 'Pilgrim Fathers,' as the first settlers in this great Puritan colony were afterwards called, is honored by all the world today.

As time went on, new colonies were formed in New England, as the lands round Massachusetts where the English were settling were called. Some were started by people anxious to grow rich, hut the greater number of colonists were people who left England in order to be free to worship as they pleased. Before the end of King James I's reign, an English nobleman called Lord Baltimore, who had become a Catholic, started a colony for Catholics. His son governed it after him, and it was called Maryland, after King Charles I's Catholic Queen, Henrietta Maria.

But England was not the only country which had sent out colonists to this part of America. After its great struggle with Spain, the little republic of Holland had become very rich and important indeed. In fact, it became the most important country of all on the seas. The first half of the seventeenth century was the great time in the history of the Dutch, just as the sixteenth century was the great time of Spain and the later seventeenth century the great time of France. The Dutch ships had nearly all the trade of the world. Even when merchants of other countries bought things from far-off lands, they got Dutch ships to carry them, so that Holland had what was called the 'carrying trade' of the world.

And just as other countries at their great times have had great writers or poets or philosophers or painters, so in the seventeenth century the Dutch painters were the greatest in Europe. The chief of them were Rubens, Rembrandt, and Van Dyck, the great portrait-painter who painted portraits of Charles I and his children and many of the great Englishmen of his time.

But the English, too, were now very great at sea since their victories over Spain, and they made up their minds to become even greater than Holland. And so a great struggle began under Cromwell. Cromwell had a Navigation Act passed by which things brought from other countries could only come in English ships. Before this the Dutch ships had done a great trade between England and America or the East, and the new Act was very bad for their trade. They were very angry, and soon a war broke out between the two countries. In the battles which followed, sometimes the great Dutch Admiral Tromp and at other times the brave English Admiral Blake was victorious.

After Cromwell and Tromp and Blake were all dead, the struggle still went on. The Dutch had an even greater admiral than Tromp, named Ruyter, and on the English side Prince Rupert fought against him. Once after a victory, Admiral Tromp had tied a broom to his mast and said he would sweep England from the seas. But after all, Holland was only a very little country, and in the end England won, the command of the seas and has kept it ever since.

Holland, too, had sent out colonists to North America, and their land, called the New Netherlands, lay between the colonies of New England and Virginia. Its chief town was called New Amsterdam. But during the war between the two countries, the English took New Amsterdam, and when peace was made they were allowed to keep it. Its name was changed to New York, after James, Duke of York, the brother of King Charles II, who became king of England afterwards and was called James II New York, which is the greatest town in America today, now became the capital of a great English colony.

The last of the colonies founded in North America, for the sake of religion, was Pennsylvania. It was founded at the end of the reign of Charles II by William Penn, a Quaker. The Quakers were looked upon as very dangerous people indeed, even worse than the Puritans.

A Sea-Fight between Admiral Blake and the Dutch (From a seventeenth-century engraving).

They lived very strict lives, always dressing very plainly. They thought it wrong to take an oath or to become soldiers, and many men among them who would not fight against the Dutch were put in prison and even whipped.

At last William Penn, a Quaker gentleman, got the king to let him have some land near New York for a colony of Quakers. He wanted to call the new colony Sylvania, or the 'Land of Woods,' but the people said it must be called after him, and so it was called Pennsylvania.

There were thirteen colonies altogether in North America at the end of the seventeenth century. The Northern colonies were different in some ways from the Southern. They did not grow tobacco on large plantations, but were divided into farms. There were not many negro slaves there, because they were not so much needed. Most of the colonists treated the Indians very badly except the people of Pennsylvania, and they began to die out. Today there are only a few hundred of the redskins left. It is a pity in some ways, for some of them were very simple and gentle people, though others were fierce and cruel.

Although so many colonies were begun by men who wanted freedom of religion, each colony had its own religion, and people who believed in a different religion were not allowed to live there, except in the one little colony of Rhode Island, which tolerated all religions like the little kingdom of Holland did. People at the time thought very little about these colonies, yet from them grew the great country of the United States, where so many millions of English people live today.

Chapter XXXVI—The Age of Louis XIV

In the year 1643, the year after the Great Civil War broke out in England, a little French prince, only four years old, became king of France. A story is told that as his father lay dying the child had said to him, 'I am Louis XIV,' and the father answered, 'Not yet.'

The little Louis XIV grew up to be a very remarkable king, but he was always thinking about himself, just as he had done when he was only four years old and standing beside his dying father. All the time that Louis was growing up Cardinal Mazarin was doing his best to go on with the work of Cardinal Richelieu and make France the greatest country in Europe.

They did their work so well, that by the time King Louis XIV was old enough to rule France himself, France was very great indeed, so great that at last it seemed that the thing which people were always trying to prevent had happened, and that the 'Balance of Power' in Europe was upset. In the end nearly all the countries of Europe were joined together to fight France. Louis XIV was not really a clever man. He was very vain and self-willed, yet even his great idea of his own importance and his determination to make other people feel it, did help to make France great.

Under Louis French trade was made much better, and for the first time France had a good navy, which became for a short time as great as either the English or the Dutch navies. Louis looked on himself as the centre of France, the sun from which everything drew its brightness and even its life. He took the sun as his emblem and was often called 'le Roi Soleil.'

Although Louis had not a great mind he had very fine manners, and everyone felt that he was a great king. He could never have done as much for France as the great Cardinals Richelieu and Mazarin had done. It was they who gave France its great time. There were great writers in France, because Richelieu and Mazarin had made France great, and just as in other countries, France's great time in history was also her great time in literature.

But it was Louis XIV who brought all the greatest men in France to his court, and many men from other countries too, so that the French court became the greatest court in Europe. French manners and French art became the fashion of the time. Other people did their best to imitate them, so that when we speak of the Age of Louis XIV we do not mean a time in the history of France only, but a time when the French led the way in everything and the other countries followed.

At the court of Louis XIV there were the two great play-writers—Moliere, who wrote comedies, that is, plays which end happily, and Racine, who wrote great tragedies, that is, plays which end in great sorrow. There was the philosopher Pascal, and there was La Fontaine, who wrote *Fables,* in. which animals are made to speak and do things like men and women. All French children still love to read the *Fables* of La Fontaine.

Louis XIV built for himself the wonderful palace of Versailles, eleven miles out of Paris. He made the French people pay him a great deal of money, so that he could build it. Visitors to Paris can still see it today with its great rooms and galleries covered with gilt and with great mirrors all along the walls of some rooms, while others have pictures painted on the walls by the artists of the time.

The great park of Versailles was filled with marble statues and wonderful fountains which are now turned on on Sundays, so that the people who come out from Paris may see how beautiful they are. For the palace of Versailles is now used as a sort of museum and belongs to the people, for there are no longer kings in France.

Louis XIV was not very friendly with the Pope. He wanted the king to have much more power over the Church in France than other Catholic kings in other countries, and he had many quarrels with the Pope through this. Yet Louis was a very Strict Catholic, so much so, that he could not bear to think of the Huguenots, who, since Henry IV had passed the Edict of Nantes, had been allowed to worship in their own way. There were thousands of Huguenots in the South of France. They were chiefly middle-class and working people. Many of them worked at making things, especially silk, in which France had a great trade with other countries.

Cardinal Richelieu had thought that the Huguenots had too much freedom, not in religion but in governing themselves, and he had taken away many of their privileges. The people of La Rochelle, the great Huguenot town, had defied him, and he had besieged their strong city

The Great Palace of Louis XIV at Versailles (From a seventeenth-century engraving).

for fourteen months. At first they were able to get food from ships which brought it into their beautiful harbor, but Richelieu built dykes right across the harbor and no more food could be got in. The people—men, women and children—died in thousands in the streets, and there were very few alive when Richelieu and his king, Louis XIII, rode into the conquered city.

Still, the cardinal did not prevent the Huguenots from worshipping in their own way. La Rochelle had grown rich and happy again when Louis XIV suddenly said that he would no longer tolerate Protestants in France. The Edict of Nantes was 'revoked,' and the freedom it had given taken away. The Huguenot churches were knocked down, and children were taken away from parents who would not promise to bring them up as Catholics. Some of the Huguenots were put to death, others were sent to work as galley slaves in the French war ships. They were chained to their oars so that they could not escape.

Many of the Huguenots made up their minds to flee away to Protestant countries, but even this was made very hard for them. The shores of France were watched, and so were the chief roads into other countries. Still, many thousands did get away, crossing into Switzerland and Holland and Germany, through forests and over mountains, where the king could not put soldiers to stop them.

Often the Huguenots disguised themselves, so that no one could tell who they were. One officer and his wife dressed themselves as orange-sellers, and travelled with a donkey carrying their oranges. Sometimes people hid themselves in empty barrels, and were carried on to ships sailing for England. So many got away, though some were caught and taken back. Louis XIV got his way, and soon there was hardly a Protestant left in France, but it was a very bad thing for the country.

Many French silk-weavers settled down at Spitalfields in London, and helped to make English trade better as others did in other countries. Many sailed away to America, finding peace and freedom like the English colonists before them. Others went to settle in the colony which the Dutch had set up at the Cape of Good Hope.

All the countries of Europe were full of horror at this persecution of the French Protestants. The Pope himself blamed Louis for it. Only James II, the Catholic brother of Charles II, and now king of England, was pleased. Charles II, England's 'Merry Monarch,' had always been much loved by the English people, but he had not really been very faithful to them. He had made secret promises to Louis XIV to try and make England Catholic again, and in return Louis had given him a great deal of money. But Charles II was wise enough to see that he could not really do this. It is said that he died a Catholic himself, but he never really had any hope of making the English Catholic.

James II was quite different. He was a very strict Catholic, and though Catholics were forbidden by the English law to help in the government of the country, James took no notice of this, but gave the best positions to Catholics.

This made the English people very angry, and when James's queen had a little baby born, they made up their minds to rebel against James, for they knew that the baby would be brought

The "Sun" King Louis XIV, of France, with his Brilliant Court (*From a painting for one of the famous Gobelin tapestries by Charles Lebrun, Court Painter to Louis XIV*).

The Embarkation of William of Orange from Holland for England, 1688 (After a contemporary painting now at Hainpton Court).

up as a Catholic, and they hated to think that they would have Catholic kings forever. So they rose in revolt against James, who fled to France, where his wife and baby had gone before him.

Then the English invited William of Orange, who had married Mary, James II's grown-up daughter, to come and rule England with his wife. And so they did. This is called the English Revolution of 1688.

William II, as he was now called, was a descendant of William the Silent, who had saved the Netherlands from Spain. He was the ruler of Holland, and he was only pleased to become king of England, too, because he wanted England to help him to save Holland, this time against the king of France.

THE WARS OF LOUIS XIV

For long before this Louis had been fighting with Holland, for he had made up his mind to join the Netherlands to France, and make the river Rhine the boundary of his country on the north as it was on the east. Louis had married a Spanish princess, who was half-sister to Charles II, the boy who soon afterwards became king of Spain. When King Philip IV of Spain, the father of Louis's wife and of Charles II. of Spain, died, Louis said that the Spanish Netherlands ought to belong to him because of his wife, and he immediately attacked them. He had a very fine general called Turenne, and in a short time the French had conquered all the chief towns of the Spanish Netherlands near France.

The other countries were very anxious about the 'Balance of Power,' when they saw the French winning town after town, and England, Sweden and Holland joined in what was called the 'Triple Alliance,' to prevent Louis conquering the Netherlands. So Louis stopped fighting for a time, but still he kept the towns he had won. He soon broke up the Triple Alliance. He made a secret treaty with Charles II, and also persuaded Sweden not to help the

Dutch. For he had made up his mind now to fight and conquer Holland.

Holland had always been a republic, but it had always elected a prince of the House of Orange as its stadtholder, as the ruler was called. The stadtholder was not a king but a kind of president. Still, as he was always chosen from the House of Orange, that house had become a kind of royal family. There were some people in Holland who did not like this, and wanted not to give very much power to the young William of Orange, who was then growing up. Two brothers called De Witt were looking after the country when Louis XIV attacked it. The De Witts were brave men and loved their country, but they had not been wise enough to see the great danger Louis XIV was going to be. The Dutch navy was fighting the French and English navy too, and was not conquered, but the Dutch army was not ready and in order. As in the days of William the Silent, the dykes were cut, the land was flooded, and the French driven off.

But the people were very angry with the De Witts. One brother was put in prison, and when the other went to visit him, the two were attacked and killed.

William of Orange now had things all his own way. He was a brave soldier and very ambitious. His whole life from this time was given to defending his country or keeping down the power of France. Yet he was not really a very noble character. He did not try to save the De Witts, but took no notice, as he did many times afterwards when cruel things were done which he could have prevented. He was a much more silent man than the William who had been called the Silent.

This was partly because of the way he had been brought up. Without father or mother or any near relation, the De Witts had brought him up alone and always watched. They thought of him as dangerous to the republic which they loved, because the House of Orange had become like a royal family. He had begged them to let him have children of his own age to play with, but they would not, and in the end he learned to hide what he felt. He did not smile at good news or cry for bad, and he kept this quiet way till the end of his life. Yet when he loved he loved passionately, and he hated just as passionately.

Above all other things he hated France and France's king. For six years there was fighting between France and Holland. The French generally won. Someone asked William, 'Do you not see that your country is lost?' 'There is one way,' he answered, 'never to see it lost, and that is to die in the last ditch.'

When, in 1678, Louis was forced by the other countries of Europe to make peace, Holland was still free. For ten years after this there was peace, but Louis was always offending someone, and trying to steal land on the borders of France. Then came the English Revolution, and William's great chance as king of England to fight Louis once more. Two years afterwards the Dutch and English fleets won a great victory over the French fleet at La Hogue. This was the end of the greatness of France on the seas.

Long after the time of Louis XIV., France became a danger to Europe under the great Napoleon, but she was never able to get together a really great fleet. But on land Louis still won victories, though William of Orange fought so well that Louis never got any real gain from his victories. At last peace was made again in 1697. William of Orange was given some towns in the north of the Spanish Netherlands, with which he could keep Louis from attacking Holland again. He would much rather have gone on fighting Louis, but by this time the English were rather tired of it. They thought that William was making use of English men and English money to save Holland.

But Louis XIV only made peace each time so as to be able to get ready for war again. And now Louis was very anxiously waiting for the death of Charles II of Spain, in order to get as much as he could of the land he ruled.

Charles II had never been strong, and people had been surprised that he had even lived to be a man. Before he died, Louis and the Austrian emperor, who was also related to the king of Spain, had arranged that one of the Emperor's sons should become king of Spain, while Louis was to have all the Spanish possessions in Italy. No one asked the Spanish people what they wished, but when Charles II died they made up their mind that they would not have any king who had been chosen for them, but that they would choose their own. They chose Philip, the young grandson of Louis XIV. He was only a boy of seventeen. Unless his elder brother died he would not become king of France, and in any case Louis XIV had had to promise that he would not join the two countries. Yet as the young King Philip was going away homesick and crying to his new kingdom, Louis said to him, 'Remember, there are no longer any Pyrenees.'

The Pyrenees are the mountains between France and Spain, and Louis meant that after this Spain would always be joined to France and help her in her wars.

William of Orange was very anxious indeed, and he wished with all his heart that the English people would once more declare war against France. Then Louis did a foolish thing. Poor King James II of England was dying in France, and Louis XIV promised him that he would do all he could to have his son, the little baby who was born in 1688, made king of England when William of Orange should die. When the English people heard of this they were very angry, and so at last William got his way, and they gave him men and money to help him to fight Louis once more.

But just at this point William died. He had never been very strong, and he had worn himself out. Mary, his queen, was dead already, and so her sister, Anne, became queen of England. The son of James II never had any chance of becoming king of England, although in the year 1715 he did cross over to Scotland, hoping to win England with the help of the Scottish Highlanders, but failed completely.

He lived nearly all his life in Italy, where he married and had children. He was always very sad, and people called him 'Old Mr. Melancholy.' He is generally called the Old Pretender, because his eldest son, Bonnie Prince Charlie, who came to England in the year 1745, just thirty years after his father, to try to win the throne of the Stewarts again, was called the Young Pretender.

When William III died, the English soldiers were not left without a great leader. The duke of Marlborough, who was tutor to Queen Anne's little boy, was placed over the army. He was a wonderful soldier. A great Frenchman said of him that he never besieged a place which he did not take, or fought a battle that he did not win. His soldiers said that the duke was 'as calm at the mouth of a cannon as at the door of a drawing-room.' His armies loved him, and the sight of his calm, determined face always made his men feel braver.

In the year 1704, Marlborough and Prince Eugene of Savoy won a great victory over the French, at the battle of Blenheim near the Danube. For Louis XIV had marched through Germany to attack Vienna, the chief town of Austria. He had an immense army, and would have defeated the army of the Emperor, but Prince Eugene, who was with his army in Italy, marched quickly to meet the French, while Marlborough made a more wonderful march still, across Europe from Holland. The great French army was defeated and half its men killed in the battle. Yet there was fighting for some years after this. At last, peace was made in the year 1718.

After thirty years of fighting, Louis had gained nothing. His grandson, Philip, kept Spain, but neither he nor any of his family who became king after him could become king of France. Neither could any French king ever become king of Spain. The Netherlands, for which Louis had fought so hard, were now given up to the House of Austria. Holland remained independent, and kept a ring of Netherland towns to keep her safe. The possessions of Spain in Italy were also given to Austria. The town of Gibraltar, on the south coast of Spain, remained to England, and the Island of Minorca and the French colony of Nova Scotia, or New Scotland, which the French had made in Canada, the part of North America to the north of New England, were also given up to the English.

Nova Scotia was only one of the colonies of the French in North America, for there was a New France as well as a New Holland. There had been quarrels before this about Nova Scotia, for the English said it belonged to them, because it was first discovered by Cabot, who was sent out by the English king Henry VII. There were quarrels, too, about it later, but England kept it in the end, and we shall see later how she won all the other French colonies in Canada as well.

Louis XIV died in 1715. He had lost all he had fought for in his great wars. He spent the last two years of his life very miserably. His eldest son and grandson died, which made the old king very sorrowful. He was still as strict a Catholic as ever, and he now persecuted some people called the Jansenists, who were Catholics, but had some peculiar beliefs which seemed like heresy to the king. The convent of Port Royal, near Paris, where some old nuns lived, had been Jansenist for many years, but Louis XIV asked the nuns to say that they were not Jansenist any longer.

They would not do this, and although they were all old ladies, he sent them off to different convents all over the country. But in spite of all his faults, Louis XIV had worked hard for France. 'L'etat c'est moi' ('I am the state'), he would often say. But although there was so much vanity in his love for France he *did* love her. With all his faults, too, he was in some ways the greatest man of the seventeenth century. His death was the end of a great time in the history of France and the history of Europe.

Chapter XXXVII—The East of Europe in the Seventeenth Century

In the second half of the seventeenth century the Turks began once more to trouble Europe. They had been troublesome in the sixteenth century, and Don John of Austria, the brother of Philip II of Spain, had won a great victory over them in the famous battle of Lepanto. Then for almost a hundred years they had left the European countries alone, chiefly because there was much trouble and disorder in their own empire, which now had its capital at Constantinople.

In the year 1656 the Turks seized Transylvania. It was the eastern part of the kingdom of Hungary, but it had become an independent little state. The Emperor Leopold helped the Transylvanians, and the Turks were driven out, but Transylvania still had to pay tribute. But the rule of the Emperor Leopold was much disliked in the part of Hungary still belonging to Austria, and some years later the Hungarians rebelled. The Turks thought this was a good chance to attack Vienna.

The Emperor begged John Sobieski, the brave king of Poland, to come and fight for him. Sobieski had already, some years before, fought against the Turks, who had taken a province from Poland. For the Turks had all the Mohammedan love of conquest, and whenever they were not weakened by disputes among themselves, were a great danger to Eastern Europe. They were always brave, and their great armies fought desperately, but fortunately they were never disciplined like the armies of the West, and when a European army under a good general fought with a Turkish army, the Europeans could always win.

While the Austrian commander was waiting at Vienna for Sobieski and his army and the Turkish army was coming nearer, he ordered that all the houses in all the suburbs round the city should be burnt, rather than that the Turks should be able to rob them. The Turks came up and began to besiege the city. The tents of the Turkish commander, made of silk and embroidered in gold and silver and with pearls and jewels, could be seen by the Austrians as they climbed the spire of the cathedral to see if Sobieski was coming, for the people were sick and starving. At last he came, and the people in Vienna could see with joy the fireworks which he set off on the top of the hill four miles away.

In the morning the Christian army under Sobieski heard Mass, and then a great standard of red with a white cross was set up. 'We have not come to save a city, but the whole of Christendom,' said Sobieski. To him it was a new crusade. The Turks prepared for the battle by killing thousands of prisoners whom they had already taken. Then they faced the army of Sobieski as it rushed down the hill upon them. Many were killed, and the rest fled away. By evening Vienna had been relieved.

John Sobieski was as humble as he was brave, and when the Emperor thanked him afterwards for his help, he bowed and said, 'I am glad to have been able to do you this small service.'

The Turks still fought for some years after this, whenever the best of the Austrian generals were busy fighting against Louis XIV; but Prince Eugene, who helped the duke of Marlborough to win the battle of Blenheim, fought them several times, and at last, in 1716, they made peace and were quiet once again for a time. Austria got nearly all Hungary back again, and Poland, too, got its lost province back.

Prince Eugene had been helped in his struggle with the Turks by the ruler of Russia, the Tsar, Peter the Great.

Victory of John III Sobieski, King of Poland against the Turks at Battle of Vienna. (By Jan Matejko; housed at the Vatican Museum.)

PETER THE GREAT

Peter The Great of Russia (*Painted by Kneller when Peter visited London in 1698*).

It was under Peter the Great that Russia first became important among the countries of Europe. It was a very large country, but it had no sea coast, and the only way its people could reach the West was through Poland. The people of Russia were chiefly Slavs, though many Tartars had become mixed with the people, and the ruling family of Russia was descended from Northern Vikings.

For more than two hundred years, until the end of the fifteenth century, the Russians had been ruled by Mongol or Turkish conquerors and then had become free again. But Russia was hardly civilized at all before the days of Peter the Great.

He was a very wonderful man. He was anxious that Russia should learn all the things which the Western nations knew, and should become important among the countries of Europe. Above all he wanted to win the lands on the Russian side of the Baltic Sea, which had been won at different times by Sweden. But the sea could only be useful to him if the Russians knew how to build ships, so Peter made up his mind to go himself to Holland and learn how ships were built.

He sailed to a place called Zaandam in Holland, and there he dressed himself like a Dutch boatman with a short jacket, a red waistcoat, and wide Dutch trousers. He lived in the one-roomed cottage of a Dutch workman, whom he had once known in Russia. But he was very noticeable, with his tall figure and handsome face and long curly hair, and crowds of people began to press round him as he watched the shipbuilders at work, so he fled away to Amsterdam, and was allowed to work in the dockyards there.

He helped in the building of a ship from beginning to end, and then the city of Amsterdam presented him with it. Peter was delighted. He called his new ship the *Amsterdam,* and sailed back with it to Russia. But he did not yet know all he wanted to about shipbuilding, and later, when William II sent him the present of a ship, Peter asked if he might come to see the English dockyards too, and so he did.

When he got back again to Russia, he taught the Russians how to build ships too. Peter wanted to live as near as possible to the West, which he admired so much, and so at the mouth of a river running into the Baltic Sea, he built himself a great new city to be his capital instead of Moscow, his capital in the east. The new city was called St. Petersburg, and it has ever since been a very important and beautiful town.

Peter got together an army too, and took back Scottish soldiers to help him to train it to fight like the armies of Western Europe. Peter was quite absolute, and he easily made the people do things as he wished. He was head of both Church and State in Russia. He got some of the German states, which did not like Sweden owning the German part of the Baltic coast, to join him in winning all the coast back from Sweden.

But the young king of Sweden was a very brave and wonderful person too. He was called Charles XII. Charles was only eighteen years old when he left the Swedish capital, Stockholm, to fight Peter the Great and his German friends. He first went against the king of Denmark, and easily conquered him. He then marched against the Russians under Peter the Great, who were besieging Narva, a town on the Baltic. The Russian army was not used yet to war, and Charles easily drove them into disorder, and took Narva. Then he marched into Poland, and took the throne from the new Polish king, Augustus of Saxony (for Sobieski was now dead), and made the Poles elect a Polish noblemen as their new king.

Then Charles made up his mind to attack Moscow, but his men suffered terribly in the severe cold of the Russian winter. Peter the Great did not attack him, but fell on the Swedish armies which came afterwards to join their king and destroyed them. He then marched across Russia, too, to where Charles was besieging a place called Pultawa. Charles was wounded in one foot, and though he tried not to let anyone know, his men saw blood dripping from his boot. He could not lead his army against Peter, but had himself carried to the battle-field. But Peter won a great battle over the Swedes without their leader.

Charles escaped into the land of the Turks, and tried to get the Sultan to help him against Russia, but he would not. Then Charles heard that his possessions on the German coast of the Baltic had been taken by the German princes. Peter the Great had won the Eastern part of the Baltic coast, and for a time there was a chance of his joining with Charles to help him to win the German part back. But Charles had now to go to Norway, which he hoped to join to Sweden, and there he died in 1718.

He was only thirty-six. When he was a boy he loved to hear about wars, and especially about Alexander the Great. He would say that he wished he could be like him. Someone said to him, 'Yes, but he only lived thirty-two years.' The boy answered, 'That does not matter, when one has won an empire.'

Charles XII was not much older than Alexander when he died. He had not won an empire, but he had gained very wonderful victories. With his death came the end of Sweden's greatness. Sweden was really like Holland, only fit to be a second-rate power. The one country was too small and the other too poor to be long among the most important countries of Europe. But for a time certain peculiar events had made both countries very great. Peter the Great died seven years after his great enemy, but Russia went on becoming more important, and is one of the great powers in Europe today.

Chapter XXXVIII—The Eighteenth Century

At the death of Louis XIV, a new period seems to begin in the history of the world. The eighteenth century was very different in many ways from the sixteenth and seventeenth centuries. People did not even pretend now to go to war about religion. Yet there were two very great wars in the middle of this century, in which nearly all the great countries of Europe joined. The stronger countries of Eastern Europe joined together or fought with each other to take the land of the smaller states, and make their own countries stronger. There was no question of right and wrong. The strong countries were fighting to get as much as they could. Kings and queens have never been so selfish before or since.

In the wars of the century England was always against France. The real reason for this was that both countries had colonies in North America and India, and each wanted to push the other out of these continents. So that while English and French armies were fighting in Europe, others were fighting in North America and India, and we shall see how in the end England won both these continents for herself.

The people of the eighteenth century were very fond of amusement and dress. The richer people went a great deal to watering-places to drink the waters and amuse themselves. Many philosophers began not to believe in God at all, and most people, even those who went to Church, did not bother themselves much about religion. But there was one good side to this. In England the worst laws against Roman Catholics and Unitarians were no longer noticed. They were not 'repealed,' but they were no longer put into practice. The Unitarians were people who believed in God, but did not believe that Jesus Christ was God. After the Revolution of 1688, the 'Dissenters,' as those Protestants who had left the English Church were called, were freed from persecution, and allowed to worship in their own chapels.

The dress of the people everywhere was still very brightly colored, and the richer people had their clothes made of very beautiful stuff's. Men wore wigs often tied with a ribbon at the back, and ladies had their hair puffed out and powdered. But in spite of all their finery the people of the eighteenth century were still very rough, and manners were not nearly so refined as they are today. Even gentlemen who were good scholars drank a great deal too much wine, and both men and women had a great passion for playing cards for money.

Just as there was no longer any great enthusiasm about religion, or even about other things, so there was no really great poetry. The best writers of the time were to be found in England, but poets like Alexander Pope, who wrote poems like the *Essay on Man,* might almost as well have written in prose. The language was clever, and the verses perfect in many ways, but it was not poetical. There were some very great writers of prose, such as Addison, Steele and Swift, and before the end of the century there were the first real English novels by men like Henry Fielding. But before the end of the century, too, there was a great change, which came to a head at the beginning of the next century, when many new poets wrote poems full of passion.

In some ways the people of today are more different from the people of the eighteenth century than the people of the sixteenth and seventeenth centuries were different from those of the Middle Ages.

The first great war of the eighteenth century was called the War of the Austrian Succession. Charles VI, the emperor of Austria, had died. He had no sons, and he left Austria and all his possessions to his beautiful young daughter, Maria Theresa. Some of these possessions had never had a woman ruling over them before, but Charles VI had written a kind of law which was called the 'Pragmatic Sanction,' saying that his daughter should rule after him in all his possessions.

Nearly all the other countries agreed to the Pragmatic Sanction, though France would not, and so when her father died Maria Theresa became Empress of Austria, queen of Hungary and Bohemia, and ruler of the Netherlands. She was only twenty-three years old when she was crowned. She had to go specially to Hungary to be crowned there with the old iron crown of that kingdom. The crown had to be padded to make it fit so small a head.

The people had always loved Maria Theresa. When she was only fourteen she had begun to be present at her father's council meetings. People often got her to ask for favors or mercy from her father when he was angry with them, and a story is told that he once said to her, ' You think that a sovereign has nothing to do but grant favors,' and the girl answered, 'I think that is the only thing that can make a crown bearable.'

Another story says that her father wanted her to marry Frederick the Great, the king of the new German kingdom of Prussia, but she loved her cousin, the duke of Lorraine, and cried when she thought she was not to be allowed to marry him. And so her father gave in, and she had been married four years when she became Empress of Austria.

But before many months had passed the other countries began to try to steal her lands from her. France, Spain and Prussia attacked her, although both Spain and Prussia had promised her father not to do so.

The little kingdom of Prussia had been got together by Frederick's great-grandfather, the elector of the little state of Brandenburg. He was always called the 'Great Elector.' His son had been made king of all the possessions he had left and the new kingdom was called Prussia. The first king of Prussia was called Frederick I. He was the grandfather of Frederick II, who was called 'the Great.' Frederick the Great's father had been called Frederick William, like the great elector. His great passion was the army. He searched everywhere for the tallest men he could find, and his soldiers often looked like giants.

FREDERICK THE GREAT

When Frederick the Great was a little boy, his father was dreadfully strict with him. He was afraid that the boy would not grow up to be a good soldier, because he liked playing the flute and dressing himself up, and other things which seemed much more amusing to him than being drilled with the hundred boys whom his father brought to the palace, so that 'Fritz,' as Frederick was called in German, could learn how to command them.

His father planned out his whole day for him. He was to get up at six, and not even turn over in bed, but get up at once, say his prayers, wash himself and have his breakfast while his hair was being combed, and all was to be finished by half-past six. Then he was to learn history for two hours, and have religious instruction for another two, and then after another wash and changing into a clean shirt and coat, he was to go in and see his father. And so on.

But the little Fritz grew very tired of all this strictness, and as he grew up into a young man his father could hardly bear to look at him. He often beat him, and once Frederick ran away, but he was brought back, and put in a kind of prison for a year. But later on the father and son began to understand each other better, and when he was dying Frederick William thanked God for having given him such a good son to have the kingdom after him.

Frederick soon showed that he was a splendid soldier and a very clever man. Under him Prussia grew stronger and stronger, and it was all through the king, and that is how he came to be called Frederick the Great.

Frederick did not see why soldiers need be giants, and was not anxious, like his father, to seize all the biggest men and make them join the army; but he looked well after his army, and made it one of the best in Europe. He was also a good ruler. Although he was absolute like all the kings of the time, except the English, he used his power well. He tolerated all religions, and tried to do justice to everybody.

Frederick became king in 1640, the same year that Maria Theresa became Empress of Austria. There belonged to Austria a province called Silesia, which the electors of Brandenburg had said for years should belong to them. Frederick thought that this was his chance to win Silesia for Prussia. He invaded it and defeated an Austrian army in a great battle. He had first offered to help Maria Theresa against her other enemies if she would give him the province, but she proudly refused. Then the Elector of Bavaria, who thought that he should be Emperor of Austria, and had never agreed to the Pragmatic Sanction, invaded Austria, and the duke of Saxony helped him by taking an army into Bohemia.

But Maria Theresa begged the nobles of Hungary to help her. They were full of love and admiration for their beautiful young queen, and declared that they would give their lives for her. She in her turn gave the Hungarians many privileges which the emperors had always refused them.

The king of England at this time was George II, who was also elector of the little German state of Hanover. Queen Anne had no children alive when she died in 1714, and the throne of England had been settled on the descendants of the Electress Sophia of Hanover, the granddaughter of James I and daughter of the elector who had been driven out of the Palatinate at the beginning of the Thirty Years' War. Her son George, the Elector of Hanover, became king of England when Queen Anne died, and after him his son George II.

Both these men were quite German, and could not even speak English. They did not even attend the meeting of the 'Cabinet,' or chief men in parliament who ruled the country, and this helped the English parliament to become more and more powerful. King George II went over himself to fight for Maria Theresa. The Elector of Bavaria had been crowned emperor, but he died in the middle of the war, and Maria Theresa's husband was crowned emperor and called Francis I.

Maria Theresa, the Young Empress of Austria

France had conquered nearly all the Netherlands, and attacked Holland, but when peace was made in 1748, all conquered lands had to be given back, except Silesia, which Frederick kept. Maria Theresa hated giving it up, but she knew there was nothing else to do at the time, and she was always very sensible. But she made up her mind to take revenge on Frederick when the time came, and in the year 1756 war broke out again. It was called the 'Seven Years' War.'

This time England was on the side of Prussia and France on the side of Austria. But the greatest help to Maria Theresa came from the Tsarina Elizabeth of Russia, the daughter of Peter the Great. The Tsarina was a very beautiful and charming woman, though almost a savage in some ways like her father, for Russia was very far from being civilized even yet. Elizabeth thought that Prussia was getting far too powerful, and besides she hated Frederick the Great, who could say very witty and cruel things, and had said things about Elizabeth which had been repeated to her. Her private life was far from good, but this did not make her any more pleased when people talked about it.

France and England fought during the war chiefly in America and India, and we must tell the story of their struggle later. England, which was growing richer as her trade improved, paid great sums of money to help Frederick to fight. Sometimes the English grumbled, but William Pitt, 'the great Commoner,' as he was called, who was the chief man in England at the time, told them that it was necessary, saying 'America must be conquered in Germany,' by which he meant that by weakening France in Europe, he could better win her colonies from her abroad.

He won many battles, but lost many too. France, Austria and Russia were all powerful enemies, but it was the cleverness of Elizabeth which kept them together. In the year 1762, Frederick was talking about 'saving the remains' of his possessions for his nephew, and he probably meant to get himself killed in battle. But just then the Tsarina died.

The new Tsar, another Peter, was a great admirer of Frederick, and immediately made

Frederick the Great in Old Age

peace with him. In the next year a general peace was made. In Europe there was no real change after all the fighting, but Frederick kept Silesia, and from this time Prussia became an equal power with France and Austria among the countries of Europe.

When next we hear of the great powers of Europe doing anything important, we find Prussia, Austria and Russia joined together ten years afterwards, to steal land from the country of Poland, which lay between their boundaries. None of these countries had any right to Poland, but part of the Polish possessions, called West Prussia, lay on the Baltic between Brandenburg and Prussia, and Frederick longed to get this for himself, and so join the two parts of his kingdom together. He knew that he would not be able to take it unless Russia and Austria got some part of Poland too.

THE PARTITION OF POLAND

Poland was a very weak country, because of its peculiar government. The king had very little power, but there were an immense number of nobles. Nothing could be done in the government of the country unless every single noble agreed to it, and this did not often happen, and so things were not done.

But the Poles were a proud and noble people, and the three great powers who now attacked them were doing a very cruel and selfish thing. There was a great deal of trouble going on in Poland when the three countries attacked it. Prussia got West Prussia, Russia a slice of the East of Poland, and Austria a province in the South.

Maria Theresa did not much like the idea of the 'partition' of Poland as it was called, but she thought that it was her duty to Austria to take part, if Prussia and Russia did so, and, she said, if she took any she must have a good share.

The Polish nobles were treated very cruelly when they refused to agree to the partition, and had to give in. The ruler of Russia at this time was the great Tsarina, Catherine II. She was the wife of the Peter who admired Frederick the Great so much. This Peter was really a very mean and miserable little man. He was more German than Russian, and often hurt the feelings of the people whom he pretended to govern. He was very rough and cruel to his wife.

Catherine was not a good woman, but she was a splendid empress. Although she was a German Protestant princess, she soon learned the Russian language and took the religion of the Greek Church, which the Russians followed, as her own. After a time she got some of the chief Russians to seize Peter and put him in prison, where he died. Most people think that Catherine had him murdered. But the Russians were proud of their Tsarina, and she did all she could to make the country greater.

For twenty years after the first partition of Poland, that part of the country which was left was very much under the power of Catherine. At last, while she was fighting the Turks, some of the Poles tried to make a new government which would make their country freer. But Catherine soon stopped this. In 1793 there was a second partition of Poland between Prussia and Russia. Frederick the Great and Maria Theresa were both dead by this time, but the later rulers of those countries were just as cruel to Poland.

After this there was only a tiny kingdom of Poland left. A brave noble called Kosciusko tried to get help for his country from France and other countries, but could not, and then he and a few brave friends died fighting against their enemies. Then a third partition was made of all that was left of Poland. Since then there has never really been a kingdom of Poland, but Polish exiles may be found in every country of Europe. The best of them are always hoping for the time when Poland shall be a nation once more. The story of the partitions of Poland show almost better than anything else the selfishness of the kings and queens of Europe in the eighteenth century.

Chapter XXXIX — The Story of India

During the Seven Years' War in Europe, England won all India for her own. India is a great peninsula in the south of Asia, and almost a continent in itself as far as size goes. It is separated from Asia by a chain of mountains in which are some of the highest peaks in the world. All through the days of Greece and Rome and the Middle Ages, people did not know much about India. It had a separate life of its own. We have seen how, about the time when the Jews were wandering west from Mesopotamia to find a home in the land of Canaan, a branch of the Aryan people, to which the Persians and Greeks and Romans and the English all belonged, was pouring into India. There were already people in India of another race, darker still than the brown-skinned branch of the Aryan people which now came in and conquered them.

The Dravidians, as these people were called, were easily conquered by the Aryans, and soon there were far more Aryans in the north. But in the high tableland in the south of India, called the Deccan, there were always more Dravidians than Aryans, and still today the people of that part of India and of the Island of Ceylon to the south of India belong chiefly to this people, who are rather like the negroes of Africa.

The Dravidians were quite savage people and not very intelligent. They believed in wicked spirits and demons, and prayed to them. The Aryans made slaves of the Dravidians, They themselves were divided into three classes or 'castes.' There were the priests or Brahmans, who really governed the others, the soldiers, and the ordinary people. The people of one 'caste' could not marry with those of another. Not even the working-class would marry with the conquered Dravidians. There were divisions again in each caste, and often the people of one division could not marry or even eat with the people of another. This caste system, as it is called, still goes on in India today.

Alexander the Great, as we know, led an army into India and won some battles, but he never made any real conquest. After this, no outside people troubled India for many years. Sometimes, in the seventh and eighth centuries, when the followers of Mohammed were conquering West Asia, North Africa, and Spain, a few Arabs would cross the Himalayas, but there was never any real conquest until in the year 1004 A.D. a Mohammedan leader from a place called Ghuzni, in the country which is now called Afghanistan, to the northwest of India, took a great army and conquered the Punjab, as the land round the great river Indus and its tributaries is called.

After this there were many Mohammedan invasions and conquests, lasting for over five hundred years, right through the Middle Ages. In this way a new people and the Mohammedan religion found their way into India. This is why today, among all the different peoples of India, so many Mohammedans are to be found, even more than there are Hindus, who keep to their old religion of the Brahmans.

In the early part of the sixteenth century a new people swarmed into India, a great band of Mongolians from the centre of Asia, and their leader made himself ruler of all India. He was called the Great Mogul, and had his capital at Delhi. The grandson of this first Mongolian conqueror who ruled when his time came was called Akbar. He was a very fine soldier and a splendid ruler. The country was happy and peaceful under him. He died two years after Queen Elizabeth, and it is strange to think that while in the countries of Europe, Protestants and Catholics were being so dreadfully persecuted for their religion, this great Eastern ruler had given toleration to Hindus and Mohammedans equally.

The rulers who came after him seemed almost more splendid, but they were very different. They were cruel, like so many Eastern kings and emperors, and thought very little of murdering anyone who offended them. The greatest of all for the magnificence of his court was the Great Mogul Aurangzib. He had stolen the throne from his father, whom he put into prison. To make himself safer, he then murdered his own three brothers. The palace of the Great Mogul at Delhi was one of the wonders of the world. Before its gates stood two great elephants carved out of stone, with immense statues of soldiers on their backs.

The great hall of the palace, where the 'Durbar' or Council met, had a roof of pure white marble held up by thirty columns also of marble. The Great Mogul had seven magnificent thrones covered with different precious stones—one with pearls, another with rubies, another with diamonds, and so on. But all this splendor could not make Aurangzib happy. In his last years he was full of fear lest someone should murder him, as he had murdered so many. Soon after his death his great empire broke up into many little states. Most of the rulers pretended to obey the Great Mogul at Delhi, but they were really independent. Where there were so many races and so many divisions, it would be easy for a strong power to come and conquer, and that is what happened.

We saw how the Portuguese, who were the first Europeans to sail to India, set up a place at Goa, where they could exchange the things they brought from Europe for the spices which they carried back from India. The Portuguese said that they alone of all the people of Europe had the right to trade with India, but it was not long before the Dutch ships began to trade with the towns on the east coast of India. In time France and England both set up trading stations in India too. The chief English stations were Calcutta and Madras on the

The Great Emperor Akbar Enters his City in State *(From an ancient Indian manuscript in the Victoria and Albert Museum).*

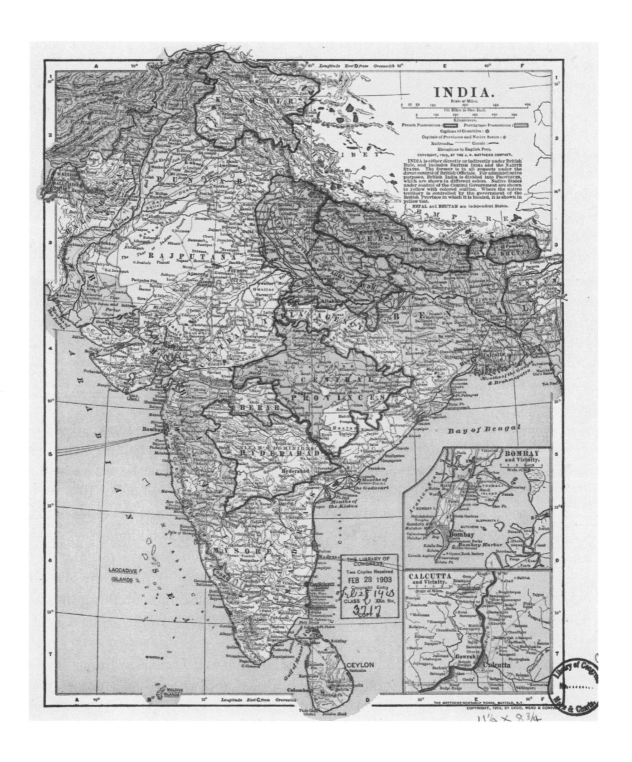

east coast, and Bombay on the west. The chief French trading-station was Pondicherry, south of Madras.

The English and French each paid some money every year to one of the native princes for permission to trade. The Frenchman Dupleix, who was in charge of Pondicherry, was the first to have the idea of how easy it would be for a strong European people to win this great country for themselves. He thought that if only the English could be driven from India, France could win this wonderful prize. The two countries were on opposite sides in the War of the Austrian Succession, and Dupleix made this an excuse for attacking the English in Madras. An English fleet was quite near, but was met by a small French fleet under another Frenchman called La Bourdonnais. The fleets fought, and though neither won, the English sailed away, and so Dupleix, with the help of La Bourdonnais, was able to take Madras, where there were very few men.

Most of the English were carried off to Pondicherry, but some escaped to another little station which the English held a few miles south of Madras. Dupleix attacked this station, which was called Fort St. David, but the little band of Englishmen held it bravely, and it was still unconquered when peace was made between France and England at the end of the War of the Austrian Succession. Dupleix was ordered to give Madras back to the English, and did so very unwillingly. The Englishmen at the trading-stations in India were working for the East India Company, which had been given the rights of all trade with India by Queen Elizabeth.

Among the clerks in the Company's service at Madras was a young man called Robert Clive. He had been the naughty boy of the family among his brothers and sisters in his English home. He was very passionate and very mischievous when he was a little boy. Once he climbed to the top of a very high steeple, and everyone who saw him was terrified, but he got down safely after all. He went to many schools but never learned very much. When he was eighteen he was sent out to India. He hated being a clerk, and felt very lonely and sad. Twice he tried to shoot himself but did not shoot straight, and then he made up his mind that he must be meant for something great. He was one of the men who escaped to Fort St. David from Madras. At last he had found something that he really liked to do, and when he went back to Madras he got the Company to have him as a soldier instead of a clerk.

There was not peace for very long between the English and French in India. They now hated each other bitterly. Their countries were at peace until the Seven Years' War broke out in 1756, but long before this there was fighting again in India. The way in which the French and English found excuses for fighting was to take part in quarrels between the native princes of the States in the Deccan which broke out at this time.

There were struggles about the crowns of the Deccan and of the Carnatic, a province in the Deccan. The French took one side and the English the other. The princes whom the

French were helping were successful at first, and great honor was done to Dupleix. He was dressed in beautiful Mohammedan robes, and a monument was put up with the story of his greatness in four languages. The natives, who had before despised the white men, had begun to see how powerful they really were. In a fight which had broken out between the French and a native prince, Dupleix with a few French soldiers had defeated a large army of natives.

The Hindus had no idea of training their soldiers, but both French and English had found out by this time that the native soldiers were almost as good as white soldiers. The natives who were trained in this way were called 'Sepoys.' When the English in Madras saw how Dupleix and his friends were succeeding, they sent soldiers to help the town of Trichi-nopoli, where the native prince called Mohammed Ali, whose side they were taking against the French, was being besieged.

Among the soldiers sent to Trichinopoli was Clive, but he saw that not much good could be done there, so he went back to Madras and asked the Governor to give him soldiers to attack Arcot, the capital of the Carnatic. Natives were watching Clive with his two hundred English soldiers and his three hundred Sepoys as he marched along the sixty-five miles to Arcot. A great storm came on, but Clive took no notice of the thunder and lightning and marched steadily on. This seemed wonderful to the natives, and they sent messengers on to Arcot to tell the natives there what a brave enemy was coming against them. The people of Arcot were so frightened that they fled away, and Clive took the empty town without any fighting at all.

But soon soldiers were sent from Trichinopoli to attack them. Clive and his men fought them for weeks. The Sepoys as well as the white soldiers loved and admired him. The Sepoys did a very fine thing. There was not much to eat except a little rice, and they said that the white soldiers must have all the rice, while they could manage quite well with the water in which it was boiled. At last one day the enemy made one last great attack. In the front of the army were great elephants with iron weapons on their heads to batter down the gates of the town. But when the English fired on them the elephants turned and fled, treading down and crushing the men of their own army. In an hour the enemy had fled and the great siege of Arcot was over.

Clive won many victories after this, and soon the English were as powerful in the Car-natic as the French had been. Dupleix was a great statesman but not a great soldier. He had had no help from France, and in a year or two he was called home in disgrace. He died broken-hearted at the thought of the empire he had tried to win for France, and which had been taken instead by the English. Meanwhile Clive had gone back to England for a rest, and had been praised and honored by everyone. On the day he landed again in India a very dreadful thing had happened, though Clive did not hear of it at once.

THE BLACK HOLE OF CALCUTTA

In Calcutta so far all had been peaceful. The English were quite friendly with the ruler or Nawab of Bengal, but in 1756 he died, and a young man called Siraj-ud-Daula became Nawab. He was really half mad and dreadfully cruel, very much like the Emperor Nero in character. He had an idea that there were great treasures shut up in the fort at Calcutta, and made up his mind to get them. He quarreled with the English and then attacked the fort. The women and children were put safely on ships in the river, all but one lady, who would not leave her husband, but the fort was taken and two hundred men in it.

Siaj-ud-Daula. The Nawab who shut up one hundred and forty-six people in the Black Hole in Calcutta (From an Indian painting).

The Nawab ordered that one hundred and forty-six of them should be shut up in a small room with only two tiny windows. It was called the 'Black Hole of Calcutta.' The night was terribly hot, and soon the poor prisoners were crying for air and water but the native soldiers at first only laughed and held torches to the windows so that they could see the people struggling inside, for they were half mad by this time. At last they brought some skin bottles of water, but they were too big to pass between the bars. Some was poured in and a few drops caught, but the fighting and shrieking grew worse than ever, until the sound died down to a moan. In the morning twenty-three people crawled out when the door was opened. The lady who would not leave her husband was among them, but he was dead inside.

When the story of this terrible night reached the other English in India, Clive set out at once with an army of Englishmen and Sepoys as before, and sailed to Calcutta. He easily conquered the Nawab and got Calcutta back. Siraj-ud-Daula made many promises, and Clive did not punish him further, but soon he found out that the Nawab was trying to get help from a French fort near against the English. So Clive besieged the fort and took it. So ended French power in the north of India.

Then Clive went against the Nawab, who had an enormous army at Plassey, ninety-six miles to the north of Calcutta. Here he won the famous battle of Plassey with three thousand men against nearly sixty thousand. Clive made Mir Jaffa, Siraj-ud-Daula's general, ruler of Bengal, but he had to pay a great deal of money to the English. It was not long before he murdered his old master, and so revenged the English for the terrible tragedy of the Black Hole of Calcutta.

Robert Clive, the Saviour of India (From a painting by Gainsliorongh).

The battle of Plassey was won in 1757, and William Pitt, who was choosing the men and arranging for the struggle with France in Europe and America, said that Clive was a 'heaven-born general.' Three years later another English commander. Eyre Coote, defeated the French in the south of India at the battle of Wandewash. After this France had no further chance in India.

But even the best Englishmen were inclined to think of India as a place from which to get money to send home to England. The Englishmen in the service of the East India Company were very badly paid, and so, although they were forbidden to trade for themselves, they did so. They were very unjust to the natives, and soon there was a great deal of misery in India. There was another massacre at Patna as bad as that of the Black Hole. This was while Clive was away in England. He went back and tried to put things in order and give more justice to the natives. But even Clive had done some things which seemed very unjust to the English at home when they heard of them, for they did not know how difficult things were in India, and how hard it was to be sure that the native princes would keep their promises.

So when Clive got back to England again he had to defend himself in Parliament against people who said he had behaved wickedly in India. In the end Parliament declared 'that Robert, Lord Clive, did render great and meritorious services to his country.' But Clive had been dreadfully upset. His old sadness came on him again, and one day he was found dead. He had killed himself.

Still things were very bad in India. The native princes had no longer any power. The Englishmen paid large sums of money to them, and they had to be content with that. All the taxes collected from the people were now paid to the East India Company, but the Englishmen did not really understand what was going on, and the native collectors took much more from the people than they should have done, and kept a great deal of the money for themselves. The people grew poorer and poorer. Then there was a great famine. The people were starving and became as thin as skeletons. Thousands died, and their bodies lay unburied and then plague broke out.

At last Warren Hastings, who was in the service of the East India Company and had fought in the battle of Plassey, was sent out as Governor. He was, like Dupleix, a statesman more than a soldier, and he did all he could to make things better. But even then things were still very bad. Much trouble came through the English not understanding the customs of the Hindus. Once a man who had cheated the English very badly was put to death. In those days stealing or cheating was still punished by death even in England. But this man was a Brahman, and to the natives it seemed a terrible thing that one of the priestly caste should be killed.

At last people in England began to think that the East India Company should not have the government of India, and a president was sent out to rule India for the government at home. In the year 1788 an attack was made on Warren Hastings, and he was tried before Parliament for misrule in India. Edmund Burke, a famous Irish member of Parliament and a splendid speaker, began with a speech in which he described the terrible sufferings of the natives and the awful behavior of Hastings. People wept while Burke spoke, and there was a terrible feeling against Hastings, but as time went on people began to understand the truth of the case, and at the end of seven years Hastings was declared 'Not guilty.' He lived a happy cheerful life in his English country home until he died when he was eighty-seven years old.

As time went on England got power over all the native princes of India. Many of them made treaties with the English by which their soldiers were put under British officers and were paid by the English. At the same time, they generally gave up some of their land altogether to the English.

The Indian Mutiny

In the year 1857 there was a terrible rebellion of the native soldiers all over the north of India.

It was partly a religious movement. Some new guns were being used, and the cartridges fired from them were greased with fat. The end of the cartridge had to be bitten off by the soldiers. Now the Hindus and the Mohammedans were forbidden by their religions to touch the fat of cows or pigs. It was now said that the cartridges were greased with the fat of these animals. The soldiers were told that this was not true, but they would not believe the English. At last they were told that the greased cartridges would not be used any more. But then they began to think that the shiny paper in which other cartridges were wrapped was also polished by the same grease and a rebellion broke out.

All over the north of India the native soldiers attacked the English—men, women, and children. There was a terrible massacre at Cawnpore, and Lucknow was only saved after a terrible siege. The English had been taken completely by surprise, but the rebellion was soon put down. There were not many English soldiers, but many of the natives remained faithful, and when they took the Sepoys prisoners it would not have been easy to carry them with them. The English were dreadfully angry, too, at the thought of their women and children, and were not sorry to kill their prisoners.

After the Mutiny it was thought better that India should be taken altogether from the East India Company, and so that company came to an end at last. Since then India has been ruled by a Viceroy or representative of the King or Queen of England. England now owns two-thirds of all the land of India, and the other third is ruled by native princes, under her. The king is called Emperor of India.

In India the English people have done very wonderful things, which the natives could never have done for themselves. Railways, roads, and bridges have been built, and it is now easy to get from one part of India to another. In old days, when a time of dry weather came, the land was burned up, and there was famine, hut the English have made canals in which water which has been stored up can be carried to the fields in dry weather.

The population of India grows very quickly, almost too quickly, for it sometimes seems that the land could never give food for all, but *now* the English have set up factories, and many of the people leave the country parts and work in the towns. Bombay is famous for its manufacture of color-stuffs and muslin. Some people are even afraid that the cotton goods made in India will take the place of those made in Manchester and the great towns of Lancashire, and that the cotton trade of that county will be ruined. These cotton goods, and Indian tea and wheat, are bought by the countries of Europe.

Many of the higher class of natives come now to be educated in England, and some of these young students think that India should be governed by its own people. The English are allowing some of the educated people to help in the government of their country, but though it may seem strange that a little country like England should govern a continent like India with its millions and millions of people, it must be remembered that these people of India are of many different races, that they do not seem able to join together in any way, and that if England or some other European country had not interfered there might have been fighting and misery for centuries yet.

On the whole, the people of India and the native princes honor and respect Great Britain, and when King George and Queen Mary paid a visit to India in the year 1912, there was a great gathering of princes at the Durbar to do them honor.[1]

---

[1] Editor's note: India gained its independence from Great Britain in 1947.

Chapter XL—The Story of Canada

To many men from the earliest times there has come a strange longing which they cannot put aside. It is a longing to go out and travel to the unknown parts of the world, to see what they are like, what people live there, what these people do, and what things grow there. It was this longing which drove Columbus across the ocean to discover America.

But Columbus was not really the first to find America. The Northmen, whose land is Norway and Sweden, had ever loved adventure, as they do still. In the last few years men from Norway have sailed right out many times to the frozen North and to the centre of the snowy South, which we call the South Pole. It was when Ethelred the Unready was ruling in England in the eleventh century that Lief Ericson sailed off towards the west, just when some of the other Northmen were swooping down upon England. After many days he and his fellow-sailors came to a land which was probably that which we now call Canada, the northern part of North America. But the Northmen sailed back to their own country, and it was nearly five hundred years before any one from Europe visited Canada again.

This time it was an Englishman, John Cabot, who set sail from Bristol and came to Canada. Again it was only a visit, and the Englishman did not try to settle there. But fishermen learned soon that good fishing was to be had near the new country, and they commenced to sail and fish round the island of Newfoundland and the coasts of North America.

Just thirty-seven years after Cabot's voyage, in 1534, a French sailor was sent by King Francis I. to see what he could find. Jacques Cartier, as he was called, was even more venturesome than Cabot. He sailed up the Gulf of St. Lawrence to the place where Montreal now stands, and it is to him that we owe the name 'Canada.' For it is said that when he met with some Red Indians who lived in the land in those days, they pointed to their huts saying 'Cannata,' meaning to point out their village to him. In their language the word 'Cannata' means 'village,' but Cartier thought they were telling him the name of the land, and so 'Cannata' or 'Canada' he called it.

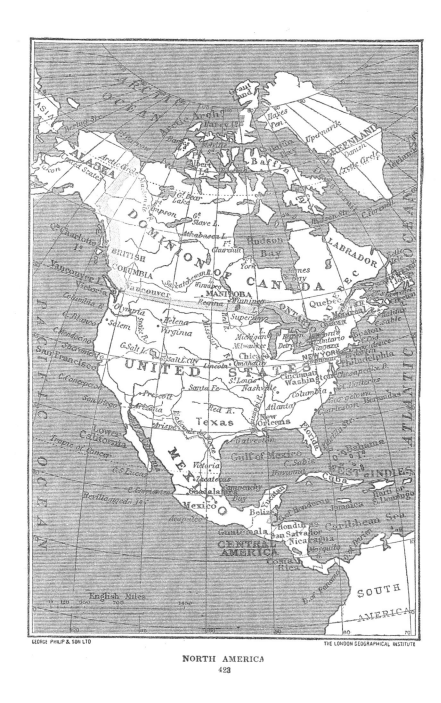

NORTH AMERICA
423

THE FIRST COLONIST IN CANADA

No one from Europe, so far, had attempted to stay in Canada, for Cartier sailed back again like Cabot, and it was almost seventy years before the next visitors came to the country and began to build themselves houses. Samuel de Champlain, who was the leader this time, is

287

The first settlement in Quebec (From a drawing in Champlain's account of his travels, published in 1613).

the first great name in the story of Canada. He will always be remembered through the beautiful lake Champlain, which he discovered, and which was called after him. Champlain was a very wise and brave man, and when he arrived in Canada in the year 1603 he at once made friends with the Indians. He had made his plans and intended to stay in Canada, for he had been sent out by a man to whom the French king had given the right to be the only one allowed to trade with Canada and sell the furs which were got from the wild animals there. The first thing to do was to find a place where he could live; and so Champlain sailed up the river St. Lawrence and round the coast until he made up his mind to settle at Port Royal, now called Annapolis, in Nova Scotia.

Champlain had soon to go back to France, but he went back again to Canada, and this time founded the city of Quebec in 1608. He had made friends with the Huron Indians, but had to fight with the fierce tribe called the Iroquois.

Champlain was a Catholic and a very religious man. He did not mind much about the fur-trader or founding towns and settlements. What he did care for was ever to find new places and to bring his religion to the people whom he met. He commenced a settlement at Montreal, and thinking to find a new way to China, sailed up the Ottawa river. But the settlements he made were not well protected, and about the time he founded Montreal the English from Virginia took Port Royal, and in 1629 an English fleet took Quebec. Champlain was taken prisoner to England, but four years later Canada was given back to the French and he returned to Quebec, where he died in 1635.

Struggles with the Indians

Champlain's work was not carried out without much fighting with the savage and treacherous Red Indians, and the warfare went on for many years longer. It was not a life to persuade many people to leave their homes in France, but many people did go. There were the missionaries, 'black robes,' as the Indians called these priests, who were the bravest colonists of all. They thought it was their duty to go out and tell the Indians about God. Yet, thirty years after Champlain's death, there were only about two thousand Frenchmen in Canada. Some of these pushed their way through the thick forests without paths, against wild beasts and savage men to the great Lake Superior, and south to where the great river Mississippi enters the ocean, and founded a colony which they called 'Louisiana' after their King Louis.

Some of the priests in Canada thought that the Indians were being made wilder and fiercer through the white man giving them brandy and other spirits to drink, and they tried to prevent it, but did not succeed very well.

One night in the August of the year 1689, the Iroquois took a terrible revenge on the French. It was a dark and stormy night, and the people in a small village near Montreal had gone to bed, when suddenly there burst in upon them a large number of Indians. Two hundred of the colonists were killed at once by one thousand five hundred Iroquois. And they were indeed happier than those who were left. For a hundred of these were carried off and tortured in the most horrible ways before they were killed.

At this time a brave Frenchman called Louis de Buade had been sent back to France; but when he returned he fought against the Iroquois so fiercely that in a few years he had so thoroughly conquered them that no Frenchman ever needed to fear them again.

The French king, Louis XIV, had been thinking what a glorious chance he had of making a great empire in America, and Louis de Buade tried to bring this about. So he attacked the English colonists in New England to win their land for France. But the fighting went very badly for the French, and when peace was made in the year 1713 by the Treaty of Utrecht, they had to give up the land where they had first settled—Nova Scotia, as well as Newfoundland and the land round Hudson Bay.

Still they held the land round the St. Lawrence, and they tried to make up for what they had to give to England by pushing farther west and founding new towns. One very brave man after terrible hardship even travelled right across Canada to the Rocky Mountains. This is still a very long journey by the fastest trains. But La Verendrye, as this man was called, had no train to go by. He simply struggled on, sometimes fighting with wild beasts, sometimes with Indians. Often he had very little to eat for days together.

George Washington

Other Frenchmen travelled south to the colony of Louisiana, and founded the large town which is called New Orleans. It was through these Frenchmen, who were trying to get as much land as they could to the South of Canada, that a young man, who afterwards became very famous, first came to learn how to fight. George Washington had not much chance of education in the things most boys and girls of his age are expected to know now. Most of what he knew he had taught himself. He could spell and write good English, which very few colonists could do. He also liked mathematics. But he learned other things which were much more valuable for him. He had finished his schooling when he was fifteen. He had on the whole been happy, though his father died when he was young. He could shoot, hunt, fish, and look after the big plantations which had belonged to his father, and now belonged partly to his half-brother and partly to himself.

Deportation of the French Catholic Acadiens from Nova Scotia

He had learned other and harder lessons. The Washingtons lived on the borders of Virginia, and life was not very safe there. They might be attacked at any time by Indians or by the Frenchmen from the north. George learned to ride about amongst these dangers without any fear, and also to be cool and calm if he was attacked by man or beast.

When he was only sixteen he was sent to look after large plantations. Even then he knew exactly what he wanted, and was so wise and sensible that grown men respected him. When he was nineteen he had an attack of the dreadful disease of smallpox, which left marks on his face till he died. He was only just a man when the Governor of Virginia chose him for a difficult task. The French, as we have seen, were pushing their settlements South, and the English colonists thought that they were taking some of the land which they looked on as their own. So George Washington was sent to tell them to go back. It was winter, and travelling was not easy even if there had been no enemy near. But he made the journey. The French officers were very polite to him, but they told him to tell the Governor that they meant to stay where they were.

So Washington went back. He did not seem to have done much, but he had looked carefully at the country, and had made up his mind where a fort should be built to keep the enemy back. Next year he was made a lieutenant-colonel and sent to fight the French and the Indians near the Ohio, where they had made their camp. He defeated them, but a month later had to give in and go back.

The next year he went back again under General Braddock to try to take Fort Duquesne, which stood where the large American town Pittsburg, with its huge smoky factories and iron foundries, now stands. General Braddock was a brave man and a good fighter, but he did not know how to fight against the French and Indians, and in the battle he was defeated, and nearly all his men were killed. It was here that Washington first showed how brave a fighter he was. All over the battlefield he could be seen on horseback cheering the men to fight harder. Many an Indian shot at him, and they could shoot well and straight, but somehow he escaped with some of his soldiers unharmed from the terrible battle.

A few months after his return he was made head of all the soldiers in Virginia. He was only twenty-three years old, but he defended the borders of Virginia against the enemy, and was one of the leaders when, three years later, Fort Duquesne was taken. The rest of his life belongs to the Story of America, which is told in the next chapter.

One of the most terrible things in this warfare between the French and English was done by the Governor of Nova Scotia. This, as we have seen, was the first French settlement made in Canada, but it had been taken by the English. A great number of the people who still lived there, however, were simple French Catholics, who were quiet, peaceful farmers and traders. They were still Frenchmen at heart, loving the French king better than the king of England. In the year that General Braddock was defeated at Fort Duquesne the Governor of Nova Scotia suddenly seized six thousand of the French settlers and drove them from their homes and right out of Nova Scotia.

In an instant their peaceful life was broken up. The country they loved, and in which they had lived so long and their fathers before them, was to be theirs no longer. Many did not know where to go in their great sorrow. Some got as far south as Louisiana. Others settled near Nova Scotia, and many years afterwards a few found their way back to the land of their birth again after terrible suffering; but most of them had seen it for the last time.

General Wolfe

But if there were Englishmen who acted with great cruelty, there were others who were so noble that their names will never be forgotten. The struggle for Canada was now at its fiercest, and although the English had won some victories, it was seen by statesmen in England that the only way to take Canada was to take Quebec. Both French and English seemed to feel that this town was the key of Canada. It was built on a high rock, which stood at the head of the Gulf of St. Lawrence. From the river it seems to be built on a precipice. On the west it is defended by steep cliffs called the Heights of Abraham, and although on the opposite side the land slopes more gently, this was naturally watched more carefully.

The French General, Montcalm, was a brave man and a clever fighter, and when he thought that Quebec was to be attacked he called together all the soldiers he could get, and brought them, with many French settlers and Indians, into the city to defend it. The leader

The Death of General Wolfe by Benjamin West; held at National Gallery of Canada.

of the English was General Wolfe, who had already fought in North America before. Before he started out from England again he met a young lady with whom he fell in love. They were to be married when the war was over and Wolfe was back again.

Wolfe was a pale slim man, rather delicate, but few men have ever been braver or cleverer. He had not nearly so many soldiers as Montcalm, and they were not soldiers who had had much training. But he had made up his mind to take Quebec. It was a dangerous thing to remain in the St. Lawrence, for in the winter the water freezes hard and the ships might be crushed to pieces. But Wolfe, although the autumn was coming on, made his camp on a little island in the river facing Quebec and waited his chance to take the city. He set his guns to fire on the city, but they did not do much harm to it, and Wolfe saw that he must try to take Quebec in some other way. So he sailed down the St. Lawrence and tried to take Montcalm's camp below the city, but he was badly beaten and many of his men were killed.

He was now ill and depressed. He could hardly drag his weak body about. But he did not mean to give in, and when he felt a little stronger he made a bold plan. Montcalm thought he was quite safe on the steep west side of the town, for he thought no army could climb the Heights of Abraham, and he did not believe that even the foot of them could be reached from the river.

But Wolfe had found that from a tiny inlet from the St. Lawrence there was a footpath up the cliffs which led to the Heights of Abraham. In the dead of night he sailed down the river with his men. Cloths had been wrapped round the oars so that no noise could be heard. No light was shown, and there was no moon. Somehow the soldiers climbed up the narrow foot-path, surprised the soldiers at the top, and when daylight came Montcalm was astounded to see nearly four thousand English soldiers on the Heights of Abraham ready to attack Quebec.

But even yet the city was not won. Montcalm brought up his soldiers for battle, and at first the English were driven back. But Wolfe made his men wait until the French came nearer and then all fire at once. Men fell along the French line, and before they could form up again the English rushed upon them. But Wolfe was wounded. As he lay dying and full of pain he heard his soldiers cry, 'They run! See how they run.' 'Who run?' the dying leader asked, and was told 'The enemy.' He was quite satisfied, and saying, 'Now God be praised, I will die in peace,' he closed his eyes and died. Montcalm was also wounded, and died the next day.

Five days afterwards, on the 11th September 1759, Quebec was given up to the English, and when the Peace of Paris was made in 1763, the whole of New France was given up to the English. This is how Canada became English instead of French.

But the country was not allowed many years of peace to settle down and grow, though the English Government, which was treating the American colonists so unreasonably, acted very wisely towards the Canadians. The country was to be governed from Quebec, and the Catholics were to be treated as well as they had ever been under the French. Only the English punishments for breaking the law were brought in, and in other things the French laws were allowed. The result of this wise treatment was soon seen, for when an army of American soldiers invaded Canada at the beginning of the American War of Independence, hoping to get the French to join them against England, they were disappointed. The Americans took Montreal, but were not able to take Quebec.

But the War of American Independence was very important for Canada. The United States and Canada became two separate countries, and many of the American colonists who would not give up the King of England left their lands and went to find new homes in Canada. The Americans would not give them any money for the farms and lands they left behind them, and these new men of Canada did not soon forget it. The new Canadians were equal to more than half all the Frenchmen in Canada, and many of them settled in the land which is now called Ontario. Here, and in the other places where they made their homes, they were given large pieces of land to live on and grow corn upon, and they were also given spades and ploughs in place of those they had left behind.

But it is easy to understand why the new Canadians did not at first get on very well with the older colonists. They were English and Protestants, while the older colonists were French and Catholics. It was not long before it was thought that it would be wise to let the people of Ontario govern themselves, while the people in Quebec made laws only for those people who lived in that part of Canada. Yet, however badly the English and French in Canada might disagree, they did not intend to join the Americans, and so when in the year 1812 the United States were at war with Great Britain and tried to take Canada their soldiers were driven back.

There were some however, though not very many, of the French Canadians who did not like being ruled by an English Governor, and rebellions took place. The leader in one of these, Louis Papineau, wished to make the people of the Quebec part of Canada join the United States; but there were very few rebels, and the rebellion was easily put down. One thing which happened just after this was the joining of Quebec to Ontario. The two provinces did not agree very well at first, but thirty years later, in 1867, other settlements in Canada joined with them. The colonies called Nova Scotia, New Brunswick, and Prince Edward Island were thinking of joining together, and Ontario and Quebec suggested that they should all join. This was agreed to, and the British Parliament passed the law which made them one on 1st July, which has ever since been kept as the birthday of the 'Dominion of Canada.'

But this was but a very small part of Canada as it is today. Other huge tracts of land lay to the north and west. Much of this belonged to the Hudson Bay Company, which was founded in 1670 to trade in furs and skins. The Company had made settlements round the lower part of Hudson Bay and over the country west of Ontario. The Dominion of Canada wanted this large and fertile country to join with the rest of Canada, and the Hudson Bay Company agreed at the end of 1869 to give up their land to the Queen for a sum of money. But this did not please many of the people who lived in the colonies the Company had founded.

One of these colonies was called the Red River Settlement, and it lay round the town which is now called Winnipeg, but was then called Fort Garry. Many of the men who lived in the Red River Settlement were 'half-breeds,' that is half French and half Indian, or partly English and partly Indian, and they feared that when the Settlement became part of Canada there would be changes that they would not like. Louis Riel, one of these half-breeds, persuaded the men to rebel. They made him their leader, and shot an Englishman who refused to join them. This made the people of the Dominion very angry, and Colonel Garnet Wolseley, who was afterwards called Lord Wolseley, was sent to punish them. He marched as far as he could, sailed over the Lake Superior, and took Fort Garry.

Three years after this all the Settlements in Canada had joined the Dominion, but Louis Riel, who had escaped in 1870, lived to persuade some people to rebel again. This second time, in 1885, there was much fighting, and Riel was caught and hanged.

In the same year the great Canadian Pacific Railway, joining the East to the far West of Canada, was opened. There has been no fighting since. Canada has gone on, growing richer and more fertile every day. New towns spring up almost like magic. New states have been formed. There are miles of wheat fields, huge canals, and railways ever growing. The Canadians are very loyal to Great Britain, and their soldiers were sent to help the British in the South African War. A royal prince, the King's uncle, represents King George in Canada. The Canadians are building great ships of war to help the British Navy, and thousands of men and women leave the shores of Britain every year to become Canadians, and live healthy, open-air lives under the fair skies of the Dominion.

Chapter XLI—American Independence

England had won Canada from the French, but she was soon to lose her own great colonies to the South of Canada. Ever since she had had colonies at all, England had said that all their trade should be hers. They were not allowed to trade with any other country but the mother-country. The colonies had never complained, but there had been a great deal of smuggling and trade with other countries, of which England had taken no notice.

Now England, after all her fighting and her many victories, was in need of money, and Grenville, the chief man in the English Parliament at the time, passed his famous 'Stamp Act.' This Act said that for all documents written or printed in the American colonies, and for all newspapers, paper should be used which had first been stamped by the English Government. The people who bought the paper had to pay for the stamp.

This was a new way of taxing the colonies, and they were very angry. They said that they would not use the paper, and in the next year it was given up. But the English Parliament passed a law saying that England had the right to make any laws she pleased for her colonies. This made the colonies still more angry. William Pitt, who had now been made Earl of Chatham, said that England had not any right to tax the colonies without their consent. Although Pitt had done so much to win India and Canada for England, he felt that the mother-country ought to leave her colonies free. He told Parliament that he 'rejoiced that America had resisted.'

It "was not long before new 'duties' or taxes were put upon certain things going to the colonies from England. The colonists must pay the tax and the English have the money. The people of America had offered to give money to the English Government to help it, but they were very angry at this new attempt to tax them. The colonists began to hate every Englishman they saw, and when a quarrel broke out in Boston between some of the people in the street and some English soldiers, in which three of the Americans were killed, the colonists called it the 'Boston Massacre.' At last all the new taxes were taken off except one on tea. The East India Company brought a great deal of tea from India, and generally they had to pay a tax when it came into England. But the Company was very poor at this time, and so the

Government let it off from paying the tax. This made the Company able to sell the tea much cheaper, and now a great quantity of tea was sent over the sea in ships to America. But the colonists were told that they must pay just this one tax of threepence on every pound of tea they bought.

Even then they would have got the tea at a very low price, but they were very indignant. They thought that the English were playing a trick, and trying to tempt them to buy the cheap tea and pay a tax at the same time. So no one bought the tea, and ship after ship sailed back to England without unloading. One ship lay at anchor in Boston Harbor. It had been there nineteen days, and yet looked as though it meant to stay there. There was a law that any ship must unload its cargo before twenty days had passed from its arrival. So the men of Boston made up their minds to attack this ship which had broken the law.

Some of them painted their faces and stuck feathers in their heads, and pretended to be Indians. They rushed on to the ship, waving pistols and tomahawks. While the English captain and sailors were staring in surprise they cut open the boxes in which the tea was, and emptied it into the sea. They emptied more than three hundred boxes altogether. Next morning tea lay drifting along all the shore of Massachusetts.

It was now England's turn to be angry. Every one felt that the men of Boston had begun a real revolution. No one would tell who the men were who had disguised themselves as Indians and done this thing, and so an order came from England that Boston was to be punished. No ship was to go in or out of its harbor, and its trade was to be taken to the town of Salem. For the future, any one giving trouble by attacking the English was to be brought

Boston 'Tea-Party'

over to England to be tried before English judges and juries. Every one felt that this was unjust, but by this time the colonists had made up their minds to fight for their liberties. Men from all the colonies met at Philadelphia, and it was agreed that they should join together and resist the English.

There was a struggle at a place called Lexington, which made the two sides bitterer than ever against each other. Some English soldiers had been sent from Boston to destroy some gunpowder and other things which the American side had collected at Concord, eighteen miles away. They had to pass by Lexington, and there they found sixty or seventy men ready to try to stop them. The English fired twice on these men, and then the Americans went away. But eight of them had been killed. The English did their work at Concord, and then set out again for Boston. On their way back, Americans were continually shooting at them from behind buildings and trees and rocks, to take revenge for the Americans they had killed on their way to Concord. Many English were killed, until at Lexington one thousand men from Boston came to their help.

There was a fight, in which more than seventy English and about fifty Americans were killed. The English really won, and most of them got safely back to Boston; but they had lost more men than the Americans, who grew more hopeful when they saw that their volunteers, who were not used to war, could fight quite well against the English soldiers.

The Battle of Bunker's Hill

The first real fight was called the 'battle of Bunker's Hill.' A few hundred volunteers, men with ordinary clothes and any guns they could get, were placed on the hills outside Boston to defend that city. Although the battle is called after Bunker's Hill, it was really fought on Breed's Hill. About four thousand soldiers attacked them. Three times the volunteers drove them down the hill, but at last the soldiers won their way up, and more than one hundred of the volunteers lay dead. Then another 'Congress' met at Philadelphia, and named Colonel George Washington General of the American Army. And so the man who had fought so well for England at Fort Duquesne was now to fight against her. He soon won Boston back, and drove the English soldiers to Halifax.

On the 4th of July 1776 the 'Congress' drew up the famous 'Declaration of Independence of the United States of America,' by which an end was put to any connection of the colonies with the mother-country. But there was still fighting to be done, and Washington had a very hard task before him.

His soldiers were badly clothed and fed. Neither side had very big armies, but the English had the soldiers who knew already something about fighting. Then some of the colonists, who were called the 'Loyalists,' were against the Declaration, and did not want to break away from England. These were a hindrance. There were many others who hated fighting, and

Portrait of George Washington by Charles Wilson Peale, 1776.

most of the volunteers only joined the army for a certain fixed time, and would then go home, often just when they might have been useful. But the English on their side did very foolish things. They seemed to think that it would be an easy thing to conquer the Americans, or to believe that they were not really in earnest. Pitt, who had known so well how to choose the best men as officers, was no longer in power, and most of the officers on the English side were very poor commanders.

Sir William Howe, the brother of Lord Howe, who had been sent by Wolfe to fight in Canada and had died there, and of Admiral Lord Howe, was a very different man from his brothers. He made up his mind to take Philadelphia, and took it. But his armies were all far apart, instead of keeping close and helping each other. One of them, under General Burgoyne, surrendered to the Americans at Saratoga in 1777. Next year the French, who were still full of anger at the great victories England had won over them in India and Canada, agreed to the Independence of the American colonies, and France and England were once more at war.

Pitt, now old and ill, begged Parliament to try to win the good-will of the Americans again. 'You cannot conquer America,' he told Parliament, and begged them to show a spirit of friendship and mercy to the colonists. But the king, George III did not like Pitt, and would not give him any power in the country. George III, who had boasted that he was 'born and bred a Briton' and was not at all German, like his father and grandfather, could not bear the idea of giving in.

George had a great deal of power over Parliament, and chose the men who governed the country. It was greatly his fault that England had been so foolish in her treatment of America. Pitt made one last great speech in the House of Lords in the April of 1778. He fell back in a fit when his speech was over, for the excitement had been too much for him, and he died a few weeks after.

After this there was never any chance of America being won back. England had to fight hard against France and Spain at sea. The French ships helped the Americans to take Yorktown, in Virginia, where Lord Cornwallis and a large army had to give in to them. Lord Cornwallis was the cleverest of the English officers who fought in the war. This was really the end of the war, though New York, which had refused to join in the Declaration of Independence, was still held by the English.

Peace was made in 1783 with both France and America. Admiral Rodney had shown by his victories over the French and Spanish fleets that England was still the greatest sea power. But she now openly agreed to American Independence, and all the thirteen colonies were now joined as a federal republic. That is, each state governed itself in its own affairs and sent representatives to the Congress, which settled the affairs in which they all had a part.

The new republic was called, and is still, the United States of America. Its capital was New York. Its first president was the hero George Washington, old and grey before his time through his labors and suffering for his country.

So England lost her first great group of colonies. A clever Frenchman once said that a colony will always break away from the mother-country when it is old enough and strong enough to look after itself, but we have no proof of this. Indeed England has many colonies today which are proud of belonging to her, but she has learned her lesson, and gives them every liberty she can.

Meanwhile the United States, which at first were the thirteen colonies on the east coast of America, have now spread right across the continent. New states were formed in 'the West.' People from the older states and from Europe went out into these wild parts round the Ohio, where the new states, called Ohio, Kentucky, and Tennessee, grew up. Although these states were called the 'West,' they are, of course, in the eastern part of the continent. They are west from the older states, but beyond them lies more than half the continent. Before the middle of the nineteenth century all this was won by the United States. The great province of Louisiana, which Napoleon took from Spain, was sold to the United States for three million pounds. Further west still, some of the land belonged to the Hudson Bay Company and some to Mexico, but the United States got it all in the end, until the republic stretched from coast to coast.

At first these settlers in the wild West led a very hard life indeed. There was plenty of rich land, which gave them food, but the only way of getting things made in other countries was to have them carried in ships along the rivers. This was a very slow way when the distances were so great, and it was not until railways were invented that the western states were able to send great quantities of the things they grew to the eastern states and to Europe, and so get back the things manufactured there, and so lead more comfortable and less rough lives.

THE END OF SLAVERY

In the new states, just as in the old Southern states, there was a great deal of cotton grown, and slaves were used on the plantations. But everywhere in the nineteenth century, as we shall see, there was a new love of freedom growing up, and people began to think it a shameful thing that men should own their fellow-men as though they were cattle.

About the time that the war between the American colonies and England broke out, a great English judge had declared that any slave setting foot on English soil became free at that moment. In a few years Parliament did away with all the slave trade in English ships, and paid twenty million pounds to slave owners in her colonies in the West Indies and South Africa to set their slaves free. It was not long before other European countries followed her example.

It was in the Southern states of America that the greatest number of the slaves were. The owners of the big plantations had dozens of them, doing the work of the house as well as the plantations. The men would work on the plantation and the women would be cooks and nurses in the house. Their little children grew up on the plantation and belonged to the master too. Many slaves were happy, for they had good masters, but they were never safe. Cruel masters might beat them, or worse still, sell their wives and children to other people. A family might be broken up and never see each other again. This was very dreadful.

At last the men of the Northern states said that all the slaves should be set free. A lady wrote a story called *Uncle Tom's Cabin,* which told all about the sufferings of the slaves, and at last the men of the North could not bear the idea that there should any longer be slaves in their country. They wanted a law passed to free all the slaves. They said that the government could give money to the slave owners to make up to them for losing their slaves.

But the men of the South were very angry. They said they would never agree to this. In the North slavery was abolished, and the men of the North were very angry against the South. John Brown, a Northerner, went to Virginia, and calling all the slaves he could find to follow him, he told them to fight for their freedom. But he was taken prisoner and hanged. He had certainly been acting against the law, but the Northerners were very indignant.

At last the Southern states said they would have a republic of their own, and elected a president. But the Northerners said they had no right to do this, and Abraham Lincoln, the president, felt that America would never be safe and strong if it were broken up like this. Abraham Lincoln was one of the greatest presidents America ever had. He had been a poor boy living in a log cabin in the wild western state of Indiana, but he had read every book he could get, and had grown to be a very wise man. He was determined to keep the states together even if slavery had to go on in the South, but the Southerners would not listen to him now.

A great Civil War broke out. There were heroes on both sides and great victories and defeats. The men of the North marched to battle singing in chorus:

'John Brown's body lies a-mouldering in the grave,
But his soul goes marching on,'

for they could never forgive the Southerners for killing John Brown. The greatest leader the South had was Jackson, who was called by his men 'Stonewall Jackson,' because they said when men were falling wounded and dead around him he stood as steady as ever, 'like a stone wall.'

In the middle of the war Lincoln declared that all men were free in North and South alike. Soon afterwards 'Stonewall' Jackson was killed, shot by mistake by his own men. At last, after two more years of fighting, the Southern army had to surrender. Almost every family in North and South alike had lost a father, or brother, or son in the war. But through much suffering two great things had been done. The states remained united and the slaves were free.

But Abraham Lincoln, who had done so much for his country, and had suffered terribly when he thought of all the unnecessary waste of men's lives, was himself to die a martyr at last. He was in the theatre at Washington one evening shortly after peace was made, when a man from the South shot at him and killed him, shouting: 'The South is avenged.' Lincoln was taken back to be buried near his old home in the wild west.

Today the United States, whose history we have been able to tell only in this short way, is one of the most wonderful countries in the world. It is covered with great cities filled with people who are among the cleverest in the world. The American love of freedom has become a proverb.

Even more than in England, perhaps, people feel there that every one should have equal chances; that it does not matter how poor a man may be, or how lowly his birth, if he has brains and character. Nearly all the greatest inventions now come from America.

New York, with its great wide straight streets and its mansions of white marble, where its rich men and millionaires live, is one of the most beautiful cities in the world. And every year millions of people pour from Europe into the United States: Russians who find that their own government does not give them enough of freedom, Italians who seek riches which their own land cannot give them, Norwegians, Swedes, Germans. Many of the most energetic people from all the countries of Europe are going to seek their fortune in 'the States.' It is interesting to see how these all settle down and mix together to form the American people, all speaking the English language, which the Pilgrim Fathers took to the land three hundred years ago.

One drawback to the good feeling in America is that many of the white people cannot yet believe that the 'coloured' people, the negro descendants of the slaves whom Lincoln freed, are their equals. There is still a great deal of ill-feeling, which we can only hope will pass away in time, and the negroes get their full share in the life of the great republic.

Chapter XLII—Australasia

One strange result of the American War of Independence was the founding of colonies in the great continent at the opposite side of the world from Great Britain—Australia. Before that time men who had committed crimes in England had been practically sold to the American colonists, who made them work on their plantations. After the war this could not be done any longer, and so, when the discoveries of Captain Cook were making people think of Australia, it was thought a good thing to send the convicts out there as colonists. In this way it happened that, in March 1787, nine ships set out for Australia carrying a large number of men who had broken the laws of England.

It was a continent that for hundreds of years had been called the southern land or Australia, for men who came to know in one way or another that such a land existed, thought it stretched to the South Pole. The Chinese knew of it in the thirteenth century, and several men are supposed to have discovered it three centuries later; but the first discoverers about whom we can be sure were Dutchmen, who in the seventeenth century sailed along the western coast. De Torres, a Spaniard, sailed through the sea which separates

Captain James Cook

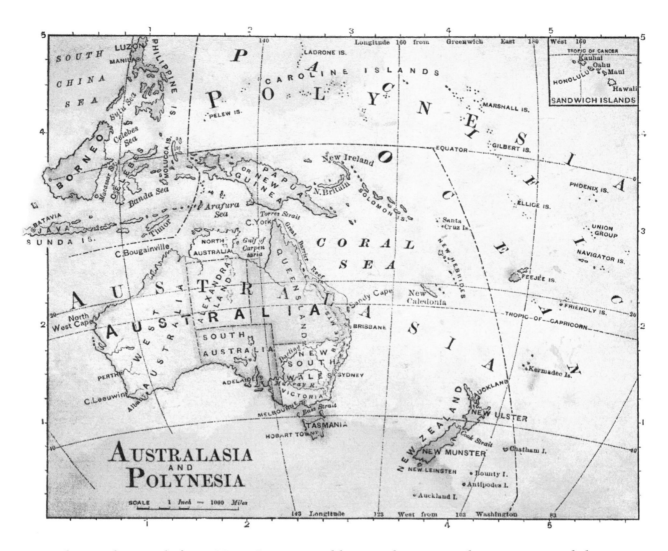

Australia on the north from New Guinea, and he may have seen the country, and the water is now called Torres Strait after him. The Dutchmen sailed from an island not far from Australia, called Java, and it was Abel Tasman who, sailing from there, discovered the island of Tasmania in 1642.

The first Englishman to visit Australia was William Dampier, who reached it in 1688. He went there again in 1699, and thought it a very poor country, with little growing on the land, and only one kind of animal. This, from his description, is now known to have been the kangaroo. The man who found out most about Australia was Captain Cook, who sailed out to make discoveries about the star which is called Venus. In October 1769 he saw the land which is now called New Zealand, and he called the water in which the ship stopped Poverty Bay, because the people who lived there would not help him in any way, and were very quick to attack him. He sailed on and came to the East coast of Australia in April 1770. He made the ship stop in a little bay which lies very near where the large town Sydney now stands. He called the bay Botany Bay, because there were so many strange plants and flowers there; but what struck him most was the strangeness of the natives.

When the ship sailed into the bay a number of them were cooking their food at a fire, but they took no notice of the ship. They did not seem to look even when the ship let down the anchor with a great noise. But when the captain tried to set foot on the shore, some of them stood up and threatened him with their spears. Even when one of the natives was shot in the leg for throwing a stone, they seemed not to be afraid, and it was with great difficulty that Captain Cook and his men could land. But they did so several times, and before sailing away they hoisted the Union Jack, to show that the land in future belonged to Great Britain.

Captain Cook sailed slowly along the coast towards the North, and he called it New South Wales, as he thought it looked like the coast of Wales. He sailed to Cape York, the point of Australia which is farthest north, and again he hoisted the Union Jack before sailing away to England. He was later sent out to Australia again, and this time he visited Tasmania as well as New Zealand; and he was making discoveries in another part of the ocean when the savage natives of a small island killed him. Brave and clever as Captain Cook was, he never forgot to be kind and thoughtful about his sailors.

It was other Englishmen who told the world all about the coasts of Australia, but the land within was not known for many years. Captain Flinders sailed round Australia in 1806, and in 1831 a ship named the *Beagle* left England with a man on board whose name will never be forgotten. Charles Darwin was sent out on this voyage to find out all he could about the rocks, plants, and animals of the countries they visited, and it was this voyage that began the work which has helped people to understand more about how the first men came to be born on earth, and has led them to think that man is only the highest of an immense number of animals which little by little, in one way or another, have grown more powerful and cleverer until the highest was born. But it is more important for the present to point out that Darwin in the *Beagle* went round Australia, New Zealand, and Tasmania, examined the coasts very carefully, and wrote down what was found out

THE FIRST COLONISTS IN AUSTRALIA

But before this many things had happened in Australia. The first colonists consisted of 564 men and 192 women convicts, and about 200 soldiers. They landed at Botany Bay, but Captain Philip, who was the head of the colony, did not find it a good place to live in; so he moved the settlement to Port Jackson, near Sydney. They had brought with them cows, horses, sheep, pigs, goats, and fowls, as well as plenty of seed to sow, and farming tools. But at first they found it very hard to make things grow, and many more convicts came, and many years passed before they found out how to till the land and settle down in comfort. In 1793 people who were not convicts began to go to New South Wales, and they were given

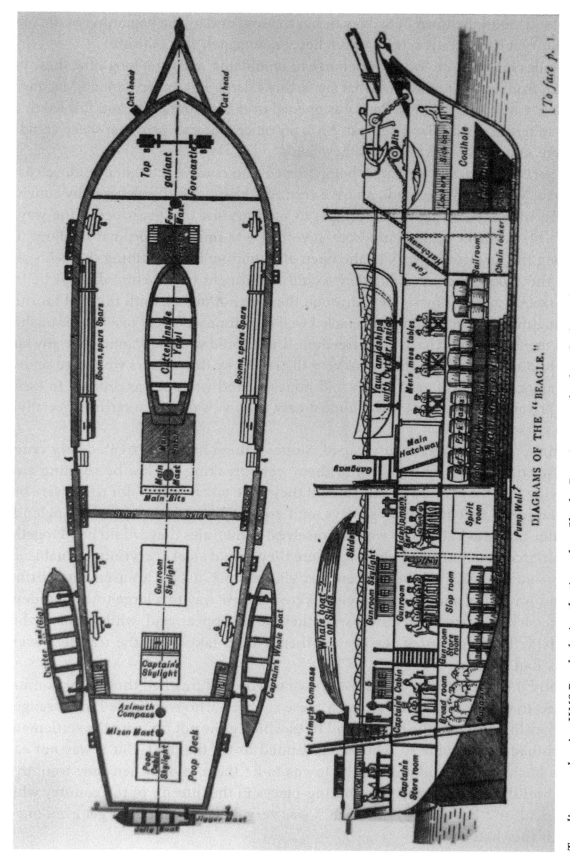

Two diagrams showing HMS Beagle during the time when Charles Darwin was on her board. *Photo of a reproduction from a book by Darwin which accompanied an exhibition about Charles Darwin in the Brno museum Anthropos.*

land and food. Soon the town of Sydney began to grow, and by the beginning of the nineteenth century it had already schools, churches, a newspaper, and a theatre.

A few miles inland from Sydney is a range of mountains, and for a long time these prevented men from trying to find out what lay farther inland. But under Captain Macquarie, who became governor in 1809, a track was opened over the mountains, and this led to the discovery of fertile pasture-land beyond. An army officer soon showed that sheep could be reared there, and settlers flocked to the new lands.

Other parts of Australia were now being turned into convict settlements: Queensland to the north, Victoria to the south, and Western Australia were all colonized by convicts, and all had in consequence, at some time, to fight against one great peril. The way in which the first convict settlements were governed was unlike an ordinary colony. The men during the day would work in the open air, building houses, tilling the fields, and watching the sheep. Then at night they would be brought back before dark to lie in a sort of barracks, guarded by soldiers through the long hot nights, until the cool morning came. Sometimes convicts who had behaved well for a time were lent to a farmer or shepherd, and then they would have more freedom. They would work very much like any farm laborer, although sometimes they were very ill-treated by the farmers who were set over them. In any case life was very dreary and hopeless, and while it was difficult to escape from the prisons in the towns, it was almost easy to run away from a farm, especially by stealing a horse.

So in time many of these men escaped. Some of them had been treated very cruelly and they meant to have revenge. All of them were breaking the law by running away, and knowing that they would be punished if they were taken again—for there were brutal things done to convicts in those days, and especially in places far from England— they did not care how cruel they were themselves. Sometimes they would band together and then march to a lonely farmhouse, where they would steal everything valuable and shoot any one who resisted. Very often they shot people just for amusement. At times they would wait till a number of travelers were on their way to a large town. Suddenly, when the coach had reached a lonely spot, they would appear, and, while some of them stood outside holding loaded revolvers, others would take from the travelers everything they had.

Naturally the free settlers, and those convicts who had finished their imprisonment and wished to start afresh, tried to catch these robbers, who were called bush-rangers, because they lived among the bushes and trees which grew not far from the settlements, and which had to be removed when men wanted to till the land. But it was not easy. Often the bushrangers paid men in the towns to let them know when they were to be attacked, and there were many good hiding-places in the interior of the country which it was difficult to find, and out of which it was very difficult indeed to get even one or two men if they had guns.

It was much worse after 1851 when gold was first found in Australia. Men flocked out from England and great quantities of gold were taken from the mines. When this was found near small settlements it was kept until there was a very large quantity, and then it was sent to the nearest large town. Men would go with it to protect it; but this did not prevent the bush-rangers waiting until the 'gold train' had reached some suitable place, when they would suddenly shoot a number of the men and force the rest to let them take the gold. Sometimes they were daring enough to march into a town and attack the bank.

One very famous bush-ranger was called Ned Kelly. His brother, Daniel, had stolen a horse in Victoria, and when the policemen came to take him, Ned shot at one and wounded him. Then he had to run away. He was joined by other bad men, and though eight thousand pounds was offered to any one who would take the men, they were not taken for two years. They were at length traced to a wooden hut in June 1880, and the police surrounded it. All but Kelly were shot, and he was taken and hanged. This was the last of the bushrangers ; but it is strange to think that they could still exist when Australia had grown so active and so rich, and when people who are still young were alive.

Long before the death of Ned Kelly Australia had begun to settle down into the condition in which it is known today. At first New South Wales included not only the whole of Australia but also New Zealand and the islands near; but before 1840 South Australia, West Australia, Tasmania, and New Zealand were cut off, and before 1860 New South Wales had become almost exactly what it is today. Queensland was the last to be treated as a colony.

Digging and Washing for Gold in Australia in 1851 (*From a drawing made in 1851*).

West Australia was the colony to which the last convicts were sent, and it was not until 1868 that transportation was stopped. Even Tasmania had for many years secured the right to be treated as a colony and not as a convict settlement.

By the year 1856 New South Wales, the oldest colony, had become a large and rich settlement: in 1850 a university was opened in Sydney, and four years later the first railway was finished and in use. The settlers now wished to choose a parliament from among themselves and to rule themselves; and in 1856 this was agreed to by the parliament of Great Britain. Each of the other colonies has grown in the same way. First a small settlement was formed; then by the industry of the settlers, most of them convicts, the settlement began to grow. Soon towns were made in other parts of the colony, and then the colony was treated as separate from the parent. New South Wales. The colony grew still larger and richer, more free settlers came, and at length it was thought great enough to rule itself.

But Australia has not grown without its troubles. The discovery of gold increased the number of free settlers to an enormous extent, and the new colonists were bold and independent men, who had respect for themselves and for little else. This made the colonies democratic, and it caused the bitter struggles between the early colonists, who now owned a great part of the land, and the more democratic, who thought that the land should be owned by as many as possible. It also did a good deal to bring nearer the struggle between those who work and those who employ, which has resulted in the victory of the workers.

When the colonies were all large and rich, many men began to feel that they ought to join together like the provinces of Canada, each colony making laws for things which concerned itself, but the colonies together making laws for other things.

For some years men talked about the new idea, but some people felt so strongly against it that it could not be brought to pass. At length, in 1900, it was agreed to, and on 1st January 1901 the Commonwealth of Australia commenced to exist. It has passed some wise laws, one of them being that every man is bound to be trained as a soldier, so that if necessary he will be able to fight for his country. The Commonwealth of Australia is very loyal. Its soldiers fought side by side with the British at Khartoum and in South Africa, and it has recently helped in providing ships for the fleet.

NEW ZEALAND

On his last voyage Captain Cook hoisted the Union Jack in New Zealand, but Great Britain did not take the country, and explorers belonging to other nations visited the islands. Then in 1814 came Samuel Marsden and a number of English missionaries, and although they taught Christianity to the natives, and in this way persuaded the different tribes to remain at peace with each other, still Great Britain would not look on New Zealand as an English colony. It was not until January 1840, when the British Government came to know that

France intended to colonize the islands, that an officer of the British Navy was told to go to New Zealand and take possession of them. The French settlers arrived a few months later, but as the land now belonged to Great Britain they became British subjects.

The Maoris, as the natives are called, are not like the natives of Australia. Tall and strongly built, they have a brown complexion, and tattoo their bodies in strange patterns. But they are very intelligent, and in the early years of the first colonists there were many struggles with them. Their courage was extraordinary, and as they had good guns it took years of fighting to make them understand that the white men had come to the islands to stay, and that they meant to be the rulers.

Most of the fighting went on in the north island. The Maoris' favorite way of fighting was to build a stockade, a sort of very strong fence, behind which they dug pits for the men to shoot from. Sometimes great numbers of white men would be killed before the Maoris could be driven from the stockade. Some of them hated Christianity as well as hating the foreigners, and so they fought with great fierceness. But others—some of them brave chiefs—fought for the English.

Although the first settlers had arrived in New Zealand in 1814, it was not until 1870 that the Maoris were finally conquered. But meanwhile many changes had taken place. Nine separate colonies had been founded in New Zealand and each had its own way of government, and they had little to do with one another. The colony was allowed to govern itself in 1852, but for years there were struggles between the New Zealand Government and the councils which ruled the nine separate states. At length, in 1876 the states were abolished, and New Zealand has since been a single colony.

It has grown steadily. The land is very good for rearing sheep, and so much of it has been divided up into strips for sheep-farming. Gold was discovered in 1853, and this brought to the colony great numbers of men who wanted to get rich quickly. Railways and telegraphs soon began to appear; good roads were made, and men were encouraged to leave England and settle in New Zealand.

Like the Australians, the men who live in New Zealand are very loyal to Great Britain, and men there were very eager to go out to South Africa to help the British army in the war. Like the Australians, too, they have added to the ships of the navy. The people of New Zealand like the Maoris now, and they get on very well together. The population has grown steadily, and New Zealand is now a rich, prosperous country, well governed and in peace.

Chapter XLIII—The French Revolution

A few years after the French had helped the United States of America to win their independence, the French nation itself began a great struggle for freedom. This struggle is the most important thing which has happened in modern times. It is called the French Revolution. All through the eighteenth century France was becoming more and more in need of money. The wars of Louis XIV had cost the nation a great deal; still Louis had left his country great.

But his great-grandson, Louis XV, who ruled after him, was very different. He lived a very bad life, and under him the French wars resulted only in losses. As we have seen, France lost India and Canada. The nation grew more and more dissatisfied. The people had not complained of having an absolute king when he had led them to victory, but now things were different. In some parts of France the peasants were very poor, though there were very few who were not free.

It is often said that it was the terrible poverty of the peasants which brought about the French Revolution, but this is not true. The peasants in many of the German states in Poland and in Russia were in a far worse state, for in those countries they were still serfs like the peasants in England in the early Middle Ages. They could not leave their villages or marry unless their lords allowed them to, and they still had to work several days each week on their lords' lands as in the early days of feudalism. Still, though the French peasants were free they were poor.

The French people had to pay great taxes at this time, and it made many of them very angry that the nobles had not to pay any at all. There was a large middle class in France, men who were educated. It was from among these that the leaders of the Revolution came.

Louis XV died in 1774, and his grandson, Louis XVI, who was only twenty, became King of France. He had been married four years before to Marie Antoinette, a beautiful young princess, and the youngest of the sixteen children of Maria Theresa. The Queen was a year younger than Louis. Louis XVI was quite different from his grandfather. He was a good and very religious man, but he was not a great king. He did not understand the troubles of France, and was not strong enough in character to face the difficulties of his position. Marie Antoinette was at first very merry. She seemed to the French people who saw her driving through the streets of Paris heartless and vain. But she was only a girl. The French never liked her, and she herself never forgot that she was an Austrian. But she too showed herself very brave, and she was always a good woman.

The American Revolution, with its declaration of the 'rights of man,' seemed a very splendid thing to many of the French. Many French soldiers and officers went over and helped the Americans against the English. Among them was a young French nobleman, the Marquis of Lafayette, who was one of the leaders in the French Revolution afterwards. Men like these thought that France too might become happy, and free, and rich again, if her people were allowed power in the government.

The old French parliament, which was called the States-General, had not met for one hundred and seventy-five years, when Louis XVI was persuaded to let it meet again on the 1st of May 1789. All France was full of joy. The people thought that a new time would commence when France had its parliament like England or America. They forgot that, even when nearly two hundred years before the States-General had been called by French kings, it had had very little real power. All over France the people were busy electing their representatives.

There were three divisions of the States-General: the Nobles, the Clergy or Priests, and the Tiers État, or Third Estate, representing the people. They were to meet at the palace of Versailles, and on the day they assembled the six hundred members of the tiers état walked in procession, dressed in black. Behind them walked the nobles, dressed in bright-colored silks and velvets, and behind them again the King and Queen, with the people of their court.

The people cheered the third estate, and were silent as the nobles passed, for it was from the third estate, the representatives of the people, that they hoped all good things would come. They cheered the King too, but grew quiet and sullen again as the Queen passed. But she made no sign, only looking up to the balcony where her eldest boy, the little eight-year-old Dauphin, who was dying, was propped up to see the procession. Before a month was over the little boy was dead, and his younger brother was now the Dauphin. Marie Antoinette shut herself up for a day, and then came bravely out again, for there were signs of trouble in this wonderful new French parliament.

The King, in his speech at the first meeting, had told the States-General that they must decide among themselves whether the three 'orders' of nobles, clergy, and the tiers état should sit together as one house or meet and vote separately. Every one knew that the nobles and the higher clergy would not be as willing to make great changes in the government as the tiers état would be. It would mean that the two votes of nobles and clergy would make the vote of the tiers état useless. So the tiers état declared that the three 'orders' must vote together. Some of the clergy joined them, but the nobles would not.

Then the tiers état, with the clergy who had joined them, declared that they were the representatives of the nation, and gave themselves the new name of the 'National Assembly.' They said that the nobles could join them if they liked, and the King could give his consent if he liked, but that it really didn't matter.

The Queen advised the King to resist, and an order was given that the hall in which the Assembly had been meeting should be closed, and that there should be no more meetings until a day when the King was to be present. When the Assembly found the door of the hall closed they refused to break up, but held their meeting in a tennis-court nearby. Here they took the famous oath that they would never separate until they had given France a constitution, by which they meant a government in which the people had some part.

Louis XVI Wearing this Revolutionary Bonnet
(From an engraving made the day after the mob invaded the Tuileries and forced the King to put on the tricolour bonnet and to drink to the health of the nation)

Louis tried to insist that the orders should vote separately, but it was no use. At Versailles and at Paris the people were growing angry, and the King had to give way. In Paris bread was dear, and there were many strangers in the city. The feeling of disorder spread, and the common people in the streets became very rough and violent. There were many men of the middle class in Paris, like the lawyer Danton, who were anxious to get rid of the King and make changes which the Assembly had not yet thought of.

Three hundred men had been chosen to select the representatives of the people of Paris in the States-General. These three hundred now made themselves the rulers of Paris. They began to collect soldiers to guard the city. Many of the roughest people joined this guard, which really became an army ready to fight the King. It was called the National Guard. The Hotel des Invalides, the home of the old soldiers, was attacked and guns and powder carried off. Then the old prison of the Bastille was attacked. Here was a great quantity of powder, and only the Governor and a few men to defend it. In a few hours they gave up the prison, but were killed as they marched out.

The news of the taking of the Bastille spread over Europe, and people understood that this was a real revolution. Marie Antoinette begged the King to flee away from France with her and her children until this dreadful time should be over, but other people advised him to stay. But many French nobles fled from France to safety, the first of many 'emigrés' who were to follow them in the next few years. The excitement spread all over France. In many of the country districts the peasants rose, murdered the 'seigneurs' or lords of the land, or drove them away from their castles. They took the land for themselves, and much of the beautiful furniture in the castles was destroyed.

Louis made up his mind to go to Paris, and did so. Lafayette rode before him on a white horse, and all along the road the people shouted, 'Long live the Nation.' It was only when the King, pale and anxious, stuck the new colors of the "Revolution, red, white, and blue, in his hat that they shouted, 'Long live the King.' Then Louis went back to Versailles, where the Queen was weeping and praying for his safety.

But it was not long before the King was back in Paris again. A terrible mob of people poured out from the city to Versailles. Lafayette followed them with some soldiers of the National Guard. The mob broke into the palace, and even into the Queen's room, but she had fled to her husband's. Lafayette drove the mob from the palace, but still they shrieked and howled to see the King, and Louis stepped out on a balcony for all to see.

Then louder cries came for the Queen, and she stepped out with her children, the only two left to her, her daughter and the six-year-old Dauphin. But the crowd cried angrily that they did not want any children, and the Queen signed to them to go back from the balcony. She stood there looking bravely down at the crowd. One man pointed a gun towards her, but did not fire.

Lafayette stepped out on the balcony and kissed her hand. He was very sad now, for the Revolution, from which he had hoped so much, was becoming a very different thing from what he had expected. The angry mob still shrieked that their king should go to Paris, and the royal family was led by the crowd to the palace of the Tuileries, where they lived for the next two years, the Queen always with her children, frightened to go beyond the gardens of the palace, the King listening to information about the doings of the Assembly, giving his consent to what he could, refusing when his conscience told him a thing was wrong.

The Assembly upset all the old arrangements in France. They did away with the old 'provinces,' and divided the country up into districts. Committees were sent out to rule these, but all were under the Assembly. But there was so much disorder that the taxes could not be collected. The Assembly was in great need of money. There were many men in it who did not believe in any religion at all, and they thought it would be an excellent plan to take the property of the Church for themselves. They did so, and the clergy were then paid wages by the state. At the same time they said that the French Church should no longer be under the Pope.

To these things Louis could not agree. At last, in despair, he agreed with the Queen that the best thing to do would to try to escape. Count Fersen, who was a great friend of the Queen's, brought them clothes to disguise themselves. The King was to be dressed plainly like a man-servant, and the Queen as a governess travelling with the two children. The Dauphin was put into girl's clothes, and his sister, who was the only one of the family who lived through the Revolution, said that he looked beautiful.

They stole quietly out at ten o'clock one night to where a coach was waiting for them. Count Fersen was the coachman. Outside Paris another coach waited for them with a German coachman, but things went wrong. The horses fell down and it took an hour to mend the harness. They missed a third carriage which was to meet them, and then a man named Drouet recognized the King. The coach rolled on, but Drouet and an innkeeper took horses and raced it to Varennes. There the royal family was stopped, just as they were practically saved. The next day they were taken back to the Tuileries again.

The King was 'suspended' for a time, that is, the Assembly said he should not have the position of king, but in a short time he was recognized as king once more. He gave his consent to the 'Constitution,' which left him very little power, and then the National Assembly, having done its work, broke up. But things in France were now in hopeless disorder. A new parliament was to meet, to which none of the members of the Assembly were to belong. New men with no experience were to rule the country.

The King and Queen were always hoping that the Emperor of Austria and the other kings of Europe would come to help them. They only agreed to the laws which were passed, thinking that in a short time foreign armies would come and free them, and all would be as it had been before in France. At last the armies did march towards France, the armies of Austria and Prussia. Leopold, the Emperor, was the brother of Marie Antoinette. Maria Theresa was now dead. But Leopold died just at this time, and his son was not so well able to help his aunt. Still, after long delays, his army came.

The King of Prussia sent an army, for he felt that these new things which the French were preaching everywhere were dangerous for every king in Europe. The French knew that the King and Queen were writing to the other countries of Europe to help them, and the leaders of the Revolution grew more and more angry, as did also the Paris mob. It was the French themselves who declared war at last. All the soldiers who could be gathered together were sent off to the borders of France and the Netherlands, and the roughest men in Paris were allowed to join the National Guard.

Before this the Paris mob had broken into the Tuileries. They had stood joking roughly in the very presence of the King and Queen, and stuck a red cap of liberty on the head of the little Dauphin. In the end they had gone away without doing any harm. Many people all over France were now sorry for the King and Queen, and kind messages poured in upon them. But once the war commenced the most violent of the people and the leaders had things all their own way. Again the mob attacked the Tuileries, and the King and Queen, with their children and the King's sister, fled for safety to the hall where the Assembly had its meetings.

Day after day they had to be crowded together in a small room used by newspaper reporters, and there they could hear the parliament discussing what should be done with them. At last they were carried off to a prison in a building called 'the Temple' in Paris. They lived here in small rooms, very different from those to which they had been used. At first a few friends were allowed to stay with them, but later these were all sent away. Madame de Lamballe, a great friend of the Queen, was driven from the Temple into another prison. By this time nearly all the nobles and friends of the King who had not escaped from France had been shut up in prison.

In the Convention,' as the new parliament was called, the most violent of the revolutionaries under Marat, a madman whose one idea was a republic in which all the people should have equal power, ordered that the friends of the King in prison should be killed. A band of two hundred men went from prison to prison and murdered them. There was only one woman killed in these dreadful 'September Massacres' as they were called. It was Marie Antoinette's friend, the Princesse de Lamballe. As Louis XVI stood staring out of the window of his prison, suddenly the head of his wife's friend was held up on a spear before his eyes. The King's first thought was to prevent the Queen from seeing it, but she had seen it and fainted away.

THE EXECUTION OF THE KING

A week or two later the Convention declared that France was a republic. For the future they spoke of Louis XVI as Louis Capet. He was a 'citizen' like any other. Then three months later Louis was brought to trial as a 'public enemy.' He was found guilty. Three hundred and sixty-one members voted for his death, and three hundred and sixty against it. He was condemned to die. Already he had been separated from the Queen and his children, but they were allowed to see him the night before he died. He was very brave and quite gentle. He made the little Dauphin promise never to take revenge for his death, and then he sent them away and gave his last hours to preparation for death. The next morning he was beheaded in a public square in Paris, assuring the great crowds who were gathered round that he 'died innocent.'

Meanwhile the Prussians and Austrians, who had thought that they had nothing to do but march on Paris, had not been very successful. They had started too late in the season; the weather was bad and their men fell sick. When the two armies at last fought at Valmy they found that the French soldiers could not be driven back, and in a few days they marched out of France again.

Then the French leaders at Paris were full of joy. They made up their minds to help all the peoples of Europe to set up republics too. Their armies overran Belgium and joined it to France. Another army did the same in Savoy, on the borders of France and Italy, and another conquered the German states on the Rhine. They then declared that they would attack England and help the English republicans to set up a republic. In this they were quite mistaken, for no one in England wanted a republic. Then came the execution of the King.

Soon France was standing alone against Europe. England, Holland, Spain, Austria, and Prussia were at war with her. The people in the south and west of France rose in rebellion, In La Vendee, a district in the west of France and running along the coast south of the river Loire, the peasants rose to defend their seigneurs and their religion. They nearly drove the republicans out of the district, but now the 'Jacobins,' the worst revolutionaries of all, got power, and what is known as the 'Reign of Terror' began.

Every one who was suspected of being against the Revolution was brought up before judges appointed for the purpose. There was no real trial. Practically every one suspected was put to death. Some were nobles but others were mere peasants. Even girls and little children and old people were put to death. In La Vendee the revolt was put down, and people were killed in hundreds for being faithful to their lords and their Church.

It took too long even to behead them all with the guillotine, the great new knife machine which had been invented during the Revolution, and so hundreds were thrown into the river to drown. Men who were violent, but not violent enough, were seized and

The Execution of King Louis XVI, illustrator: Charles Monnet.

316

condemned to death in their turn. Madame Roland, the wife of one of the leaders, had exclaimed when she was led out to die, 'O Liberty, what crimes are committed in thy name.' For in the end she too was guillotined. But the Queen's turn had come before this. Her children had been taken from her in prison, and she too was tried and condemned to death. She was old and white before her time, and blind in one eye through the cold and damp of her last prison. For her last days were spent not even in the Temple, but in the common prison.

From there she was drawn, sitting on a cart, with her hands tied, to be guillotined before the Paris mob. Her little boy died in prison after being treated with the greatest cruelty, but her daughter was at last sent to her mother's relations in Austria. A girl from Normandy, called Charlotte Corday, travelled up from the country to Paris, and stabbed Marat to the heart for his cruelty. She was killed in her turn. Danton and Robespierre, great leaders of the Revolution, were killed too.

At last the Reign of Terror came to an end. France was winning victories on all her boundaries. Now that Robespierre was gone, the people all over France asked for a complete change of government. They turned against the Jacobins who were left, and many of these were massacred in their turn. After a time in which religion had been attacked so cruelly, the people were now again crowding to the churches. Many of the emigrés came back to France. It was thought even that the little Dauphin, who was still alive in prison, might be made king, but this was not to be.

At last a new constitution was set up. It consisted of two houses of parliament, and at the head five men called the Directors. But in the lower house of the new parliament many of the Jacobins were to sit again. There was a great deal of disorder at the elections, and a young officer called Napoleon Bonaparte was called in by Barras, the head of the government, to put down an insurrection. In this way this young officer became important. We shall see what a great part he played in the history of France and the world in the next twenty years.

Chapter XLIV—The Story of Napoleon

Napoleon bonaparte was born of a good family in the island of Corsica, in the year 1769, the year after Maria Antoinette was married to Louis XVI of France. Corsica had for many years been fighting for its independence against Genoa, but had at last been sold by that state to France. So Napoleon Bonaparte, though he was Italian by birth, was a subject of the French king. When he was a boy he was fond of playing with a drum and sword, and his father made up his mind that he should be a soldier. When he was ten years old he was sent to France to be trained at schools for boys intending to join the army, and he became a lieutenant in an artillery regiment when he was sixteen.

When the Revolution broke out, Napoleon, although he had never been very fond of France because of its conquest of Corsica, was filled with enthusiasm for it. Corsica sent representatives to the tiers état, and all the reforms which were made in France were carried out in Corsica too. In the first years after the beginning of the Revolution, Napoleon Bonaparte lived quietly in lodgings at Auxonne, where his regiment was stationed, and did all he could to educate his young brother Louis, who lived with him. Their father was by this time dead, and Napoleon was looked upon as the head of his family, although he was only the second son.

The other officers in his regiment were royalists, and Napoleon was very lonely, for he could not mix freely with them. He had always been fond of history, and he read now all he could find, being especially fond of Julius Caesar's own account of his wars in Gaul. He had to take his sister home to Corsica when the convent at which she was a pupil was broken up by the revolutionaries, as so many convents and monasteries were. But it was not long before all the Bonapartes had to leave Corsica, for Paoli, the chief man in the island, turned against France after the death of the king, and joined himself with England to fight against France. The Bonapartes went to France.

Napoleon had a better chance of rising quickly as an officer, because the army was in great need of good officers, through the loss of so many royalists. He first won great praise for himself by the way in which he helped in the attack on the royalists at Toulon in 1793.

They had let British and Spanish soldiers into the town, and the republicans were afraid that more and more might come, and that a great attack might be made on France from this port. The first officers sent against Toulon did very little good. One of them was an artist and knew nothing about fighting. It was Napoleon who pointed out the weak side of the town, where the attack could be made. The town was conquered, and an English invasion of France by way of Toulon was now impossible.

After this Napoleon helped a great deal in fortifying places along the coast of France. He still spent all his spare time in studying the science of war. The help which he gave the Directory in putting down the insurrection in Paris in 1795 made him great. He had fallen in love with Josephine de Beauharnais, the widow of a French noble who had been executed during the Revolution. Josephine was very lively and beautiful, and one of the greatest women in France at the time. She was a friend of Barras, the chief man in the Directory, and he persuaded her to marry Napoleon. She was six years older than Napoleon and did not care much for the thin, pale-faced officer, but she at last agreed to marry him, though she would not go with him two days after the marriage to Italy, where he had got the command of the French army.

The attack on Italy was part of the war against Austria, to whom most of the north of Italy belonged. Two other armies were to march through Germany and attack Vienna. Napoleon was only one of the generals of the republic, but he knew that he was the best soldier of his time, and he had already made up his mind to imitate Julius Caesar and to make himself dictator of France, and of as much of Europe as he could win. It was a wonderful plan for this young Corsican officer even to think of, and more wonderful still is the fact that he nearly carried it out, and that for years he kept all Europe struggling to overthrow his power.

The Emperor of Austria had the King of Sardinia to help him in the north of Italy, but Napoleon always tried to keep his enemy split up, and prevented the army of Piedmont, which was under the rule of the King of Sardinia, from joining the Austrian army, and soon the King of Sardinia made his peace with Napoleon, giving Piedmont up to France.

Napoleon then easily conquered the Austrians, and took the north of Italy. He made the people pay him money, and he chose some of the most beautiful of the art treasures of Italy to send back to France. Before this Prussia and Spain had been frightened into making peace with France, and Spain and Holland were even helping that country at this time; but England was still the greatest power on the sea, and victories were won over both the Spanish and Dutch fleets. Now, in 1797, Austria made peace, and agreed to give up the north of Italy to France.

THE GREAT LORD NELSON

England was now left alone to fight the French. When Napoleon got back to Paris it was quite plain that he could do just what he liked. But he did not have himself made dictator yet. He pretended that he was going to invade England, but he really intended to sail to Egypt, conquer it and Syria, and from there perhaps win both India and Europe. When Napoleon sailed off to the East, part of the British fleet under Sir Horatio Nelson followed it.

Nelson was soon to show himself the greatest of English seamen. He was a small, delicate-looking man, but he was a splendid sailor and soldier, and had been at sea since he was twelve years old. A story is told of him that, when he was still a young midshipman, he was on a ship which sailed into the ice-bound seas near the North Pole. He and another boy stole away one night to see if they could find and shoot a bear. A fog came on, and the captain was very anxious when he knew that the boys were missing, but when the fog melted away he saw them far off, ready to attack a bear.

The captain called to them to come back to the ship, and the other boy did so, but Nelson cried out, begging the captain to let him have just one blow at the bear. But the captain had a shot fired which frightened the bear away. When Nelson got back to the ship the captain scolded him, but he said sorrowfully, 'I wanted to kill the bear and take its skin home to my father.' Horatio Nelson never knew what it was to be afraid.

When the fleet under Nelson came up with the French fleet they were anchored in the Bay of Aboukir, close to the shore of Egypt. Napoleon was already fighting on the land, and winning Egypt from the Mamelukes. Nelson ordered five of his ships to sail in between the French ships and the shore, 'for,' he said, 'where the French ships had room to swing the English had room to anchor.' In this way the French ships were caught between two fires.

The battle began at sunset and went on all night. By morning eleven of the thirteen French ships had been destroyed or taken. The French Admiral's flagship had blown up and the Admiral himself had been killed. It was on this ship that the ten-year-old boy, Casablanca, died standing at his post on the burning ship until his father should give him leave to go. His father was already dead, though Casablanca did not know it, and the brave boy died too.

Nelson was wounded in the forehead, but he had won the great Battle of the Nile. After this no other fleet had any chance against the English in the Mediterranean. Meanwhile Napoleon went on from Egypt to Syria, which he meant to win from Turkey, but he could not take Acre, which the English officer, Sir Sidney Smith, helped to defend.

Then suddenly Napoleon slipped back to France in a fast sailing ship. He was much needed there, for trouble was threatening the Directors from all sides. Napoleon was greeted with joy as the conqueror of Egypt. He was wise enough not to say much about Syria.

When Napoleon had left France, England was the only country at war with the Republic, but he came back to find that a new 'coalition' had now been formed against her. England of course was in it, for it was England from the first who was most determined to resist the attacks of France on the lands of Europe. Russia and Austria were the other chief members of the coalition.

While Napoleon was away the Directory had been in great need of money, and they had actually sent an army to attack Rome, where there were a few republicans. The old Pope,

Pius II, was a very good and gentle man and Rome had been quite happy under him, far happier than it was now when the French turned it into a republic, and then took as much money and as many of its art treasures as they could get. The people of Europe were horrified to hear that the Pope had even been roughly treated, his staff dragged from his hand and his ring from his finger. He was carried off to Siena, and then to Valence in France, where he stayed till he died. The French soon made themselves hated in Rome.

For the same reason they set up a united republic in Switzerland, calling it the Helvetian Republic. The cantons, as the divisions of Switzerland were called, were each used to governing themselves, and did not want this new form of government. The kingdom of Naples, whose queen, Marie Caroline, was a sister of Marie Antoinette, was also turned into a republic, though here again very few of the people wished for this change.

When the coalition began to fight, the French were defeated in North Italy by the great Russian general Suvarov. Suvarov was a very wonderful general. He never dreamed of failure, and when he had fought and won a battle he always still had strength to pursue the enemy as they fled. His men took the same courage from him. His commands before a battle are almost amusing from the confident way they would begin with such words as: 'The hostile army will be taken prisoners.'

The King and Queen of Naples were given back their kingdom, and Nelson's fleet stood by to defend them. In Switzerland an Austrian officer led an Austrian and Russian army against the French, but could not drive them out. Still things were going very badly with the French when Napoleon got back from Egypt. The people were quite tired of the Directory. The Abbé Sieyès, a priest, who had been making constitutions ever since the Revolution began, had another one ready now.

The worst of 'paper' constitutions—that is, constitutions which are drawn up out of a man's head without any experience of how they work—is that they very seldom will work at all. This new constitution of the 'year VIII' as it was called (for now in France the years were counted from the 'year I,' the first year of the destruction of the monarchy and the setting up of the republic), was carefully drawn up so that power was divided between many people, and nobody had any real power at all.

Napoleon thought it would be a very good constitution indeed with one change. At the head of all the other parts of the constitution there should be a 'First Consul,' and he should be Napoleon himself. Napoleon had his great army behind him, ready to fight for him to a man, and the French people had no chance to say 'No,' even if they had wished. But they were tired of disorder, and were only too glad to have a strong man to govern them. For the 'First Consul' was just as absolute as any king of France had ever been. Four years afterwards he was given the name of Emperor, but he was the all-powerful ruler of France from the moment he became First Consul at the end of the year 1799.

The few serfs who were still remaining in France at the Revolution became free. The property which had been taken from the Church and given to other people was not given back, but the churches which had not been given away were. Peace was made with the Pope, and the Catholic religion was made the religion of the state again, but the priests were to be servants of the state and paid by the government, as they are still in France today.

So many changes which the Revolution had made remained, but there was no real democracy or self-government, which was what the republicans had fought so hard for. Each district in France was governed by men chosen by Napoleon, so that he had the whole government of the country in his hands, just as much as Louis XIV had had. The people were not more free under Napoleon in many ways than they had been before.

The freedom of the press, which the revolutionaries had given, by which any man could publish any book he liked, was now stopped. Every book had to have the consent of people appointed by the Emperor. Then, too, Napoleon could imprison or send any one out of the country just as he liked. He had his spies everywhere to watch the people and inform him if any one was dangerous to the government.

As time went on too, Napoleon became more and more anxious to have a magnificent court. The old nobles who were willing to come back were gladly received, for Napoleon liked to have men with high-sounding names around him. The revolutionaries had said there should be no new titles, but Napoleon loved to make men dukes for their services to him, and so a new nobility grew up around him.

His coronation with Josephine in 1804 was a very gorgeous affair. Napoleon had persuaded the new Pope, Pius VII, to go to Paris for the coronation, but when the moment came he preferred to put the crown on his head himself. Napoleon was dressed for the ceremony in a red velvet coat, and over it a purple robe of velvet trimmed with ermine, while Josephine knelt beside him in white satin and diamonds.

Napoleon Bonaparte (*After the painting by Delaroche*).

Russia had by this time made peace with Napoleon, for the Tsar Paul admired him very much, and had only really been led to declare war against France because Napoleon had attacked the Turks, and Russia thought that the western countries of Europe should leave the east alone, and that if any one won land from Turkey it should be Russia herself.

So now Napoleon had England and Austria to fight. He knew that a large Austrian army was at the foot of the Italian side of the Alps, near the Mount St. Bernard, a very difficult place. But he led his men across. It was a very difficult march with cannons and baggage, but Napoleon's soldiers could do almost anything. They fought the Austrians, and won the great battle of Marengo. In Germany another of Napoleon's generals won the battle of Hohenlinden,

The Solemn Coronation of the Emperor Napoleon in the Cathedral of Notre Dame at Paris in 1804. *The Pope, Pius VII, came to Paris to crown Napoleon as Emperor of the French, but at the moment of the actual crowning, Napoleon, in this pride, waved the Pope on one side, and crowned himself and his wife the Empress Josephine (From the painting by David).*

and now Austria too made peace, leaving Napoleon with all his conquests. And so once more England was left to fight France alone.

Russia had persuaded Sweden, Prussia, and Denmark, all the countries with ships on the Baltic, to complain of the way in which England treated their ships. England had forbidden ships of countries which were not at war to carry things between countries which were at war, and other things which were quite right. For if England had not forbidden these things, a country like Sweden could have helped France very much against her without declaring war. But now these countries complained, and England had to fight them.

A fleet was sent to Denmark under Nelson, but over him was Sir Hyde Parker, who was not nearly so fine a fighter or officer as Nelson. He sent messages to the Danes, hoping to be able to make an agreement without fighting. This made Nelson very impatient. But the Danes were obstinate, and so a great battle was fought outside the harbor of the city of Copenhagen, the capital of Denmark. It was a hard fight, and in the middle of it Sir Hyde Parker, fearing that the English would be defeated, put up a signal; 'Cease Action.' Nelson did not see it at first, and when some one told him of it, he put a telescope to his blind eye (for he had lost one eye and an arm too in battle some years before), and said, 'I do not see the signal,' and so went on fighting.

He was right, for the English won a great victory. The Danes promised to give up their fleet, and now Napoleon had no more hope of destroying England's power on the seas. Soon after, the Tsar Paul died, and his son Alexander became king. Though Alexander admired Napoleon too, he was much under the influence of his mother and her friends, and he was persuaded to give up the friendship with France. So England had her way after all about the ships of the countries which were not at war.

Just at this point the younger Pitt, the son of the great Earl of Chatham, gave up his position as head of the government in England. It was he who had been so determined to fight the French, and Napoleon took advantage of his absence to arrange a peace with England. A peace was signed, but it did not last long. Napoleon never meant it to. He hated England with a bitter hatred. So far he had been able to conquer the old-fashioned armies of the European countries, but everywhere the English had won by sea.

These victories of the English were partly owing to the fact that the English were a real nation, while the feeling of nationality was not awake yet in Europe, except perhaps in France itself. The armies of Austria made war on Napoleon because their Emperor told them to, but they had no great interest in the battle. Later on, when the peoples of Europe began to hate Napoleon, things were different.

The younger Pitt came back to power in 1804 and immediately began to plan another coalition, but even before this Napoleon was building a great fleet of flat-bottomed boats, in which he hoped to carry soldiers across to England and conquer it. He knew that England had no great army to meet his, but already Englishmen everywhere were offering themselves as volunteers and drilling hard, so as to be able to fight the French when they came.

Napoleon ordered Spain, whose weak king, Charles IV, was entirely in his power, to build a fleet too. The French and Spanish fleets were to sail to the West Indies, and Napoleon hoped that the greater part of the British fleet would follow them. Then the remaining French fleet would easily destroy the English fleet in the Channel, and land the 'Army of England' in England. But things went wrong. The English fleet watched the others too well, and the whole plan failed. Meanwhile Pitt had got his coalition, when Russia and Austria joined him once more in war against Napoleon. One thing which made the other countries very angry was the way that Napoleon behaved when in 1804 he found out a plot to kill him and put the uncle of Louis XVI on the French throne.

This uncle, who was called Louis XVIII by the Royalists, was in England, and Napoleon could not get at him, but he ordered French soldiers to arrest the Duke d'Enghien, a young prince of the French royal family, who was living in one of the German states. Napoleon had no right to arrest a prisoner in any other country. This was an insult in itself, but people were still more horrified to hear that the young prince had been shot by order of Napoleon, although he had not had anything to do with the plot.

THE DEATH OF NELSON

In October 1805 Napoleon, seeing that he could not land his army in England, sent it across Europe to fight the Austrians in Bavaria. It won a great victory at Ulm, but two days after Nelson won another victory at sea, the victory of Trafalgar. The battle of Trafalgar was fought off the Spanish coast near the Cape of Trafalgar. The English under Nelson fought the united fleets of France and Spain. The ships fought close together in a terrible struggle, and the English almost completely destroyed the enemies' fleets. At the beginning of the fight Nelson ordered the famous signal to be made to all his ships, 'England expects every man to do his duty.' But Nelson, at the head of his line of ships on his own ship the *Victory,* was wounded in the breast. His coat was covered with medals, which he had refused to take off when some one suggested that the enemy would recognize him through them and shoot specially at him. But as he was carried down below deck to die, he covered them and his face with a handkerchief lest his men should see that he was dying and be discouraged. Before he died he knew that the victory had been won. Almost his last words were, 'Thank God I have done my duty,' and then he asked his friend Captain Hardy to kiss him.

We may still see Nelson's ship, the *Victory,* at anchor outside Portsmouth harbor. Very quaint it seems to us today, when we compare

Nelson (After the painting by Hoppner).

our own ironclad men-of-war with this battleship of a hundred years ago.

In spite of Trafalgar Napoleon seemed all-powerful, for after Ulm he won a very brilliant victory at Austerlitz, and once more Austria and Russia made peace with him. At the beginning of the French revolutionary wars, the leaders of the Revolution had tried to set up republics all around France, but now Napoleon did away with the republics and turned them into kingdoms, as he had really made France again.

But they were not to be independent kingdoms. Most of them were ruled by Napoleon's brothers, or his generals, and all of course had to do exactly what the Emperor told them. All Napoleon really cared for now was victory and power. He drove the King and Queen from Naples and put his brother Joseph there as 'King of the Two Sicilies.' Holland, or the Batavian Republic, now became a kingdom again under his brother Louis.

The Electorate of Hanover, which belonged to the English King, was taken, and for a time given to Prussia, but later, with some other states joined to it, became the kingdom of Westphalia, and over this another brother, Jerome Bonaparte, reigned as king. Napoleon had himself crowned King of North Italy. The smaller German states he joined together under his protection, and called them the 'Confederation of the Rhine.'

As though to make all these changes in Europe the more remarkable still, the Emperor of Austria gave up his title of Holy Roman Emperor, which had been so carefully treasured and handed down through the Middle Ages, and called himself for the future the hereditary Emperor of Austria. Napoleon would dearly have loved the title of Roman Emperor for himself. All this Russia and Austria had to agree to, when the coalition broke up in 1806. Soon after this William Pitt died. Charles James Fox, one of the greatest statesmen of the day, who had at first been enthusiastic about the French Revolution because of its cry for 'freedom,' now tried to make peace with Napoleon too, but failed.

Now at last the King of Prussia, Frederick William III, declared war too against Napoleon, but his army was completely defeated at the battle of Jena, and Napoleon marched to Berlin, the Prussian capital. Then Russia joined the army of Prussia, but both were defeated, and Napoleon and Alexander of Russia met and made the Peace of Tilsit. They met in a raft on the middle of the river at Tilsit. Napoleon cleverly did all he could to make the young Tsar admire him. When he had done this, he flattered him by suggesting that they two should divide Europe and Asia between them.

Napoleon's idea was that he himself should be Emperor of the West, by which he meant all Europe except Russia and Sweden, while Alexander should be Emperor of the East, and be allowed to win power over Sweden and Turkey. The idea pleased Alexander very much. For five years Napoleon and Alexander were friends. Napoleon's first idea after the Peace of Tilsit was to try once more to ruin England. He forbade every country in Europe to trade with Britain. As every country in Europe depended very much on the things brought to them in English ships, this would have been very difficult. The countries of Europe still bought things brought in English ships, and had to pay more for them because of the extra difficulties. Even Napoleon had to buy cloth for his soldiers' clothes from England.

The two most faithful friends which England had were Sweden and the little kingdom of Portugal. Alexander of Russia was left to deal with Sweden. Alexander attacked Sweden, whose brave king, Gustavus IV, was made to abdicate because he would not give up his friendship with England. His uncle was made King of Sweden, but had to agree that one of Napoleon's generals should be king after him. He had to give up Finland too, which was now taken by Russia. While Napoleon made up his mind to punish Portugal, he thought it would be easy enough. He made up his mind to send a French army into Spain, and he asked the chief officer of the Spanish king to join a Spanish army with it. These two armies poured into Portugal, and the royal family and all the greatest men of Portugal took refuge in the fleet. Some English ships came to protect them, and they sailed off to Brazil.

Meanwhile there was much quarrelling between the king, Charles IV of Spain, who was almost an imbecile, and his son Ferdinand, who was not much better. Napoleon asked them both to meet him at Bayonne, and there he threatened Ferdinand, who called himself already King of Spain, because his father had abdicated, that if he also did not give up his claim to the throne in a few hours, he should be treated as a rebel.

So Ferdinand gave up his rights to his father again, but Charles IV had already sold his kingdom to Napoleon for a palace in France and a pension. Then Napoleon offered the crown of Spain to Louis his brother, remarking that the climate of Holland did not suit him. But Louis refused, and it was then given to Joseph Bonaparte, who gave up his kingdom of the Two Sicilies to one of Napoleon's generals.

Spain's Struggle with Napoleon

But while Napoleon had been busy making all these arrangements he had forgotten all about the Spanish people. It was a dreadful mistake. They were very angry indeed when they heard that their country was being bought and sold in this way. National feeling in Spain rose against Napoleon. The people were determined to fight this conqueror and tyrant. Every peasant took up arms, and though the armies of Spain were made up of men who had not fought before, they soon showed themselves able to fight the French armies on equal terms. The siege of Saragossa, the capital of Aragon, is among the famous sieges of history.

There were only a few hundred Spanish soldiers to hold its low brick wall against a large French army, but women and children and monks and nuns, as well as the ordinary men of the city, did their part to help. The children carried the cartridges which the nuns made. When the hospital where the wounded soldiers lay was set on fire, the women carried the men from their beds through the flames. At another place an army of 18,000 French had to surrender their arms to an army of young Spanish soldiers quite new to war. The tale of these things spread through Europe. The English sent armies too to help the Spaniards, and so began the 'Peninsular War.'

In this war there fought on the English side Sir Arthur Wellesley, who afterwards became famous as the Duke of Wellington. He had already won great victories for England over the natives in India, who had risen against the English when Napoleon had sent them word that he was coming to help them to 'drive the English out of India.' Wellesley landed in Portugal in August 1808, and drove the French armies right out of that country. This was a great gain, for now England had a country from which she could attack Napoleon overland.

Sir Arthur Wellesley was called back to England, but Sir John Moore, in the same winter, prevented Napoleon, who had now come unexpectedly, from conquering the South. Sir John Moore had to lead his men over the ridges of the hills of Galicia to Corunna, where he expected English ships to take his worn-out soldiers back to England. It was one of the greatest retreats of history. The hills were covered with snow. Every now and then the English had to turn and fight the foremost of those following them. Napoleon did not follow long, for he had to go back to Germany, but one of his generals took his place. At last, when they reached the coast, the English army turned and fought one more great battle. They won, but the noble Sir John Moore was killed. Every child knows the poem which tells about his burial.

Then Sir Arthur Wellesley came back to Spain. For five years he fought against the French generals there. The Spanish armies were not much use to him, but the ordinary peasants and working people helped him very much. He had to fight the great battles himself, but wherever a few French soldiers were met by peasants they were attacked and killed, for the Spaniards were now full of hate for the French, who had tried to buy and sell their nation.

During five years Napoleon had to leave 250,000 soldiers to fight in Spain, while he himself was fighting in other places. He always thought that his officers there were fighting badly. It was a long time before he understood what a great soldier Wellesley was, though at last he said, so the story tells us, 'This Wellesley seems to be a man indeed.' He did not then know that this same Wellesley, as Duke of Wellington, was to overthrow his power at last.

The example of Spain filled the peoples of Europe with enthusiasm. Up to now there had not been any real national feeling in any country of Europe except England. In the east of Europe, as we have seen, districts were bought and sold and handed about from one country to another. But now things were different. The peoples in Europe began to hate Napoleon just as the people of Spain did. The French Revolution itself, though it now seemed a failure, had spread new ideas of freedom among the peoples of Europe.

Napoleon himself, though he would have no government by the people, which was what the leaders of the Revolution had wanted, made many reforms in the countries he conquered. Better laws and justice were given. In France much better schools were set up, and Napoleon tried to have even the poor boys in the countries he conquered educated, though he thought that education did not matter at all for girls. They were best at home with their mothers, he thought. He was very old-fashioned indeed on this subject. But perhaps the greatest reform of all was the setting free of many serfs in the east of Europe. With this freedom the peasants began to feel a hope and pride in the countries to which they belonged.

The defeat of the Prussians at Jena made that people very angry, and a great Prussian statesman named Stein now arose and made many reforms in Prussia. The serfs were free and every young man was trained in the army. Many of these things were what Napoleon himself had advised in other countries, but when he found people doing these things for themselves he was afraid, for he knew that the love of freedom would grow and that the nations would rise against him. So he made the King of Prussia send Stein away.

But he could not destroy the work he had begun. A new love of freedom spread through all Germany, a sort of excitement like that which had moved the men of the Renaissance. New German poets like the great Goethe began to write, and the young men of Germany joined themselves in secret clubs and societies, determined to drive the hated foreigners out of their land. The little district of Tyrol had belonged to Austria for four hundred years, but now it had been given to the King of Bavaria. It rose in revolt.

Tyrol is a country of mountains where simple peasants lived, but it was the peasants who were now showing themselves so brave everywhere. They were led by Andrew Hofer, a village innkeeper, a tall man, strong as a giant. The peasants rose under him and won their country back for a time, but they were defeated later, and Hofer was shot.

Meanwhile Napoleon had defeated the Austrians once more at the battle of Wagram. The Emperor of Austria was forced to make peace, and he was forced too to allow an Austrian princess, the Archduchess Marie Louise, to marry Napoleon. The Empress Josephine had not had any children since her marriage with Napoleon, and he longed above all things to have a son to hold his empire after him. So now he divorced Josephine in spite of her begging him not to do so. She lived quietly by herself after this, and the Emperor sometimes visited her. He was full of joy when Marie Louise had a son, who is generally called the young Napoleon. He did not know that, while his son was still a little child, he would lose the empire he had meant to hand on to him.

THE FALL OF NAPOLEON

Napoleon seemed now more powerful than ever. The English armies which were sent to help in Europe were not sent to the right places, for the second Lord Chatham, the son of the elder Pitt and brother of the younger, was not a clever man, and it was he who had the arrangement of the war. But now, at last, the friendship between Alexander of Russia and Napoleon came to an end. Alexander would not help Napoleon to try to ruin the English trade, and so Napoleon made up his mind to attack Russia itself.

He led what he called his Grand Army of half a million of his best soldiers trained now in many years of war. Half of these were French, the rest soldiers from the countries he had conquered. When he reached Dresden with his army, Marie Louise and the little King of Rome, as the baby was called, were with him. The Emperor of Austria, the King of Prussia, and other kings were present to do him honor. It was for the last time.

And now Napoleon led his great army into Russia. He was sure of victory, but he did not know Russia. On he marched across the vast country, but the heat was terrible, for in Russia the summers are very hot and the winters terribly cold. Many horses died and many soldiers deserted, and the Russian generals instead of fighting led Napoleon on across the vast country. Winter was coming on, and Napoleon thought of staying where he was till the spring. But he was impatient. He must conquer Russia and take Moscow at once, and so he pushed on.

One battle there was in which he conquered the Russians, but lost thirty thousand men himself. A week later the Grand Army, or what was left of it, reached Moscow. Food had run short, but now all hoped to get as much as they wanted. Napoleon expected that the Tsar would come to meet him, and surrender himself and the keys of the capital. But what was his surprise when he reached the city to find the streets empty. There were no people, and worse still, there was no food. Indeed the city was breaking into flames, for the Russians had preferred to burn their town rather than give it up to Napoleon.

And now there was nothing to do but turn back and march across that dreary land through the terrible frost and snow, west again. A Russian army blocked the way, and in another battle thousands more men were lost. There was nothing to eat but horse-flesh, and the soldiers' clothes froze on them. Napoleon, in the grey overcoat which he always wore, was pale and haggard with anxiety. All the way the Russians attacked the outer parts of the army without giving battle. At the river Beresina the bridge had been cut down, and the Russians were waiting at the other side. The French built a bridge and struggled across the icy water, but the Russians attacked them, and thousands were driven back into the river and drowned.

Napoleon never showed any sign of weakness, but led the remnant of his army on until, at the town of Vilna, he heard bad news, and at last left his army and pushed on as fast as he could to Paris. After this the army fell into disorder, and only a few thousands of the half million men, whom Napoleon had led so proudly into Russia, crossed the river Niemen and left it again. At Paris Napoleon said that things had gone well, but that the cold of the winter had caused losses in the army. But he could not deceive Europe.

The Prussian people now rose and forced the government to declare war once more on Napoleon. Russia joined them, and then Austria. The armies against Napoleon were more dangerous than ever before, but he did not give up hope. He was still able to get together an enormous army, and he won one more victory at Dresden, but at the great 'Battle of the Nations' at Leipzig he was defeated and driven across the Rhine.

Even now the countries of Europe would have been glad to leave him France for himself, but he would not agree, and so the armies followed him into France. Even now he won brilliant victories, but he could no longer keep his enemies divided, and fight them one by one, as he had so often and so cleverly done before. His generals told him it was madness to resist, and at last the great Emperor, who had defied Europe so long, had to confess that he was beaten.

At first he offered to abdicate in favor of his son, but none would agree to this. He had to abdicate altogether. But even now the people of Europe hardly dared to suggest that he should become as other men. He was still to be called 'Emperor,' but he was to be kept quite safe on the little island of Elba, which was to be the only land left to him. There Napoleon went, and the brother of Louis XVI came to be King of France, and was called Louis XVIII.

A congress of representatives of the five great countries of Europe, Russia, Prussia, Austria, France, and Great Britain, met at Vienna. There were many things to settle after the terrible confusion of the last twenty-five years, and the representatives soon began to quarrel. Meanwhile Napoleon was lonely in Elba, alone with thoughts, which drove him nearly mad, of all he had lost and all he had nearly won. Marie Louise had gone home to Austria and taken her baby with her. She had refused to follow her husband to the lonely island of Elba. Napoleon had joked as he looked down one day from the top of the highest hill in Elba, saying with a smile, 'It must be confessed that my island is very small.'

But at last he could bear it no longer. He made up his mind to have one last try for power. He had heard that the new King of France, Louis XVIII, was not a man whom the French would love or admire. He knew, too, that his own soldiers had loved him, and remembered how the men of his Imperial Guard had wept when he bade them good-bye. He would go to France and try to win it back again.

Soon news came to Vienna that Napoleon had landed in France and was marching to Paris, and that the French soldiers were trooping to his standard, and Louis XVIII had fled. The Congress broke up. Nothing could be done until he was conquered again. Wellington, who had driven the French right out of Spain in 1818, was the man to save Europe. For a hundred days Napoleon ruled at Paris, getting together once more an enormous army, while Prussia and England and Austria and Russia did the same.

But Napoleon was the quickest, and he made up his mind to attack the Prussians under their general, Blücher, in Belgium, then the English under Wellington, before the two armies could join together, and before the Russians and Austrians, who were marching across Europe, should come up to them. He attacked the Prussians at Ligny and defeated them. Blücher then drew his army back towards Wavre, but Napoleon thought he had gone to Namur. Napoleon sent some regiments towards Namur to prevent Blücher joining the English. He then turned to attack Wellington at a place called Quatre Bras, or the Four Roads.

The Duke of Wellington

Wellington had already fought with one of Napoleon's officers, but neither side won, and now Wellington drew off towards Waterloo, a plain near Brussels. Here Napoleon followed and attacked, and on the 18th of June the great battle of Waterloo was fought. It was the first time that Napoleon and Wellington had met to fight each other.

The English army was posted on a ridge of hills. On the road below he left men to guard the farmhouse of La Haye Sainte, and still further to the right more men to guard the farm and castle of Hougoumont. The French were drawn up on a ridge at the other side of the valley. Both generals were sure of victory.

At half-past eleven in the morning the battle began. Napoleon's plan of battle was to stagger the enemy's front with artillery, and then, before they had recovered, to send in bodies of cavalry to break them up or ride them down. But he could hardly do this with the two farms in the way. The French, therefore, made many determined attacks on La Haye Sainte and Hougoumont, but could not take them. It was a tremendous struggle, and very equal, but at half-past four in the afternoon Blücher with his Prussians, tired after a long march but fresh enough to fight, came up and attacked the right of the French army. Soon after Wellington cried, 'Up, guards, and at them!' and the fifteen hundred English guards whom he had kept in reserve till then dashed on to the French ranks. The line broke, and the French turned and fled.

Only the Imperial Guards stood close round the Emperor. The British begged them to surrender, for they hated to cut down such brave men. 'The Guard dies but does not surrender,' was the answer. At last Napoleon rode sadly from the field. He had lost everything. True, twenty-five thousand English and Prussians lay dead on the field, and Wellington wept as the list was read to him.

But it was the end of the great struggle, and Napoleon knew it. He tried to get away in a ship to America, but the shores of France were too closely watched. At last he gave himself up to the English officers on the battleship the Bellerophon, which sailed to Plymouth. Meanwhile it had been decided that he should be sent to the island of St. Helena, half-way between the coasts of Africa and South America. There he would be safe. He lived there for six years, with sentinels posted round his house, and an English officer visiting him every day to make sure that he was still there. English battleships lay at anchor round the island to make doubly sure.

For the most part he was calm, and spent much of his time writing down his 'memoirs,' the story of his life, as it seemed to him. There is much that is true and much that is false in his story. Near him were always the portraits of Josephine, who died soon after Waterloo, and Marie Louise and his son, the young Napoleon, who was never to be emperor after all. Napoleon was buried at St. Helena, but years afterwards the French people, remembering his greatness, for he was, after all, one of the greatest men who have ever lived, had his body carried to Paris and buried there in a gorgeous tomb, with a circle of great marble figures looking down on the spot where the body of the Emperor lies.

CHAPTER XLV—THE REMAKING OF EUROPE

The Congress at Vienna had now to begin again the work of putting order into the Europe with which Napoleon had been playing chess for so many years. France was reduced to the size it had been in 1789, before the revolutionary wars began. Many of the provinces she had conquered on the Rhine were more French than German, but most of the German states were formed into a loose 'Confederation,' and these were included in it. The part of Poland which had been taken from Prussia was given to Alexander of Russia. Holland and Belgium were joined together as one kingdom, and given to the royal House of Orange, the former rulers of Holland.

Holland and Belgium were two quite different nations in race and in religion, but no notice was taken of nationality, although it was really the spirit of nationalism which had overthrown Napoleon at last. The north of Italy was given back to Austria, and Savoy to the King of Sardinia. The King and Queen of Naples went back to their kingdom. Spain had already been given back to Ferdinand VII.

The great kings of Europe looked on the French Revolution as a thing which was over. It was to them a kind of bad dream. Some of its ideas had already become part of the laws of the countries, but the 'Holy Alliance,' in which the Emperor of Austria, the Tsar of Russia, and the King of Prussia joined, made it quite clear that they believed in absolute government. They would try to do good things for the people, but the people must not do anything for themselves.

So the nineteenth century began, but the ideas of the French Revolution were not dead, and all the nations have been slowly winning the liberty and equality which the Revolution had tried to teach. Louis XVIII was restored to the throne of France once more, but it was understood that he was to give the nation a 'constitution.' France was to have a parliament of two houses like England.

Louis XVIII was a sensible and rather clever man. He had spent his days in exile since the Revolution in Russia, until he was driven away twice by the changing plans of both tsars, and afterwards in England. He was prepared to be very tolerant and moderate, but the lower house of his first parliament was very violent. The elections had been made while emigrés were pouring back to France, and many of the people, especially in the south, were full of relief that the old ways, as they thought, had come back. Many of the people who were known to have been in favor of the Revolution were massacred by the peasants, who were full of revenge for all they and their Church had suffered. These massacres were afterwards spoken of as the 'White Terror.' The lower house insisted on the trial of some of Napoleon's greatest friends, and the brave Marshal Ney was tried and shot. Many others were driven from the country. But at last Louis dissolved this parliament, and the next was much more moderate.

The other countries of Europe had left a large army in France, and France had to pay a great sum of money to help to make up to these countries for the expenses of the wars against Napoleon. But now the army was withdrawn, and things were quiet in France for some years. Perhaps the thing which the French people felt most in the conditions of peace of 1815, was that most of the beautiful works of art which Napoleon had stolen from all over Europe and brought to Paris had to be sent back.

Louis XVIII reigned in France until he died in 1824, and his brother became king and was called Charles X.

Charles X was not such a wise man as Louis XVIII. He was not content to rule as a constitutional king. 'I would rather hew wood' he said, 'than be a king like the king of England.' It was under Charles that France won Algiers in the North of Africa, the most prosperous of the French possessions today, but nothing could make Charles popular. He stopped the freedom of the Press, and Paris rose in revolt. Once more the 'tricolor,' the flag of the Revolution, was seen in the streets.

The soldiers and the citizens fought, but the soldiers had never really had much enthusiasm for fighting against the tricolor. The citizens won, for many of the soldiers went over to them. The palace of the Tuileries was again attacked, but the king was not there. When he sent word that he was ready to grant freedom to the Press again he was told that it was too late. He fled to England, where William IV was now king.

Many of the Parisians had hoped for a republic once more, but this was not yet to be, and the French Crown was offered to the duke of Orleans, a member of the royal family, who had fought as a young man when the armies of the Revolution were attacked by the invaders at Valmy. But Louis Philippe, though he reigned until 1848, never really suited the French. They wanted more reforms than he could grant. Once more in 1848 an attack was made on the palace of the Tuileries, and Louis Philippe had to abdicate in his turn. He was seventy-five when he fled away with his queen into exile.

France now became a republic again with Louis Napoleon, the nephew of the Emperor Napoleon, as its president. He was the son of Louis Bonaparte, the former king of Holland. Napoleon's own son, the 'king of Rome,' had died at the age of twenty. He had always been a delicate boy, and he died worn out with longing to be able to do something to win his father's empire back. It was not long before Prince Louis Napoleon was able to have himself proclaimed Emperor.

He was called Napoleon III, as though he had a right to succeed to the son of Napoleon, who was therefore spoken of as Napoleon II. So France was ruled by an emperor once more, though not for long.

Meanwhile, changes in Europe had followed both the revolution of 1830 and this of 1848. Belgium had rebelled against being joined with Holland, and had become a separate kingdom under a German prince, the uncle of Princess Victoria, who became Queen of England in 1837. Hanover could not be held by women, and so no longer belonged to the English sovereign. It was soon joined to Prussia. Poland, filled with the spirit of nationality and wish for freedom, rose against Russia, but the rebellion was put down. With the death of Ferdinand VII in 1833 Spain also got a constitution for a time.

Before this the nations of Europe had been roused to enthusiasm by the struggle of the Greek people for independence against the Turks. The Sultan at Constantinople left the government of the conquered states in the hands of rulers who governed them very much as they liked. These rulers, who were of course Mohammedans, were often very cruel to the Christian people like the Greeks, who had borne their rule for centuries. But the new spirit of nationalism was now felt by the Greeks, and they rose in rebellion against the Turks. Terrible fighting took place, for the Greeks were as cruel as the Turks once they had risen, just as slaves are vicious when they have once risen against their masters.

At first the countries of Europe did not interfere, although Russia, and England especially, were in favor of the Greeks. But volunteers from these countries went to help the Greeks. Among them was the poet Lord Byron, who was full of the memories of the great days of Greece and enthusiasm for its writers. The modern Greeks could hardly be looked upon as the descendants of the old Greeks, for so many Romans and other peoples had since mingled with the people. Still, in Greece itself there was a new enthusiasm for the study of the old Greek literature and language.

The population of Greece was now largely made up of herdsmen and of soldiers, many of whom were brigands constantly worrying the Turkish rulers. Lord Byron hoped that the glories of old Greece might be restored, and was full of this dream when he landed in Greece to help them to fight in 1824. He went to Mesolonghi, one of the strongest places on the west coast of Greece, but he caught fever in the low swampy land and died.

Still he had given the Greeks hope and courage. Mesolonghi was besieged by sea and land. The siege lasted a year, and then all the food and powder were gone, but the Greeks would not surrender. They preferred to die, and when they could hold out no longer, men, women, and children dashed out on the Turks, and died fighting outside the town they had defended so long. At last England, France, and Russia sent help to the Greeks, and a great battle was fought in the bay of Navarino. The Turks were defeated, but there were some years of fighting yet. England did not want to make Turkey too weak, because this would make Russia too strong, but at last in 1833 it was arranged that Greece should be a free kingdom under Otto of Bavaria, a prince only seventeen years old, as its first king. This new kingdom was to have a constitution too, so the work of the French Revolution was being slowly but surely done.

Hungary, the beautiful country which had so long been under the rule of Austria, though it belonged to quite a different race from the people of that country, now fought for freedom too. For many years the Hungarians had chosen the Emperor to rule them, but now it had become a matter of course, and they had no share in their own government and there was no freedom of the Press.

Louis Kossuth, the Hungarian Patriot

In the year 1887, a young Hungarian, Louis Kossuth, set up a newspaper, in which the new ideas of liberty found a voice. This did not please the Austrian government, and Kossuth was put in prison for two years. At last he was set free, and started his newspaper again. The people looked on him as a leader. When the revolution of 1848 took place in France, the Hungarians hoped more and more for liberty, and Louis Kossuth was sent with some other chosen men to ask for reform in Hungary. The Emperor promised, for he was frightened at the moment, but he broke his promises, and then Hungary rose with Louis Kossuth as its leader in a war against Austria.

The peasants flocked armed with knives and hatchets to fight for their country. They defeated the Austrians many times, but Austria got help from Russia and thousands of soldiers marched into Hungary. The Hungarians had to give in. Many of the leaders of the rebellion were shot, but Louis Kossuth escaped from the country. The United States sent a ship to carry him over to their land, but afterwards he went to live in Italy, where he died in 1894. But thirty years before this, Hungary had won her freedom after all. Though she remains under the Austrian Emperor her government is quite independent of the government of Austria, and the countries ruled over by the Emperor are now called together Austria-Hungary.

Soon after Napoleon III became Emperor of France the French people joined the English in a war with Russia. Russia had won Finland and so become the chief country on the shores of the Baltic. She longed to capture Constantinople and launch her ships on the Bosphorus. Turkey was in a very weak state. The Tsar Nicholas told the English that Turkey was 'a sick man, a very sick man.' He felt that it would be easy to steal all he wanted from the 'sick man.' He was willing that England should take Egypt and the island of Crete, and would have liked to take the Turkish provinces in Europe for himself. But England did not want Russia to become too strong, and refused. One reason why England did not care for the Russians to grow too strong was that Russia is the nearest country in Europe to India, which she might try to attack through the passes of the Himalayas. Russia made the Turkish treatment of the Christians in her provinces an excuse for attacking the Turkish fleet in the Black Sea, in the year 1854. The Turkish fleet was destroyed and four thousand Turks were killed. So England and France made ready to attack Russia in the peninsula of the Crimea, and so began the famous Crimean War.

The English commander was Lord Raglan, who had lost his arm at Waterloo. The English and French knew nothing about the Crimea, but they landed in September 1854 at a place near the mouth of the river Alma. The Russians were drawn up on a ridge of hills on the other side of the river. They fired on the English and French all the time they were crossing the river, but they went bravely on up the hill and broke the Russian line and so won the first battle of the war. Then they marched on to Balaclava, where again they defeated the Russians. But the battle of Balaclava is best remembered because of the famous charge of the Light Brigade.

Through some mistake the brigade, a company of cavalry, was ordered to cross a mile and a half of the battlefield, where it would be fired on all the time, and charge the Russian guns. It was a terrible order, for horse-soldiers cannot attack artillery in such a way, but though they knew it was a mistake, the brigade knew too that a soldier's first duty is obedience. They made the charge and few came back to tell the tale. Everybody knows Tennyson's poem on the 'Charge of the Light Brigade.' Their courage will never be forgotten. The French general looking on said, 'It is magnificent, but it is not war.'

As winter came on the English and French were besieging Sebastopol. The cold was terrible, and the soldiers were short of clothes. Some ships carrying clothes and blankets were wrecked in Balaclava Bay, and the things were all lost. When some things did arrive it was seen that terrible mistakes had been made. Once a great case of boots was unpacked. They were all for the right foot! The men fell ill and thousands died.

FLORENCE NIGHTINGALE

It was now that Miss Florence Nightingale, an English lady, took nurses out to care for the sick and wounded soldiers at Scutari, where the Turkish barracks had been made into a hospital. But at last, after a siege of three hundred and forty-nine days, Sebastopol was taken. So ended the Crimean War. The Black Sea was opened to ships of all countries, and Russia was allowed to keep only six warships on it.

Ever since the Crimean War the Christian nations under the Turks in Europe have been longing for their freedom. In 1877 Russia joined the Christians in their struggle, and Roumania, Servia, and Montenegro won their independence. Other provinces were put under the protection of Austria and afterwards became part of Austria-Hungary. Bulgaria got its own government, but had to pay tribute. It is now quite free. Even today the people of Albania and the districts to the north of Greece are struggling for their freedom from the Turks. They are being helped by the Servians and Bulgarians and other peoples who have already won their freedom. There are many who feel that things will not be right until the 'sick man of Europe' is driven out of Europe altogether. The Turks are a brave if fierce people, but Christian peoples have never been happy under their rule.

Immediately after the Revolution of 1848 in France, which once more filled the minds of men all over Europe with the longing for freedom, nearly every one of the German states demanded a 'constitution' from their princes. There was a feeling, too, that after all the Germans of all these little states belonged to one race, and that they would be much stronger if they could join together and become one nation. A great meeting was held at Frankfort to discuss this thing, but there were too many quarrels.

Some people wanted to include Austria. Others felt that the Austrians were not really Germans, and wanted all the other states to join with Prussia at their head. This is what happened afterwards, but for the time the idea was given up. But as the years went on the Germans were more and more inclined to unite.

The King of Prussia, William I had for his chief statesman a great man called Ottovon Bismarck. Bismarck was one of the greatest statesmen of modern times. He was stern and strong, and when he made up his mind to do a thing he did it. 'The German problem,' he said, 'cannot be solved by parliamentary decrees, but by blood and iron.' He knew that before Prussia could make itself the head of a new German empire, there must be a war with Austria. In 1863 Christian IX, the father of the Princess Alexandra, who married the Prince of Wales, afterwards King Edward VII of England, became king of Denmark.

For many years the little states of Schleswig and Holstein, which were really German, had belonged to Denmark, but now Prussia and Austria fought Denmark for them. The Danes fought as they had always done, splendidly, but Denmark is too small a country to fight against two great powers, and in the end they had to give up Schleswig and Holstein to the enemy. Then Austria and Prussia fought for the states themselves in the 'Seven Weeks War.' The wonderful army which Bismarck had made for Prussia won the victory, and Austria gave up all power in Germany.

The new Prussian province of Schleswig-Holstein gave Germany more power on the Baltic coast. Right across the province there is now a canal which saves the German ships from sailing round the stormy coast of Denmark. It is in the harbor of Kiel that Germany is now building her 'Dreadnoughts,' the great warships which many Englishmen fear are being prepared to attack England's supremacy on the seas.

When France under its Emperor Napoleon III saw the growing power of Germany, it grew alarmed. Bismarck was glad of the chance of war, and in 1870 a war between France and Prussia broke out. The French people were still full of the memory of Napoleon and the great victories which his armies had won. They did not realize how strong the army of Prussia had grown and how weak their own now was. They went into the war with a light heart.

The German states joined readily with Prussia and sent their armies to help the strong Prussian army against France. In all the battles which the Germans won the conquering army was larger than the French army it defeated. But the Germans were really better prepared for war in every way. The French won the first battle, in which the young Prince Imperial, the son of Napoleon III, fought nobly, but it was their only victory. At the great battle of Sedan the French were surrounded, and though they fought madly the better trained soldiers of Prussia conquered them.

Napoleon III went wherever the shots were thickest. He was hoping to be killed, but at last he made up his mind to surrender, and sent the message to old King William: 'Not having been able to die in the midst of my troops, there is nothing left for me but to give up my sword into the hands of your Majesty.' An emperor who could not win battles would never be tolerated by the French. This Napoleon III knew, and he left France for ever with the Empress Eugenie. He died three years afterwards in England, broken-hearted. The Empress Eugenie lived for many years in England, loved and admired by all who knew her. But the young Prince Imperial was killed in the Zulu War, fighting nobly for the English people who had given his father and mother a home in their exile.

But though the Emperor had surrendered, Paris determined to resist. For four months the siege went on. The starving Parisians ate horses and paid large sums of money for dogs and cats and rats. But at last they had to give in, and when peace was made they had to give up Alsace and Lorraine, two more of those Rhine provinces which were much more French than German. The French have never forgiven the Germans for their defeat in the Franco-Prussian War, and to get back Alsace and Lorraine is the dream of many Frenchmen today. The provinces themselves are still loyal to the French, and it is said that if a visitor asks a peasant girl there today to what country she belongs, she will look cautiously round to see that no one is listening and then whisper eagerly 'France.' But one great result of the Franco-Prussian War was, that now, at last, France became a republic and has been one ever since. After nearly a hundred years the freedom which the first

"Discussing the War in a Paris Café" — *a scene from the brief interim between the Battle of Sedan and Siege of Paris during the Franco-Prussian War.*

leaders of the Revolution of 1789 had longed for, and which had caused so much suffering to France and to Europe, was won.

At the same time the war made Germany a nation. While the Prussian king was at the palace of Versailles, where he stayed during the siege of Paris, news came the people of the German states had made up their minds to unite in one empire, and King William I of Prussia became the first Emperor of Germany. Each state still governs itself, and has its own prince and its own court, but in all things connected with war, and peace, and trade the government of the Emperor decides for all. So after many centuries the German states, which had remained separate since the Middle Ages, became at last a nation.

THE MAKING OF ITALY

Meanwhile Italy, that other country which had been for so long broken up and in the power of other peoples, was becoming a nation too. Early in the nineteenth century the same longing for freedom which had begun to spread through the other countries of Europe was felt in Italy too. Young men like Joseph Mazzini, the first great hero of Italian independence, longed to see their country freed from the foreigner and united as one nation. His one thought was the sorrows of Italy. He always wore black clothes to show how he mourned for her. A society was formed of Italians who would work for their country's freedom. It was called "Young Italy," and its watchword was, 'God and the People.'

After the Revolution of 1830 some of the Italians rose, but only a few, and they were easily put down. Before this, Mazzini had gone into exile after being in prison for some months, for 'Young Italy' was a secret society and it had been found out that he belonged to it. He went like so many exiles to England, where he stayed until a new movement began in Italy, after the Revolution in France in 1848. All North Italy rose against Austria, and Mazzini went to Rome and set up a republic.

The Pope, Pius IX had at first been very much in sympathy with the idea of the liberty of the people, but had afterwards become frightened at the violence of some of the leaders. He now fled from Rome. But in the north, Austria brought a great army and defeated the Italians, and Prince Louis Napoleon brought an army of Frenchmen and won back Rome for the Pope, in spite of the splendid fighting of Garibaldi, another leader of the 'Young Italy' movement. He, too, had been exiled soon after Mazzini, and had spent many years in war in South America, until he also came back to Italy, when he heard that the people were ready to fight for their freedom.

When, after weeks of fighting, he was at last driven from Rome, he fled with his wife Anita, whom he dearly loved, trying to reach Venice, but could not do so, and he was hunted from place to place, over mountains and through forests until his wife died worn out. At last he got away to America, where he stayed until ten years later Italy made a last and successful attempt to win its freedom.

Many of the leaders of the 'Young Italy' movement would have liked to have made an Italian republic, but they hoped to get help from the other countries of Europe, and they knew they would only get it if they tried to set up a kingdom, and not a republic. If they had won in their rising in 1849, Charles Albert of Sardinia was to have been ruler of the lands conquered from Austria, but Austria forced Charles Albert to abdicate and his son Victor Emmanuel became King of Sardinia. Charles Albert went into exile, and died without knowing that success was to come and that his son was to be king of all Italy.

Victor Emmanuel had for his chief statesman Cavour, the third great leader in winning the freedom of Italy. He saw that Italy could only conquer Austria if she were helped by other countries. In 1859 a French army under Napoleon III marched into Italy to help Cavour against Austria. Nearly all Lombardy was won by them, and then Napoleon, who thought he had done enough, made peace with the Austrians. This would have left Venice and other parts of North Italy to them, but Cavour was terribly angry at Napoleon's behavior, and the people of North Italy all wanted Victor Emmanuel for their king.

Garibaldi helped in the struggle, a dark fierce man in the famous red shirt which he always wore. At last all of North Italy, except Venice, belonged to Victor Emmanuel. There were still the Papal States, Naples and Sicily, to win. Garibaldi begged of the North Italians for money to get men and weapons to fight against the King of Naples, who was of course a foreigner belonging to the French royal family. Garibaldi took his men to Sicily and called on the peasants to rise. The islanders rose and drove the Neapolitan officers away. Sicily was won for Victor Emmanuel.

Then the leader crossed to Naples; the royal family fled and the people followed Garibaldi. But at the royal palace there were still royal troops. They might at any moment have fired, but Garibaldi stood up in his carriage looking steadily at them. Then they, too, gave way to the enthusiasm of the people for 'Young Italy.' Great cries of 'Viva Garibaldi! ('Long live Garibaldi!') were heard on every side, and Naples was won also for Victor Emmanuel. The greater part of the Papal States had been taken too. All Italy except Rome was now joined under one ruler for the first time since the fall of the Roman Empire. In 1870, when France being at war could no longer send an army to defend the Pope, Rome was taken too, and became the capital of the new kingdom.

An offer was made to the Pope to pay him yearly a large sum of money. He was to have his court like a king, and his soldiers, but he was not to rule over any part of the land. But the Pope would not agree to this. He still lives in his palace of the Vatican, but has never given his consent to the loss of the Papal States. This question of the 'Temporal Power,' as the Pope's rule over the Papal

Garibaldi, the Italian Patriot
(From his statue at Florence).

States was called, is still discussed among Catholics today. There are many who think that the Pope can rule better and more spiritually over the Church now that he is no longer a temporal prince, but others think that he has been robbed of his rights. Especially in Roman society does the quarrel go on. The people are divided between the 'Whites,' who are all for the Pope, and the 'Blacks,' who are in favor of the king. Meanwhile the royal and papal courts go on side by side. Certainly it would have been impossible for the great dream of Italian unity to come true if the temporal power had been kept.

And so now at last all Europe was divided into nations, and all had 'constitutions ' more or less free, except the one country of Russia. Nowhere any longer were there serfs, except indeed in Russia until 1861, when there, too, the Tsar set them free. But in Russia alone there is very little freedom of government yet. The Tsar is as absolute as any king before the French Revolution, or more so. There is no freedom of the Press in Russia and no freedom of thought. For years all men or women who have dared to speak against the government have been sent as prisoners to Siberia, that great tract of land stretching across the north of Asia which Russia won in the sixteenth century. There the exiles used to be driven in crowds, marching in chains for thousands of miles to the prisons they were never more to leave. Prisoners are still sent to Siberia, but they go by the wonderful Trans-Siberian Railway, which stretches from Europe to the Pacific Ocean. Many Russian exiles are to be found in all the countries of Europe, waiting and hoping till their country too shall be free. There are some who have grown desperate and would destroy all governments if they could.

Everywhere else the peoples of Europe are free, and so, too, in America and Africa and Australia. At the beginning of the nineteenth century all South America, except two little districts in the north which belonged to England, were under Spain and Portugal. The people were partly Spanish and Portuguese, but there were many more natives, and many, too, 'half-breeds,' or 'Creoles,' people descended from Spaniards who had married natives. When the United States won their freedom from England and the news of the French Revolution reached South America, ideas of revolution began to spread through South America too. Then when the Spanish and Portuguese kings were deposed by Napoleon, the South Americans hardly knew who were supposed to be their rulers. This encouraged the ideas of independence which were already spreading. The Portuguese royal family fled to Brazil, but soon after they had returned to Portugal. Brazil became a separate state with a Portuguese prince as its constitutional emperor. At last, in 1889, Brazil became a republic.

But things were not done so peacefully in the greater part of South America which belonged to Spain. In these provinces there were many royalists as well as republicans, and there were many bitter struggles before the republicans won. One of the great heroes of the struggle was a man named San Martin. For four years he fought against the royalists in the rich country round La Plata, the great 'silver' river, but in 1816 he was able to set up the republic of Argentina. Then Chili arose, but the royalists of Peru defeated the republicans there. There were many strange people in South America, and the leader of the Chilians was

Colton Map of South America, 1855

an Irishman named O'Higgins. But San Martin marched to his help across the great mountain range of the Andes, and Chili, too, won its independence. After many bitter struggles, Venezuela also won its freedom, though it was twice won back again, and then Bolivar, the hero of Venezuela, joined with San Martin to win Peru.

At last Spanish South America was divided into nine republics. At first they were often governed by dictators, soldiers who had helped to win their freedom for them; but in the end they all became really free republics, and South America rapidly became rich and strong. So here, too, the work of the French Revolution spread.

And now even the peoples of Asia are waking up to the idea of freedom, and we may hope that before long all the peoples of the earth will have their liberty.

Chapter XLVI—Africa—The Land of Mystery

Meanwhile another vast land was becoming of greater importance in the world's history.

Africa as we know it today can only look back on a history of about forty years. Within that time the nations of Europe have agreed to cut it up into pieces, in each of which some European nation rules. Of all that vast continent only two states are ruled by natives, the republic of Liberia and Abyssinia. Liberia is the place where slaves who had been set free were allowed to settle down and begin their lives over again in freedom. From 1821 up to about fifty years ago ships sailed across the ocean from America, bringing hundreds of old negro men and women and children to their new home in that Africa from which their forefathers had been stolen so many years before.

The other native state, Abyssinia, is much older, and one of their old stories says that the Queen of Sheba who visited King Solomon was a queen of Abyssinia. Since the struggle with Italy, which ended in the terrible defeat of the Italians in 1896, no one has tried to rob the Abyssinians of their independence.

In the rest of Africa, Germany and Portugal each have two pieces south of the Equator, one on the east and one on the west side. Between them are the South African Union and other states under Great Britain. At Lake Tanganyika, where this country ends, is the Congo Free State, which belongs to Belgium. North of the Equator Great Britain has British East Africa and Uganda, stretching up to Egypt, to the west of which is the huge desert land reaching to the west coast and belonging to France. Morocco, Algeria and Tunis are also under France, Tripoli and the westerly part of Africa under Italy, while there are other strips of land on the west coast belonging to France, Great Britain and Germany. We must now see how all these lands came to be ruled by the nations of Europe.

Although the continent of Africa is about three times as large as Europe, and nearly two hundred times the size of England and Wales, and has a huge number of people living in it, it is a land of mystery. Part of it, indeed, is called the 'Dark Continent'; but in many ways the whole is dark. There is so little known of it—so much that can never be known. The people who first lived in Africa were probably a small black race, and many of this sort of people still live in the part of Africa farthest from the sea.

The parts we know best are the parts near the sea. Besides Egypt, the Northern sea states—Morocco, Tunis and Tripoli, which were called 'Barbary' from the ' Barber' people who live there—were the only places which people knew much about before the sixteenth century. We have seen how the Arabs conquered Egypt in the seventh century, and then pushed their way along the North African coastlands and on into Spain. But after the Moorish power was ended in Spain, Barbary, except Morocco, was taken by the Spaniards at the beginning of the sixteenth century. But it never really became Spanish, and almost immediately afterwards Algeria, Tunis and Tripoli were taken by the Turks, who had also now conquered Egypt. Morocco alone remained independent, and some of the Moors from that state journeyed south as far as Timbuktu.

The Barbary Pirates

But the Turks have always seemed to stop the growth of the lands they have conquered, and the only thing that shows that these states were alive until the nineteenth century was the bands of pirates who sailed out in their swift low boats and attacked any ship which was not well protected with guns. The pirates were quite fearless, and even when the French and English joined against them they could not conquer them at first. They were not always only people from Barbary. Men from European countries joined them, too, now and then. They not only attacked ships; sometimes they would swoop down on a town, kill whoever tried to resist them, and carry other people off and sell them as slaves, or make their friends buy them back for immense ransoms. They often attacked Spain and Sicily and parts of Italy, but even got as far as Ireland sometimes.

Of course if the nations of Europe had really joined to conquer them they could have done so, but they did not. Tunis was really a pirate state, and pirates ruled the chief coast towns of all these states. Twice in the nineteenth century a British fleet attacked Algiers, which was one of their chief strongholds; but they were not really put down until France conquered first Algeria and then Tunis. France now really rules both of these states, though there is a native ruler in Tunisia who governs under the French. The French power has in the last few years been recognized as the chief in Morocco, though Spain is allowed to govern certain parts. For many years in the last century several European nations wanted to be the chief power in Morocco, and Germany was the last to agree to the French ruling there. In 1912 the Italians invaded Tripoli and took it from the Turkish rulers after some fierce fighting.

EGYPT

Egypt has had quite a different past from the Barbary States. When the Arabs took Egypt it was at first ruled by governors sent by the Caliphs, but in time the governors passed on their power to their sons and became the real rulers of the country independent of the Caliphs. Saladin, against whom Richard I fought in the Crusades, was one of these rulers of Egypt.

Many other rulers came after Saladin, but they were often weak men, and in 1517 the Turks conquered Egypt, and they kept it till Napoleon's famous attack on Egypt in 1798.

Some years before this, however, a Scotsman named James Bruce, who had had a life filled with strange adventures, had travelled through Egypt. He had spent two years at the court of the pirate rulers of Algiers, and he then travelled through Tunis to Tripoli. He took ships to the island of Crete, but was wrecked and had to swim back to the African shore. He had made up his mind to see where the Nile, the great river of Egypt, began.

It was not an easy thing he had set himself to do. But he had many things in his favor. He was used to danger. He was taller and bigger than most men, very strong, and very good at sports. He knew several languages well, and also had a little knowledge of how to cure diseases. He arrived in Alexandria in 1768, and was able to make friends with the ruler of Egypt. The country was filled with wild men, but Bruce went among them without fear. He saw the old Egyptian city of Thebes, and went across the desert to Arabia dressed as a Turkish soldier. Then he returned and went to Abyssinia, where every one was kind to him. He stayed there two years. The King of Abyssinia did not want him to go away, but at last allowed him to, and then Bruce travelled to the place where—not the Nile, but—the 'Blue Nile' begins. He had done a great deal, but he had not done what he thought. The White Nile is really the Nile of the ancient peoples, and although he did not find its source he travelled still further across the desert and found the place where the Blue Nile joins the White Nile, a place which British people will always remember, for there stands Khartum, where General Gordon died.

Poor Bruce, after all his hardships, found that people would not believe his story when he got back to London. Even when he wrote all his adventures down in a book many people still refused to believe him. He went back very sad to his home in Scotland. But now we know that all he said was true.

THE END OF EGYPT'S INDEPENDENCE

Napoleon's soldiers did not stay long in Egypt. They were driven out by the English and the Turks, and then Mehemet Ali made himself ruler. He was terribly cruel, and when a British army fought against him he cut off the heads of the soldiers and stuck them on pieces of wood in Alexandria. The strange thing is that after beginning his rule with so much cruelty

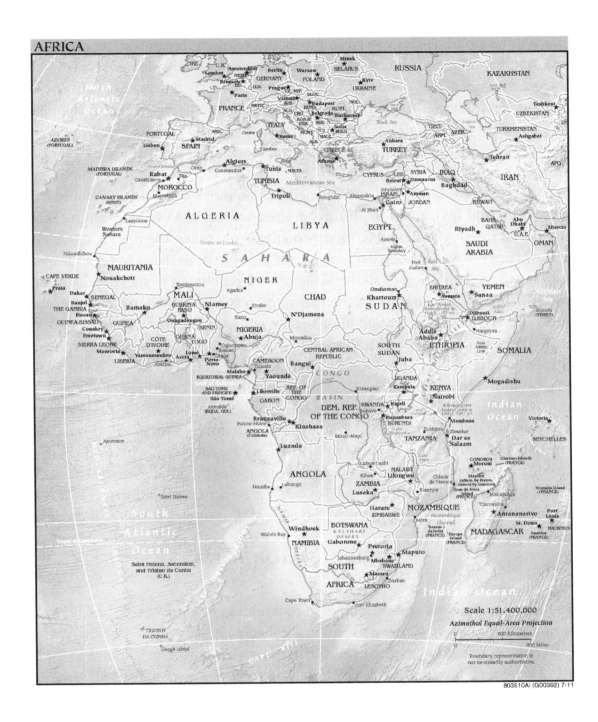

he really became a good ruler, and when he died in 1848 all the land along the Nile and the roads by which people travelled were quite safe even for Christians.

It was through the grandson of Mehemet Ali, Ismail, that Egypt lost its independence. He had been to school in France, and had there learned many new ways of obtaining and spending money. Eastern people are generally extravagant; but Ismail had become worse through his life in Paris. He found that it was easy for a country to borrow money, and so he got as much as he could. He borrowed so much and so often that at last the great countries of Europe saw that they must interfere if Egypt was ever to pay its debts.

But before this Ismail had done many good things for Egypt. He got Englishmen to teach the Egyptians new ways, and letters were sent by post for the first time in the history of Egypt. He built railways, lighthouses and telegraphs; and the great canal at Suez, through which ships sail on their way to India and Australia, was opened in 1869, six years after he began to rule.

In 1875 Egypt was in a very bad state. Ismail had no money, and no one would lend him any more. So he sold his part of the profits in the Suez Canal to Great Britain. This made England take an interest in Egyptian money matters, and when the men who were sent to find out how Ismail was spending his money told how great his debts were, an Englishman was put to see to the collection of all the taxes, and a Frenchman to see that the money was spent wisely. After three years Ismail tried secretly to stir up rebellions in Cairo, and then the English and French asked the Sultan of Turkey, who was supposed to be Ismail's king, to appoint another ruler for Egypt. This the Sultan did at once, and England and France helped the new ruler to govern Egypt until the Arab soldiers rose in rebellion. The British fleet then attacked Alexandria in 1882, and the English, seeing that they could not conquer the rebellious Arabs in this way alone, made up their minds to send soldiers to Egypt. France refused to send any and so did Italy; and British soldiers had to do the work alone. England in this way came to be the only nation to help the Khedive, as the ruler of Egypt is called, to govern in peace. Sir Evelyn Baring, who is now Lord Cromer, was the Englishman sent out to represent Great Britain in 1884, and until a few years ago he remained in Egypt. He was so wise that law and order are everywhere now in Egypt, and the country is rich and prosperous.

GENERAL GORDON

But many Englishmen have lost their lives in making Egypt a greater and better state. The most famous of these was General Gordon. He had fought in the Crimean War and in China before he was sent to Egypt, in 1874, to act as governor for the Khedive in the land to the south. He went at once to the country he was to rule, and worked hard for six years putting down the slave trade, drawing maps of the unknown country and learning to know the strange peoples of the desert. He succeeded in this so well that he could make these people do things which no one else could persuade them to do. He was always in great danger.

Once a rebellion broke out at a place called Darfur, and Gordon went as fast as he could to put it down. He had only a few soldiers, and when he came near to the rebels he left his soldiers behind and went with only one *man* to speak to the rebels. This man he took because he did not know the language of these people. After he had spoken to them for a little time the rebels went quietly away. He tried to make peace in a war between Egypt and Abyssinia, but was taken prisoner. During each of the last three years of his rule he had to ride about three thousand miles on camels or mules, and he was quite tired out when he gave up his command in 1880. He spent a short time in South Africa, paid a visit to Palestine, and then at the beginning of 1884 was asked by the British government to go out to Egypt once more.

When Gordon left Egypt, a man whom he had once had to send away for ruling badly under him had been made governor of the Sudan, as the country south of Egypt is called. Soon his unjust rule made people very angry, and an Egyptian who had been ill-treated now rose and got the people to rebel. He said that he himself was the 'Mahdi,' the successor of Mahommed. A large army was sent to fight against him, but it was defeated, and hundreds and hundreds of soldiers were killed. Soon the Mahdi became master of nearly the whole of the Sudan except Khartum, and Great Britain advised the Khedive to give up the Sudan altogether. Gordon was sent to see how the soldiers in the forts scattered over the Su-

Death of General Gordon at Khartoum *by Jean Leon Gerome Ferris.*

dan could be got away to Egypt without being killed by the Mahdi. He arrived at Khartum on the 18th of February, and all the natives welcomed him, thinking that he had come to deliver them from the Mahdi. Soon the soldiers of the Mahdi surrounded Khartum, but not before Gordon had got the women and children safely away.

There had been an army not far off at Suakin, but it was taken away, and the forts north of Khartum were taken, so Gordon was cut off from all help. He had only one other white man with him. The rest were natives. There was not much food in Khartum, and the fort was not built to stand against a strong attack. Yet the months dragged on, and still he would not surrender. There alone in the midst of the desert, among men of a different race and religion, he held out, doing, as he said, 'the best for the honor of his country,' waiting and hoping that help would come.

On the 5th of January 1885 the last morsel of food was eaten, and the starving men grew weaker day by day, but would not give in. But the waters of the Nile had risen and broken one of the walls, and when the Mahdi and his followers rushed in on 26th January the men were too weak to resist. Gordon and many others were killed. 'I am quite happy, thank God,' he had written in a letter which he left behind for his sister; 'I have tried to do my duty.'

Two days after his death the help he had hoped for arrived, but it was too late, and many long years were to pass before the Egyptian army, trained and drilled by British officers and helped by British soldiers, was to avenge the death of Gordon. Little by little this army was built up; step by step it marched forward into the Sudan until Sir Herbert (now Lord) Kitchener felt that it was strong enough to attack the Mahdi's stronghold at Omdurman, two miles north of Khartum. The followers of the Mahdi fought so bravely that ten thousand were killed before they gave in; but at last the black flag which used to fly at Omdurman was captured and sent home to Queen Victoria. The Mahdi's power was destroyed forever. This was in 1898. On Sunday, 4th September, two days after the victory, General Kitchener, with a man from each regiment, crossed the Nile to Khartum, hoisted the flags of Great Britain and Egypt, and held a service in memory of General Gordon on the spot where he died.

Since then Egypt has grown still more prosperous under the direction of Great Britain. A university was founded at Khartum a few years ago, and the place which was the scene of so terrible a tragedy is now a peaceful and prosperous town. Lord Cromer resigned his position as representative of Great Britain in 1907, and now Lord Kitchener, who did so much to give Egypt peace and safety, has taken his place.

The Citadel and tombs in Cairo, Egypt in the late 1800s.

THE EXPLORERS

So far only a fringe of Africa has been mentioned. The story of the rest of this huge continent is chiefly the story of the brave men who spent their lives in trying to learn something of its mystery. It is strange to think that the explorers who have discovered what is known about Africa nearly all, and certainly all the greatest, lived within the last hundred years. It is true that in the fifteenth century the brave Portuguese sailor, Bartholomew Diaz, sailed round the Cape of Good Hope and stopped at many places on the coast, and Portuguese missionaries made their way into Abyssinia. And it is also true that the Dutch, two centuries later, settled in Cape Town. But behind these coast lands lay the 'Dark Continent' about which the people of Europe knew nothing until the nineteenth century.

Mungo Park

One of the first explorers to go to Africa was a young Scottish doctor named Mungo Park. It was only a year after the death of Bruce, who discovered the source of the Blue Nile, that Mungo Park started out to follow the course of the Niger, a river of West Africa. He reached the Gambia river, and having anchored his ship as far up as he could sail, he set out on horseback with a negro servant and a slave boy.

The natives warned him not to travel into the desert, but he went on. He had to make friends with the native chiefs whom he met. Once he had to give up his best coat because a chief liked the yellow buttons so much. He travelled through part of the country where war was going on, and the negro servant ran away. Mungo Park was taken prisoner and badly treated, but at last got away. But he had no food or drink. When he thought he must surely die he came at last to 'the long-sought majestic Niger glittering in the morning sun.' He travelled still further, but he was nearly dead from hunger and from the suffering caused by the bites of mosquitoes, and so he sadly turned back.

He had followed the great river three hundred miles, and after a few years in England he went out again. Once more he had to go through terrible sufferings. He started with a good many men this time, but many died, and with only seven left he went on, determined 'to discover the termination of the Niger or perish in the attempt.' His end was very sad. The little party was sailing down a river when they saw the whole bank covered with natives who shot arrows and threw spears at them, and all but one man, seeing no way of escape, jumped overboard and were drowned.

David Livingstone

It was thirty-six years before the next great explorer went to Africa. This was David Livingstone, who was also a Scotsman like Mungo Park. He had had a hard time as a boy. He left school when he was only ten years old, and worked for many years in a cotton mill before he was able to go to college, to study to become a missionary. He wished to go to China, but when he had studied for a long time, and had become a doctor, he was sent out to Africa. This was in 1841. He was twenty-eight years old then, and a strange man to look at.

He looked rough, but he was really very gentle, and he was always bubbling over with fun. He travelled great distances on his first journey, his winning manner helping him to make friends with the natives, and he soon made up his mind that he could do most good by travelling as far as possible, and handing over the knowledge he had won for others to follow. He had not been in Africa very long before he was attacked by a lion, which crushed his arm so that it never really got well.

He got married in Africa and still continued his journeys. Sometimes he stayed a little time in one place, and once after he had done this the whole tribe of people followed him when he went away, because they loved him so much. In 1849 he crossed the great Kalahari desert, and reached Lake Ngami, which he was the first white man to see. This was only one of the many discoveries he made. He reached the Zambesi river in 1851, and later on he made up his mind to follow it, see where it began, and where it entered the sea.

It is impossible to tell of all his journeyings, how he crossed Africa to the Portuguese town Loanda on the west, and then followed the Zambesi right to the east coast. When he reached Loanda he was nearly dead. He had suffered terribly from fever, and for many days had had hardly anything to eat. After a short rest he set off again, always writing down carefully what he had found out, and again he was nearly dead when he reached another Portuguese town on the west. But he left his men there, and two months later had the joy of reaching the place where the Zambesi runs into the sea.

After a year in England he went to Africa again in 1858, and he was very angry when he saw the terrible cruelties of the slave trade. The Arabs who bought and sold the negroes as slaves treated them worse than beasts. Livingstone made up his mind to do all he could to put an end to the slave trade in Africa. Wherever he went he set the slaves free, but once he had to stand by while Arab traders killed hundreds of women. He had lost the four goats he had taken with him, his medicine chest was stolen, and he could do nothing to help himself. He was not heard of for a long time, and people thought that he must be dead. So a brave man called Henry Morton Stanley was sent out by the owner of a great newspaper to try and find him. When Livingstone, worn out, thin from fever, and half-starved, reached Ujiji on Lake Tanganyika, what was his joy to find Stanley waiting for him with food and medicine.

He seemed to get new life from the meeting, and started afresh to find new places. Stanley had to leave him in 1872, and Livingstone was never seen again by white men. He travelled from Tanganyika to Bangweolo. But there fever and the terrible disease of dysentery came on again. He grew worse and worse, so that the natives had to carry him. On 27th April he wrote for the last time in his diary. On 30th April he could just wind his watch, and the next day the natives found him kneeling by the side of his bed, dead. They carried the body and all the dead man's books to the coast, where they could give them into the keeping of white men, for they were anxious to do all they could to show their love and respect for their dead teacher. The body was brought to England and buried in Westminster Abbey. Stanley went

Dr. Livingstone meets Stanley.

out to Africa the next year and discovered the Edward Nyanza: 'Nyanza' is the African name for 'lake.' He went right across the centre of the continent.

It was the travels of these brave men that made the people of Europe begin to wish to take the land of Africa for themselves. At the beginning of the nineteenth century Great Britain got Cape Colony by the Peace of Paris. It was a strange people the British had to rule there. The Dutch settlers of the seventeenth century had married with French Huguenots, who came later, and these independent and rather hard men were jealous of the English settlers who now flocked to South Africa. They hated the English for putting an end to slavery and the slave trade, and in 1835 a great number of them moved together, or 'trekked,' as they say in Africa, northwards to Natal, where they founded a republic.

But not many years later Natal was made a British colony, and many pieces of land where the natives were rebellious were added to Cape Colony. Others of the Dutch, or 'Boers,' as they were called, when they settled in Africa, founded the Orange Free State, east of Natal. Great Britain took that in 1848, but gave it back to the Boers to rule, six years later. Other Boers settled north of the Orange Free State and founded the Transvaal Republic; but they fought so much with the natives that Great Britain took it from them in 1877. This did not help the English very much for they had now to struggle with the natives. The warlike Zulus, a very savage tribe, rose under their King Cetchwayo, and after defeating the English in one terrible battle they were beaten in 1880, and Zululand was added to Natal.

This was a chance for the Transvaal. They had been afraid of the Zulus before, but now that they were beaten, the Boers rebelled against the English. They soon beat the few British soldiers in South Africa. They had been fighting for years against the natives, and knew better than the English how to fight in that country. The British Government, while new soldiers were still on the way to South Africa, gave back to the Transvaal the right to govern itself. This looked to the Boers as if Great Britain had been really beaten, and they did not take much notice of the conditions on which Great Britain had given them back their independence.

It was only a few years later (in 1884) that Germany seized a big piece of Africa, both on the west and east coasts. Gold-mines were now discovered in the Transvaal and gold-seekers soon poured in from England. Johannesburg, the town in the centre of the district, grew by leaps and bounds. The Boers had always been clever to take advantage of any chance, so they put large taxes on the newcomers but would not allow them any share in governing the country. But the 'Outlanders,' as the Dutch called the newcomers, came by and by to feel very angry against this unjust treatment.

THE IDEAL OF CECIL RHODES

There was at this time in South Africa a young man named Cecil Rhodes who saw all the difficulties. He had gone out to South Africa when he was only seventeen, because of his delicate health. He soon got sufficient money from gold-digging to be able to do what he liked, and his one thought was that all the strange and splendid country he had seen should be for Great Britain. His health grew better and he went to Oxford to complete his education; but it broke down again and he was told he had only six months to live. He went back to South Africa and entered the Cape Colony Parliament, and when he was after a time strong enough to go back to Oxford to take his degree he was already a statesman. He was becoming richer all this time from the Kimberly diamond-fields.

He saw the danger of the Transvaal blocking the way to the north and the equal danger that the German colonies on the east and west coasts should meet, and he persuaded the British Government to take the huge tract of land called Bechuanaland under its protection. In 1889 he founded a South African Company which had great powers over the land now called Rhodesia—after Rhodes himself. Rhodesia stretched up to the German colony on the east coast and the Congo Free State. Bechuanaland and Rhodesia kept the way to the north quite open for Great Britain, and Englishmen began to dream of a great belt of land which should unite Egypt with Cape Colony and be all for Great Britain.

Rhodes became Prime Minister, or chief man, in the Government of Cape Colony in 1890. The Outlanders were now thoroughly angry about their grievances, and one of them. Dr. Jameson, collected a band of men and tried to get their rights by fighting for them. The Boers easily beat them, and then, after such a short battle, began to think even more badly about the British. The Boers all over South Africa were roused, and at last Sir Alfred Milner was sent to try and make peace between them and the English settlers. President Kruger was then head of the Transvaal, and he flatly refused to make the condition of the Outlanders any better.

The Boer War

No one in Great Britain was expecting trouble when suddenly the Boers demanded things which could not be granted, and in 1899 war broke out between Great Britain and the Transvaal. The Boers were good fighters. They could shoot straight and ride for days without being tired out. There were very few British soldiers in South Africa, and soon they had to retreat to Ladysmith in Natal. Fresh soldiers were at once sent out from England under Sir Redvers Buller. Some of them were sent to Kimberley in the diamond-fields and some to help the soldiers in Ladysmith. Others tried to stop the Boers who were invading Cape Colony. But disasters came everywhere. The British soldiers, brave as they were, did not know the country, and were easily beaten by the Boers. More soldiers were sent out in 1900, and the great general, Lord Roberts, was sent to lead them, with Lord Kitchener, who had avenged Gordon in Egypt, as his chief assistant.

Soldiers came also from Canada, Australia, and New Zealand. Things began to look brighter for the British when in February Lord Roberts surrounded the Boer general Cronje at Paardeberg and made him give in. There were four thousand Boers taken prisoners in this battle on 29th February, and, the day before, Ladysmith had been relieved by Sir Redvers Buller. The British army now in the Orange Free State (for all the Boer states were helping the Transvaal) found no resistance, but fever had broken out and many soldiers died. The Free State was now taken, and Lord Roberts marched into the Transvaal. The march

Lord Roberts stepping on the gangway from the Dunottar Castle *on his arrival at Cape town.*

was made quickly, and sometimes the Boers won in small battles, but in June the last real Boer army was beaten, and President Kruger had fled.

The Transvaal was taken, Kruger sailed to Europe, and it was thought the war was over. But for two years the struggle still went on. The Boers split up their army into small bands and attacked whenever and wherever they could. Lord Roberts had gone back to England, and Lord Kitchener built small forts all over the country. There were many small battles, and sometimes still the Boers won. Then at length, in March 1902, the Boers saw they could hold out no longer and went to Pretoria to ask for peace. The agreement was signed on the 21st of May, and the war was at last at an end.

Since 1902 the peoples of South Africa have been allowed to govern themselves, and Cape Colony, Natal, the Transvaal, and the Orange Free State have joined together, just as the first colonies in Canada did. There are still some things on which the Boers and the English do not agree, but they are learning to live together in peace, and the Union of South Africa, which is the name of the four colonies, is growing more and more prosperous. A railway from Cairo in Egypt is getting longer every day and will soon meet one from Cape Colony. When the two join the heart of the 'Dark Continent' will be robbed of some of its mystery.

The **Big Hole, Open Mine** *or* **Kimberley Mine** *(in the language of Afrikaans: Groot Gat) is an open pit and underground mine in Kimberly, South Africa, and claimed to be the largest hole excavated by hand.*

Chapter XLVII—The Story of China and Japan

It was not until the nineteenth century that the countries of Europe had any real connection with the two great countries of Asia, China and Japan. Yet the Chinese had a civilization older than any in Europe. Their country is larger than all the countries of Europe put together, and more than four hundred millions of people live in it. The Chinese are a Mongolian people like the Turks. They have yellow skins and straight black hair, which until lately hung in long plaits down their backs from the centre of their heads, the rest of the head being shaven. The children's heads are shaven too, and until their hair has grown long enough to be put into a 'pigtail' it stands up in little tufts from the middle of their heads. But now most of the Chinese have had their pigtails cut off to show their liking for the new freedom which is finding its way into their land.

We may often see Chinamen in the streets of our big towns today, but before the nineteenth century this never happened. For the Chinese had got to a certain state of civilization and for hundreds of years they had gone no farther. They wanted to have nothing to do with foreigners and to live their own life in their own way.

Yet hundreds of years before the birth of Christ the Chinese knew how to write. Before that time, too, they could build suspension bridges and had made the wonderful 'Great Wall' —fifteen hundred miles long—with towers and fortifications. The wall was really a road on top, and along it the caravans travelled which traded between Siberia and China. They had silk manufactures and made beautiful china, and they had discovered the art of printing five hundred years before it was discovered in Europe. But China had never gone much farther, and Europe knew little about her except the stories which Marco Polo told after his famous journey to the court of the Great Khan, which these people had not believed.

In the sixteenth century, traders from Portugal stopped at places on the Chinese coast, and later the English followed. In the seventeenth century tea was brought from China to Europe. No one had ever seen it before. But the Chinese would not let people go far into

Commodore Perry

their country. When, in the sixteenth century, a curious Portuguese succeeded in getting to Peking, the capital of China, he had his head cut off. And still in the nineteenth century it was the same. The Chinese took no notice of all the wonderful things which were happening in Europe, but went quietly on in their own way.

Japan, too, when people began to be interested in it, in the nineteenth century, was just as anxious to keep itself free from the foreigner, but the Japanese soon showed that they were a very different people from the Chinese. Their history does not go so far back. They are probably a people of mixed race, but they must have some Chinese blood in their veins, and are rather like the Chinese to look at. Some people think that there is a large Aryan element in their blood. We know that the Japanese had taken possession of their beautiful islands at least in the first century after the birth of Christ.

Their history was not unlike that of the peoples of Europe in the early Middle Ages. There was an emperor called the Mikado over all the land, but a kind of feudalism grew up in which great lords got all power. The Portuguese traders went to Japan also in the sixteenth century and the Jesuits sent their missionaries to teach the people Christianity, but not much progress was made. Japan, like China, did not like foreigners. But in 1853 the United States sent some warships under Commodore Perry with a letter from the President to the Mikado asking him to make friends with the United States. He pointed out to them how near the two countries really were. The Japanese did not like the idea, but when a few months later the Americans came for their answer the Japanese said 'Yes,' for they knew that they had no fleet to fight against the nations of Europe and America if they chose to fight them.

Soon America, Great Britain, Russia, and Holland all had permission to trade at certain ports with Japan. In 1862 some Japanese were sent to journey through Europe and America. Everything was new and wonderful to them. Their own land was very charming, full of flowers. It was from Japan that chrysanthemums were first brought to Europe. The people themselves were small but quaint and pretty, and wore graceful clothes of cotton or silk with great wide sashes. Theirs is a land of sunshine though the top of their great mountain Fujiyama is covered with snow. They were fine artists and everything in Japan then, as now, seemed pretty and clean.

But in the middle of the nineteenth century the Japanese knew nothing of modern inventions, and these first men from Japan who came to Europe were full of enthusiasm when they went back. But there were many men in Japan who still hated the idea of imitating

A Great Battle in Japanese history, Painted by a Japanese Artist (From a great painting, 12 feet long, of the Battle of Ogaki, by a famous Japanese artist. This was one of the greatest battles in Japanese history: it was fought in the 17th century, and gave the Shogun (a kind of hereditary Prime Minister) the supreme power in Japan, even over the Mikado, which he held until the awakening of Japan to Western ideas in the 19th century).

Western ways. These men joined together and overthrew the power of the great lords. The Emperor got all power again, and they hoped he would send the foreigners away. But he did not. The old Mikado died and the new one was full of enthusiasm too for the things which were to be learned from the West.

Soon Japan had a navy and an army imitated from those of the countries of Europe. A new system of education was set up and every child in Japan was sent to school. Tokyo, the capital of Japan, became the largest city in Asia and one of the greatest in the world. It has electric light, telephones, and telegraphs, all learned from the West. By degrees, too, Japan has won a parliament, through which the people can use their power, though the Mikado is still more powerful and important in some ways than most 'constitutional' kings. The Japanese people have great respect and reverence for those above them and for old people generally. They are very honorable too and very brave. In some ways they are the most wonderful people of our modern world for the quick eager way they have learned so many new things in so short a time. Japan, a small nation, after all about as big as Great Britain, first proved her new-found strength in a struggle with China.

All this time China remained as obstinate as ever, hating all new things. In 1840 she had been obliged to open up some of her ports to British trade and had given up the city of Hong Kong to Great Britain, but this was only after a war between the English and Chinese called the 'Opium War.' British traders carried opium, which they got from the poppy-fields of North India, into China. Now opium is a drug which makes people sleepy and stupid when they eat it and ruins the health of people who get into the habit of using it. It makes people intoxicated in a worse way even than too much wine or beer. Some of the Chinese people grew very fond of opium and the Emperor tried to prevent the British from bringing it into China. A short war took place and then the Chinese had to give in.

A few years later there was another war, in which France and England together destroyed some of the Chinese forts and marched to Peking. The Chinese Emperor had put some English in prison. These were released, but to give the Chinese a lesson the wonderful summer palace of the Emperor at Peking was destroyed by the soldiers. More ports were then opened. Soon afterwards the English helped the Chinese soldiers to put down a rebellion of thousands of Chinese who had risen against the government, following their leader, who was a madman who thought he was a prophet and ought to rule over China. This time English and Chinese soldiers marched together against the rebels, and peace was made. At last the United States and the great European countries were allowed to send ambassadors to live in Peking, as they do to all the capitals of other countries.

The Chino-Japanese war broke out in 1894. It was about the peninsula of Korea, which lies between the two countries. It did not belong to either, but the Japanese heard that the Chinese were making ready to invade it. The Japanese sent word to China that this must not be, but the Chinese went on with their preparations. Then war came. Everybody thought that little Japan would be crushed by the great power of China, but the Japanese won on land and sea. The Japanese fleet won a great victory over the Chinese in Korea Bay, and then the Chinese ships sailed off to Port Arthur in Manchuria. But the Japanese landed and took the town which is now one terminus of the Trans-Siberian railway. Then China begged for peace. The Japanese were admired by all Europe. Her young soldiers had fought like heroes. A story is told of one boy who was blowing the bugle as he stood by his captain. A bullet struck him in the chest, but still he blew till he dropped dead.

But the Japanese had never really feared China. They knew that Russia wanted to take China for herself, and indeed no sooner was the treaty of peace signed between China and Japan, than Russia got France and Germany to join her in taking all that Japan had won. The Japanese waited their time. Meanwhile, in the year 1900, many Chinese, angry at the way in which the European countries had interfered in China, rose to attack the houses in Peking where the European ambassadors lived. The German ambassador was murdered in the street. Many missionaries who were trying to convert China to Christianity were murdered in the same way, or burnt in their houses with their wives and children. Many of the ambassadors were besieged in Peking, but were saved when the armies of six countries, with Japan amongst them, marched to their help.

So far the relations between China and Europe have not been a success, yet the Chinese are a splendid people in many ways, full of energy and industry. When they become Christians they are splendid men indeed. And just lately men in China have risen to demand freedom too, like the peoples of the West. A new constitution has been planned. We do not yet know how it will work, but the Chinese sent a touching request for prayers to be said in England for their success in their new way of life. On Sunday, 27th April 1913, prayers were said in most of the churches throughout Great Britain for, in the words of the Chinese message, 'the newly established government, for the President yet to be elected, for the constitution of the Republic, that the Government may be recognized by the Powers, that peace may reign within our country, that strong, virtuous men may be elected to office, that the Government may be established on a strong foundation.'

With Japan, as we have seen, things are quite different. In the year 1904 the Japanese felt themselves strong enough to demand their rights from Russia, and the Russo-Japanese war began. Before this every one had feared Russia. People had believed that she had a wonderful army, but neither her army nor her navy was a match for those of Japan. At the beginning of the war, the Japanese defeated the Russian fleet, and landed their armies in Korea. Terrible battles followed, in any one of which the Russians lost more soldiers than were killed altogether in the Boer War. When peace was made Korea was given to Japan. Before this Japan and England had made a treaty of friendship. Both were determined to prevent the power of Russia from growing. England feared that Russia might attack her empire in India, and both were determined that China should be left with the Chinese. For this and other reasons the friendship between England and Japan is very close. Both are island nations and have very much in common.

CHAPTER XLVIII—OUR WORLD TODAY

Our world today is very different from the world of even a hundred years ago. Children who have not had time to see many changes can hardly understand how different it is. A hundred years ago steam-engines were only just being thought of. Before that things had had to be carried along-rough roads in wagons from place to place. People who were rich enough travelled on horseback or in carriages, and for ordinary travelers in the eighteenth century there were stage-coaches which travelled between the biggest towns very slowly and painfully, for all over England and in other countries too the roads were very bad. Now, when we want to go to another town we step into a railway train which carries us there at the rate of from thirty to sixty miles an hour.

Even when the roads had begun to be made better, and the 'ruts four foot deep' got rid of towards the end of the eighteenth century, it took three whole days for a letter to be carried from Bath to London. Now we can post a letter in any town in England or Scotland and know that it will reach London by the next morning. In those days families did not break up and scatter all over the world. When they did, it was very difficult for them to get news of each other. Even after Queen Victoria began to reign in England people had generally to pay at least a shilling for a letter to be sent to another part of England; but then it was arranged that letters could be sent to any part of the British Isles for a penny, and now a penny stamp will carry a letter to our friends in any of the British colonies, so that, though people are separated by such enormous distances, they feel in some ways nearer to each other than people in different parts of England did a hundred years ago.

The first real passenger train began to run in England in 1830. It went at the rate of twenty miles an hour, which seemed very terrible and dangerous to people then, and, sad to say, one man was killed on the opening day of this railway, between Liverpool and Manchester. Now our express trains go at the rate of sixty miles an hour. By this time it was found that steam could be used to drive ships instead of waiting for wind to fill their sails. It was thought very wonderful when a steamer called the Great Western crossed the Atlantic from Bristol to New York in fifteen days. Now it is regularly done in a week.

Political Map of the World, November 2011

More wonderful than the discovery of steam was that of electricity. Through it people can send messages by telegram so that news can be had in a few minutes from places miles away, and through its use on the telephone people can speak to each other from place to place, even from cities so far apart as Paris and London. Cables, enclosing telegraph wires, have been laid down on the ocean floor from England to America, and 'cablegrams' can be sent so that in a few hours people in any part of America can have news from friends in Europe. Submarine cables are now laid between many places all over the world. But in the last few years an inventor called Marconi has discovered that messages can be sent by electricity between two instruments without any wires at all. This would have seemed like magic to people a hundred years ago.

Guglielmo Marconi, *winner of the 1906 Nobel Prize for Physics for his work with wireless telegraphy. He is considered the inventor of the radio.*

It is a very wonderful and important discovery. Already it has been very useful. Ships in distress which have wireless instruments can ask for help from other ships miles away. It was through the wireless messages by Phillips, the heroic telegraphist on the great steamer the Titanic, which was wrecked in 1912, that help came from the Carpathia, and the people who had been got into the boats before the steamer sank were saved. Almost like magic, too, it seems that photographs can also be sent by electricity, so that photographs of a football match or any interesting event can be sent from the place it has happened in, such as Leeds or Manchester, and the pictures will be published in the London evening newspapers an hour or two later.

The daily newspaper, again, is a thing that was quite new to our great-grandfathers. There were daily papers in London at the end of the eighteenth century, but they were few and expensive. After the middle of the nineteenth century they became common in other large towns, and now very few people feel quite happy without their morning and evening paper, in which they may read the things that have happened all over the world the day before, things the news of which would have taken weeks and months, and even years, to come to us before the days of telegrams. Electricity is used of course, too, for light and heat, and new houses nearly everywhere have electric light, while even gas-light was not known a hundred years ago when people used candles or oil lamps.

In the last few years, too, it has been discovered that man can travel through the air quicker and more smoothly than by the quickest express trains. The great invention of the airship has come to us within the last few years. Every few weeks some improvement is made, and airmen are learning to manage their ships more easily. But as yet things are only at the beginning, and already many brave airmen have lost their lives, as brave pioneers must often do. People talk of the days when nations will no longer fight at sea with the great iron-clad warships, which also were first built in the nineteenth century, but will fight their battles in the air with fleets of airships. Balloons were invented at the end of the eighteenth century. In them also men can go through the air, but at first they could only go like sailing-ships in the direction in which they were sent by the wind. Now, however, in the last few years airmen have discovered how to make balloons go in any direction they wish, and the 'dirigible' balloons are thought to be more useful by many people than even airships. Several airmen have now crossed the English Channel, and prizes are being offered for the first flight right round England and Scotland, and the first flight across the Atlantic.

On December 17, 1903, at 10:30 am at Kitty Hawk, North Carolina, this airplane arose for a few seconds to make the first powered, heavier-than-air controlled flight in history. The first flight lasted 12 seconds and flew a distance of 120 feet.

So we live in a world of change and adventure. Brave and clever people are doing wonderful things every day to try to make the world a more comfortable place. But even more wonderful than these changes in the things around us— changes most of which have begun in England and have spread all over the world—are the changes which have come over the minds of men. In most countries now men may believe as they like, and religion is a matter for each person to settle for himself. This spirit of toleration and freedom is the thing which we ought to value most of all the things which make our world today different from the world of a hundred years ago. At the beginning of the nineteenth century the laws against Catholics, which prevented them from taking part in the government of their countries, were withdrawn in England and Ireland. For hundreds of years the Catholics in England and Ireland had been looked upon almost as criminals, and very hard laws had been passed against them. This was especially terrible in Ireland, where nearly all the people were Catholic. Up to this time the Irish had had their own parliament, but only Protestants could sit in it or even vote for the people who became members of parliament. But now this was changed, and at last the Catholic Irish were given the ordinary rights of citizens. The Irish parliament was, however, given up, and Ireland for the future sent members to the English parliament, as Scotland had already done for a hundred years. Many of the Irish have never been pleased with this arrangement, and Ireland may soon have 'Home Rule' again. But Catholic emancipation was only one sign of a new spirit which was passing over the world.

The new democratic spirit is seen too in the education of children. In nearly all countries now children are sent to schools which the governments keep up, so that even the poorest people can give their children a good education. A hundred years ago very many of the people could not read or write at all, and especially miserable were the children of poor people in England at the end of the eighteenth century and the beginning of the nineteenth. In the second half of the eighteenth century manufacturers had grown very quickly in England. Things which had before been made by people in their homes in the country were now made much more quickly in great factories built in the towns. This was through the invention of new machines.

It was now found that even children could help to work these machines, and little children of six and seven years old were crowded into the factories, working from early morning till dark. But soon this was changed. Laws were passed which said that children should no longer work in the factories until they were older, and then only for a few hours. Now no boy or girl is allowed to leave school until fourteen years of age, and so every child has a chance of learning things which will help him or her to live a wise and happy life.

Photographer Lewis Wickes: Little spinner in Bibb Mill No. 1,
Macon, Ga. *She was so small she had to climb up on to the spinning frame to mend broken threads. Jan. 19, 1909. Location: Macon, Georgia (United States)*

The children of the British Empire, whether in Great Britain or the colonies, have also the joy of feeling that they belong to a great race, that all over the world people speaking their language and loving their country are living their lives in their own way. They can like and admire the people of other nations, but they cannot help loving the people of their own empire. It is this feeling of loyalty to the nation and the empire that led to the setting up of 'boy scouts ' in England, a great movement which has now spread to other countries. For while we wish that peace may be kept between the nations, we naturally feel determined to be ready to defend our empire if that peace is broken.

In reading history children nearly always feel glad that they were born in their own time and not in the past, when there was so much cruelty and bloodshed. For, unfortunately, in many parts of the story of the world it is tales of cruelty and intolerance which have to be told. But then, too, there are the tales of the heroes, and saints, and martyrs, the pioneers and discoverers, and all who have done their part to make our world today a better place. This is one of the great lessons of history, that we too should do our part honorably and well, and in reading the story of the world, think not only of the romance of the past and present, but of the romance of the future too.

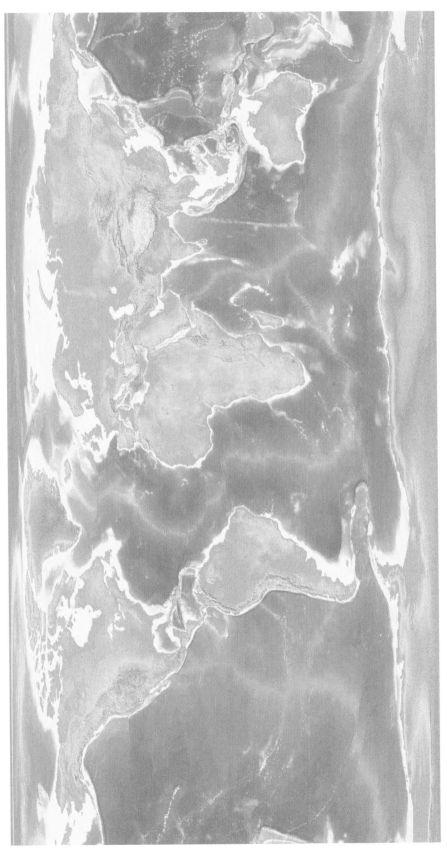

Topographical Map of the World

Index

CPSIA information can be obtained at www.ICGtesting.com
Printed in the USA
BVOW10*0715160615

404120BV00007B/2/P

9 780988 510630